the lives of
ROBERT RYAN

the lives of

ROBERT RYAN

J.R. JONES

Wesleyan University Press | Middletown, Connecticut

Wesleyan University Press
Middletown, CT 06459
www.wesleyan.edu/wespress
© 2015 J.R. Jones

All rights reserved
Manufactured in the United States of America
Designed by Mindy Basinger Hill
Typeset in Garamond Premier Pro

Wesleyan University Press is a member of the Green Press Initiative.
The paper used in this book meets their minimum requirement
for recycled paper.

Portions of this book appeared previously in "The Dark Shadings
of Robert Ryan: A Brief Biography," *Noir City*, Vol. 6, No. 2, Summer
2011, and in "The Actor's Letter" and "The Essential Robert Ryan,"
Chicago Reader, October 29, 2009.

Library of Congress Cataloging-in-Publication Data

Jones, J.R., 1963–
The lives of Robert Ryan / J.R. Jones.
      pages cm
Includes bibliographical references and index.
Includes filmography.
ISBN 978-0-8195-7372-8 (cloth: alk. paper)—
ISBN 978-0-8195-7373-5 (ebook)
1. Ryan, Robert, 1909–1973.   2. Actors—United States—Biography.
I. Title.
PN2287.R88J66 2015
791.4302'8092—dc23
[B]   2014033019

5   4   3   2

For Margaret

Contents

Introduction

He was well liked in Hollywood but hardly well known. Tall and trim, with a winning Irish grin and a politician's firm handshake, he listened more than he spoke, his small brown eyes taking everything in. By the mid-1950s he had worked with some of the best directors in the business—Jean Renoir, Pare Lorentz, Jacques Tourneur, Joseph Losey, Fred Zinnemann, Max Ophuls, Robert Wise, Nicholas Ray, Fritz Lang, Budd Boetticher, Anthony Mann, Samuel Fuller—and none of them had an ill word for Bob Ryan. He dug into his part, he showed up on time, he delivered on the first take. He was generous with other actors, patient with young performers who might be having trouble. He got to know the crew and looked out for their interests; in stressful situations he was always good for a wisecrack to break the tension. But at 6 PM every night he disappeared, home to his wife and three children in the San Fernando Valley. Even his close friends found him a puzzle; director Harold Kennedy echoed many when he called Ryan "the most private person I have ever known."[1]

Forty years after Ryan's death, his artistic reputation has only grown. Martin Scorsese called him "one of the greatest actors in the history of American film,"[2] and when Film Forum in New York mounted a twenty-three-film Ryan retrospective in August 2011, critics recognized it as a powerful body of work with its own thematic coherence. Schooled by the great Austrian theater director Max Reinhardt, Ryan was hired by RKO (Radio-Keith-Orpheum) Radio Pictures in 1942 and groomed as a handsome male lead, but all that changed with his unnerving performance as a bigoted army sergeant concealing his murder of a Jewish civilian in the film noir classic *Crossfire* (1947). His career ignited just as noir was developing into a shadowy interrogation of American values; with his strength, intelligence, and willingness to explore the soul's darker corners, he invested the genre with a string of neurotic and troubling portrayals that still reverberate through the popular culture.

Ryan liked to upset the easy morality of genre pictures, and he was drawn to men with complicated motives: the insecure millionaire who validates himself by controlling his wife's every move in *Caught* (1949), the closeted crime lord coveting the cop who's out to get him in *House of Bamboo* (1955), and the ruthless California rancher who avenges the attack on Pearl Harbor by killing a Japanese farmer in *Bad Day at Black Rock* (1955). Long after Ryan had grown frustrated with his sinister screen persona, he continued to play men twisted by hatred or bigotry if they promised great drama that would change minds. By all accounts he was a good man, but often he expressed his goodness by playing evil men—with an alarming relish and conviction. That curiosity and daring set him apart from his '40s and '50s peers; his coiled performances widened the parameters of what moviegoers might expect from a leading man and helped pave the way for such volatile personalities as Robert De Niro, Harvey Keitel, and Tommy Lee Jones.

His reputation as a heavy obscures his great versatility: by the time Ryan died in 1973, he had played everything from Jay Gatsby to John the Baptist. Against his agent's advice, he grabbed the role of Ty Ty Walden, the elderly patriarch of *God's Little Acre* (1958), and turned in a tender and funny performance as the grizzled old coot. In search of acting challenges, he struck out into legitimate theater, playing political satire (Jean Giraudoux's *Tiger at the Gates*), theological drama (T. S. Eliot's *Murder in the Cathedral*), and his beloved Shakespeare (*Antony and Cleopatra* with Katharine Hepburn, *Coriolanus* with director John Houseman). Near the end of his career he was hailed for two performances on the New York stage, as the scheming newspaper editor in Ben Hecht and Charles MacArthur's comedy *The Front Page* and the angry, self-pitying father in Eugene O'Neill's tragic *Long Day's Journey into Night*.

Such was his life on the stage and screen. In public Ryan was the antithesis of the right-wing characters he often portrayed; raised in the Chicago Democratic machine, married to a Quaker woman of strong pacifist ideals, he campaigned tirelessly for liberal causes throughout his career, tracing a careful route through the political booby traps of the blacklist era and into the tumultuous '60s. His experience as a Marine Corps drill instructor during World War II turned him against the war machine forever; he championed "world peace through world law" as a member of the United World Federalists, and in the late '50s he cofounded the Hollywood chapter of the National Committee for a Sane Nuclear Policy. Playing a violent, racist hick in the late-period noir *Odds against Tomorrow* (1959), he grew close to Harry Belafonte and got involved in the civil rights struggle. In the mid-1960s he spoke out against the Vietnam War, stumping for Eugene McCarthy in the New Hampshire primary that drove Lyndon Johnson from the White House—even as, on-screen, he played hardened military men in *Battle of the Bulge, Anzio,* and *The Dirty Dozen.*

His partner in all this was Jessica Cadwalader, a freethinker from Berkeley, California, who, having married Ryan, abandoned an acting career and became a writer, publishing five novels. He trusted and admired her; to some extent she became his social conscience, inspiring him in his political work. Their civic ambition manifested itself most impressively with the Oakwood School, a progressive grade school they launched in North Hollywood in 1951 with a handful of other parents. Combining his star power and her determination, the couple managed to guide the school through its rocky first years, when political conflicts among the parents of the enrolled students threatened to tear it apart. They invested heavily in the project, donating thousands of dollars to keep it afloat and immersing themselves in the scholarship of education. Their own children graduated from Oakwood, now considered one of the better private schools in Los Angeles. Ryan often told people the school was the most important thing he had ever done.

His private life Ryan reserved for himself and his family, avoiding the Hollywood social scene to concentrate on raising his children. Movie magazines invariably portrayed him as a contented spouse and dad, and there was some element of truth in this; interviewed at home in the mid-1960s, he remarked with touching sincerity, "All my best friends live in this house."[3] But there was a dark side to Ryan as well. He could be silent and withdrawn; he drank too much and suffered from debilitating depressions—"Black Irish moods," he called them. Jessica grappled with similar problems, and through the '50s a good deal of the hands-on parenting in the Ryans' home was administered by Solomon and Williana Smith, a childless black couple who lived with the family. Millard Lampell, one of Ryan's few close friends in the '60s, shrewdly observed, "I think Robert would [have liked] to be remembered as a loving husband and a good father, neither of which he always was."[4]

Ryan's own father, who died in 1936, taught him by example that a man keeps his problems to himself, and as Ryan matured and became a celebrity, he grew increasingly adept at compartmentalizing his life. This permitted and, to some extent, encouraged the sharp contradictions in his character. He loved acting more than anything else, but his tireless political activities sprang from a gnawing sense that his chosen profession really was shallow and narcissistic. He recoiled from the hobnobbing and false friendships of the movie business, then fumed when the good roles went to more enterprising actors. He kept his frustrations buttoned up, and when they had a chance to burst out in some of his more unhinged characters, they hinted at a man with more issues than he would ever let on. "Every actor has at least two selves," he said. "There's the *outside* self that takes part in family life and society and the *inside* self who is someone else."[5]

I gained an unexpected insight into Ryan's inner life in 2009, when I got the chance to read an undated, twenty-page manuscript he had written for his children and then filed away and forgotten. Uncovered by his youngest child, Lisa, and passed along to Michael Miner, my colleague at the *Chicago Reader,* it was a brief history of Ryan's years growing up in the city, warmly nostalgic in its recollections of the North Side and his extended Irish family. But it also contained references that, as I began to investigate, led me to a scandal undocumented in any account of Ryan's life. His father, Timothy, and three uncles operated the politically well-connected Ryan Company, a firm that specialized in rail and sewer tunnel construction. In April 1931 Timothy Ryan was personally responsible for a South Side project where a disastrous subterranean fire lasting some twenty hours claimed the lives of twelve men and injured another fifty.

One should always take care when connecting an actor's life to his roles. But if Ryan was indeed the puzzle that so many claimed, this tragic story supplies at least one piece of it, helping us understand the power and insight he brought to so many of his tortured characters. Conscience runs like a gold thread through many of his key performances. Nicholas Ray's *On Dangerous Ground* (1952) presents Ryan as a brutal policeman forced to reckon with his rage when he meets a blind woman, played by Ida Lupino, who challenges him to find his better self. In *The Professionals* (1967) he's a horse wrangler who hires on to help rescue a kidnapped woman but antagonizes his partners by peeling away the heroic façade of their mission; in *The Wild Bunch* (1969) he's an outlaw who can barely live with himself after cutting a deal with the law to track down his old friend. More broadly, Ryan's political and social conscience sharply influenced his choice of roles, especially after he was freed from his RKO contract in the early 1950s and could exercise somewhat more control over the films he was making.

Even more revealing than Ryan's manuscript are the several unpublished memoirs Jessica Ryan left behind at the time of her death in 1972. Witty and acutely observed, these pieces illuminate her husband's character and her own, particularly their aversion to Hollywood social life. They provide the clearest picture of Ryan's political skills, honed from years of exposure to the inner workings of machine politics. They also offer a rare female perspective on a Hollywood dominated by men and, in Ryan's case, populated by such macho characters as Mann, Fuller, Lee Marvin, Robert Mitchum, Richard Brooks, André de Toth, Sam Peckinpah, and John Wayne. Ryan may have been famous for his tough-guy roles in westerns and crime pictures, but when his wife passed away, his sense of self began to crumble.

The more I explored the Ryans' lives, the more I realized that here was not just the story of a movie star but a pocket history of American liberalism, stretching from a war against fascism in Europe that united the country to a war against communism in Southeast Asia that bitterly divided it. This struggle played out in Ryan's screen life, which he began as an eager army flyboy in *Bombardier* (1943) and ended as a right-wing millionaire conspiring to kill President Kennedy in *Executive Action* (1973). It defined his public life, where he fought the good fight in the coldest years of the Cold War, his compromises as revealing as his victories. It also animated a good deal of his inner life, a place where men guard their secrets and, sometimes, take them to their final rest.

the lives of
ROBERT RYAN

one

Inferno

The day Robert Ryan turned nine, the entire nation celebrated. All weekend long had come word that the Armistice was about to be signed, bringing home a million American soldiers from the trenches of France. In Chicago, where the boy lived, whistles began to sound and guns to go off in the predawn darkness of Monday, November 11, 1918. Women ran from their homes with overcoats tossed over their nightgowns, beating on pots and pans. The elevated trains coming from the Loop tied down their whistles and went screaming through the neighborhoods, confirming that the nation was at peace. People who ventured downtown for work were sent home by their employers, and by noon the neighborhood parties were rolling.[1] In Uptown, on the city's North Side, young Bob ran around telling people this was his birthday and returned home with a few dollars in change. His parents, Tim and Mabel, made him give back most of the money, but even so this was a great day. Everyone had called this "the war to end war"—if that were true, then he would never have to die in a trench.

The Ryans had no need for their neighbors' charity; they were respectable, middle-class people who had worked their way up. Bob's great-grandparents, Lawrence and Ellen Fitzpatrick Ryan, had immigrated from County Tipperary, Ireland, in 1852 during the Great Famine and settled in Pittsburgh, where times were tough (their son John would later tell Bob about the "No Irish Need Apply" signs that greeted them on their arrival). The family moved to Chicago four years later and eventually retreated about thirty miles south to the heavily Irish Catholic river town of Lockport, Illinois, along the Illinois and Michigan Canal.

John and his older brother, Timothy E. Ryan, worked together as boat builders in the 1860s, then went their separate ways as John established his own business in town and Timothy (known as "T. E.") returned to Chicago to try his hand at real estate speculation. John served as superintendent of the canal at one point and, with his wife, Johanna, raised a family of eight children. He liked his glass. "Although my grandfather drank a quart of whiskey a day for sixty-five years, he was never drunk or out of control,"[2] Bob later recorded in a memoir for his children.

Up in Chicago, T. E. Ryan prospered, cofounding the real estate firm of Ryan and Walsh and building his family a mansion on Macalister Place on the Near West Side. He also established himself as a political brawler in the city's well-oiled Democratic machine. Through the 1890s he won five terms as West Side assessor, and from 1902 to 1906 he served as Democratic committeeman for the Nineteenth Ward. T. E. was widely regarded as boss of the West Side, so popular and influential that, during the World's Columbian Exposition in 1893, he was named grand marshal of the Irish Day parade. A portrait reproduced in an 1899 guidebook to state politics shows a handsome man with swept-back hair, a handlebar mustache, and a hungry glint in his eye. "One of the most popular men on the West Side," the guidebook reported, "and a politician whose power is as strong as ever."[3] His success exerted an irresistible pull on John's sons, and one by one they all drifted to Chicago.

Timothy Aloysius Ryan was the second of John's children, born in 1875, and in the 1890s he headed north to board with his illustrious uncle and get into business in the city. Tim proved to be an eager political protégé: in 1899 he was appointed chief clerk in the city attorney's office, and five years later he ran for the state board of equalization in the Eighth Congressional District, billing himself as "T. A." Ryan. His uncle bankrolled all this, apparently seeing in his tall and handsome young nephew a rising political star. Tim got himself started in the construction business and ran an unsuccessful campaign for West Town assessor, his uncle's former position. "Father's duties have always been somewhat vague in everyone's mind," Bob wrote. "In his twenties he seems to have been occupied principally with fancy vests, horse racing, attending prizefights, and a great deal of social drinking. In short, a rather well-known and well-liked man about town."[4]

By 1907, Chicago was home to five of John and Johanna's sons. They were big men—one of Bob's uncles stood six feet eight inches tall—with ambitions

Timothy Aloysius Ryan, the actor's father. Informed once that a gubernatorial candidate had been accused of embezzling fifty thousand dollars, he remarked, "Any man who could only steal fifty thousand dollars in that job isn't smart enough to be governor." *Robert Ryan Family*

to match. Larry, Tim's younger brother by eight years, had come north to clerk for T. E.'s real estate firm, and Tom, Joe, and John Jr. wanted to start their own construction firm so they might capitalize on their uncle's political influence. But the brothers' relationship with their uncle ruptured. According to Bob, Larry's job "involved handling some funds and he was ultimately accused by his uncle of a minor embezzlement. Larry was about as liable to have done this as to burn down the Holy Name Cathedral. Father sided with his brother and left his uncle's bed, board, and generous patronage for good."[5] From T. E.'s power base in the west, Tim and Larry relocated to the relatively unpopulated North Side, where they banded together with their siblings to turn the newly christened Ryan Company into a going concern.

Tim was thirty-two the night Larry introduced him to Mabel Bushnell, a lovely twenty-four-year-old secretary at the *Chicago Tribune*. Raised in Escanaba, a port town on Michigan's Upper Peninsula, Mabel was descended from some of the first English families of New York, though her father was a cruel and alcoholic newspaper editor from Gladstone, Michigan, whose career ultimately had given way to a tougher life as a tramp printer operating out of Rhinelander, Wisconsin. Tim took Mabel out on the town, squiring her to restaurants and theaters, springing for hansom cabs. He wanted her badly, but

Robert Bushnell Ryan (circa 1912). "I was a completely
nonaggressive youngster," he later recalled. *Robert Ryan Family*

she took a dim view of his boozing, not to mention his political ambitions. Tim agreed to swear off liquor and politics, and in 1908 they were married, in a ceremony conducted by both a priest and a protestant minister. They moved into the apartment on Kenmore, and Robert Bushnell Ryan arrived late the next year—November 11, 1909.

Two years later Mabel gave birth to a second child, John Bushnell, and the two boys slept in the same bed. "Very early in my life I remember the lamplighter," Bob wrote, "a solitary youth who went around lighting the street lamps."[6] He and Jack enjoyed an idyllic life in Uptown, frolicking every summer on Foster Avenue Beach and running up and down the alley behind their house, an avenue for commercial activity. "Almost all heavy hauling was done by horse and wagon," Bob remembered, and the alley "was full of various dobbins hauling ice, garbage, groceries, etc. In the hot summers the horses wore straw hats. The horses got to know the various stops and often would break in a new driver by showing him where to go."[7]

The brothers' friendship ended in June 1917 when Jack—"a rather solemn, gentle little fellow," Bob wrote—died of lobar pneumonia, probably brought on by flu. He was not quite six years old. "I remember the terrible day that he died,"* Bob would write, "and the feeling of my mother and father that he might have been saved."[8] Devastated by the boy's death, Tim and Mabel vacated their little apartment at 4822 Kenmore, blocks from Lake Michigan, and moved slightly northwest to a one-bedroom on Winona Street. "The neighborhood was somewhat less desirable," Bob wrote. "But nothing mattered. We had to move and we did."[9] His parents, craving a portrait of little Jack, took a photograph they had of their sons on a dock and had Bob airbrushed away.

Now Bob slept alone, in a Murphy bed that folded out from the wall, like the one Charlie Chaplin had wrestled with in his two-reeler *One a.m.* He went to school alone, having transferred from Goudy Public School, which he remembered as mostly Jewish, to Swift Public School nearer his home. His parents were Victorian people, reserved even with their own child; and as the years passed, Bob learned to keep his own company, reading endlessly and roaming around the new neighborhood.

---

*His death predated by only a few months the first recorded cases of the Spanish influenza, which would kill at least half a million people in the United States alone.

One unique attraction was the Essanay Film Manufacturing Company on Argyle, founded a decade earlier and now the city's premiere movie studio. Chaplin had made films for Essanay in 1915, and Gloria Swanson and Wallace Beery had gotten their start there; Bob would remember seeing them all on the streets of Uptown. He and his school friends even spent their Saturday afternoons appearing as extras in the two-reel comedies of child star Mary McAllister, each earning the princely sum of $2.50 a day.

He was naturally quiet, even withdrawn, and his parents worried over his introverted nature. Mabel gave him a violin that once had belonged to her brother and every Friday marched Bob to the elevated train and downtown to Kimball Hall for a lesson. His teacher, a Scandinavian player for the Chicago Symphony, couldn't do anything with him. Tim, knowing full well that a boy carrying a violin down the streets of Chicago would be a magnet for bullies, signed Bob up for boxing lessons at the Illinois Athletic Club, where a coach by the name of Johnny Behr taught him how to fight. Bob loved boxing: he was smart and quick in the ring, and he realized that if you didn't worry about the punch it didn't hurt as much. "Athletic prowess did a lot for my ego and my acceptance in school," he later told an interviewer. "The ability to defend yourself lessens the chance you'll ever have to use it."[10]

Chicago could be an ugly place. Eight months after the Armistice was signed, Bob saw the city erupt again, this time in violence. Temperatures in the nineties had irritated tensions on the Near South Side between blacks confined to the Twenty-Fifth Street Beach and their white neighbors on the Twenty-Ninth Street Beach. On July 27, 1919, a black boy rafting near the shore at Twenty-Ninth Street was killed by a white man hurling rocks, and the incident touched off five days of murderous rioting. "As rumors of atrocities circulated throughout the city, members of both races craved vengeance," wrote historian William M. Tuttle Jr. "White gunmen in automobiles sped through the black belt shooting indiscriminately as they passed, and black snipers fired back. Roaming mobs shot, beat, and stabbed to death their victims."[11]

Thirty-eight people died, and more than five hundred were injured. An official report would blame much of the initial violence on Irish athletic clubs such as Ragen's Colts and the Hamburg Club, but the rage had spread like an infection, creeping into the West and North Sides. (Just south of Uptown lay one of the North Side's isolated pockets of blacks.) For a boy not yet ten, the riot must have been a frightening experience. Not only could war go on forever, it could happen right in your own backyard.

THE RYAN FAMILY'S FORTUNES began to turn in 1920 when Tim's friend Ed Kelly was appointed chief engineer of the Chicago Sanitary District. Son of a policeman, Kelly had started out with the district at age eighteen, and though he had studied engineering at night school, he displayed more talent as a South Side politician, having founded and been elected president of the two-hundred-member Brighton Park Athletic Club. The Irish athletic clubs were mainly social, organizing team sports, but they were also politically oriented, and Kelly soon made a name for himself in the Cook County Democratic Party. By the time he became chief engineer, he had put in more than thirty years with the district. His spotty formal training was much noted in the press (one muckraking journalist accused him of farming out his technical work to consultants). Yet Kelly understood and had mastered the operating principle of Chicago politics: take care of your friends and they'll take care of you.

Under Kelly, the Ryan Company won lucrative city jobs paving streets and building sewer tunnels. Tim, who supervised sewer construction, worked from 5:30 AM until 8 or 9 PM at night; he and his son barely saw each other except for weekends. With his winning manner and many connections, Tim was critical to the operation, though according to Bob, the man who really ran the company was his Uncle Tom, "a rather cold and shrewd businessman."[12] Flush with the company's profits, Tim and Mabel decided to move again, this time to a bigger apartment, in the northerly Edgewater neighborhood, that was only a block from the lake. They bought their own automobile and furnished their new home well. During the summers Bob went to Camp Kentucky in Wisconsin, while his parents enjoyed golfing weekends in Crystal Lake, northwest of the city. Mabel might have succeeded in keeping Tim away from drink, but politics was another matter, and Kelly could always rely on T. A. Ryan as a Democratic Party committeeman for the Twenty-Fifth Ward.

Haunted by the memory of little Jack, Tim and Mabel would never have another child, choosing instead to spoil and smother Bob. "You cannot know the difficulties that attend an only child," he would write years later, in a letter to his own children. "Two big grown-ups are beaming in on him all the time—even when he isn't there. It is a feeling of being watched that lingers throughout life."[13] He hid in the darkness of the movies, spending countless afternoons at the Riveria Theater on Broadway or the smaller Bryn Mawr near the "L" stop. The charm and dash of Douglas Fairbanks were his greatest tonic, and he never missed a picture: *The Mark of Zorro, The Three Musketeers, Robin Hood.* Bob had seen how motion pictures were made and was fascinated by the results. Yet he could barely conceive of the movies as an occupation; his father and uncles considered the Ryan Company a legacy for their children.

After Bob graduated from Swift in 1923, his father pulled some strings to get him a summer job as a fireman on a freight locomotive, which satisfied the thirteen-year-old boy's appetite for freedom and Tim's desire that he learn the value of a dollar. Rumors of petting parties at the local public high school had persuaded Mabel that Bob needed a private education, and that fall his parents enrolled him at Loyola Academy, a Jesuit college prep school for young men that was located near the Loyola University campus to their north. The experience would shape him not only as a person but also as an artist.

Loyola was heavily Irish Catholic, the sons of an aspiring middle class, and the class of 1927 would produce an unusual number of Jesuit priests. Tim must have been pleased that his son would be schooled in the Catholic faith, though Mabel valued Loyola more for its academic reputation. The priests were known as stern taskmasters, and the curriculum was tough—along with the arts and sciences, the boys learned Latin, Greek, and Christian doctrine. Later in life, when Bob Ryan's interests had turned to education, he would take a more skeptical view of Jesuit schooling. "The fathers were well-seasoned men who had a good deal of authority that they seldom used," he remembered. "Huge areas of a fruitful life were almost ignored. Jesuit education was books and drill and writing and *some* discussion."[14]

At the new school Bob began to distinguish himself in athletics, especially after a growth spurt propelled him to a height of six-foot-three, only an inch shorter than his father. He played football all four years and competed in track and field. Formidably big and agile on the gridiron, he was an All-City tackle his senior year. In school he struggled with Latin and especially chemistry but excelled in English, joining the literary society and working on the school magazine, *The Prep.* He read voraciously. "Truly, I may say that a man's best friends are his books," he wrote in the magazine his junior year. "Your companions may desert you, but your books will remain with you always and will never cease to be that source of enjoyment that they were when you first received them."[15]

Ryan with his parents, Mabel and Tim. "You cannot know the difficulties that attend an only child," he later wrote. "It is a feeling of being watched that lingers throughout life." *Robert Ryan Family*

The book that changed his life was *Hamlet,* which he spent an entire semester studying under the instruction of his beloved English teacher, Father Joseph P. Conroy. The priest led the boys through the Elizabethan verse into the dark heart of the play, the young prince charged by the ghost of his dead father to avenge the treachery of his uncle, Claudius, and the unfaithfulness of his mother, Gertrude. *Hamlet* was full of moral conundrums, the hero torn between his conscience and his thirst for revenge. Bob was captivated: such rich language, such profound thoughts, such high drama. By the end of the semester he could recite practically the entire text. He fell in love with theater, reading Shakespeare, Chekhov, Shaw, and O'Neill, a writer who spoke to his own Irish melancholy. Their work awakened in him a hunger for self-expression, and he wondered if, instead of following his father into construction, he might become a playwright himself.

The money kept rolling in at the Ryan Company, and before long the family bought a Cadillac, then a Pierce-Arrow with a chauffeur to drive Tim to work. Bob got his own Ford and tooled around in bell-bottom suits and a fur coat. Tim became a patron of the Chicago Opera Association; he took Mabel to New York City to see all the shows. (Bob shared their love of musical theater; among his favorite performers were Fanny Brice and the great Irish-American showman George M. Cohan.) Tim Ryan, Bob wrote in a letter to his own children, "was always generous and kind to me—in a day when father-son relationships were not thought of as they are now." His father was "a big man (6' 4"—250 lbs.) with a radiant personality and strong sense of humor, and was idolized by many people. His other side was only displayed at home and was very hard to take."

Bob wouldn't elaborate on this statement, but he would note his father's ambivalence toward the construction business, which hardly inspired one to join him. "Dad, I think, would have been content to have enough money to live well, eat well, play bridge, and tell stories to his rather small circle of friends."[16] Friction between father and son began to build as Bob's graduation from Loyola drew near. Tim had mapped out his son's future: he would stay at home, earn a professional degree at Loyola or DePaul or the University of Chicago, and find a good living for himself as the next generation of the Ryan Company. Bob insisted on going east to school and won admission to Dartmouth College in Hanover, New Hampshire.

That summer he accepted an invitation from his former camp counselor, a wealthy Yale graduate named Frank Scully, to work at a dude ranch Scully was trying to start on some land his family owned in Missoula, Montana. Bob took the train out West, spent the summer sharpening his horseman skills, and even found time for a first romance with a girl named Thora Maloney. He would remember his awe at seeing "plains that never ended—where one seemed to be becalmed in a purple ocean. As we got into the foothills of the Rockies and finally saw some of the high peaks I was aware of a lift of spirit that I shall never forget. It was strange to be so far from home and yet to feel as if I was coming home."[17]

Back in Chicago he gathered his belongings for school and at long last left his parents behind. His father was pained to see him leave. "He didn't get the point—packing off 1,300 miles to the state of New Hampshire when there were five colleges to be had within an hour's drive," Bob would write. "Mother must have sensed that I *should* go—though I hope she didn't know how much I *wanted* to go."[18]

At Dartmouth he pledged Psi Upsilon (one of his fraternity brothers was Nelson Rockefeller) and went out for track and football. But his real claim to fame was boxing: in his freshman year he won the college its first heavyweight title. His grades were unspectacular; he maintained a C average, studying Greek, French, English, physics, evolution, philosophy, and citizenship. The following summer he returned to Scully's ranch, pursuing romance with another girl, Thula Clifton, and in the fall he played football again, though his career ended ignominiously after he broke his knee in a game against Columbia University. The injury threw his schoolwork into disarray, and in December 1928 he withdrew from all his classes without receiving any grades, standard procedure for someone flunking out.

For the next eight months Bob returned home to his parents, who had moved to a new apartment on Lake Shore Drive. Tim insisted that Bob work, so he got a job as a salesman, first for a steel company and then for a cemetery. "I'm offering a permanent product," he would tell his customers.[19] That fall he reenrolled at Dartmouth, starting over as a sophomore, and though he would continue to box, he had resolved to get serious about his studies.

A month after he returned, the stock market crashed. October 23 brought the first wave of sell-offs, then on October 29—"Black Thursday"—the bottom dropped out. Crowds gathered outside the Chicago Stock Exchange, where a record one million shares changed hands in a single day. The Ryan

Company was privately held and, at that point, worth at least $4 million. But each of the brothers was personally invested in the market, and they were all wiped out. All they had left was the promise of more construction work.

Even that seemed precarious: earlier that year Assistant State's Attorney John E. Northrup had returned indictments against Ed Kelly and a dozen other men at the sanitary district, charging that they had defrauded taxpayers of $5 million over the past eight years and done a healthy business in bribes and kickbacks from contractors. "A well-greased palm was essential to doing business with the department," wrote Kelly's biographer, Roger Biles. "Some trustees received gifts of twenty-five cases of liquor a month from favored contractors." Others "admitted financing lengthy European vacations with illegally solicited contributions."[20] Kelly would later concede to the IRS that from 1919 to 1929 his income was $724,368, though his salary for that period totaled only $151,000.

More than seven hundred people were called to testify, many of them against their will. Witnesses exposed gaping discrepancies between the district's stated expenditures and what contractors were actually paid: the payroll was said to be padded by as much as 75 percent. The trial revealed that bids were submitted in plain envelopes that were later opened and altered so that favored firms could be awarded lucrative contracts. Elmer Lynn Williams, publisher of the muckraking newsletter *Lightnin',* alleged that the district's central auto service had provided high-ranking officials with "young women procured for these tired business men by an older woman who was on the pay roll. The taxpayers were charged for vanity cases, whiskey and the time of the 'entertainers.' "[21]

None of the Ryan brothers was ever implicated, but the scandal soiled the reputations of everyone doing business with the district. Kelly escaped conviction only when the judge in the case, who was pals with a local Democratic boss, quashed the indictments and Northrup, forced to reassemble his case before the statute of limitations ran out, dropped the chief engineer as a defendant. Years of hardball Chicago politics had turned Tim Ryan into a cynic when it came to graft; informed once that a gubernatorial candidate had been accused of embezzling fifty thousand dollars, he remarked, "Any man who could only steal fifty thousand dollars in that job isn't smart enough to be governor."[22]

EIGHTEEN MONTHS AFTER THE CRASH, in April 1931, Tim suffered another devastating blow. One of his sewer projects for the city, southwest of the Loop in the Pilsen neighborhood, was engulfed in a horrific fire that burned for nearly twenty-four hours and claimed at least a dozen lives. Bob would come to view the disaster as a key factor in his father's death.

The Ryan Company had contracted to build the Twenty-Second Street section of a huge, $2.1 million concrete intercepting sewer that would travel southwest to the sanitary drainage and ship canal. During construction each block-long section of the ovoid, seventeen-foot tunnel was sealed off to maintain air pressure and prevent collapse; the only exit was a short, perpendicular work tunnel that led to an elevator shaft. The cause of the fire was never officially determined, but according to several newspaper reports—including one that cited Tim Ryan as its source—a cement worker had dropped a candle (used to detect air leaks) into a pile of sawdust. Timber and sawdust were major components in tunnel construction: wooden forms used to mold the concrete were braced against the earthen walls and anchored in place with sawdust packs. The fire began to spread underneath the concrete, pumping black smoke into the tunnel.

At street level a foreman noticed a ribbon of smoke drifting up from the elevator shaft and, fearing an electrical fire, sent three electricians down to check the wiring; they found nothing wrong. Tim learned of the fire around 6 PM, and the first workmen to flee the tunnel reported a smell of burning insulation, which led him and his crew to believe the cause was indeed electrical. Morris Cahill, the construction superintendent, warned them that if the fire reached the east end of the tunnel and destroyed the hoses maintaining the air pressure belowground, the entire tunnel section would collapse.

According to the *Daily News*, loyal employees begged Ryan to let them extinguish the fire: "We'll be okay, boss. Let us go, please. It'll mean your contract if we don't."[23] Without waiting for Ryan's permission, an assistant foreman led a party of men down into the tunnel; Cahill made three trips down but each time was overcome by smoke. With no word from the men below, Ryan summoned the fire department around 7 PM.

"My men are in there!" Tim exclaimed as the first engine company arrived on the scene. "What are we going to do?"[24] Confusion over the fire's cause and ignorance of its severity may have been as deadly as the blaze itself: the first two rescue parties descended into the tunnel without the benefit of gas masks. The operation went on for hours, slowed by the thick smoke and the difficulty of getting at the burning material. When the fire broke out, panicked workmen had retreated into the metal chambers at either end of the tunnel section, which were sealed by an air lock and offered fresh air pumped in from street level thirty-five feet above. As the fire raged out of control, it pushed firefighters back into the chambers as well, and the trapped men waited through the night, praying and trying to lie still.

By midnight the construction site looked like the scene of a mining disaster. A light wagon trained its searchlight on the mouth of the elevator shaft, and thousands of spectators, some of them distraught family members of Ryan employees, were being held back by a police cordon. Hospital squads had arrived on the scene and set up shop in a neighboring lumberyard. More than two dozen firefighters had already been taken to Saint Anthony Hospital, and the fire department had by now dispatched a full quarter of its forces to the site.

Firefighters attacked the superstructure over the elevator shaft and eventually managed to tear the roof off in an effort to provide more ventilation. Mining equipment arrived, and mine workers from around the city converged on the site to volunteer their services. After the utility companies shut off the electricity and the Twenty-Second Street gas main (located a perilous ten feet from the tunnel), crews of men with picks, shovels, and pneumatic drills started three new ventilation holes in the concrete—one above each air chamber and another at the center of the tunnel.

No plan was too far-fetched: a professional diver who lived on the North Side was recruited to venture into the tunnel in his wet suit, but after only a few minutes he signaled for help and was brought back up—the rubber was melting. A description in the *Chicago Evening Post* sounds like a scene from Dante: "Terrific heat developed in the cramped quarters underground. Blazing timbers fell. . . . Water, poured above the tunnel in a vain effort to cool it and dissipate some of the fumes, eddied, four feet deep in spots, and made it impossible to see even inches ahead in the thick white mist."[25] Sometime during the night, the air supply inside the east air chamber failed, and the laborers and firefighters trapped inside decided to make a break for it, but most them died of smoke inhalation before they could reach the elevator shaft.

Outside, the rescue effort was beginning to reach across state lines. Henry Sonnenschein, secretary to Mayor Anton Cermak, brought word from his boss, who was vacationing in Miami Beach, that the city would spare no expense in addressing the crisis, which threatened to become a citywide calamity if the fire breached the east and west walls of the tunnel into the remainder of the sewer line. By 3 AM a rescue squad from the federal mining bureau had roared out of Vincennes, Indiana, for Chicago, escorted by state police. A squad from the state mining bureau in Springfield boarded a special train with right-of-way cleared to the site of the disaster. But the critical arrival, just after dawn on Tuesday, was an experimental smoke-ejector truck designed by an inventor in Kenosha, Wisconsin. A modified fire truck, the smoke ejector was essentially a gigantic vacuum cleaner on wheels, and its long, flexible fourteen-inch tubes were extended down the mine shaft to suck the smoke out of the tunnel.

The crowd roared later that morning when sixteen men trapped in the metal chamber and already given up for dead began emerging from the elevator shaft. Early that afternoon rescuers recovered the last dead man from the tunnel: Captain James O'Neill, one of the first firefighters on the scene, who had been trapped in the east chamber and was trampled near the air lock by the stampeding workmen as they tried to escape. The final death toll was four firemen and seven laborers, plus a policeman who had been run over by an ambulance. Nearly fifty other people had been injured, some seriously. Later that afternoon, the young widow of Edward Pratt, a firefighter whose body had been recovered overnight, broke past the police cordon and tried to hurl herself down the elevator shaft.

By that time Tim had been summoned to the county morgue, where Dr. Herman N. Bundesen, the Cook County coroner, was convening an inquest to determine how the fire had started and how the eleven men had died. Bundesen had a long history with Ed Kelly, having worked for the sanitary district during the Whoopee Era; according to journalist Elmer Lynn Williams, he had proved himself "one of the pliable tools of the machine."[26] Kelly, still holding firm in his capacity as chief sanitary engineer, served as technical advisor to the inquest.

Called to testify, Tim Ryan wept as he recalled the first crews of firefighters going after his trapped workmen: "I saw men going down into that reeking tunnel without gas masks—without masks. I never saw such courage displayed in my life."[27] Neither he nor his construction superintendent could state with certainty what caused the fire, and the news accounts of a workman igniting a pile of sawdust never were introduced.

When the inquest reconvened a week later in a courtroom at City Hall, the panel ruled that all eleven men had died of smoke inhalation but declared the cause of the fire unknown. "Unofficially," reported the *Chicago American*, "the jury members expressed the view that no human agency was at fault in the fire and tragedy that followed; that all precautionary measures were maintained by the contractors to safeguard life."[28] The city was indemnified against liability for the workmen's deaths; the Ryan Company would pay any settlements to the families through its compensation insurance. A pall hung over the firm, exacerbated by the Kelly corruption charges still crawling through the court system.

IN THE QUIET SECLUSION OF HANOVER, Bob must have been even more determined not to join the Ryan Company. His grades had improved substantially; he was earning mostly B's now and the occasional A in English or comparative literature. He had reclaimed his record as an intercollegiate boxing champion and—encouraged by his coach, Eddie Shevlin—even entertained thoughts of becoming a professional fighter. But his father talked him out of it: most boxers, he pointed out to Bob, were washed up at thirty. Bob was tired of athletics anyway. Having defended the heavyweight title in his sophomore and junior years, he retired from the ring to devote himself to his degree in dramatic literature.*

His best friends were still his books. The 1920s had brought a great revival of interest in Herman Melville, and Bob was floored by *Moby-Dick*. Something in Ahab's lonely obsession spoke to him; his daughter, Lisa, would remember him ritually reading the book every year.[29] He adored Joyce, especially *Ulysses,* but his tastes also ran to more popular fare; at Dartmouth he sold a professor and several of his classmates on Joseph Moncure March's 1928 narrative poem *The Set-Up,* about a black boxer who runs afoul of gangsters.[30]

As an admired upperclassman, Bob drove around campus in a Buick roadster, took up smoking a pipe, and made bathtub gin. Prohibition had been in effect since 1919, and overturning it had become a touchstone for Democrats. In a nod to his father's electoral ambitions, he ran for class marshal on the

---

*Countless news stories would misreport that Ryan retired from collegiate boxing undefeated; in fact, Dartmouth yearbooks indicate he lost to his opponent at Western Maryland College on a close decision in the 1930 season and fought his opponent at University of New Hampshire to a draw in the 1931 season.

As an undergraduate at Dartmouth College, Ryan became an intercollegiate boxing champ and ran for class marshal on the slogan "Rum, Rebellion, and Ryan."
Robert Ryan Family

slogan "Rum, Rebellion, and Ryan." His flyers declared him in favor of "free beer, free love, and free wheeling." But that summer would bring him closer to genuine lawlessness than he could stomach. "I answered an ad," he later recalled. "An oil man wanted a chauffeur. He took one look at me and said I was it. I ferried him around for two weeks before I discovered he was a bootlegger and that he was taking me along as a bodyguard."[31] Bob soon quit the job.

Without the athletics, his academic performance improved; he made Phi Beta Kappa in his junior and senior years, wrote an essay on Shakespeare that was anthologized in a collection of undergraduate writing, and won a hundred-dollar prize for his experimental one-act play *The Visitor,* whose title character was the grim reaper and whose one and only performance took place in the college's Robinson Hall. Now twenty-two, Bob had hung onto his blissful ignorance for as long as possible, but he began to understand that he would be graduating into harder times than any he had ever known. The Ryans' life of luxury had evaporated as the country spiraled into depression. Tim wanted Bob to come home and help with the business, but Bob resisted. He would do anything but seal himself up inside an office.

After graduating in June 1932, Bob took what little money he had and moved to Greenwich Village with two fraternity brothers, intending to find a job as a newspaper reporter and work on his playwriting. A third of the country was out of work, and along the streets of New York people queued at breadlines and soup kitchens. Bob couldn't figure out what he wanted to do with his life; he only knew he couldn't go into business. He fought a professional bout under an assumed name to raise some cash, but otherwise the boxing went nowhere. A girlfriend got him gigs modeling for true-confession magazines and department store ads—he later claimed to be the first man in America to model French jockey shorts—but his pals gave him so much grief over this that he quit. For a while he worked as a sandhog, pushing rock barges through tunnels under the Hudson River.

In this economic climate the pampered young man oscillated between realism and sheer fantasy. Some pals from Psi Upsilon persuaded him to come in with them on a gold mine in Libby, Montana, and Bob moved out West to prospect with a friend. The living was rough; they had to break ice on a stream for bathing water. After four months they had managed to extract about eight dollars' worth of gold. When Bob heard about a cowpuncher job in Missoula paying that much every week, he gave up on the mine, and eventually he returned to New York City, wearing a long beard and hitting up his classmates for money to get back on his feet.

Magazine profiles would offer differing accounts of how Bob managed to wind up a sailor aboard *The City of New York,* a diesel freighter making runs to South Africa, in 1933. According to one, he was strolling along the Brooklyn waterfront one day, visiting a friend, and when he saw the ship loading on the wharf, he impulsively asked for a job.[32] According to another, he "accepted drinks one night from a jovial tramp steamer captain" and "woke next morning bound for Lourenzo Marques, Portuguese East Africa."[33] In any event, Bob shipped out as an engine room wiper, cleaning up oil that leaked from the cylinders and various pumps, oiling the pumps, and fetching coffee. Owned by the private Farrell Lines, *The City of New York* headed down the East Coast to New Orleans and then across the Atlantic, carrying manufactured goods. It probably docked in Cape Town, East London, and Durban, and it returned to New York two or three months later with shipments of raw asbestos or chrome.[34]

Bob might have been surrendering to his love of Melville and Eugene O'Neill, who had written of the seafaring life in *Anna Christie* and *The Hairy Ape.* He spent more than two years at sea, collecting stories of hardship and adventure. The equatorial heat was unbearable; once he had to intervene when a delirious female passenger tried to push her baby through a porthole. Another time, after the ship's store of food spoiled, he subsisted for days on lime juice.

Whenever Bob heard from his parents, the news was grim. In December

1934 his Uncle Tom died, leaving the presidency of the Ryan Company to Tim. Soon after that both Joe Ryan and John Ryan died. The pressure of the construction industry was crushing them out like the cigarettes Bob now smoked daily. In January 1936, not long after returning home from a run, he received a phone call from his mother: his father had been hit by a car, and Bob was to return to Chicago at once to look after him and help out with a subway tunnel project. Bob made an inglorious return to Chicago as a common sandhog, pushing rock barges beneath the streets of the city by day and struggling to understand the business by night.

Tim's accident had exacerbated a heart condition, and on April 27, 1936, he died of a coronary occlusion at Passavant Memorial Hospital. He was sixty. Writing to his children, Bob would quickly recount the stock market crash and the tunnel disaster, adding, "I am sure that both of these events caused my father's early death."[35] Tim was laid to rest in Calvary Cemetery in the north suburb of Evanston, beside his little son Jack.

Bob knew he had to look after his mother and made a game effort to help his uncle Larry, now president of the Ryan Company and the last surviving brother at the firm. But he wanted out of the tunnels: one time, as he was breaking up rocks with a sledgehammer, he turned over a rock to find an abandoned dynamite charge. Another time he worked forty-eight hours straight when a power plant failure imperiled the air pressure in a tunnel. Eventually, he quit the company, drifting from one job to the next. One oft-repeated story had him working as a collector for a loan shark on the blighted West Side and, moved by the poverty he saw, coming back to return one family's money. He was working as a gang boss on a WPA road paving crew for thirty dollars a week when his uncle Larry Ryan died in December 1937, only fifty-five years old. The Ryan Company would endure into the 1940s, but there was nothing left of the brothers now except their name.

Frustrated with her son's career drift, Mabel finally called on Tim's old friend Ed Kelly, who had not only survived the sanitary district scandal but ascended through a city council vote to become mayor of Chicago. After Anton Cermak was fatally wounded during an assassination attempt on President-elect Roosevelt in February 1933, Kelly had been pushed through the council by his old friend Patrick Nash, the Twenty-Eighth Ward alderman, and they controlled a formidable vote-getting operation that gave them enormous power over the city. Bob would remember Big Ed Kelly as an avatar of ward politics and no dreamer. One night in 1928, when Bob was home from college, he had been sitting in his parents' living room when Kelly came calling for Tim, having just met Al Smith, the progressive New York governor and Democratic nominee for president. "He's talking about things like welfare and human rights and all that shit," Kelly complained.[36]

As mayor, Kelly had relaxed enforcement of gambling laws; according to the Chicago Crime Commission, the administration pocketed $20 million from organized crime one year to ignore illegal operations. At the same time Kelly had forged an alliance with Roosevelt and brought much-needed New Deal funding to the city. He went out on a limb politically with his vocal advocacy of open housing and school integration. To some extent this was pure politics: his success at drawing blacks away from the Republican Party contributed to his success at the polls. But Kelly acted too, appointing blacks to more influential posts, working to integrate the police department, and, at one point, shutting down a local screening of D. W. Griffith's *The Birth of a Nation*. "The time is not far away," he told one audience, "when we shall forget the color of a man's skin and see him only in the light of intelligence in his mind and soul."[37]

Now Big Ed would come through for the Ryans one more time, with a white-collar patronage job for Tim's aimless son. Bob joined the Department of Education as an assistant vice superintendent, though his job consisted of little more than filling requisitions for school supplies. Under the leadership of James B. McCahey, a coal company executive and crony of the mayor's, the board had developed a reputation to rival the sanitary district's; local muckraker Elmer Lynn Williams called it "the most corrupt Board of Education that ever cursed the Chicago schools."[38] Down in his little basement office, Ryan recalled, he "had little to do except combat hangovers,"[39] so he spent a good deal of time writing, an infraction ignored by the other patronage hires. The boredom drove him mad—this was everything he'd struggled to avoid in his vagabonding days. He was pushing thirty, his father was dead, and he still hadn't decided what to do with his life.

The answer came to him one afternoon when he ran into a friend and she talked him into taking a role in a local theater production. Despite his passion for theater, Bob could be painfully inhibited; he still winced at the memory of delivering a speech in grade school and hearing laughter ripple through the audience when his voice cracked. But he took the role, and something happened. "I never even thought of acting until I was twenty-eight," he later recalled. "The first minute I got on the stage, I thought, 'Bing! This is it.'"[40]

Electrified by the experience, Bob signed up for acting classes with Edward Boyle, a stock company actor who charged five dollars a week. "What an audience most likes to feel in an actor is decision," Boyle would tell him. "Always keep saying to yourself, 'Decision, decision, decision.'"[41] After Bob's mother informed him that the Stickney School, whose upper classes were college preparatory instruction for girls, would have to cancel its senior class play because the drama coach had taken ill, Bob managed to convince the principal that he was an experienced stage director and took over the production. The play was J. M. Barrie's comic fantasy *Dear Brutus,* and the performance, on May 6, 1938, went off reasonably well. "With kindest regards for the first person who ever wanted my autograph," Bob would write on a program for a friend.[42]

Bob silently hatched a plan that would get him out of Chicago for good: over the next couple of years, he would save a few thousand dollars, move to Los Angeles, and enroll in the acting school at the Pasadena Playhouse. In another era he might have set his sights on New York, but Bob was still smitten with the movies. "The very mention of them excites the imagination and stirs the blood," he'd written in a high school essay. "We may walk out of our own world into another."[43] By now his focus had shifted from Douglas Fairbanks to the new generation of talking actors: Clark Gable, Spencer Tracy, and James Cagney, the latter of whom had become a star playing a Chicago gangster in *The Public Enemy.*

His ticket out of town arrived in summer 1938. Years later a couple of news stories about Ryan would refer to an inheritance, but the story most frequently told had him unexpectedly striking it rich on a friend's oil well near Niles, Michigan, his three hundred dollars' worth of stock paying a sudden dividend of two thousand dollars. His mother was dumbfounded when he informed her of his plan. "You can't earn a living that way," she insisted. "This little acting group you play with is nice, as a hobby. But I know you. You can't act."[44] Act he would, and before long he had kissed his mother good-bye and boarded a westbound train from Union Station. Surely his father would have disapproved. "How sharper than a serpent's tooth it is / To have a thankless child!"[45] But then, if his father hadn't struck out on his own as a young man, he would have spent his life caulking boats in Lockport, Illinois. Whatever sort of life Bob found for himself in Los Angeles, at the very least it would be his own.

two

The Mysterious Spirit

She was gorgeous. Five-foot-seven at least, with dark red hair and cutting, observant brown eyes. Ryan first spotted her in the hallway of the Max Reinhardt School of the Theater on Sunset Boulevard. He had arrived in Los Angeles to discover that the theater school at the Pasadena Playhouse was full, but a fellow named Jack Smart, whom he had met through a girlfriend in Chicago, recommended the Reinhardt School, which had opened just that summer. As Ryan liked to tell it, he decided to enroll the moment he saw the girl in the hallway. Through a school administrator he managed to arrange an introduction; her name was Jessica Cadwalader, she was studying acting as well, and they would begin classes together the next day with Professor Reinhardt. Feeling impetuous, Ryan asked her to dinner, and she accepted.

Jessica Cadwalader was twenty-three, born in Los Angeles to Quaker parents and, after they divorced, raised in Berkeley by her mother. She had graduated from the private Anna Head School, where she had been a tennis champ, and shortly thereafter she boarded a bus for New York City, where she found an apartment in the Murray Hill neighborhood of Midtown Manhattan, took modeling jobs through a Park Avenue agency, and tried to establish herself as an actress under the name Jessica Cheyney. For some time she had performed with the Wayfarers, a theater group in San Francisco. Now she was back in Los Angeles looking for movie work; she had been an extra in the W. C. Fields comedy *Poppy* (1936) and gotten a line, only to see it cut, in the Gary Cooper drama *The Adventures of Marco Polo* (1938). She was formidably well read despite the fact that she had never attended college, and she looked a little startled at dinner when Ryan informed her that the piece he had been rehearsing for the first class was no less than Hamlet's second soliloquy. He wanted to get Reinhardt's attention.

As Jessica already knew, Reinhardt's attention was a force to be reckoned with. Quiet and stout, with hypnotic blue eyes, the aging Austrian studied you so intensely, and listened with such force, that he seemed to be penetrating your very soul. Reinhardt had made his name in Europe and the United States with spectacular, expressionist stagings of *Everyman* (for the Salzburg Festival, which he cofounded in 1920 with Richard Strauss), *The Miracle,* and *A Midsummer Night's Dream.* His 1934 production of the latter at the Hollywood Bowl became the talk of the town, and the following year Warner Bros. hired him to direct a lavish screen version with James Cagney, Olivia de Havilland, and Mickey Rooney. Born to Jewish parents in Austria-Hungary, Reinhardt had fled the Third Reich in 1938 and settled in Los Angeles. Though he never managed to land another movie assignment, he continued to direct stage productions on both coasts; in fact, the new school would serve as a workshop for plays he wanted to mount commercially.

Jessica braced herself the next day as her new friend from Chicago came forward to butcher Hamlet's second soliloquy: "O villain, villain, smiling, damned villain! My tables—meet it is I set it down / That one may smile, and smile, and be a villain!"[1] Reinhardt's only response was, "With training . . ."[2] Ryan took this as a great triumph when Jessica spoke to him afterward. "There is a young man who has just enrolled that I like very much," she reportedly wrote to her mother, "but he's the worst actor I've ever seen in my life."[3]

Meeting with Ryan later, Reinhardt told the young man he had a quality that reached out over the footlights, and with enormous work and commitment he might one day become a great performer.[4] These were the right words coming from the right man at the right time, and from that moment onward Ryan entrusted himself to Reinhardt. "Max Reinhardt was not only my first teacher," he would write near the end of his life (forgetting Ed Boyle in Chicago), "but remains to this day, thirty-two years later, the most tremendous and important person who has ever influenced my career and my work."[5] Though Reinhardt was best known for his elaborate productions, incorporating music, choreography, and lighting effects, Ryan saw that the old man was also deeply and personally invested in his smaller projects. "His own obsession was the inner life of man," Ryan wrote, "the mysterious spirit that both flickers and flames in all of us."[6]

Reinhardt felt that human emotion was stifled by bourgeois life. "Unconsciously we feel how a hearty laugh liberates us," he wrote in an essay on acting, "how a good cry or an outbreak of anger relieves us. We have an absolute need of emotion and its expression. Against this our upbringing constantly works. Its first commandment is—Hide what goes on within you. Never let it be seen that you are stirred up, that you are hungry or thirsty; every grief, every joy, every rage, all that is fundamental and craves utterance, must be repressed."[7]

How profoundly this idea must have struck his new student from Chicago, this powerfully built but painfully shy man whose parents had shown him the good life but always taught him to keep his feelings to himself. "Only the actor who cannot lie, who is himself undisguised, and who profoundly unlocks his heart deserves the laurel," Reinhardt wrote.[8] Not until years later, after working with numerous pedestrian directors, would Ryan recognize what an enormous gift Reinhardt had given him so early in his development. Yet implicit in that gift lay a great moral and emotional challenge.

Reinhardt cut an imposing figure, yet he tended to put people at ease because he listened so closely. "He never listened passively," recalled the composer Bronislaw Kaper, "he listened actively, with the greatest interest reflected in his eyes and his half open lips."[9] In fact, Reinhardt's ability to listen defined his whole approach to acting. "The best piece of advice I've ever received as an actor was given me by Max Reinhardt," Ryan told a reporter years later. "He put it in one word—'Listen.' If you really hear what other actors say to you, your own reaction and the proper reading of your lines will be easy."[10]

Actors who worked with Reinhardt, among them Stella Adler and Otto Preminger, testified to his talent for bringing an actor out of himself, quite literally—for locating personal traits that one might heighten and project onstage. If you engaged Reinhardt imaginatively, he invested himself in your performance, and you immediately felt the thrill of shared discovery. "He was most effective when he liked an actor, and perhaps only when he liked him," remembered Preminger. "If he felt that the actor really wanted to be directed by him, then his imagination, the variety of advice, the way he worked the actor in the scene and *for* the scene, was just fantastic. I don't think any director ever had that gift. Maybe it was because he was an actor originally."[11]

The Reinhardt School offered a well-rounded education, and Ryan threw himself into his studies, learning about lighting, set design, and direction. But acting was his great love now. His workshop teacher, Vladimir Sokoloff, had performed with the Moscow Art Theatre under the great director Constantin Stanislavski, and from him learned the principle that movement expressed a character's motivation better than anything else. Yet Sokoloff's classes were more traditional than the Stanislavski-inspired "method acting" then gaining traction at the Group Theatre in New York, in which the performer used powerful personal memories to trigger onstage responses. " 'The Method' would have driven Sokoloff out of his skull," Ryan later mused. "He taught action, not 'memory of emotion.' "[12]

Under Sokoloff's instruction the young man improved rapidly, and during the fall 1938 semester Reinhardt cast him as Silvio and Jessica as Beatrice in a workshop production of Carlo Goldoni's *At Your Service.* Ryan played Bottom in *A Midsummer Night's Dream* and the father in Pirandello's *Six Characters in Search of an Author,* "at one of whose unforgettable rehearsals," wrote Gottfried Reinhardt, "my father showed Bob Ryan how literally to collapse after the discovery of his daughter in a brothel, how to fold up like a jackknife and to exit, his torso bent horizontal, a destroyed human being." Clearly Reinhardt appreciated the physicality of this boxer who had graduated to the stage, and Ryan would embrace the idea of movement as character.

ALL THROUGH this great artistic awakening, Ryan was falling in love with Jessica Cadwalader. Their courtship took a rocky turn when he invited her to dinner at the Brown Derby and a miscommunication resulted in each of them sitting alone, waiting for the other to materialize, on successive days. When he called her to complain about being stood up, she hung up on him and went to San Francisco with a girlfriend. But before long the two thespians had become inseparable, going out for drinks when they could afford it or talking all night about books and movies and politics and, of course, acting. Ryan had never met anyone like her; she was introverted, but smart as a whip and passionately idealistic. The more time he spent with her, the more he wanted her in his life. For some reason she always called him Robert; friends and family had called him Bob for years, but to Jessica he would always be Robert Ryan.

Ryan might have thought he had experienced the West in his Montana adventures, but Jessica's people were real westerners. Her maternal grandmother, Anno, told Jessica all about the old days. Born Annie Neal in 1859 to an undertaker in Atchison, Kansas, she had been worshipping at the town's

Jessica Cadwalader (late 1930s). Ryan met her in the lobby of the Max Reinhardt School of the Theater on Sunset Boulevard; they spent the next thirty-three years together. *Robert Ryan Family*

Episcopal church one Sunday morning when she met George Washington Cheyney, a young Philadelphian five years her senior whose wealthy family, alarmed by his indolence, had set him up as manager of a silver mine that some of his father's colleagues owned in Tombstone, Arizona. On his travels back and forth, George Cheyney changed trains in Atchison, and before long he and Annie had married and moved to Tombstone, to a large house on the hill overlooking the town.

By then Tombstone was the fastest-growing boomtown in the Southwest, with a fair amount of culture alongside the roughnecks who poured in hoping to strike it rich. There were decent restaurants, an ice cream parlor, and opera performances at Schieffelin Hall, named for the prospecting family that had founded the town. Jessica pressed her grandmother for details about the famous shootout at the OK Corral in 1881. "I never knew anything about all that riff-raff," Anno replied. Her husband "did not think such goings-on should be talked about in front of ladies. . . . I have a feeling George said it was good riddance to bad rubbish."[13] Later Jessica dug up a history of Tombstone that described one George Cheyney ducking behind a counter during the armed robbery of an assayer's office.

As superintendent of the Tombstone Mill and Mining Company, George Cheyney branched out from Tombstone and developed a new mine in the Oro

Blanco Mining District, but in the late 1880s Tombstone's mining industry collapsed after the miners began to hit water and the town's pumping plant was destroyed in a fire. George ran for Congress as a Republican in 1890 and served as school superintendent for the territory, then moved his family to Tucson, where he was appointed postmaster in 1898 and four years later ran a successful campaign for probate judge. Shortly after his election George traveled to San Francisco, seeking treatment for a liver ailment from a Tucson physician who had moved there, and died at age forty-nine from cirrhosis.

Three years later his second daughter, Frances—Jessica's mother—married Richard Bacon Cadwalader, a young Quaker in his early twenties who had come West from Cincinnati with his mother, Ella Bacon Cadwalader, after suffering a nervous breakdown in his first semester at Harvard. Ella Cadwalader fought against the union between Richard and Frances, but when Anno traveled from Tucson to Los Angeles to visit her sister, she took the young lovers along and had them married by an Episcopal clergyman. This would have been the ultimate horror for Ella and her husband, Pierce Jonah Cadwalader, whose family had followed the Society of Friends since the seventeenth century and been part of the influential Philadelphia Quakers Meeting.

In 1907, Frances gave birth to a son, Richard Jr., and seven years later, on October 26, 1914, Jessica Dorothy Cadwalader arrived. The family was living in Tucson when Richard Jr., only ten years old, died of influenza in September 1917 (just three months earlier, little Jack Ryan had succumbed in Chicago). Jessica grew up an only child, an introvert, and a voracious reader, closely instructed in her religious beliefs by her great aunt Dora, whom she remembered as "a great and determined Quaker lady."[14] From childhood Jessica learned to value peace over war, mercy over revenge; she learned that God's spirit, dwelling within her, not only permitted but obliged her to work for peace. Dora liked to recite the "Quality of Mercy" speech from *The Merchant of Venice,* in which Portia describes mercy as "twice blest: / It blesseth him that gives and him that takes."[15]

Since the beginning the Society of Friends had preached the equality of men and women, allowing women into ecclesiastical positions, and in America the Quakers had provided not only the idealism but also some of the early leaders of the women's movement: the Philadelphia abolitionist Lucretia Mott, who had helped organize the 1848 Seneca Falls Convention on women's rights; the great speaker and activist Susan B. Anthony, who spent a lifetime trying to win women the vote; and Alice Paul, who helped pass the Nineteenth Amendment in 1920 and wrote the Equal Rights Amendment proposed to Congress three years later.* Dora wanted Jessica to get a good education and become a lawyer like Dora's brother, Jonah; there was no reason she should have to spend her life in her husband's shadow.

ON SATURDAY, MARCH 11, 1939, Bob and Jessica exchanged vows at St. Thomas Episcopal Church in West Hollywood, with their mothers, the Reinhardts, the Sokoloffs, and about fifty of their fellow students attending (including Nanette Fabray, the other big star who would emerge from their graduating class). Anno must have been there as well, a reminder to Ryan of the iron female will surging through his bride's family. A respectable matron in Tombstone and an example to her children in late middle age, Anno had decided upon her seventieth birthday to please no one but herself. "That evening she drank her first highball and smoked her first cigarette," her grand-daughter wrote. "She went on doing both to the end, chain smoking without inhaling, puffing out great clouds of smoke to wreathe her white head, looking like something between a Chinese ancient and an old madame, while the cigarette ashes spilled down the front of her massive bosom."[16]

Two more productions—Goldoni's *Servant of Two Masters,* which had been one of Reinhardt's early triumphs, and *Holiday,* a romantic comedy by Phillip Barry that had become a screen hit for Katharine Hepburn and Cary Grant—followed before the end of the year's study, at which point the two newlyweds began to reckon with the question of money. As the story goes, word came shortly after their wedding that Ryan's oil well in Michigan had run dry, which meant an end to their steady dividend.

They supported themselves as best they could: Ryan worked as an assistant director to Reinhardt and taught boxing lessons for a dollar a pop, but Jessica was the real breadwinner, modeling for a photographer and then hiring on with vaudeville producers Franchon and Marco as a chorus girl at the Paramount Theater. "It was a rugged job, and she hated it," Ryan would write, "but it made it possible for me to work and study and pound on doors and try a little longer to make somebody believe I could really act."[17] The

---

*For more on this fascinating topic, see Martha Hope Bacon, *Mothers of Feminism: The Story of Quaker Women in America* (San Francisco: Harper and Row, 1986).

first agent Ryan approached told him to go out the door and come back in again. "Make an entrance. Get it?" When Ryan did, the agent said, "Go back to Chicago."[18]

From the house they had rented after their marriage, they moved to a small cottage and then to an apartment above someone's garage. Their situation was precarious, but Ryan was relatively sanguine. "I thought of what had happened to my father and knew that it was worse than useless to worry," he recalled. "The moment I stopped worrying, things began to come right for us."[19]

In late December 1939, Reinhardt cast Ryan in a commercial production of Somerset Maugham's drawing room farce *Too Many Husbands,* to open the following month at the Belasco Theater in Los Angeles. Promoted as "a saucy comedy with music," the play centered on a woman who believes her first husband has been killed in action during the Great War and takes a second, only to have the first return home; by then she has a child by each man. Marsha Hunt, a young actress who had recently signed to MGM, went to see a friend in the play and was struck by Ryan and the other male lead, former Olympic shot putter Bruce Bennett. "They were remarkable, both of them," Hunt recalled. "Tall, wonderfully good-looking but, most of all, graceful in their movements onstage."[20] The engagement brought Ryan his first serious attention around town, and by the end of its run a casting director for Paramount Pictures had recommended him to director Edward Dmytryk for the lead in *Golden Gloves,* an upcoming picture about amateur boxing.

Golden Gloves told the story of a young fighter, mixed up with a crooked promoter, who sees the error of his ways and throws in with a crusading journalist to clean up the sport.[†] Dmytryk shot a screen test with Ryan as the fighter, then decided to give the role to Richard Denning; as a consolation prize he cast Ryan as Denning's opponent in the climactic bout. They began shooting the fight in mid-December and finished in seven days; given nothing but a soundstage and three hundred extras, Dmytryk managed to evoke an entire stadium by dimming the lights on the audience, as at a real fight, and using bee smokers to create a cigarette haze over the crowd. Dmytryk was impressed with Ryan in the ring: "He was 6' 4", weighed 198 pounds, boxed beautifully, and hit like a mule. He tapped Denning in the ribs during their

---

[†]The picture was loosely based on the story of Arch Ward, a *Chicago Tribune* sports editor who had founded the tournament in the 1920s.

fight, and Dick made three trips to the hospital for X-rays. To this day he insists his ribs were broken, though the pictures showed nary a crack."[21]

With the role came a contract as a stock player at Paramount for $125 a week, and the chance to experience a moviemaking operation from the inside. As Ryan sat with photographers and makeup artists and casting people, his physical attributes were evaluated with cold precision. At thirty years old, he was a seriously handsome Black Irishman, lean and muscular, with a strong jaw and a warm, brilliant smile. Yet his forehead was already lined from years of hard labor, and his brown, crinkly eyes were rather small in his face; if he narrowed them even slightly, they took on a beady, menacing quality. His height was impressive but hardly ideal for someone trying to get a leg up in supporting roles. "The men stars wouldn't have me in a picture with them," he recalled. "I towered over so many of them."[22]

Paramount threw him bit roles: one morning in January 1940 he shot a scene for *Queen of the Mob,* based on the story of Kate "Ma" Barker and the Barker-Karpis gang, and a month later he put in two days playing an ambulance driver, barely glimpsed on-screen, in the Bob Hope comedy *The Ghost Breakers.* From mid-March to early May he was a Canadian mountie in Cecil B. DeMille's *North West Mounted Police,* starring Gary Cooper and Madeleine Carroll, and that same month he played a train passenger in the nondescript western *The Texas Rangers Ride Again.* Ryan was disappointed but not exactly surprised when Paramount cut him loose after six months. Rather than hanging around Hollywood, waiting for something to happen, he and Jessica resolved to look for stage work in New York.

Back in Manhattan, the couple scraped by on Jessica's modeling gigs and whatever Ryan could find. A year after Hitler's invasion of Poland had ignited the war in Europe, President Roosevelt succeeded in passing the Selective Service Act, which established the country's first peacetime draft and required the registration of all men from twenty-one to thirty-five years old. As a married man, Ryan was unlikely to be drafted soon or at all, but Jessica was horrified by the idea of him going to war. Ryan "believed that people should fight their own fights," their son, Cheyney, later wrote. "Hence, if you believed in a war, you should be ready to fight it yourself." Yet Jessica had been raised to believe that all war was immoral. "For her, war was not a story of people fighting their own fights. It was one of the privileged sending others to pay the costs while they reaped the benefits and attacked the patriotism of others along the way."[23]

By June 1941 they had hired on at the Millpond Playhouse, a summer stock theater in Roslyn, Long Island. The productions tended toward mystery and comedy; the company, Ryan recalled, was "appalling, being mostly bad amateurs."[24] In *The Barker* he played a carnival barker and Jessica a hootchie cootchie dancer; two weeks later they costarred again in something called *Petticoat Fever.* Millpond staged a mystery play Jessica had written, *The Dark Corner,* and in the comedy *Angel Child,* Ryan costarred with twenty-two-year-old Cameron Mitchell. The highlight of the season was William Saroyan's philosophical barroom comedy *The Time of Your Life,* starring Ryan as the rich drunk, Joe, who encourages the other barflies to live life to the fullest.

The Ryans bailed out soon afterward, landing first at the Robin Hood Theater in Arden, Delaware, and then at the Cape Playhouse in Dennis, Massachusetts, where Ryan won a romantic role opposite the celebrated Luise Rainer in J. M. Barrie's comic fantasy *A Kiss for Cinderella.* Set in London during World War I, the class-conscious fantasy told the story of a poor cleaning woman, played by Rainer, who dreams that she is Cinderella and the neighborhood constable, to be played by Ryan, is Prince Charming. *This guy is going to be a big star,* thought Robert Wallsten, a fellow cast member, as he watched Ryan rehearse. "I had no idea about his dramatic ability, and playing this Irish bobby was not a very serious role. But he had a corner on that Irish charm, and there was that magic grin. . . . It was the smile that was so warm and engulfing, and so endearing."[25] Wallsten would become one of the Ryans' oldest friends.

From Dennis the production moved to the Maplewood Theatre in Maplewood, New Jersey, where Ryan caught an extraordinary break. Rainer had been married to Clifford Odets, a founder of the Group Theatre and one of the most daring American playwrights of the day (*Waiting for Lefty, Awake and Sing!*); with the recent demise of the Group, Odets had sold his play *Clash by Night* to showbiz impresario Billy Rose, who was mounting a Broadway production with Lee Strasberg, another Group founder, as director. The play dealt with an unhappy working-class couple on Staten Island, but in a larger sense it considered the restive political mood in America as the war in Europe raged on. Tallulah Bankhead, hailed for her recent performance in Lillian Hellman's *The Little Foxes,* had signed to play the bored and frustrated wife; Lee J. Cobb, among the Group's most gifted actors, was cast as her dense but devoted husband; and Joseph Schildkraut, a longtime stage and screen veteran who had won an Oscar playing Alfred Dreyfus in *The Life of Émile Zola,* was the husband's cynical friend, who moves in on the wife. For the minor role of Joe Doyle, a young neighbor with romantic problems of his own, Rainer urged Odets to consider her handsome young lead in *A Kiss for Cinderella.*

Rose took Bankhead out to Maplewood to see the show, and she liked Ryan. Soon after *A Kiss for Cinderella* closed on September 23, 1941, he was rehearsing *Clash by Night* in New York City. One can only imagine his excitement: four months earlier he had been slugging it out at the Millpond Playhouse, and now he would be making his Broadway debut in a cutting-edge social drama, alongside some of the most respected talents in the American theater. He had seen Bankhead in *The Little Foxes* and thought her an extraordinary actress.[26] A world-class diva, she could be witheringly cruel to colleagues, but she took a shine to him during rehearsals. When he introduced her to Jessica, who had been modeling to help meet the rent, Bankhead quipped, "If I was fifteen years younger I'd take him away from you."[27] The Ryans laughed, though Jessica couldn't have been too pleased. She would spend the next thirty years meeting women who were less frank but similarly inclined.

"Tallulah was a stereotype of what the public thinks star actresses are like: they really aren't except in her case," Ryan would remember. "She liked some kind of excitement going on and didn't much care where it came from." At the same time Bankhead was a consummate professional, the first to arrive and the last to leave, and always with her part down cold. She might challenge Strasberg or Odets in rehearsal, yet in performance she could be remarkably generous toward other players. "She was a great experience," Ryan would conclude, "and she came along at a most important time in my life."[28]

Unfortunately, the production quickly degenerated into a snake pit of professional rivalries and personal grudges, from which Ryan was lucky enough to be excepted. Bankhead despised Billy Rose, a diminutive casting-couch type whose theatrical résumé consisted mainly of brassy revues. "He approached the Odets play as if he were putting on a rodeo," she later wrote.[29] An elegant presence onstage, Bankhead had taken the role of the drab housewife as a dramatic stretch, but when the play began its out-of-town tryouts in Detroit, critics decided she had been miscast, favoring Lee Cobb's performance as the husband. "That was when the shit hit the fan," Ryan remembered.[30] Bankhead and Katherine Locke, who played Ryan's girlfriend, soon fell out, united by nothing except their dislike of Schildkraut, whom Locke later accused of putting the moves on her.[31]

Though some of these conflicts sprang from ego or personal enmity, the production was built on an artistic fault line that would become more apparent in years to come: on one side were the more traditionally trained actors such as Ryan, Bankhead, and Schildkraut, and on the other were proponents of the Method such as Cobb and Strasberg, the latter of whom would institutionalize the techniques of tapping into one's own emotional experience when he founded the Actors Studio six years later. Method acting could be fresh, genuine, even explosive, but it could also be unpredictable and inconsistent from night to night. Cobb, the most ardent Method actor among the cast, often seemed to be working through his role onstage, and for someone such as Bankhead, playing against him was one curveball after another. Ryan sympathized with her, and later in his career, colleagues would note his annoyance and even anger over onstage surprises.

From Detroit, *Clash by Night* moved on to Baltimore, Pittsburgh, and Philadelphia, where Bankhead came down with pneumonia and the show was shut down (as the star, she had no understudy). While the cast and crew cooled their heels in New York, waiting for her to recover, Ryan scored an interview for the lead role in a Hollywood prestige picture to begin shooting the next year. Pare Lorentz—whose acclaimed documentary shorts *The Plow That Broke the Plains* (1936) and *The River* (1938) had won him a brief but controversial tenure as director of the US Film Office—had signed with RKO Radio Pictures to direct a dramatic feature about a war veteran trying to make ends meet during the Depression, to be titled *Name, Age and Occupation.* For six months he had been crisscrossing the country in search of an actor skillful enough to play the role but credible enough to function in the semidocumentary format Lorentz envisioned. Finally, he turned to his friend John Houseman, an erudite British producer who had collaborated famously with Orson Welles.

Working for the Federal Theatre Project, Houseman and Welles had staged the "voodoo" *Macbeth* (1935), which transplanted the Shakespeare play to a Caribbean island, and the proletarian musical *The Cradle Will Rock* (1937), which proved too hot for the government and inspired them to launch the independent Mercury Theatre. Houseman and Welles had gone on to create the CBS radio broadcast *The War of the Worlds,* which had terrified the nation with its too-convincing account of a martian invasion, and the RKO drama *Citizen Kane* (1941), whose critical acclaim had now emboldened the studio to bankroll Lorentz's ambitious project. Houseman arranged for Lorentz and himself to spend a week interviewing actors in a Manhattan hotel suite. When Ryan arrived to read for the part, his acting must have impressed them, but what really won over Lorentz was Ryan's endless litany of soul-crushing jobs in the depths of the Depression. Here was a man who not only could play the part but already had lived it.

In the 1972 memoir *Run-Through,* Houseman would remember traveling by train with Lorentz through western Kansas and hearing on the radio in the club car that the Imperial Japanese Navy had attacked the US air base at Pearl Harbor, Hawaii, killing and wounding thousands of Americans. The next day the United States and United Kingdom declared war on Japan. Three weeks later, *Clash by Night* opened on Broadway at the Belasco Theatre, its take on the national mood decisively outpaced by world events. Reviews were scathing, though the players got good notices for their work, Ryan included; most critics went to town on Odets, citing a lack of passion and fresh characterization. The play closed on February 7, 1942, after only forty-nine performances, but not before Ryan was seen by such luminaries as Greta Garbo, Judith Anderson, Ruth Gordon, and Thornton Wilder.

"Ryan's was a small part," remembered Tony Randall, then a young actor starting out in New York, "but he was very, very good."[32] According to one news story, Ryan was "showered" with offers from New York producers, including one from the Theater Guild to appear in a new play with Katharine Hepburn.[33] The attention went to his head. He would remember "swaggering" into Bankhead's dressing room one night and "demanding to know how long it was going to take before I was a really great actor. I expected her to say a year or so. But instead she said very quietly, 'In 15 or 20 years you may be a good actor, Bob—if you're lucky.'"[34]

three

Bombs Away

Soon after the Odets play breathed its last, Ryan found himself in Tennessee shooting locations for *Name, Age and Occupation* with director Pare Lorentz and actress Frances Dee. The movie's story dated back to a novel Lorentz had begun in 1931: an eighteen-year-old boy from North Carolina fights overseas in the Great War but finds nothing waiting for him back home except a series of dehumanizing farm and factory jobs. As Houseman explained, the movie would explore "the condition of the US industrial worker with special emphasis on the economic and emotional effects of the production line."[1]

Lorentz already had tried mixing actors with real people, to less than stellar effect, in his documentary *The Fight for Life* (1940), about the Chicago Maternity Center and infant mortality in the slums. But George Schaefer, president of Radio-Keith-Orpheum, was prepared to take a gamble on the director; before Ryan even reported for work, Lorentz and cinematographer Floyd Crosby had spent twenty days shooting industrial operations at Ford's River Rouge Plant and a US Army facility. Location shooting continued through the spring, and in June the company arrived in Los Angeles to spend four weeks shooting interiors on the Pathé lot in Culver City.

That same month, fed up with Schaefer's artistic pretensions and dismal bottom line, the RKO board replaced him with N. Peter Rathvon and installed Ned Depinet as president of the movie division, RKO Radio Pictures. Charles Koerner, the new, commercial-minded head of production, immediately targeted two runaway films: *It's All True,* which Orson Welles had been shooting in Brazil since early that year, and *Name, Age and Occupation.* Lorentz, observed director Edward Dmytryk, was "a fine critic, a top maker

Ryan on location with director Pare Lorentz for the ill-fated *Name, Age and Occupation*. Their RKO colleague Edward Dmytryk called Lorentz "a fine critic, a top maker of documentaries, but completely lost in straight drama. After 90 of shooting, he was 87 days behind schedule." *Robert Ryan Family*

of documentaries, but completely lost in straight drama. After 90 days of shooting, he was 87 days behind schedule."[2]

In late June, RKO halted production of *Name, Age and Occupation* and asked Lorentz for a financial accounting.[3] He must have seen the writing on the wall when Koerner announced his production plans for 1942–43: $12 million was budgeted for only forty-five features, and in contrast to the literary projects favored by his predecessor, RKO would be aiming for good, solid box office by making patriotic movies for the home front. *Name, Age and Occupation,* with its Depression setting and heavy themes, hardly filled that bill, and after screening rushes, RKO executives killed the project.

They liked Ryan, however, and signed him to a $600-a-week contract; under Schaefer the movie division had developed a shortage of leading men, exacerbated now by the many actors enlisting in the armed forces. "Without the talent shortage I would very likely have still been grubbing around New York for 40 a week jobs where I more or less belonged at my stage of the game,"

Ryan confessed·in a letter to a friend.[4] He and Jessica moved their belongings back to Los Angeles and rented a house in Silverlake, which they shared with Ryan's fifty-nine-year-old mother, Mabel. By October he had his first assignment from RKO, a picture about the US Army Air Forces called *Bombardier*. With this new job, the couple decided the time had come for children. Before long Jessica was pregnant, but she miscarried early the next year, another sad bond for two partners who had each lost a sibling in childhood.

With *Clash by Night* and now *Name, Age and Occupation*, Ryan had been involved with two prestigious dramas that crashed and burned yet elevated him professionally. Two years after his pink slip from Paramount, he was back in Hollywood earning nearly five times as much from RKO. Boom times had returned to Hollywood with the US military mobilization against Germany and Japan: as defense plants hummed in the nation's industrial centers, workers with good wages packed the movie palaces in search of solace, inspiration, or just relief from their worries. The studios cooperated eagerly with the Office of War Information to rally moviegoers to the war effort, and of the seven features Ryan would make over the next sixteen months, every one addressed the war in some way.

Even as he cranked out these patriotic pictures, Ryan waited for his own draft notice to arrive. After Pearl Harbor the draft age had been widened to include all men from twenty to forty-four years old; he was thirty-two, but Congress and public opinion favored drafting single men over husbands and fathers. In February 1942 the director of selective service, Lewis B. Hershey, had ruled that movies were "an activity essential in certain instances to the national health, and in other instances to war production" and had granted deferments for essential "actors, directors, writers, producers, camera men, sound engineers and other technicians."[5] The outcry in Congress and around the country was immediate, and within forty-eight hours the board of the Screen Actors Guild had voted to oppose the order, arguing that "actors and everyone else in the motion picture industry should be subject to the same rules for the draft as the rest of the country."[6] Hershey soon reversed the policy, but California draft boards were generally cooperative toward the big studios.

Bombardier had been in development for two years already and took as its inspiration not a play or novel but a piece of military hardware, the top secret Norden bombsight, which used a mechanical computer to calculate precision bombing at high altitudes. Pat O'Brien starred as an air force major preaching the virtues of the new contraption, and Randolph Scott was his friendly antagonist, a captain who favors traditional dive-bombing attacks. Ryan was cast as a jaunty young cadet at the new aerial bombardment training school (one scene has him reciting for O'Brien a pledge similar to that taken by real-life bombardiers, that he will "protect the secrecy of the American bombsight, if need be with my life itself," as strings swell and O'Brien looks on in misty-eyed sanctification).

Most of the movie was shot on Kirtland Army Air Base in New Mexico, whose bombardier training program was the model for the one in the movie. RKO vetted the script with the Office of War Information in exchange for access to planes and other resources; one fascinating scene in *Bombardier* shows Ryan's cadet practicing atop a bomb trainer, a twelve-foot frame on wheels that simulates bombing trajectories as it rolls toward a small, motorized metal box representing the target. In return the army got a wholesome, rousing picture that reasoned away any qualms one might have had about raining death from above. One cadet is torn by letters from his mother, who belongs to a peace organization and fears for his soul. "Peace isn't as cheap a bargain, Paul, as the price those people put on it," his commander explains. "Those people lock themselves up in a dream world. You see, there are millions of other mothers that are looking to you."

Ryan put in five weeks on the shoot, though the cast was large and he didn't get much time in the foreground. At one point he bursts into a funeral service for a young trainee to announce in close-up, "The Japs have bombed Pearl Harbor!" During the climax, as Scott and Ryan fly a nighttime scouting mission over Japan in advance of the squadron, their plane is hit; instead of bailing out with the others, Ryan stays behind to dismantle the bombsight with a pistol (actual military protocol) and dies in a giant fireball when the plane crashes. The absurd ending has Scott, captured behind enemy lines, escaping from the Japanese to drive a flaming truck around the munitions plant for the benefit of O'Brien's squadron above. With its fiery payoff, *Bombardier* validated Charles Koerner's new production strategy when it opened the following spring: budgeted at $907,000, it grossed $2.1 million.

More so than the bit parts at Paramount, Ryan's roles at RKO gave him a chance to learn the craft of screen acting, which favored subtlety of expression and demanded incredible mental focus. "On the stage you can coast along," he explained to a journalist years later.

You don't have to concentrate so intensely on small details as you do in a movie. . . . Let's say in this scene, you're talking to me and I'm supposed to be taking a sip from this cup while I listen to you. . . . on the stage, it doesn't make any difference when the cup goes back into the saucer because nobody can hear it. But in a movie scene, while I'm listening to your lines and thinking of the line I have to say next, I must also remember to time the return of the cup to the saucer so that it won't get there until after you finish the last word from your speech, and not a split-second before you finish. If the cup hits the saucer while you're still talking, the clack it makes on the soundtrack will clash with your last words and ruin the scene. A half-hour later we have to do the same scene over again for a close-up or from a different camera angle and it has to be done exactly the same as we did it before.[7]

But even more than acting experience, Ryan took away from *Bombardier* a long, warm friendship with Pat O'Brien, who liked the young man's professionalism and soon began lobbying to have him in his pictures. They shared some striking similarities, including a birthday (O'Brien was exactly ten years older), a Catholic upbringing in the Midwest (he had attended Marquette Academy and Marquette University in Milwaukee), and a love of Chicago (he had met his wife, Eloise, while appearing in a show at the Selwyn Theater in 1927). O'Brien had been summoned from the New York stage to Hollywood by Howard Hughes, who cast him as Hildy Johnson in the movie version of Ben Hecht and Charles MacArthur's *The Front Page* (1931). O'Brien soon moved to Warner Bros. and became a professional Irishman, costarring no fewer than eight times with his pal James Cagney, before memorably embodying the title Norwegian in *Knute Rockne, All American* (1940).

That hit allowed him to end a long, frustrating relationship with Warners and eventually sign with RKO. "I loved that RKO lot, as did most who worked there," O'Brien later wrote. "It exuded more friendliness and warm camaraderie than any studio in which I ever worked."[8] In addition to Cagney, O'Brien was tight with Frank McHugh, a pudgy comic actor who had been with them at Warners, and Spencer Tracy, an old classmate at Marquette Academy. Ryan got to meet them all, though he was never social enough to be considered part of this "Irish mafia." When Ryan asked O'Brien if his natural reticence would hurt him in the movie business, O'Brien pointed to Cagney, who was equally private but remained one of Hollywood's biggest stars. "That was all I needed to know," Ryan recalled. "I became a Cagney."[9]

Ryan's next assignment brought him into close quarters with another big talent. *The Sky's the Limit,* which began shooting in February 1943, starred Fred Astaire as a heroic Flying Tiger who goes AWOL during a publicity tour of the United States and falls for news photographer Joan Leslie; chasing after him are his two pilot buddies, played by Ryan and Richard Davies. Ryan's character, Reggie Felton, is a snide comedian: riding in a parade, he prepares to poke Davies in the eyes Three Stooges–style but then remembers where he is and flashes the crowd a "V for Victory" sign. He spends most of his screen time needling Astaire, and in one memorable scene, set in an army canteen, blackmails him into doing a "swami dance" atop their table. Choreographed by Astaire, the dance took several days to film, during which Ryan sat in a chair looking up at the great performer. Ryan even scored some waltz lessons from Astaire when the scene called for him to share a dance with Leslie.

Behind the Rising Sun, which began shooting in late April, was the darkest and most interesting of Ryan's wartime releases, an anti-Japanese propaganda picture of some journalistic substance but even more racial hysteria. Its source material was a 1941 book by James R. Young, an American journalist who had spent thirteen years working for the influential *Japan Advertiser* before his reporting from occupied China, published in a variety of Japanese papers, got him arrested in Tokyo and held by police for sixty-one days. *Behind the Rising Sun* offered a variety of insights into Japanese culture and a ringing indictment of the Imperial Army's misadventure on the continent. Young's sympathy and affection for the people of Japan was evident throughout, yet Doubleday Doran had packaged the book with a cover drawing of a slit-eyed, hideously grinning man, a fan in one hand and a revolver in the other.

After directing Ryan in *Golden Gloves* over at Paramount, Eddie Dmytryk had landed at RKO and, with screenwriter Emmet Lavery, had assembled an anti-German propaganda piece called *Hitler's Children,* about the Hitler Youth movement. For *Behind the Rising Sun* the two men banged out a script that bore little resemblance to the book, but incorporated various incendiary news stories from prewar Japan. "On a not very original plot, we strung ten or twelve incidents calculated to increase the flow of patriotic juices," Dmytryk recalled.[10] One of them involved a fighting match between an American boxer and a Japanese sumo wrestler, and Dmytryk had just the guy to play the boxer.

The not-very-original plot involved a Tokyo businessman (J. Carrol Naish), whose son Taro (Tom Neal) returns from the United States with an engineering degree from Cornell, falls for a pretty secretary (Margo), and clashes with his father over her. Nearly all the Japanese characters were played by American actors in eye makeup; Neal is particularly unconvincing, bounding down a ship's gangplank to announce in pure Americanese, "Gee, Dad, it's good to see you!" Later Taro serves with the Imperial Army in an occupied province of North China, where he hardens himself against atrocity. Confronted by an American reporter (Gloria Holden) in his office, he watches from a window as soldiers throw a child into the air and—Dmytryk implies with a jump cut—catch it on a bayonet. "They're not my men," Taro replies. "It's not my responsibility."

Billed fourth in the credits, Ryan played Lefty O'Doyle, a bushy-headed American baseball coach in Tokyo, and of the few incidents or observations from Young's book that found their way into the movie, many involved him. When Taro shows up at a game with his sweetheart, O'Doyle points out the flag display interrupting the game on the field. "Can you beat it?" he asks them. "Telling them that baseball isn't just baseball anymore? They mustn't come here to enjoy it just as a sport. They must come here to enjoy it as a military exercise." Another scene, lifted directly from the book, takes place during a late-night poker game at a geisha house where O'Doyle, who's had a few drinks too many, loses his temper over a mewling cat and fires his pistol into the darkness, scaring it away. Almost immediately a trio of police appear at the door to grill and browbeat him and his companions about the fired gun and the "arreged cat."

The big fight scene, which began shooting one Saturday afternoon in mid-May and continued the following Monday, would wind up the movie's oddest and best-remembered moment. O'Doyle is called upon to defend the honor of an American engineering executive who has clashed with Taro; defending Taro's honor is a towering sumo wrestler, played—in eye makeup—by Austrian-American wrestling champ Mike Mazurki.* At thirty-six, Mazurki stood an inch taller than Ryan and was built like a brick wall. The ensuing fight is less a match than a melee, O'Doyle throwing roundhouse punches as the wrestler kicks, chops, and grapples with him. In the end the boxer triumphs, yet even this wacky contest has a sharp edge: for dishonoring Japan, the wrestler is later executed.

---

*Though still working his way up in bit roles, Mazurki would play heavies in movies and TV for another fifty years, most memorably in *Murder, My Sweet* (1944).

Ryan triumphs as the American boxer pitted against Japanese sumo wrestler Mike Mazurki in RKO's propaganda item *Behind the Rising Sun* (1943). When Ryan joined the Marine Corps, his reputation from the picture preceded him. *Wisconsin Center for Film and Theater Research*

THREE DAYS BEFORE MIXING IT UP with Mazurki, Ryan was inducted into the US Army. His draft notice finally had arrived, and RKO had arranged for a deferment so he could finish *Behind the Rising Sun* and *The Iron Major,* which were shooting simultaneously. The latter film was RKO's attempt to score with Pat O'Brien playing another legendary college football coach—in this case Frank Cavanaugh, whose long career was interrupted only by his meritorious service in France. O'Brien had lobbied for Ryan to play Timothy Donovan, a football hero under Cavanaugh who later became a priest and served alongside him as an army chaplain. Ryan ages unpersuasively from his early twenties to his sixties, with the usual graying temples, and brings the story to a close with a mawkish prayer promising his late friend Cavanaugh that the fight for freedom continues: "We thank you, Cav, and we salute you. God rest your gallant soul."

Another deferment was granted so Ryan could appear in the low-budget

Gangway for Tomorrow, an inspirational tale for the home front about five random folks riding in a carpool to their jobs at a defense plant. As they travel, flashbacks reveal stories from their past; Margo had a pretty good one, playing a French cabaret singer and resistance member who escapes from the Nazis, but Ryan's was a hokey number about an auto racer who wipes out in the Indianapolis 500 and has to stay home while his two buddies join the Army Air Corps. Originally titled "An American Story," the picture wore its Office of War Information credentials on its sleeve: in the final moments the workers arrive at the plant, lock arms, and head through the gates to the strains of "The Battle Hymn of the Republic."

By summer *Bombardier* had opened to tremendous box office, and preview screenings of *The Sky's the Limit* and *Behind the Rising Sun* had brought Ryan overwhelmingly positive response cards from patrons. David Hempstead, producer of *The Sky's the Limit,* was about to start an A picture with Ginger Rogers called *Tender Comrade,* and he urged her to consider Ryan for the male lead. Written by the talented Dalton Trumbo, *Tender Comrade* told the story of four women working in a Los Angeles airplane factory who decide to rent a house together; interspersed with this were flashbacks focusing on Rogers and her man, who's preparing to go to war. For an unknown actor this would be quite an assignment—seventeen solitary love scenes with one of Hollywood's biggest stars.

Rogers had caught a preview of *The Sky's the Limit* at the invitation of her old dance partner Fred Astaire; she thought Ryan was too tall and too mean looking, but she agreed to let him read for the part. When Ryan showed up to audition, he found about a hundred other actors waiting. Yet as he and Rogers talked and played scenes together, she slipped Hempstead a note: *I think this is the guy.* Later, when Hempstead offered Ryan the job, he gave him the slip of paper, which Ryan kept to the end of his life.

Tender Comrade would be Eddie Dmytryk's first A picture, and he spent a full month, from mid-August to mid-September, directing Ryan's love scenes with Rogers. The first of them neatly demonstrated Ryan's skill at expressing character through action: Jo (Rogers), alone one night in her studio apartment, hears a knock at her door and is overjoyed to discover it's her husband, Chris (Ryan), home on furlough; as he steps into the room, he swings his overnight bag into the air and sends it sailing across the room onto her bed. Ryan plays straight man to Rogers in the forced comic scenes detailing their

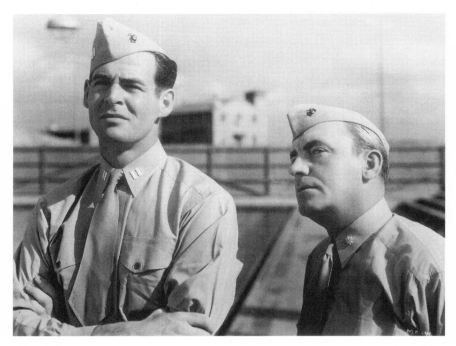

Ryan and Pat O'Brien in *Marine Raiders*. O'Brien mentored the younger actor at RKO, but they wound up on opposite sides when the House Un-American Activities Committee came to Hollywood. *Franklin Jarlett Collection*

early relationship, but he comes into his own as the couple begin wrestling with the fact that he wants to enlist. "I've never felt so at-home in a role in my life," Ryan told *Photoplay*. "Y'know, a lot of these scenes are retakes of things that have happened between Jessica and myself."[11]

Trumbo was one of Hollywood's more politically outspoken writers—he had participated in the founding of the Screen Writers Guild, the movie industry's bitterest labor battle of the mid-1930s—and with *Tender Comrade* he added a provocative subtext to the standard women's picture. Jo (Rogers) can barely contain her heartache after Chris ships out; but while he's gone, she comes up with the idea of pooling her rent money with three fellow riveters. They agree to a majority vote on all matters, and Jo proposes that they share their resources further: "Now the four of us here have two cars, two sets of tires wearing out. We could sell one car and use the other on a share-and-share alike basis." Rogers, a determined anticommunist, had balked at Trumbo's original line: "Share and share alike—that's American."

Ryan was scheduled to report for duty on October 20, but as the date approached, RKO offered him yet another script. Pat O'Brien wanted Ryan to costar with him in a war picture called *Marine Raiders,* about the Marines' new amphibious commando units. The script was lousy, with tedious love scenes and chest-thumping heroics. In one jungle scene Ryan's impetuous captain finds a fellow marine who has been killed and desecrated by the Japanese; enraged, he goes charging into the enemy's position spraying machine gun fire.

To play something like this at Camp Pendleton in San Diego County, where *Marine Raiders* would be shot as less fortunate men actually shipped out for the Pacific, must have filled Ryan with the sort of manly shame he had felt as a male model. Stars the stature of James Stewart and Robert Montgomery had enlisted and taken combat assignments; even Pat O'Brien put himself in harm's way entertaining troops in northern Africa and Southeast Asia. As part of the deal struck by RKO, Ryan asked to be discharged from the army so that he could enlist in the Marines, which would mean a greater chance of seeing combat. The Marines, in turn, would give him a deferment until January 1, 1944, so that he could make the picture.

Marine Raiders didn't wrap until late January, however, and by that time the Marines had granted Ryan a second deferment through February 15. Shortly before the picture was completed, the commanding general at Camp Elliott in San Diego wrote to Marine Corps Commandant Alexander Vandergrift to request a third deferment through April 15, so that Ryan could appear opposite Rosalind Russell in *Sister Kenny,* a biopic of the Australian nurse who had developed a radical new treatment for polio. Vandergrift would have none of this, and Ryan was ordered to report for duty on the fifteenth as previously agreed. RKO was offering him a "duration contract," which meant that he would be welcomed back to the studio upon his discharge from the service. *Behind the Rising Sun* had been released in August and, partly on the strength of Ryan's much-talked-about fight scene, turned a jaw-dropping $1.5 million profit.

In a movie magazine piece that appeared under her byline, Jessica recalled "the dreary building in downtown Los Angeles" where she dropped Robert off for his Marine Corps induction. "It was that ungodly hour of the morning, at which time all good men seem to have to go to the aid of their country."[12] They said their good-byes, she drove away weeping, and Ryan finally joined the war.

four

You Know the Kind

If Ryan had any hope of remaining unnoticed in the ranks, they were diminished when he learned from a fellow recruit at the LA induction center that a letter from the Marine Corps—which Ryan had never gotten—listed toiletries and other items they should bring with them. A private on duty offered to pick up some things for him, and Ryan got off the bus in San Diego carrying his belongings in a brown paper bag. A Marine Corps photographer was there to meet him, snapping pictures as he turned in his travel orders, got fitted for fatigues, sat for a regulation army haircut, went through a classification interview, and picked up his gear from the quartermaster's depot. After that he was on his own and wondering how he would be received. When he had been at the base earlier, shooting *Marine Raiders,* an officer had told him that movie boys were liable to get roughed up in the Corps, but Ryan didn't have any trouble. He mentioned this to a bunkmate; the man replied, "Most of these guys saw you bat that Jap around in *Behind the Rising Sun.*"[1]

Basic training commenced at Camp Pendleton, about an hour north of the San Diego base. Established as a Spanish mission in 1769 and built up through land grants into the vast Rancho Santa Margarita, the property had been purchased in 1942 by the US government, which was converting it into the nation's largest Marine Corps base. It was enormous—about two hundred square miles, with eighteen miles of shoreline for amphibious training. According to Pendleton historians Robert Witty and Neil Morgan, the terrain "stretches eastward across twelve miles of rolling hills, broad valleys, swampy stream beds, and steep-sided canyons, rising on its northeast perimeter to a height of 2,500 feet."[2] By the time Ryan arrived, Pendleton had sent two divisions into the war and was home to more than 86,000 people.

He and Jessica had resolved to keep a stiff upper lip in each other's absence, but by the fourth week Ryan had written asking her to visit him that Sunday, and she endured the four-hour bus ride to meet with him at the reception center. They went outside, and he spread his poncho over the grass so they could sit and talk. He had learned how to use an automatic rifle, Thompson submachine gun, mortar, bayonet, and hand grenade. The infiltration course, in Wire Mountain Canyon, forced recruits to crawl through three trenches and penetrate a single and then a double apron of barbed wire while dynamite charges went off all around them and live rounds were fired over their heads. The obstacle course, built over a cactus patch, included a 125-foot wooden tunnel, a house whose only exit was through the roof, and a 100-foot cable bridge. He was mastering more mundane skills as well—how to mend his clothes, for instance—and drilling with his platoon. As the tallest marine, he was named honor man and placed in the front rank to set the pace; he took direction well, of course, and had to admit that the theatricality of it appealed to him.

Following a ten-day furlough in April, Ryan got his first assignment: effective immediately, he would be a "recreation assistant" at Pendleton. This was good news for Jessica, who wanted him out of harm's way and far from the trigger of a gun, but not for him. The whole idea of enlisting in the Marines was to erase the stigma of all those deferments; now he would be running a sixteen-millimeter projector and directing amateur plays. After fifteen weeks of this, during which time the D-Day landing commenced, he was transferred to the San Diego base, where he continued to thread a projector and also performed on *Halls of Montezuma,* a weekly radio show broadcast coast to coast. Once Jessica realized he was unlikely to see action, she decided to leave Mabel on her own in Silverlake and moved to San Diego, where she occupied a "tiny box of a house on the pier at Pacific Beach."[3]

By this time Jessica had stopped acting entirely. Back when they were with Reinhardt, she had been considered the better actor, but over the years she had watched Robert work and grow, and she was proud of his success. She had been at it for ten years now, and once Robert had started pulling down $600 a week at RKO, she decided she had had enough. She hated the stage fright and the tedium and the itinerant lifestyle. Instead she would turn to her second love, writing. In addition to the first-person piece about Robert's induction, which would appear in the October 1944 issue of *Movieland,* she began placing stories in fan magazines such as *Photoplay* and *Motion Picture* and women's magazines such as *Coronet* and *Mademoiselle.* Her immediate success would bring a weird parity to the marriage, since Robert had started out writing and, frustrated, turned to acting.

Serving on the sidelines must have gotten to Ryan, because on August 25—the day Paris was liberated—he applied for a commission as a second lieutenant to serve on an aviation ground crew. "I feel that my background would qualify me for any branch of ground duty not requiring technical knowledge or expertise," he wrote on his application.[4] A complete physical found him fit for overseas duty, and his commanding officer wrote him no fewer than three letters of recommendation. He waited the rest of the year for an answer. The Marine Corps was hardly generous with promotions, and he had no way of knowing whether the scuttlebutt about his deferments would hurt his chances, or what RKO might be doing behind the scenes to protect its investment.

In January 1945, as the Battle of the Bulge raged, Ryan was assigned to the Fortieth replacement draft; he would be shipping out as an infantryman, a development he would later describe to a friend as "swell."[5] His application for a commission was turned down a week later. Ryan would be leaving for the Pacific in late February, which was alarming news to his wife and mother. But things didn't work out that way: as he would tell his Dartmouth class newsletter, "I was yanked out of the infantry with the proverbial foot on the gangplank and put to instructing troops in bayonet, judo, boxing and such at Camp Pendleton."[6] Now classified as a combat conditioner, Ryan would spend his days training men for battle; in May he was promoted to private first class, and in August he was reclassified again, as a combat swimming instructor.

Thousands of Americans spent the war this way—not quite at home, not quite at battle. "Theirs is the task of the damned," wrote Richard Brooks in a prefatory note to his novel *The Brick Foxhole.* "These men see others trained and shipped off to ports of embarkation, but they themselves are always left behind. They brood over it, and in the end they become disappointed, introverted, and embittered."[7] Ryan read the book with great interest when it was published in May 1945; the author was actually stationed at Pendleton, and according to scuttlebutt, the publication had brought him a court-martial. At the center of

Robert and Jessica (circa 1944). While he drilled recruits at Camp Pendleton, she struck out on her own as a magazine writer and novelist. *Robert Ryan Family*

The Brick Foxhole was an ugly sequence in which soldiers at liberty in Washington, D C, go home with a homosexual man for some late-night drinking and wind up beating him to death. Ryan was struck immediately by the book's frank depiction of the bilious prejudice on open display at Pendleton.

Of particular fascination was the character of Montgomery Crawford, the bullying sergeant who drags the other men into this murderous episode. Monty has served as a beat cop in Chicago and likes people to know he's killed a Jew and two black men in the line of duty. He "always shot niggers in the belly because then they didn't die right away and they squirmed like hell." Ryan had known guys like this before—cruel, jingoistic, worshipful of authority. Monty "shook hands with too firm a grip and he would openly cry when the post band played 'God Bless America.'"[8]

Ryan tracked Brooks down to tender his compliments, and the two met in the library at Camp Pendleton. Brooks was tall and athletic—for a while he had considered a career as a pro baseball player—and favored a pipe that belied his short temper. Born to Russian Jewish parents in Philadelphia, he had grown up in poverty and gotten his start as a writer during the Depression by riding the rails and reporting on his experiences for local newspapers. From there he had moved into radio drama in New York and, in a weird coincidence, cofounded and then quit the dreaded Millpond Playhouse the summer before the Ryans performed there. Out on the West Coast Brooks found work writing for NBC Radio in Los Angeles, and as a screenwriter at Universal he knocked out a couple of jungle pictures for Maria Montez before enlisting in the Marines. Rumors of a court-martial over *The Brick Foxhole* were true, though the Marines, realizing that more publicity would only enlarge the book's audience, had ultimately dropped the case.

Brooks undoubtedly knew Ryan from his good-guy roles at RKO, and to his surprise the actor told him that, if *The Brick Foxhole* were ever filmed, he wanted to play Monty. Anyone could see the physical resemblance—Brooks had described Monty as "more than six feet tall" with "a pair of small, bright eyes"[9]—but why would a lead player want a role like this? "I know that son of a bitch," Ryan explained. "No one knows him better than I do."[10]

In fact, Ryan's experience as a combat conditioner—teaching men to kill and wondering if they would ever come back alive—was turning him against the military. When he wrote to his old Dartmouth pal Al Dickerson in early summer 1945, he took a dim view of his own contribution to the war. "I certainly haven't made any 'sacrifice,'" he admitted, "especially when you add the fact that I have sat on my ass stateside for 16 months while a lot of my buddies went on to Saipan and Iwo. . . . I will not bore you with the too well known complaints against the military. War is a stupid institution when it isn't being sinful and tragic and catastrophic."[11] By the time he got out of the Marines he would come to share much of Jessica's pacifist philosophy.

Meanwhile Jessica had come into her own as a writer. To Ryan's surprise she announced one day that she had written a mystery novel and wanted him to read it. *The Man Who Asked Why* was a "literary mystery," mindful of formula but written with intelligence and wit. Its eccentric sleuth, Gregory Sergievitch Pavlov, "looked like a retired clown"[12] but was in fact an eccentric professor of languages, transparently based on the Ryans' dear friend and acting teacher

Vladimir Sokoloff. Ryan passed the manuscript along to someone he knew at Doubleday Doran (publisher of *Behind the Rising Sun*), and to his and Jessica's delight the book was accepted for publication as part of Doubleday's Crime Club imprint, scheduled to appear in November.

In August the war, and the very concept of war, attained new levels of sin, tragedy, and catastrophe when President Truman ordered the atomic bombing of Hiroshima and Nagasaki. The blast in Hiroshima on August 6 flattened nearly five square miles and killed seventy thousand people, with tens of thousands more to die from burns and radiation by the end of the year. Few in America could grasp the devastation, but one thing everyone understood was that now Japan would surrender. RKO wasted no time in reasserting its claim to Ryan's services; the day after Nagasaki was bombed, the Marine Corps director of public information dispatched a letter to the commandant asking that Ryan be allowed to make a "marine rehabilitation picture" called *They Dream of Home.** This request was denied, and ten days later Ryan was assigned to the Seventy-Ninth Replacement Draft. His feelings about shipping out may have been different this time, though, because Jessica had discovered that she was pregnant.

Two weeks after receiving his new assignment, Ryan reported to the Bureau of Medicine and Surgery complaining of neck and back pain. According to the doctor's summary, Ryan said that he had wrenched his back in May 1939, while lifting a car to change a tire, and subsequently suffered periodic attacks that had sidelined him for two to four days, but that "he did not mention this condition on induction because he considered it of minor importance and he wished to get into the service."[13] Diagnosed with epiphysitis of the spine, he was pronounced unfit for service and recommended for discharge. By this time the Fourth Division had begun arriving home, and Pendleton was discharging 175 men daily. On October 30, 1945, Ryan won an honorable discharge and returned to civilian life, the prospect of fatherhood, and a steady job at RKO. The studio had already slotted him for a melodrama called *Desirable Woman* that would give him a chance to work with Joan Bennett and the great French director Jean Renoir.

Years later, press accounts would note simply that Ryan had enlisted in

---

*The film would ultimately be released as *Till the End of Time* (1946), starring Robert Mitchum and directed by Edward Dmytryk.

the Marines, which was true but hardly the whole story. His wife's pacifism, his employer's opportunism, and his own professional ambition had kept him out of uniform for nine months, but then he had served and sought a combat assignment. He would note with disdain how his friend John Wayne had avoided doing his duty, and his own stint in the Marines would become a much-valued credential as he became more vocal in his commitment to peace. When his teenage son, Cheyney, asked him why he had served, Ryan's only response was, "What else was I gonna do?"[14]

SON OF THE GREAT PAINTER, Jean Renoir had directed some of the best French films of the 1930s — *The Crime of Monsieur Lange, Grand Illusion, The Rules of the Game*—before fleeing the Nazi invasion in 1940. Since then he had bounced around Hollywood, making one picture at Twentieth Century Fox, another for RKO, and two more as independent productions released through United Artists. His first UA project, *The Southerner,* was a moving tale of struggling cotton farmers in Texas, but in general Renoir found the Hollywood of the war years to be rocky soil for his kind of left-wing humanism. (His limited fluency in English didn't help.) After finishing *Diary of a Chambermaid* for UA, he returned to RKO at the invitation of Joan Bennett to direct *Desirable Woman,* a romantic melodrama that had been in development for some time. Renoir had enjoyed working at RKO, and he looked forward to collaborating with producer Val Lewton, who had delivered for the studio with a series of artful, low-budget horror films (*Cat People, I Walked with a Zombie, The Seventh Victim*).

Ryan's excitement about the picture only grew as he got to know the director. "One of the most remarkable men I've ever met," he would say of Renoir. "Working with him opened my eyes to aspects of character that were subtler than those I was accustomed to."[15] His character was notably darker than anything he had played on-screen, a shell-shocked Coast Guard lieutenant now relegated to patrolling the misty Pacific coast on horseback. In one scene a friend at the base hesitantly informs him that the ship he was serving on has gone down, and the lieutenant is crushed. Not long afterward, on one of his lonely rides, he passes a wrecked ship, where he encounters a beautiful woman gathering firewood (Bennett). She brings him home to meet her husband (Charles Bickford), a famous painter now blind and embittered, and the lieutenant, consumed by lust for the woman, becomes an uneasy companion to the fractious couple.

In fact, Val Lewton had never really been interested in the project, and by the time principal photography commenced in late January 1946, he had been replaced by producer Jack Gross, who let Renoir do pretty much as he pleased. A month into the shoot, Charles Koerner—the head of production who had axed Pare Lorentz and Orson Welles—died suddenly of leukemia, which left Renoir even more unsupervised. He had never made a picture with so much improvisation on the set. "I wanted to try to tell a love story based purely on physical attraction, a story in which emotions played no part," Renoir said.[16] The open adultery of the source novel, *None So Blind,* already had been scrubbed away by the Production Code Administration, but there was something haunting about the lovers' wordless attraction playing out right under the blind man's nose.

Renoir also was intrigued by the story's sense of solitude, something he felt was increasingly prized amid the chaos of modern life. "Solitude is the richer for the fact that it does not exist," Renoir wrote. "The void is peopled with ghosts, and they are ghosts from our past. They are very strong, strong enough to shape the present in their image."[17] One scene showed the lieutenant, Scott, in his bed at the base, consumed by a nightmare. In a feverish montage, an Allied ship hits a mine and goes down, the image of a whirlpool pulls the eye in, bodies and ropes drop through the water, and Scott strides across the ocean floor in slow motion, stepping over the skeletons of his dead crewmates, on his way toward a lovely woman in a flowing gown. Before they can kiss, there's an eruption of flame, an inferno that jolts Scott out of his dream.

Ryan—whose brother, father, and uncles all had preceded him to the grave—knew all about ghosts, and his strong streak of willful self-isolation made him an ideal collaborator for this kind of story. He would marvel at Renoir's ability to "discover the true personality of the actor" and integrate it into a performance, a skill he would recognize in no other director but Max Reinhardt.[18] Renoir found a neurotic quality in Ryan that had never been captured on-screen and would become the key element in his screen persona. Lying in bed, Scott confesses to his commanding officer that the nightmares have become chronic since he was released from the hospital. Ryan's gaze shifts back and forth between two fixed points—the officer's face and something awful a million miles away—as the tension gathers in his voice. The doctors have pronounced Scott healed. "But my head!" he exclaims in anguish, gesturing at it as if it were strange to his body.

The picture wrapped in late March, leaving Ryan free to tend to his expect-

Joan Bennett, Jean Renoir, and Ryan rehearsing *The Woman on the Beach* (1947). "One of the most remarkable men I've ever met," Ryan called Renoir. "Working with him opened my eyes to aspects of character that were subtler than those I was accustomed to." *Franklin Jarlett Collection*

ant wife. On Saturday, April 13, Jessica gave birth to a healthy baby boy, whom they named after his grandfather, Timothy, in the Irish tradition. Ryan's next picture, a mediocre western called *Trail Street*, didn't start shooting for three months, so the couple had plenty of time to care for and enjoy their new child and each other. Now that Ryan was back from the military, he worked either six days a week or not at all, loafing around in his mismatched pajamas until noon and working out later in the day. Jessica usually started writing in the morning—her second mystery novel, *Exit Harlequin*, was scheduled for publication in January 1947—and worked until mid-afternoon. Determined homebodies, she and Robert relaxed in each other's company, smoking, drinking, reading, and talking into the night.

Trail Street starred Randolph Scott as western hero Bat Masterson; Ryan got second billing as the villain, and whiskered "Gabby" Hayes dispensed cornpone comedy as Scott's sidekick. (Four-month-old Tim Ryan made his screen debut as a baby being held by a woman in the frontier town.) Director

Ray Enright had spent twenty years in the business without making a notable picture; he was quite a comedown after Jean Renoir. At the same time, Ryan's collaboration with Renoir was in trouble. *Desirable Woman* was test screened on August 2 in Santa Barbara, where it was laughed at and jeered by an audience full of students. Renoir would confess later that he was the first to get cold feet, and he offered to reedit the film. Five or six weeks later, he emerged with a version that was shown to two disinterested parties: screenwriter John Huston, who argued that the lieutenant's war trauma should be eliminated entirely, and director Mark Robson, who argued that it was central to the story. Renoir listened to Robson and moved the lieutenant's fiery nightmare to the beginning of the picture.*

By late November, when Ryan and Bennett were called in for reshoots, Renoir had lost confidence in his original conception, and the love relationship became more conventional. Several dialogue scenes that explained the characters' motivations were excised, which gave the action a detached quality. This garbled, seventy-minute cut of the picture, retitled *The Woman on the Beach,* would flop at the box office eight months later and end Renoir's association with RKO. By then Renoir had grown close to the Ryans—Jessica adored him and his wife, Dido—and the two couples would keep in touch long after the Renoirs returned to France. "Bob Ryan is a marvelous person," Renoir would later attest. "Professionally he's absolutely honest in everything he does."[19] Almost everything—Ryan admired Renoir too deeply ever to tell him he thought *The Woman on the Beach* was a failure.

THE MOVIE BUSINESS boomed in 1946 as servicemen rejoined their families, which may explain why Peter Rathvon, the new president of Radio-Keith-Orpheum, allowed most of the year to pass before finally choosing forty-one-year-old Dore Schary to replace the late Charles Koerner as head of production. Schary was a comer: born to Russian Jewish immigrants in Newark, New Jersey, he had written plays in New York before arriving in Los Angeles to write for the screen and winning an Oscar for the MGM classic *Boys Town* (1938). Since then the tall, bespectacled young man had supervised B-movie production for Louis B. Mayer at MGM, and independent producer

---

*A definitive genesis of the movie can be found in Janet Bergstrom's "Oneiric Cinema: *The Woman on the Beach," Film History* 11 (1)(1999): 114–125.

David O. Selznick had tapped Schary to head his new company Vanguard Pictures. Schary had great story sense, and he knew how to get the most out of a dollar. Selznick was generous enough to let RKO buy out Schary's contract, and on January 1, 1947, Schary took charge of the studio's production slate.

Two days later the United States experienced a dramatic political shift when the Eightieth Congress convened, its opening session carried for the first time on broadcast television. President Truman, battered by union struggles as he served out Franklin Roosevelt's fourth presidential term, had been rebuked at the polls in November, when Republicans picked up fifty-five congressional seats and took control of the House of Representatives. Once the new Congress was sworn in, Republicans wasted no time in mounting a frontal assault on the Roosevelt legacy, and the House Un-American Activities Committee (HUAC), created in 1938 to investigate subversion against the US government, announced that a top priority would be uncovering communist influence in the motion picture industry.

A liberal Democrat, Schary took little notice of this as he moved into position at RKO. His formula for success involved socially conscious films that could be made on relatively small budgets, and the first script he sent into production was a murder mystery adapted from *The Brick Foxhole,* the novel that had so intrigued Ryan when he read it in the Marines. Producer Adrian Scott, who had scored at RKO with the Dick Powell mysteries *Murder, My Sweet* (1944) and *Cornered* (1945), had read *The Brick Foxhole* and was struck by the sequence in which soldiers beat a homosexual man to death. This would never get past the Production Code Administration, but what if the victim were a Jew instead? Scott hired screenwriter John Paxton to take a crack at the novel; their project, *Cradle of Fear,* would be the first Hollywood picture to deal openly with anti-Semitism in the United States.

The script had gone nowhere with Charles Koerner in charge, and market research indicated that only 8 percent of moviegoers would go for such a picture (compared to 70 percent for *Sister Kenny,* the Rosalind Russell drama RKO was still trying to get made three years after the Marines had refused to let Ryan appear in it). Schary was a different story—he read *Cradle of Fear* one night and pulled the trigger on it the next day, naming Scott as producer and Eddie Dmytryk as director. The budget was around $500,000, but half of that would go for the stars Schary felt would be needed to sell such a controversial picture to the public. Scott and Dmytryk would have to get *Cradle of Fear* in the can with what remained, shooting for about twenty days on existing sets.

"What's-a-matter, Jewboy? You 'fraid we'll drink up all your stinkin' wonderful liquor?" Montgomery (Ryan) and Floyd (Steve Brodie) close in on their victim, Samuels (Sam Levene), in *Crossfire*. *Franklin Jarlett Collection*

Paxton would remember his excitement after Schary gave them the go-ahead, as "a little parade went off around the lot (the writer just tagged along) looking for sets that could be borrowed or adapted, or stolen. An unusual procedure with front office blessing."[20]

Ryan got along well with Schary, and when he learned the picture was in preproduction, he begged the new chief to let him play Montgomery. Schary must have been surprised: this wasn't the sort of role that would lead to more love scenes with Ginger Rogers. Monty was repellent—ingratiating one moment, bullying the next, especially when he and his drunken pals are boozing it up with Samuels, who has met them at a bar and invited them back to his place. "Sammy, let me tell you something," Monty slurs. "Not many civilians will take a soldier into their house like this for a quiet talk. Well, let me tell you something. A guy that's afraid to take a soldier into his house, he stinks. And I mean, he *stinks!*" Things only get worse from there: when Samuels tries to get rid of them, Monty snaps, "What's-a-matter, Jewboy? You 'fraid we'll drink up all your stinkin' wonderful liquor?" The word had never been uttered in a Hollywood picture.

The role might well blow up in Ryan's face. But he loved the script, valued the idea behind the picture, and knew he was the man to play Monty. "I thought such a part would make an actor—not break him," he later wrote.[21] He lobbied Dmytryk—who, by this time, had directed him in his first picture (*Golden Gloves*), his biggest hit (*Behind the Rising Sun*), and his first romance (*Tender Comrade*). Schary and Dmytryk acceded, billing Ryan third behind Robert Young as Finlay, the pipe-smoking police detective who investigates the crime, and Robert Mitchum as Keeley, a jaded sergeant who tries to save the confused young Private Mitchell from being framed by Monty. Schary also brought in some first-rate supporting players: Sam Levene as Samuels; sultry, blond Gloria Grahame (*It's a Wonderful Life*) as a hooker who briefly adopts the private during his nocturnal wanderings; and, in the picture's second-creepiest role, craggy Paul Kelly as a man who hangs around her apartment and keeps changing his story about their relationship.

When the picture came out, Ryan would publish two stories under his own byline, in publications no less divergent than *Movieland* and the *Daily Worker,* that explained his rationale for taking the role. "Convictions are nice things to have," he wrote in the *Worker,* "but when close friends tell you that you're jeopardizing your career by taking a role you believe in—well, it makes you stop and think." The picture was unlikely to convert any hardened anti-Semites, he conceded. "No one picture, no one book, no one speech could accomplish that. It's the cumulative effect that counts."[22] In *Movieland* he argued that the picture's subject was broader than anti-Semitism: "We all stand to lose if fascism comes. Not just the Jews. The Irish, the Catholics—and I'm both of those—the Negroes, labor, the foreign born, everyone is done for whose color, or religion, occupation or political belief is distasteful to some new paperhanger-turned-Strong Man."[23]

Once he had been cast, Ryan dove into the part. He studied back issues of *Social Justice,* a frequently anti-Semitic magazine edited by the Roman Catholic priest and populist demagogue Father Charles Coughlin. Launched in 1936, it had serialized the fraudulent *Protocols of the Elders of Zion,* which purported to be a Jewish plan for global conquest, and published one article by Coughlin that borrowed passages from a speech by Joseph Goebbels, Hitler's propaganda minister, about the threat posed by communism, atheism, and the Jewish people. Ryan also paid a visit to Jean Renoir, who was still wrestling with *The Woman on the Beach,* and asked him about the fascist sympathizers he had known in France. Renoir spent the afternoon telling him stories, and Ryan came away convinced that the key to Montgomery was a deep-seated sense of inferiority.

If Schary wanted to test the limits of his authority at RKO, he succeeded; in early February, Rathvon sent him a memo expressing his doubts that *Cradle of Fear* would do anything to reduce racial intolerance. "Prejudiced Gentiles are not going to identify themselves with Monty and so feel ashamed of their prejudices," wrote Rathvon, a smart and cultured man whom Schary respected. "Rather they may be resentful because they feel we have distorted the problem by using such an extreme example of race hatred."[24]

On another front, Darryl F. Zanuck, president of Twentieth Century Fox, informed Schary that Fox had a picture about anti-Semitism on the boards, *Gentleman's Agreement,* and suggested he cease and desist. "We exchanged a few notes," Schary recalled, "then a phone call during which I was compelled to tell him he had not discovered anti-Semitism and that it would take far more than two pictures to eradicate it."[25] Determined to beat *Gentleman's Agreement* out of the box, Schary stepped up production on *Cradle of Fear;* principal photography would begin Monday, March 3.

Scott and Dmytryk went over the script carefully, working out every shot in advance to save time on the set. Once the cameras began rolling, Dmytryk fell into a pattern of shooting for about six-and-a-half hours each day, then using the last couple of hours to rehearse the next day's scenes; this gave the crew time to set up the first shot and enabled the players to come in the next morning ready to go. The sets looked cheap, so Dmytryk placed his key lighting low in the frame to throw lots of shadows; for a scene in which Monty bullies his accomplice, Floyd, the only light source was a table lamp, revealing some of the uglier lines in Ryan's face. Dmytryk also chose his lenses to make Monty look increasingly crazed: at first his close-ups were shot with a fifty-millimeter lens, but this was reduced to forty, thirty-five, and ultimately twenty-five-millimeter. "When the 25mm lens was used, Ryan's face was also greased with cocoa butter," Dmytryk recalled. "The shiny skin, with every pore delineated, gave him a truly menacing appearance."[26]

The real menace, though, lay in Ryan's deft underplaying. Critics would stress the intelligence he brought to his heavy roles, but in the case of Monty, an ignorant blowhard, the defining characteristic was an animal cunning. In his first two speaking scenes, Monty is interrogated by Detective Finlay, and in both instances he hastens to defend his pal Mitchell, whose wallet has been found at the crime scene, even as he directs suspicion toward him and away from himself. In the second interrogation, with Sergeant Keeley looking on, Monty grows angry at Finlay's questioning and barks at him, promising, "You won't pin anything on Mitch, not in a hundred years!" Catching himself, he drops his gaze, glances back and forth at the two men, and apologizes, pleading, "It's just that I'm worried sick about Mitch."

This was Ryan's first picture with Mitchum, whose roughneck adventures during the Depression (boxing, riding the rails, doing time on a chain gang) were even more dramatic than his. The men liked and respected each other, but their upbringings set them apart; Mitchum had grown up poor and dropped out of high school, and his politics were more conservative. Ryan might have held forth on the dangers of fascism, but according to Dmytryk, when a reporter on the set asked Mitchum why he was making the picture, the actor replied, "Because I hate cops."[27] In fact, he was annoyed at having been lured back from a Florida vacation by Scott with the promise of a great part, only to learn it was no such thing (Scott confessed that they needed him for his box office clout). Mitchum must have realized at some point that Ryan was walking away with the picture.

The only real complication to emerge during production was how to get rid of Monty after the detective has tricked him into exposing himself. Screenwriter John Paxton wanted to add a scene in which Monty goes to trial, but Schary scotched this idea. Schary later claimed that the picture's original ending had MPs cornering Monty and shooting him down "like a rat," which might have increased the audience's sympathy for him.[28] Instead Monty breaks away from the cops and runs out into the street; from a second-floor window, the detective orders him to halt and then calmly dispatches him with a single bullet in the back. Paxton was appalled when he saw this, but he had no say in the matter. Schary also changed the release title to *Crossfire,* which had no relevance to the story but sounded great.

Principal photography wrapped on Saturday, March 29, after only twenty-four shooting days. The project had come together so quickly that there was no time for the sort of front-office meddling that might have watered down the story. A few weeks later Ryan attended a rough-cut screening with Scott, Dmytryk, and a handful of RKO executives. None of the other cast members was there, but he was eager to get a look at his performance. Watching the story unfold, Ryan knew he had nailed the character. About fifteen minutes into the picture, the detective interrogates Monty, asking him about the victim. "I've seen a lot of guys like him," Monty explains, conspiratorially. "Guys that played it safe during the war? Scrounged around keepin' themselves in civvies? Got swell apartments, swell dames? You know the kind. . . . Some of them are named Samuels, some of them got funnier names." Later, as Monty smacks Floyd around, his rage boils over: "I don't like Jews! And I don't like nobody who likes Jews!"

After the screening was over and the lights came up, the room was silent. Finally, one of the RKO suits spoke up: "It's a brave thing you've done, Ryan. You're gambling with your career, of course." Another piped up: "Really courageous."[29] Taken aback, Ryan walked out of the screening room, crossed the lot, picked up his car, and headed home. Given what he had seen in the Marines, talk of bravery embarrassed him. But the executives' remarks were the first reaction he had received outside of the cast and crew, and their subtext was obvious: if the public turned against Ryan, RKO would simply cut him loose.

five

We Will Succeed, You Will Not

Jessica Ryan hated guns: she had no intention of letting her lovely Tim play with toy guns, learning to fantasize about combat and killing. Robert, a capable marksman in the Marines, didn't feel that strongly, but he had no fondness for firearms either. "He went hunting once with his father and shot something," his son Cheyney remembered. "He said he'd never do it again."[1]

Regardless, the RKO publicists liked nothing better than to send Ryan on a hunting expedition. The previous November he had driven up to Oregon with actor Lex Barker to be photographed hunting geese, and that spring Jessica swallowed her pride and accompanied him on a jaunt out to the desert with a photographer for *Photoplay* and actress Jane Greer, who had just starred in *Out of the Past* for RKO. Jessica posed at the wheel of a jeep and stood by as Robert held up a dead jackrabbit for Greer's inspection; the resulting story claimed that she and Greer each had bagged a rabbit as well.[2] This was followed by another trip to a ranch in the San Fernando Valley to hunt pheasants for a four-page pictorial in *Screen Guide;* one photo showed the couple heading out from their car, Jessica scowling as she carries a rifle at her waist, the barrel pointed to her side.[3]

After *Crossfire,* Ryan strapped on his six-guns again for *Return of the Bad Men,* another B western with Randolph Scott and "Gabby" Hayes. He couldn't wait to finish with this tired oater and move on to *Berlin Express,* an espionage thriller scheduled to begin shooting overseas in July. Dore Schary had been mightily impressed by the documentary authenticity of Roberto Rossellini's Italian postwar drama *Open City* (1945), and he wanted *Berlin Express* to be the first drama filmed inside Germany since the fall of the Third

Reich. (Director Billy Wilder would be arriving at the same time to shoot *A Foreign Affair* for Paramount.) *Berlin Express* centered on an international group of passengers riding a US military train from Paris to Berlin, and like *Crossfire,* it would mix genre entertainment with liberal politics, stressing the imperative of world peace.

Ryan would be gone for more than two months, flying from New York to London and then traveling with cast and crew to Paris, Frankfurt, and Berlin. He was excited about the picture and eager to get a firsthand look at the ravages of war. General George Marshall had just delivered a commencement address at Harvard in which he stressed the danger of allowing the European economy to deteriorate any further; he called for a massive economic aid plan to rehabilitate the victors and the vanquished alike. *Berlin Express* would carry Ryan right into the heart of this debate. He finished *Return of the Bad Men* in mid-July 1947, and yet another photographer arrived, this time at the house in Silverlake, to shoot him packing his bags and bidding Jessica and Tim farewell on his way to the LA airport.[4] Jessica was afraid of airplanes and begged him to take a train east, but Ryan never passed up a chance to fly.

The producer, thirty-seven-year-old Bert Granet, was shouldering quite an operation. Military permits were required at each point of travel through occupied Germany, which meant that twenty-seven cast and crew members had to be screened by the FBI* and then cleared by the army and State Department.[5] Cinematic resources in Europe were so scarce that nearly all camera and lighting equipment had to be brought over, along with one hundred thousand feet of film that required cool, safe storage in nations where any kind of storage space was prized. Because local film laboratories were so dodgy, all footage had to be shipped back to the United States for processing, so none of the completed scenes could be viewed until the expedition returned to Hollywood.[6] Lodging and automobiles were in short supply (there was only one camera truck available in all of Paris); even simple items such as nails, lumber, and rope had to be bought on the black market.

A native Parisian, director Jacques Tourneur had come to Hollywood in the 1930s and distinguished himself at RKO with subtle, low-budget chillers such as *Cat People* (1942) and *I Walked with a Zombie* (1943). He had just

---

*In response to my Freedom of Information Act request, the FBI reported that its central records system contained no file for Ryan.

completed his masterpiece, the wistful film noir *Out of the Past*. Unfortunately, *Berlin Express* didn't have much of a script; inspired by a *Life* magazine story, it would be a rather awkward marriage of journalism and Hitchcock-style suspense, its harsh scenes of a ravaged Germany punctuating an increasingly far-fetched tale in which a German diplomat critical to the reunification effort is kidnapped by right-wing terrorists. The four heroes pulling together to foil this plot were obvious stand-ins for the occupying powers: Ryan is an American agricultural expert, Roman Toporow a Russian military officer, Robert Coote a British veteran of Dunkirk, and actress Merle Oberon the French secretary of the kidnapped politician.

Decades later Granet left behind in his papers an account of the personal chaos inspired by Oberon during the trip. The delicate British beauty had outmaneuvered him already by getting Schary to name her husband, Lucien Ballard, as cinematographer; the couple would be rooming together. The company was lodged at the Hôtel George V, just off the Champs-Élysées, but Oberon, in a standard movie-star power play, insisted that she and Ballard stay at the palatial Hôtel Ritz on the Place Vendôme. Ballard, an Oklahoman of part-Cherokee descent, was tall, athletic, cultured, and handsome; he had won Oberon's heart by inventing a small spotlight that attached to the camera and helped minimize her facial scars from a 1937 car accident.*

"By the time we settled in Paris, Merle had developed a deep passion for Robert Ryan," wrote Granet. "He was tough looking but at heart he was a happily married pussycat. He was not even fair game for someone of Merle's sexual talents. She would tease him then cool it."[7] Born in Bombay to a Welsh father and an Indian mother, Oberon had spent her adult life concealing the mixed parentage that would have ended her career as an actress in Britain and the United States. For six years she had been married to the great British producer Alexander Korda, who cast her opposite Laurence Olivier in *Wuthering Heights* (1939), but in 1945 she had left Korda for Ballard. She obsessed over her beauty and exulted in her status, spoiling herself with clothing and gems. Oberon was high-strung and wildly romantic—among her previous lovers were Leslie Howard, David Niven, George Brent, and the heroic RAF pilot Richard Hillary.

During the company's stay in Paris, wrote Granet, Oberon urged him and

---

*Cinematographers still refer to this device as "the obie."

Ryan with Merle Oberon in *Berlin Express* (1948). Their affair unfolded amid the chaos and deprivation of postwar France and Germany. *Film Noir Foundation*

his wife, Charlotte, to throw a dinner party in their suite and invite Ryan. That evening she arrived hours late, dressed to the nines in a black evening gown and accompanied by a dapper Englishman; later she confessed to Charlotte that she was trying to make Ryan jealous. "By the time we were shooting in Frankfurt, she had successfully bedded Ryan," Granet reported. "Since Lucien . . . was constantly on location, all he could do was develop suspicions. Merle successfully made him believe that it was Charles Korvin who was making a pass at her."[8]

Korvin, a Hungarian actor playing one of the villains, had already shot two pictures with Oberon, and the two despised each other. More than thirty years later, after her death, Korvin told celebrity biographers Charles Higham and Roy Moseley that Oberon deserted Ballard on more than one occasion to spend the night with Ryan, first on the cross-country train from Paris and then in Frankfurt (where the crew lodged at hotels in the center of town and the cast was billeted at a castle in Bad Nauheim, thirty-five kilometers north of the city). "I know that she slept with Ryan both in Hollywood and in Europe and I thought it unfair and cruel of her," Korvin remembered. "I objected to the affair and so did everyone else on the picture."[9]

Political argument only added to the tension. When Ryan asked his fellow cast members how they felt about General Marshall's vision for postwar Europe, the idea of economic aid for Germany got a cool reception. Coote and Oberon had endured the London blitz. Korvin and Paul Lukas, both Hungarian, had been personally touched by the Holocaust, and Toporow, who was Polish, loathed the Germans and the Russians alike. "How can you let 80 million people starve?" Ryan would ask.[10] Invariably they dismissed him as naïve or softhearted; mass starvation, said one, would be no less than the German people deserved.

Their resolve began to melt away as they got a look at Frankfurt: entire neighborhoods reduced to rubble, middle-class people reduced to beggars. More than fifty-five hundred had been killed in the bombardment, and the medieval city center, the Römer, had been completely destroyed. In *Berlin Express*, Ryan and Oberon venture into the neighborhood and discover a maze of shoulder-high rubble, like a bizarre sculpture garden. Another scene shows Ryan staring grimly out a bus window as people walk the streets with suitcases full of belongings for sale; in the train station he tosses away a cigarette and two shabby men race like pigeons to scoop it up. The children they encountered on location were "emaciated, shocked and sick," Ryan later wrote, with "old faces and rickety bodies."[11] By the end of the first week, he remembered, no one talked anymore about the justice of letting people starve.

From Frankfurt the company flew to Berlin, where principal photography began on Saturday, August 2. This time the company stayed in Zehlendorf, about fifteen miles from downtown, near the US occupation forces headquarters, and cast members were chauffeured about in a car that had belonged to Hitler's foreign minister, Joachim von Ribbentrop. More than three years after the Allied bombing, Berlin was still a boneyard of gray, jagged, hollowed-out buildings, block after block, mile after mile. Unter den Linden, once the capital city's most majestic boulevard, was bare now, its namesake linden trees destroyed or chopped down for firewood. The great Reichstag was an empty shell, the lush Hotel Adlon bombed out and boarded up. Out for a stroll one night, Ryan fell into a bomb crater.

The poverty on the streets was overwhelming: Germans clustered around the locations, pleading for work as grips or extras. One well-known theater actor offered to work for a pair of pants, then came back the next day and said he wanted food for his family instead. Granet gave him both, and a check. "It is hard to visualize a world where the standard of currency is simply the cigarette," he wrote.[12] Chocolate bars were equally prized, and Ryan used them to pay the woman who ironed his shirts. "There seemed to be very little bitterness on the part of the Germans who worked with us," Ryan wrote. "A grip, hoisting a heavy prop one day, laughed and said, 'There goes my 1,500 calories.'"[13]

Apart from soldiers and government staffers, most of the other Americans in Berlin were journalists, who congregated at the press club and treated the movie people with smirking condescension. "As our visit wore on, the frost melted," Ryan would write. "Fortunately there were no jokers in our company. Nobody tried to dress up like Hitler and make a speech from the famous balcony. Nobody got drunk or was carted off to jail."[14] The Russians were suspicious when cast and crew arrived to shoot in the Soviet sector, though Ryan saw no evidence of the military might he had expected, "no streets bristling with machine guns, no bayonets—as a matter of fact, almost no Russians."[15] Their chilly reception contrasted sharply with the picture's final scene, in which the American and the Russian mend their ongoing political quarrel with a brotherly wave outside the Brandenberg Gate.

The last week in Berlin the company enjoyed a picnic on the Rhine River, courtesy of the US Army, and a party at the press club, attended by reporters and military people. There followed another nine days of photography in Frankfurt and four more in Paris. According to Granet, Ballard and Korvin came to blows during one train trip. When the company arrived in London, Oberon refused to fly back to New York and persuaded Granet to send her, Ballard, and Ryan on the *Queen Mary* out of Southampton. News photographers snapped photos of Ryan, grinning angrily and fiddling with his hat, as he escorted Oberon through Waterloo Station.

Decades later, when the affair had become a distant memory, Ryan would share with Harold Kennedy, his theatrical colleague and drinking buddy, a curious anecdote about his Atlantic crossing with a beautiful costar and her cameraman husband. As Ryan framed it, the woman had been making passes at him throughout the journey and cornered him late one night as he was taking the air on deck; getting no response to her come-ons, she pounced, knocked him down, and refused to let him up. Suddenly her husband "materialized on the deck, lifted her up, reached down and took hold of Bob's shoulder, assisted him to his feet, and then, after apologizing to him profusely, blackened both of the lady's eyes."[16]

Ryan had an Irishman's way with a story—he wasn't the sort of man to stand by while someone was hitting a woman—but then Granet also reported rumors of noisy fights between Ballard and Oberon on the voyage home, and said that she returned to Hollywood with broken teeth. Ryan was staying on in New York for a few days to do promotional work for *Crossfire*. When the *Queen Mary* docked on Tuesday, September 9, the first thing he did was to call Jessica in Los Angeles. She put Tim on the phone to hear his father's voice, and she must have informed Ryan, if she hadn't already, that she was expecting another child.

WHILE RYAN WAS IN EUROPE, *Crossfire* had exploded. The picture opened in late July at the Rivoli, a 2,092-seat movie palace on Broadway, and broke box office records in its first week. "One of the most startling pictures ever to come out of Hollywood," wrote the *New York Morning Telegraph*. "A film to be praised, praised again, and seen by all," wrote the *New York Post*. "An important, stirring film," declared the *Daily Mirror*. "Robert Ryan gives one of the performances of the year."[17] The picture had transformed his reputation overnight: critics and colleagues who had regarded him as a confident but unspectacular leading man now recognized him as an exciting, first-class character actor. There was talk of an Oscar nomination. "I came back to the sort of reception reserved by the New York press for people who had done something," he later recalled. "Everybody wanted an interview; photographers were everywhere."[18]

Ryan made a rare personal appearance at the Rivoli, where *Crossfire* was in its eighth week. "It was the first time I had seen the picture with an audience, and I was elated at the reaction," he said. Afterward, when he was introduced to the crowd and walked onstage, the room suddenly quieted. Monty was the black, unfathomable heart of the picture; moviegoers who reacted to the anti-Semitism in *Crossfire* inevitably zeroed in on Ryan as the embodiment of all that fear and hatred. "I'm really not that kind of a guy," he said, bringing down the house.[19]

By fall *Crossfire* had gone into general release and was performing well across the country, racking up impressive numbers not only in the more liberal metropolitan centers but in many small towns and in such conservative communities as Memphis, Omaha, and Oklahoma City. The RKO sales force played down the picture's anti-Semitic angle, stressing the mystery element and Ryan's costar Robert Mitchum, whose popularity was on the rise. There were pockets of resistance—"We never have had any racial troubles in this town and I don't want to put anything before the people that might put ideas into their heads," declared one theater owner—but RKO pursued a sharply effective strategy of establishing the picture in one cluster of towns and then expanding it to the next.[20]

Given the taboo-smashing nature of the story, some conflict was inevitable. The US Navy found the idea of an American soldier murdering a Jewish civilian so inflammatory that it banned *Crossfire,* refusing to screen it for troops at bases foreign or domestic. The army allowed it to be shown to soldiers at home but nixed any screenings overseas, arguing it might be seen by foreigners on the bases and reflect poorly on the United States. The Motion Picture Export Association, which cleared movies for the international market, turned down *Crossfire,* citing the same concerns. And though most leaders of the American Jewish community hailed the picture—in Chicago, the Anti-Defamation League had launched a vigorous campaign encouraging local lodges to sponsor private screenings for civic leaders—some argued that *Crossfire* might harden anti-Semitic feelings and even provoke bigots to violence.

This opinion emerged most strongly in the American Jewish Committee's monthly magazine *Commentary.* Editor Eliot Cohen noted the malign magnetism of Ryan's hypnotic performance: "You're drawn to him. He's big, he catches your eye. His personality overshadows the others. A plain, husky fellow, not much education, visibly troubled, up against a world too smart for him, fighting shrewdly, stupidly, blindly against the 'others' who hem him in—before his crime, after his crime. (For the millions near enough like him to identify with him, will Montgomery be the simple bully and villain the producer intended, assuming that was his intention? The chances are just as good that he will be taken as a kind of hero-victim—the movie equivalent of the Hemingway-Faulkner-Farrell male, hounded and struck down by a world he never made.)"[21]

Ryan was less concerned with anti-Semites or the Jews they hated than with the much larger middle ground of Gentiles who were innocent but ignorant. "What I hope for is that the mass of Americans—those who have never come directly, first-hand, against intolerance—will think about those who daily are exposed to it, and will reflect on their actions to those groups in a new light," he wrote in the *Daily Worker*. "Most Americans aren't intolerant, but neither are they concerned with those who are. Pictures like this will help show how senseless, how ignorant, how detrimental to fundamental American principles . . . any kind of bigotry is. When people fully realize that, they will stop the careless thinking and the even more careless talk."[22]

One thing Ryan had understood better than the friends who had discouraged him from playing Monty: a controversial role can help an actor's career. Ray Milland had won an Oscar playing a raging alcoholic in *The Lost Weekend* (1945). Yet, as Ryan pointed out in yet another first-person piece about *Crossfire*, Stephen Crane's *The Red Badge of Courage* had never been filmed because no movie star wanted to play a coward.* "The controversial role, like no other, can meet the needs of the actor who feels the void of not achieving professional stature," he wrote, inadvertently revealing the career frustration that had driven his choice. "It gives one the feeling of accomplishment, of acting with a purpose."[23] When he reflected on the risk taken by Dore Schary, Adrian Scott, Eddie Dmytryk, and John Paxton, who had dreamed up the picture, his own gamble paled in comparison.

Ryan looked forward to more such projects, but the political winds were shifting. That fall Schary was approached by two investigators from the House Un-American Activities Committee—"rather gray-looking gentlemen," he wrote.[24] The committee was moving forward with its hearings into communist infiltration of the movie industry, and they wanted to know if he might have any relevant information about Ryan. Schary pointed out that Ryan was a former marine, a credential he felt spoke for itself. They asked him about Scott and Dmytryk, the producer and director of *Crossfire*. They requested

---

*When John Huston finally brought the novel to the screen in 1951, his star was the legendary war hero Audie Murphy.

screenings of *Crossfire* and *The Farmer's Daughter,* a Loretta Young comedy that RKO had released in March, and afterward they declared both pictures to be "pro-Communist."[25]

Schary later wrote that he gave the investigators nothing and expressed his lack of regard for the committee. On September 22, Schary, Scott, and Dmytryk all received subpoenas to testify in Washington. Forty other Hollywood professionals were summoned as well, ranging from such right-wingers as Adolphe Menjou, Ayn Rand, Leo McCarey, and Walt Disney to such left-wingers as Charles Chaplin, Clifford Odets, Robert Rossen, and Bertolt Brecht. The Red-baiting *Hollywood Reporter* labeled nineteen of the forty-three—including Scott and Dmytryk—as "unfriendly" witnesses on the basis of their previous public statements about the committee. The hearings would convene a month later.

Ryan always would attribute his narrow escape from the blacklist to his war record and his Irish-Catholic heritage (the committee's equation of communists and Jews was well known). He had just been investigated by the FBI and cleared for travel in the Soviet sector of Berlin. The fact was that Scott and Dmytryk *had* been Communist Party members, whereas Ryan (for all his willingness to publish in the *Worker*) was a solid Democrat who could always be counted on to inject a note of ward-heeling realism into the unmoored radicalism of friends and colleagues. During this period, Jessica would write, he had "his first brush with the doubletalk, the rigid doctrinaire attitudes, the attitude of take over or destroy, of some people involved who were or had been truly Communist-minded. At the same time he would not nudge one inch from the position of defending their right to believe as they did."[26] Ryan quickly threw in with the Committee for the First Amendment (CFA), an organization formed by his screenwriter pal Philip Dunne, as well as John Huston and director William Wyler, to protest the hearings.

Wyler hosted an overflow meeting of the new group at his Beverly Hills home in early October. Outside, FBI agents took down license plate numbers,[27] yet the CFA was a safely liberal group: it defended civil liberties in general, not the "Hollywood Nineteen" in particular, and the founders actively discouraged communists and fellow travelers from joining. The group resolved to protest the congressional probe in full-page newspaper ads and organized a large delegation of celebrities to fly east for the hearings. Ryan was stuck in town shooting interiors for *Berlin Express,* but he agreed to take part in

Hollywood Fights Back, a pair of radio programs to be broadcast nationwide on October 26 and November 2.

Even before that, on Wednesday, October 15, Ryan appeared at the giant "Keep America Free!" rally at the Shrine Auditorium, which benefited a defense fund for the Nineteen. Presented by the Progressive Citizens of America (PCA)—a more radical group that was the Communist Party's last real lobbying presence in Hollywood—the rally drew some seven thousand people.[28] "We protest the threat to personal liberty and the dignity of American citizenship represented by this police committee of Dies, Wood, Rankin, and Thomas," Ryan declared, naming the congressmen on the committee as he read a proclamation from the PCA. "We demand, in the name of all Americans, that the House Committee on Un-American Activities be abolished, while there still remains the freedom to abolish it."[29]

The following Monday the hearings commenced in the Caucus Room of the Capitol Building, with every seat filled and the proceedings recorded by newsreel cameras, nationwide radio, and a battery of reporters and press photographers. J. Parnell Thomas, the New Jersey Republican who had assumed chairmanship of the committee with the Eightieth Congress, presided over the hearings, which got off to a bang when studio head Jack Warner volunteered the names of twelve people who had been identified as communists and fired from Warner Bros. His action stunned the Hollywood community, especially his colleagues at the Motion Pictures Producers' Association (MPPA), which had agreed to close ranks against the committee. As the week progressed, the committee called a succession of friendly witnesses, who named some three dozen people as communists.

The week's events failed to dent the enthusiasm of the Committee for the First Amendment, whose members took heart from editorials condemning the hearings in the *New York Times,* the *Washington Post,* and other dailies. On Sunday morning the CFA's star contingent—including Humphrey Bogart, Lauren Bacall, Myrna Loy, Gene Kelly, Judy Garland, and Danny Kaye—took off for New York and then Washington, having already recorded their contributions for the *Hollywood Fights Back* broadcast. Ryan delivered his thirty-second bit live in the studio: "President Roosevelt called the Un-American Committee a sordid procedure, and that describes it pretty accurately," he declared. "Decent people dragged through the mud of insinuation and slander. The testimony of crackpots and subversives accepted and given out to the press as if it were the gospel truth. Reputations ruined and people hounded out of their jobs."[30]

The tide of public opinion began to turn against the Nineteen on Monday morning, when writer John Howard Lawson accused the committee of Nazi tactics, was charged with contempt of Congress, and had to be forcibly removed from the chamber. As all this was going on, Dmytryk turned to Schary and asked, "What are my chances at the studio now?"

"You have an ironclad contract," Schary replied.[31]

Adrian Scott brought a four-page statement defending *Crossfire* and noting the anti-Semitism of Mississippi Democrat John E. Rankin, a committee member, which Thomas refused to let him read. Both Scott and Dmytryk were asked repeatedly if they were communists; they declined to answer, citing their Fifth Amendment rights, and were charged with contempt. Schary, asked if he would knowingly employ communists at RKO, replied that he would, "up until the time it is proved that a communist is a man dedicated to the overthrow of the government by force or violence, or by any illegal methods."[32]

Seven more unfriendly witnesses defied the committee and were cited for contempt, among them screenwriter Dalton Trumbo—whose wartime romance *Tender Comrade* (1944), directed by Dmytryk, had given Ryan his first big break. The committee had absurdly labeled the movie communist propaganda for its story of four women sharing a house while their men fight in World War II. When Thomas suddenly suspended the hearings on October 30, with Brecht having broken rank and eight witnesses still to be heard, *Variety* reported that one factor was the reluctance of several committee members to release a long-promised list of subversive pictures. Once these innocuous and well-known titles were made public, the members argued, the committee would become "a laughing stock."[33]

If Ryan was afraid of the committee, he didn't show it: while the hearings were in progress, he and his *Crossfire* costar Gloria Grahame spoke at the annual convention of the American Jewish Labor Council, which would turn up on the US attorney general's list of communist (but not subversive) organizations.[34] The studio moguls, however, were badly spooked by the hearings. On November 24—the same day the House of Representatives voted 346 to 17 to uphold the contempt citations—the Motion Picture Producers' Association met at the Waldorf-Astoria Hotel in New York to hammer out a strategy. President Eric Johnston insisted that the studios purge their ranks;

Schary led the charge against him, backed by independent producers Samuel Goldwyn and Walter Wanger, but Johnston carried the day. The MPPA announced that members would no longer employ known communists and would fire the unfriendly witnesses (now labeled the Hollywood Ten), whose actions "have been a disservice to their employers and have impaired their usefulness to the industry."[35]

RKO was the first studio to act, firing Scott and Dmytryk. Schary refused to drop the ax, so Floyd Odlum, chairman of the board, handed the job to Schary's boss, RKO president Peter Rathvon. Every studio contract included a vaguely worded morals clause allowing the studio to terminate any employee deemed to have disgraced the company. Barred from the lot, their current projects canceled or reassigned to other producers, Scott and Dmytryk turned their attention to the pressing matter of defending themselves against the contempt citations, which could land them in federal prison.

Support for the unfriendly witnesses wilted. Humphrey Bogart, whose iconic tough-guy persona had been a potent weapon for the CFA, issued a statement describing the PR tour to New York and Washington as "ill-advised and even foolish."[36] He had never been a communist or communist sympathizer, he declared, and he detested communism. The statement caused a collective shudder in Hollywood—if a star of Bogart's magnitude felt the need to distance himself from the Ten in such strident terms, could anyone be safe? Donations to the Committee for the First Amendment dried up immediately, and members reported pressure to resign. Within three months the organization would fold.

Amid all this, *Berlin Express* was still shooting on the RKO lot. The picture's final scene, with the American and the Russian expressing their fellowship outside the Brandenberg Gate, must have seemed like fantasy now. Closer to the mark was the little speech delivered to the kidnapped peacemaker by the malevolent leader of the right-wing underground: "I too believe in unity. But unlike you I know that people will only unite when they are faced with a crisis, like war. Well, we are still at war; you are not. So we are united; you are not. So we will succeed; you will not."

RYAN LIKED TO TELL INTERVIEWERS he wasn't "a chaser" (which was true—the way women responded to him, he never had to chase anyone). For a man so proud of his family, the affair with Merle Oberon was a strange anomaly, an ongoing adulterous relationship that became an open secret among the cast and crew. Charles Korvin contended that the affair continued on the RKO lot, though production records suggest some turbulence as the picture was drawing to a close. On Wednesday, November 5, Oberon went home sick at noon, forcing Tourneur to scrap the rest of the day's scenes. The following Monday she didn't show up for work, and that Friday she left in the middle of the afternoon. According to biographers Higgins and Moseley, she and Ryan never saw each other again after *Berlin Express,*[37] though Ryan and Lucien Ballard would make four more pictures together.*

Somehow RKO managed to keep the whole mess out of the scandal sheets; however, the much-feared gossip columnist Louella Parsons twitted Ryan about it in a February 1948 profile. ("There had been a lot of talk about feuding in the 'Berlin Express' troupe, and I asked Bob if that were true," wrote Parsons. "I had heard that he and Merle Oberon had been particularly bitter in their quarrel.")[38] From that point on, Ryan's movie-magazine pictorials stressed fatherhood, with Tim becoming a frequent participant. How Bob and Jessica dealt with the affair would remain private, but soon after he returned from Europe, they decided to buy a house in the San Fernando Valley, far from the Hollywood social scene.

A certain amount of hobnobbing was required to keep one's career going, but Jessica didn't like actors or the parties they threw. "As a wife, you met the same people over and over again," she wrote in a later memoir, "because they didn't recognize you unless you were standing right beside your husband, and even then they weren't always sure you were the wife. It was spooky." By now she had published her second mystery for Doubleday and was working on a third, but no one was interested in that. She would start conversations with people and then see their eyes darting about in search of someone more important. "If you were a wife you got very tactful about releasing any poor sap quickly to go do business . . . and then ended up sitting tensely with other tense wives trying their best to look as if they were having a good time."[39]

She reached her limit one night when she and Robert attended a swank party and she was immediately shunted off to the side with her friends Amanda Dunne and Joan Houseman. Robert, Philip Dunne, and John Houseman were off somewhere having lively conversations. "That night Joan Houseman's

---

**Inferno (1953), *The Proud Ones* (1956), *Hour of the Gun* (1967), and *The Wild Bunch* (1969).

solution to the condition of non-being was to retreat to a corner of the vast living room of the vast house and get quietly smashed," Jessica wrote, "while she stared at the crowd with an expression of splendid French contempt."[40] Amanda and Jessica began tossing back drinks as well, until Amanda stood up suddenly, looking as if she might be ill, and went off in search of a bathroom.

Left alone, Jessica strolled into the host's library to find some reading material, and before long Amanda burst into the room, looking rather crazed. "There's a room full of dead animals out there!" she exclaimed. Jessica followed her back into a coatroom where all the women's furs were hung. This was too much for Jessica, and she told Robert she was going out for some air. "Once outside in the car, I went quietly into hysterics," she wrote. "The condition of non-being produces intense anxiety."[41]

On Kling Street, just east of Cahuenga Boulevard in North Hollywood, the Ryans found an A-frame ranch house with a paved terrace and a bare, spacious yard. "It was the biggest house we could get with the most ground for the least money at a time when we still did not trust—*I* didn't trust—that the money would keep coming in," Jessica wrote. "Robert never doubted it, but he had never been as poor as I had been."[42] The couple landscaped the place themselves (planting ivy that eventually ran riot over the house) and began adding wings. The shed in the backyard was converted into Ryan's private office and workout room. This was the first time Ryan had actually owned a home—his parents had rented all their lives—and the suburban locale suited his reclusive nature.

The place was modest but comfortable, with plenty of room for the kids to run around; he and Jessica installed a sandbox, a swing set, and a wading pool. "Facing the garden is a wide, airy living room with almost one whole wall of glass, opening onto the terrace," noted a visiting journalist. "A beautiful antique chest dominates one end. The chairs and divans are tailored and comfortable; the tables low and wide . . . The muted greens and grays and blues of walls, carpets, and upholstery are brightened by huge bouquets of fresh garden flowers."[43]

Ryan made sure the reporter understood that social gatherings at their home were limited to their close circle of friends, not the movers and shakers of the picture business. He and Jessica were perfectly happy with each other's company. Philip Dunne would marvel at Ryan's "tremendous devotion to his family. He was the most family-oriented man I ever knew."[44]

Ryan tending to chores at the new house on Kling Street in North Hollywood. His years there with Jessica and their young children were among his happiest. *Robert Ryan Family*

In December 1947, Ryan made a quick trip to Chicago to address the national Conference of Christians and Jews, pinch-hitting for Dore Schary. "He began to be asked to speak before Jewish groups to discuss anti-Semitism," Jessica recalled. "In the beginning, the doing of it appeared to be for publicity for the movie . . . but when that phase was over, they wouldn't let him go. For a long time there he was playing what he called the Synagogue Circuit."[45]

From there Ryan flew to New York to see some plays. Since *Crossfire* had hit, he had been fielding offers from Broadway, but his calendar for 1948 already was filling up with pictures. RKO announced that he would costar with Cary Grant, Frank Sinatra, and Robert Mitchum in *Honored Glory,* an episodic drama about nine unidentified men, killed in action during World War II, whose stories make them candidates for the Tomb of the Unknown Soldier (the film would never be made).[46] MGM wanted to borrow Ryan for the revenge drama *Act of Violence.* And Schary, who had been trumpeting *Crossfire* as proof that A pictures could be made on B budgets, was ready to move forward with his next such experiment: *The Set-Up,* a boxing drama about a washed-up fighter staring down his bleak future. The source material was Joseph Moncure March's narrative poem of the same title, a favorite of Ryan's at Dartmouth.

His first assignment that year was RKO's antiwar parable *The Boy with Green Hair,* adapted from a short story by Betsy Beaton. Filmed in Technicolor, it starred eleven-year-old Dean Stockwell as a schoolboy who has been passed from relative to relative while his parents are overseas.* Eventually he lands in a bucolic small town with a kindly old Irish-American gent (Pat O'Brien) and begins to make a life for himself, but then he learns the truth about his parents—they were killed in London during the blitz—and the trauma turns his hair green overnight.

The project had originated with Adrian Scott, himself the adoptive father of a traumatized British war orphan; but after Scott was fired by RKO, Schary handed *The Boy with Green Hair* over to producer Stephen Ames and first-time movie director Joseph Losey. A senior at Dartmouth when Ryan was a freshman, Losey had studied with Bertolt Brecht in Germany and in 1935 had traveled to the Soviet Union, where he staged Clifford Odets's *Waiting for Lefty* in Moscow. His latest theatrical project had been an acclaimed Broadway production of Brecht's *Galileo,* performed in English for the first time and starring Charles Laughton.

Fresh from the rubble and hungry children of Frankfurt and Berlin, Ryan couldn't have been more sympathetic to *The Boy with Green Hair.* His second-billed part consisted of only one extended scene with Stockwell, which took two days to shoot; even so, it would remain one of the picture's best-liked sequences. At a police station one night, cops fire questions at Peter, the brooding and now bald-headed boy. Ryan plays Dr. Evans, a laid-back child psychologist who arrives with a brown-bag dinner and asks the cops to leave them alone. Children who grew up around the actor would remember his uncondescending manner toward them, and he incorporates it here to fine effect. Evans wordlessly changes the lighting in the room, taking an overhead spot off them, and asks Peter to move to a chair so he can have the bench for his dinner. "Chocolate malted milk," he notes, frowning into the cup. "I'm sure I asked for strawberry." They both know it's a game, but Peter is starving; he takes the malted and digs into a hamburger, and his responses to the doctor's questions trigger a series of flashbacks.

---

*Stockwell had just won a special Golden Globe Award for his performance as Gregory Peck's son in *Gentleman's Agreement.*

The Boy with Green Hair can be cloying and moralistic, but there are genuine moments of fear and anger as well. Peter, having learned of his parents' death, is stocking shelves at a local grocery and overhears three women debating the Cold War. Losey follows his face, shooting him through cabinets and shelves as the women's voices hover off-screen. "People say another war means the end of the world," says one. "War will come, want it or not," her friend replies. "The only question is when." A third adds: "Just in time to get more youngsters like Peter." This so frightens the boy that he drops a bottle of milk, which smashes on the floor. A low-angle shot shows the three ladies gathered above, grinning in amusement.

The central scene is a powerfully weird and stylized dream sequence in which Peter awakes in a forest clearing and encounters the very war orphans he and his classmates have been studying on posters in school. One girl has lost a leg; another holds an Asian infant. The oldest orphan explains to Peter that his green hair marks him as a messenger: "You must tell all the people — the Russians, Americans, Chinese, British, French, all the people all over the world — that there must not ever be another war."

The Boy with Green Hair crystallized a public sentiment for world government that had been growing in the United States since the end of the war. Norman Cousins, editor of the *Saturday Review of Literature* and a founder of the United World Federalists, had framed the issue before any other journalist. His celebrated editorial "Modern Man Is Obsolete," written the night after Hiroshima was destroyed, argued that the event marked "the violent death of one stage in mankind's history and the beginning of another." Now that man had the power to incinerate whole cities, he would have to evolve past the need for war, which would mean eradicating global inequality and establishing world government. To this end, Cousins wrote, modern man "will have to recognize the flat truth that the greatest obsolescence of all in the Atomic Age is national sovereignty."[47] By 1946 a Gallup poll found that 52 percent of Americans favored the liquidation of the US military in favor of an international peacekeeping force. Ryan was one of them, and he would get to know Cousins later that year when he joined the Federalists, a rapidly growing organization that advocated "world peace through world law."

The week before Ryan shot his scene for *The Boy with Green Hair,* the Academy of Motion Picture Arts and Sciences announced the Oscar nominations for 1947. *Crossfire* was honored in five categories: best picture, best director, best screenplay, best supporting actress (Grahame), and best supporting actor

Jessica and Robert attend the 1948 Academy Awards ceremony. "We don't ask actors home," she would later write. "We haven't, Robert or I, much to say to them privately." *Franklin Jarlett Collection*

(Ryan). But as more than one industry observer noted, this good fortune put RKO in a ticklish position, given that it had fired the picture's producer and director. There was another twist as well: in every category except Ryan's, *Crossfire* was competing with *Gentleman's Agreement,* the Fox production Schary had beaten to the box office by four-and-a-half months. Released in December and carefully marketed with *Crossfire* as its model, *Gentleman's Agreement* was still doing big business across the country and had topped the nominations race with a total of eight.

Though RKO had beaten Fox to the punch, *Gentleman's Agreement* had effectively stolen *Crossfire*'s thunder as an exposé of anti-Semitism, to Ryan's great irritation.[48] Adapted from a novel by Laura Z. Hobson, it starred Gregory Peck as a journalist who poses as a Jew in order to write a magazine story. In some respects *Gentleman's Agreement* was bolder than *Crossfire;* it confronted prejudice head-on instead of sneaking it into a murder mystery, and in contrast to the other film's psychopathology, it revealed more casual and insidious forms of bigotry. It was also the kind of picture Academy voters could feel good about honoring: this was no crummy little crime story shot on borrowed sets, but a big, long prestige drama set in the penthouses and boardrooms of Manhattan, produced by the great Darryl F. Zanuck.

The other nominees for best supporting actor were Charles Bickford as the starchy butler in RKO's *The Farmer's Daughter,* Thomas Gomez as the warmhearted carny in Universal's *Ride the Pink Horse,* Richard Widmark as the giggling killer in Fox's *Kiss of Death,* and Edmund Gwenn as Kris Kringle in Fox's *Miracle on 34th Street.* Ryan relished the attention, though his chances of winning seemed fairly slim: he would be dividing the psycho vote with Widmark, and really, who was going to choose a Jew-hating murderer over Santa Claus?

Cheyney Ryan arrived on March 10, at Cedars of Lebanon Hospital in Los Angeles, and ten days later Jessica had recovered sufficiently to accompany her husband to the Shrine Auditorium. As most had predicted, Gwenn won best supporting actor. *Crossfire* was shut out by *Gentleman's Agreement,* which took best picture, best director (Elia Kazan), and best supporting actress (Celeste Holm). According to Dmytryk, the right-wing Motion Picture Alliance for the Preservation of American Ideals had conducted a vigorous campaign against *Crossfire.*[49] The picture had made the year-end lists of all the major critics and collected honors ranging from an Edgar Allan Poe Award (for best mystery film) to a Cannes Film Festival award (for best social film). But in Hollywood, *Crossfire* was still a double-edged sword. A few months earlier, when MPPA president Eric Johnston had praised the picture in a speech, the legal counsel for the Hollywood Ten had puckishly invited him to serve as a character witness for Scott and Dmytryk. Johnston declined.

six

Caught

The Shrine Auditorium may have been a temple of self-congratulation on Oscar night, but outside its walls the movie business was in serious trouble. Ticket sales had boomed after the war when soldiers were streaming home, but in 1947 domestic box office revenue plummeted as people like the Ryans started families and moved into the suburbs. Britain and other countries, hoping to revive their own war-ravaged film industries, levied tariffs on US imports, diminishing the once-lucrative European market. And the federal government renewed its antitrust campaign against the major film studios, pressuring them to sell their theater chains. If that happened, the entire business model for the studio system would collapse.[1]

Dore Schary had come to RKO promising to cut costs, and the board of directors reaffirmed its confidence in him after the HUAC hearings. But in his first year as production chief, the studio's annual profit had plunged from $12 million to $5 million. In February 1948 the trade papers reported that Floyd Odlum, RKO's chairman and majority stockholder since 1936, would sell his controlling interest in the studio to Howard Hughes, the aviation giant and mercurial moviemaker who had produced such landmark pictures as *Hell's Angels* (1930) and *Scarface* (1932).

In early May, Ryan made a quick trip to New York for the *Berlin Express* premiere, and by the time he returned to the West Coast, Hughes had struck a deal with Odlum, purchasing 24 percent of RKO for the grand sum of $8.8 million—then the largest cash transaction in the history of the movie business. The announcement sent shock waves through the studio: Hughes had a reputation as a controlling and capricious moviemaker. For years his pet project had been *The Outlaw,* a sexually suggestive western starring Jane Russell and her thirty-eight-inch bust; shot over a maddening nine months in 1940 and 1941, the picture had been held up first by the Production Code Administration and then by various state censorship boards, finally winning wide release in 1946. Hughes's latest infatuation was starlet Faith Domergue, and many thought he was buying RKO in order to distribute *Vendetta,* the film he had been constructing around her to the tune of $2 million.

Hughes moved quickly to tamp down the paranoia raging around the Gower Street lot: Peter Rathvon, president of Radio-Keith-Orpheum, issued a memo to all employees assuring them that the new owner had "no hungry relatives looking for your jobs, nor substitutes waiting to step into the RKO management."[2] Schary, whose contract permitted him to leave the studio in the event of an ownership change, was particularly apprehensive about the prospect of Hughes, an anticommunist and anti-Semite, meddling in his production slate. But when Rathvon arranged a meeting between the two men at his home, Hughes promised Schary that nothing would change under his leadership. In early June, Schary issued a reassuring memo to studio personnel: "I have had a number of talks with Mr. Howard Hughes, and we are in complete agreement on present policy and on the projected program for RKO."[3]

While all this transpired, Ryan was on loan to MGM, making *Act of Violence* with director Fred Zinnemann. Like *Crossfire* it was a hard-bitten suspense film that touched on the harsh realities of the war, with Ryan as a fearsome heavy, though in this case the theme was not bigotry but betrayal. Ryan and bug-eyed Van Heflin play survivors of a Nazi prison camp, once comrades but now deadly enemies. Just as *Crossfire* began with a shadowy silhouette of Ryan beating someone to death, the new movie opened with a predawn sequence of a mysterious figure in trench coat and fedora limping across a New York street, climbing the stairs of a seedy tenement building, and extracting a pistol from a bureau drawer. Ryan's face is revealed finally in close-up as he holds the gun before him, and thick white letters scream out the title: ACT OF VIOLENCE.

Pictures about returning soldiers had become commonplace (a year earlier, *The Best Years of Our Lives* had won seven Oscars), but seldom were they so bitter. Ryan's character, Joe Parkson, catches a Greyhound bus to the West Coast and arrives in the small town of Santa Lisa, where he's immediately halted by a cop as he tries to cross the street: it's Memorial Day, and a parade is passing. "I liked the idea of this man, who was the veteran of an unhuman [*sic*] experience in the war, having to step back because a few old guys were walking past him, carrying the American flag, as though they owned it," Zinnemann recalled.[4] Parkson has come to town to murder Frank Enley (Heflin), a local contractor, family man, and pillar of the community. Enley is a war hero in Santa Lisa, but Parkson knows the truth about him: when starvation drove Parkson and other POWs to attempt a tunnel escape, Enley ratted them out to the commandant.

As Enley, Heflin had nabbed the better role, yet Parkson was iconic—an avenging angel, slouching toward Southern California to be born. Early in the picture he shows up at the contractor's home to find only his flinty wife, Edith (twenty-one-year-old Janet Leigh). Sweating and absurdly out of place in his noirish getup, Parkson forces his way in. "He's got it nice here, hasn't he?" Parkson observes as he peers around their pleasant home. "Real nice." Edith tells him to get lost, and in a rage Parkson spills the whole story, his eyes drilling through her. He remembers how he and ten other prisoners were ambushed by guards, tortured with bayonets, and left on the ground to die. Only he survived, listening to the others all night: "One of them lasted till morning. By then you couldn't tell his voice belonged to a man. He sounded like a dog that got hit by a truck and left in the street." This last detail reduces Edith to tears, and Parkson leaves her to weep in her sparkling kitchen.

Written by Collier Young, the story had bounced around Hollywood (it was briefly a vehicle for Gregory Peck and Humphrey Bogart at Warner Bros.) before landing at MGM with Zinnemann directing and Robert Surtees as cinematographer. The two men had worked together in the early '30s as camera operators at Berlin's EFA Studio, where Zinnemann was mentored and powerfully influenced by the pioneering documentary maker Robert Flaherty (*Nanook of the North*). Since then, Zinnemann, a Viennese Jew, had fled the Nazis and found an unlikely home for his grim style at the MGM fantasy factory: *The Seventh Cross* (1943) starred Spencer Tracy, Hume Cronyn, and Jessica Tandy as Germans who have escaped from a concentration camp; and *The Search* (1945), with Montgomery Clift, was about a boy who has survived Auschwitz and goes looking for his mother across the German countryside. Only after the war would Zinnemann discover that his own parents had died in a concentration camp.

From Flaherty, Zinnemann had learned the value of authentic locations, and this new picture would give him and Surtees a chance to photograph

Ryan and Janet Leigh in *Act of Violence* (1948). The flinty young
actress gave as good as she got when she and Ryan faced off in
this film and *The Naked Spur* (1953). *Franklin Jarlett Collection*

the real LA, where Enley flees and descends into the criminal underworld.
Zinnemann would recall "the many sleepless nights we spent shooting exteriors in the eerie slums of downtown Los Angeles,"[5] most notably the Bunker
Hill district, with its hilly terrain, its slanting, funicular railway cars, and its
long flights of cement steps hugging the run-down buildings. Other scenes
were shot at the Hill Street railroad tunnel, the Santa Fe freight yards, and as
far afield as Big Bear Lake in San Bernardino County. This sense of realism
extended to the actors as well. "No make-up of any kind was used on any
member of the cast," wrote Surtees. "We tried to maintain on the screen a
high standard of skin texture."[6] The technique heightened the hard set of
Ryan's face, with its lined brow and sneering mouth.

As a Catholic, Ryan had no trouble grasping this study in guilt and damna-
tion. Enley's confession to Edith, detailing the hunger and desperation inside
the camp, was the sort of thing most Americans wanted to forget about. "The
Nazis even paid me a price," Enley exclaims. "They gave me food, and I ate
it. . . . There were six widows, there were ten men dead, and I couldn't even stop
eating." Parkson turns out to be similarly cursed by his thirst for vengeance.
In his cheap hotel room he is visited by Ann (Phyllis Thaxter), his girl in New

York, who has followed him to LA in the hope of derailing his homicidal plan. She appeals to his conscience, begging him to let go of his hatred. Ryan plays the scene in near silence, considering her words, and looks up in shock when she refers to him being "as crippled in your mind as you are in your—" Then the telephone rings, bringing news of a rendezvous with Enley, and Parkson's face hints at a smile as he's pulled back into his wicked dream.

BY THE TIME *Act of Violence* wrapped in mid-July, RKO was in chaos. Dore Schary had resigned on July 7, less than a month after his calming memo to employees, when Hughes ordered him to suspend production of one picture and fire contract player Barbara Bel Geddes from another (for which she and Ryan had already done some test scenes).[7] Following a weekend meeting with the board, Hughes announced that all production would shut down from August to October as he reorganized the studio. Three hundred RKO employees were immediately terminated, and *Variety* reported that another seven hundred would be fired in the near future;[8] by the time Hughes was finished, the studio workforce of twenty-five hundred would be reduced to six hundred.[9] Numerous contract players were let go; by the following winter, only six remained, among them Ryan, Gloria Grahame, western star Tim Holt, and Robert Mitchum (whose contract RKO shared with producer David O. Selznick).[10]

Hughes could be a ruthless enemy but also a staunch ally, and he was vocal in his admiration for Ryan and Mitchum; he backed Mitchum after the actor was busted for marijuana possession in September 1948. With his connections to the Defense Department, Hughes was a good man to have in your corner during the Red Scare. But he was a strange individual: one time Ryan, summoned to the millionaire's house, found him shuffling around with empty tissue boxes on his feet; when Ryan asked about them, Hughes told him they were disposable and thus more sanitary than socks. On another occasion Hughes invited the Ryans over for a dinner party; they arrived to a house full of guests but no Hughes. After an hour and a half of cocktails, the guests were called in to dinner. Finally, the host arrived and greeted his guests. "I'm so glad that you're here tonight, Mrs. Ryan," Jessica remembered him saying. Then he left the room, and no one saw him again.[11]

Ryan returned to RKO expecting to begin principal photography for his coveted boxing drama *The Set-Up*, but like everything else it had been shelved when Hughes shut down the studio. Instead Ryan found himself swept into a bizarre professional intrigue that not only touched on intimate details of Hughes's private life but also provided Ryan with one of the more neurotic roles of his career: Smith Ohlrig, the controlling multimillionaire in Max Ophuls's caustic melodrama *Caught.*

Ophuls, another German Jewish exile, was one of many directors Hughes had walked on and discarded over the years. Despite an impressive track record in Germany and later France, Ophuls's first assignment in Hollywood didn't materialize until 1946, when his fellow émigré Preston Sturges hired him at California Pictures Corporation, the small indie Sturges had formed with Hughes, to develop and direct *Vendetta,* Hughes's project for his nineteen-year-old lover, Faith Domergue. When production began, Ophuls—a master stylist who favored long, sinuous tracking shots and dramatic use of perspective—immediately fell behind schedule and soon was relieved by Sturges, who had wanted to direct the picture himself anyway. Hughes took to ridiculing Ophuls,* referring to him as "the Oaf."[12]

Since then Ophuls had gained a foothold in Hollywood, directing the hit swashbuckler *The Exile* and the sublime romance *Letter from an Unknown Woman* for Universal. Charlie Einfeld, founder of the small Enterprise Studio, engaged Ophuls to develop a screen adaptation of *Wild Calendar,* a popular novel by Libbie Block in which a middle-class woman marries her wealthy playboy of a cousin and, following his heart attack, takes up with another man. Einfeld had bought the rights at the suggestion of Ginger Rogers, who wanted to star, and commissioned a script by Abraham Polonsky; when Rogers dropped out, Einfeld gave the property to Ophuls, who threw away Polonsky's script and started over with Arthur Laurents. "I'm not going to make a picture from that lousy book," Ophuls told Laurents over lunch. "I'm going to make a picture about Howard Hughes."[13]

Enterprise approached RKO for a loan of Ryan and Barbara Bel Geddes, but Peter Rathvon, who had taken over as production chief temporarily, didn't like the script and nixed the deal. Ryan must have been eager to make the picture; its producer, Wolfgang Reinhardt, was the son of his beloved acting teacher Max Reinhardt (who had died in 1943). After Einfeld invited

---

*Hughes fell out with Sturges too, and their partnership collapsed before the picture could be completed; when Hughes finally released *Vendetta* through RKO in 1950, it was directed by Mel Ferrer.

Ryan over to the studio to discuss the situation, they placed a conference call to pitch the project to Hughes, who was notoriously hard to see in person. Hughes read the script and insisted that certain of his own idiosyncrasies (the sneakers, the rumpled clothing, the refusal to drink anything but milk) be deleted, but in the end he approved the loan. "Max could have Ryan and Bel Geddes," Laurents recalled, "but the dailies had to be delivered to Mr. Hughes in person at his house at midnight by the editor."[14] When Rathvon learned that Hughes had overruled him, he resigned.[15]

By the time Ryan reported for work on July 30, *Caught* was already twelve days behind schedule; John Berry had taken over as director after Ophuls came down with shingles, but then Ophuls recovered, took over the picture again, and junked all of Berry's footage. Enterprise was sliding toward bankruptcy after the recent flop of its Ingrid Bergman vehicle *Arch of Triumph,* and Ophuls was under serious pressure to get his picture back on track; the twelve days abandoned would have to be made up in four. Luckily for Ophuls, he had a trio of highly professional stars in Ryan, Bel Geddes, and James Mason, making his US screen debut as a compassionate ghetto doctor who completes the story's love triangle. Mason was a superb actor, though according to Laurents he wore a false chest to make himself look more manly. Ryan, who had no need for a false chest, once confided to his friend Robert Wallsten that Bel Geddes came on to him before the shoot, explaining that she liked to sleep with her leading men. "I'm sorry to tell you," Ryan replied, "but I have a wife and children."[16]

Ophuls was himself a disciple of Max Reinhardt, and Ryan's performance delighted him. "Max was very fond of Robert Ryan," recalled assistant director Albert van Schmus. "He thought that he was a natural human being in front of the camera. And that's what Max wanted, in that particular part at least."[17] Smith Ohlrig, the millionaire, was a complicated role; for the story to work, viewers would have to believe that Leonora had married him for love as well as money. When Leonora and Ohlrig first meet, he takes her on an aggressively fast midnight drive and interrogates her mercilessly, mocking her charm school training; Ryan captures the strange mix of charm, confidence, and vulnerability that made Hughes irresistible to so many women.

A later scene in a psychiatrist's office tells a different story: Ohlrig is a serious head case, warped by his wealth and icy in his calculation of other people's motives. He's come to the shrink hoping to alleviate his recent heart trouble, and when the doctor suggests his attacks are an attention-getting device, Ohlrig leaps off the couch in a rage. "What are some of your other little gems?" he exclaims. "I must destroy everyone I can't own? I'm afraid all anyone wants is my money? I'll never marry because I'd only be married for my money?" To prove the doctor wrong, Ohlrig picks up the phone and directs an assistant to offer Leonora a wedding proposal.

Leonora soon finds herself confined to Ohlrig's mansion on Long Island as he goes about his business and mercilessly antagonized when he deigns to come home—in one case, late at night, barking orders, with an entourage of business associates. His ensuing confrontation with Leonora plays out in the game room, where Ryan, in a wonderful bit of business, banks a billiard ball around the edges of a pool table as Ohlrig calculates Leonora's motives for marrying him and her options for breaking free. "Every one of my corporations, every single one, has a different staff, a different lawyer, a different accountant," he explains. "Not one of them knows anything about each other. I run it all. Each one has his place and he stays there. . . . And that's what you've got to learn, Leonora. You're better paid than any of them."

BACK AT RKO, Ohlrig's real-life counterpart was remaking the studio in his own image. Hughes had installed two of his men, C. J. Tevlin and Bicknell Lockhart, on an executive committee overseeing the studio, and through them he declared that the era of Dore Schary's "message pictures" was over. Studio president Ned Depinet moved to New York to replace Peter Rathvon as corporate president, and longtime veteran Sid Rogell became head of production at RKO Radio Pictures. Yet the new owner's management style caused no end of frustration. With his phobia of germs, Hughes kept counsel from his house or his office at the nearby Samuel Goldwyn Studio; RKO executives couldn't reach him, which caused endless delays on critical decisions, but when he decided he was ready to talk, he would phone them at home in the middle of the night.

Cameras finally rolled again that fall as Hughes launched a slate of six modestly budgeted A pictures—the second of which, *The Set-Up*, began shooting in mid-October. Ryan had been coveting this assignment ever since he learned that RKO owned the rights to Joseph Moncure March's pungent narrative poem. When it made the *New York Times* best-seller list in 1928, there hadn't been an African-American heavyweight champion since Jack Johnson thirteen years earlier, and as March later observed, "The fight racket was still tainted by a strong residue of race prejudice."[18] Pansy Jones, the tragic hero of *The Set-Up,* is a black middleweight nearing the end of an undistinguished career,

> A dark-skinned jinx
> With eyes like a lynx,
> A heart like a lion,
> And a face like the Sphinx:
> Battered, flat, massive:
> Grim,
> Always impassive.[19]

Pansy has lost so many fights lately that his manager doesn't even bother to tell him when he cuts a deal with Tony Diamond, a local racketeer, for Pansy to throw his next bout. To everyone's astonishment, however, Pansy comes on strong and knocks out his opponent. Walking home from the fight, Pansy is stalked by Diamond and one of his boys; they chase him down to the subway, where Pansy falls onto the tracks and dies under the wheels of a train.

Soon after publishing *The Set-Up,* March had come to Hollywood as a screenwriter and contributed story and dialogue to Hughes's early triumph *Hell's Angels;* since then, however, he had fallen into an unbroken run of forgettable pictures. When he heard that *The Set-Up* was being produced, he offered his services to RKO, but instead the job went to first-timer Art Cohn, a former sportswriter, and Pansy Jones became Bill "Stoker" Thompson, a two-bit fighter who has spent twenty years getting pummeled in bottom-of-the-card bouts. Julie, his disillusioned wife, begs him to retire before he gets killed, but Stoker still dreams of getting a title shot and thinks he can beat Tiger Nelson, the young up-and-comer he faces that night in the heartless tank town of Paradise City. "I thought the story was wonderful," Ryan later told an interviewer, "because it had none of the usual mawkish glamour that is falsely attached to prize fight stories. It's not a glamorous business."[20]

RKO offered the script to Fred Zinnemann, but after *Act of Violence* the director was tired of brutality. Instead the job went to Robert Wise, an RKO contract director who had gotten his start as an editor (*The Hunchback of Notre Dame, Citizen Kane, The Magnificent Ambersons*). In keeping with the poem, Wise wanted the hero to be a black man, and he had his eye on Canada Lee, a former boxer who had played John Garfield's sparring partner in *Body and Soul.* But at that point no black actor had ever starred in a big studio release, and as Wise recalled, Ryan was "dying to do it."[21] Even without the racial element, *The Set-Up* could be a relevant picture, exposing the seedy world of small-time boxing: the corruption, the bloodthirsty crowds, the athletes chewed up and spit out.

Wise and Cohn had plenty of time to research the picture while RKO was shut down. They saw fights at Hollywood Legion Stadium, and Wise toured the small arenas in Long Beach, observing the crowds and hanging out in the dressing rooms with the fighters. [22] *The Set-Up* would be heavily populated with vivid minor characters: Shanley (Darryl Hickman), a nervous teenager facing his first professional bout; Luther Hawkins (James Edwards), a black boxer in his prime, his route to the top all mapped out; "Gunboat" Johnson (David Clarke), an old-timer with a face full of scar tissue who leaves for the ring promising he will be champ someday and returns on a stretcher, unable to remember his name.

At the center of this ensemble, however, was Stoker Thompson, a dull-witted, good-hearted man and the most sympathetic figure Ryan had ever played onscreen. "I liked the character of Stoker," he later wrote. "I liked his decency in a pretty grim business."[23] Ryan's moving performance was even more impressive coming on the heels of *Caught:* Smith Ohlrig is rich, ruthless, and articulate, whereas Stoker is poor, empathetic, and plainspoken. Except for his opening argument with Julie (Audrey Totter) in their cheap room at the Hotel Cozy, his dialogue is sparse and mostly functional, which forces Ryan to communicate almost everything about the character physically. In the lengthy dressing room sequence he hugs the periphery, watching the other fighters and silently weighing the price he's paid for a life in the ring.

After the fashion of Alfred Hitchcock's recent mystery *Rope, The Set-Up* would transpire in real time, from 9:05 to 10:16 PM, with the four-round bout between Stoker and Tiger Nelson commencing at the midpoint of the picture. Ryan had boxed on-screen already in *Golden Gloves* and *Behind the Rising Sun,* but this would be his most demanding match. "I had to learn to fight like a professional instead of an amateur, and that took months of training," he wrote.[24] He and Hal Baylor, playing Nelson, rehearsed carefully with fight choreographer Johnny Indrisano, a former welterweight boxer who had found a second career in Hollywood. Wise spent about a week on the scene, using three cameras—one for a long shot, another for a two-shot, and a handheld camera to crowd the fighters—and edited the sequence himself. The result was thrilling, more intense and chaotic than any boxing match ever filmed. One former prizefighter on the set told Ryan, "This is so true it makes me sick."[25]

The photojournalist Weegee (aka Arthur Fellig) was cast in a nonspeaking role as the timekeeper, and in a story for the *Los Angeles Mirror* he described the shoot as "a social register of the fighting racket," observed by no less than eight former professionals. "HOW THAT GUY CAN FIGHT," Weejee said of Ryan. "Usually on a fight story the make-up men (they prefer to be called ARTISTS) are busy painting on BLACK EYES ... but here it was different ... they were busy painting OUT real black eyes, as the fighters forgot about the camera and were really slugging it out."[26] Stoker is supposed to go down in the third round, but he hasn't gotten the message and gives Nelson a run for his money. Back in Stoker's corner, his manager (George Tobias) and corner man (Percy Shelton) spill the beans about the fix and beg him to lie down, but by now the struggle has taken on a life of its own.

Stoker wins by a knockout in the fourth, cheating the stony-faced racketeer Little Boy (Alan Baxter) out of the dive he was promised. As soon as the fight is over and the arena empties out, the power dynamic is suddenly reversed; when Stoker learns that his manager and corner man have vanished, the victory drains from his face, leaving only fear. Little Boy and his goons pay Stoker a visit in the dressing room, now silent and nearly deserted, and the racketeer promises they will be waiting for him outside. Once they're gone, Stoker races through the arena in a panic* and tries to escape into the alley, but they're waiting for him, along with Tiger Nelson. They close in, backing Stoker up against the corrugated metal shutter of a loading dock, his face slack with terror. For an actor such as Ryan, whose strength was key to his screen persona, it was a shockingly vulnerable moment. He would never have another quite like it.

"He takes more pride in that movie than any other he ever made," Jessica Ryan wrote. "It was an original."[27] Howard Hughes certainly thought so: the following March, as RKO was readying the picture for release, he sued United Artists for copyright infringement, arguing that its forthcoming drama *Champion* (directed by Wise's friend Mark Robson) duplicated key scenes from *The Set-Up*. A federal judge ruled for Hughes, ordering UA to delete from *Champion* a sequence in which the hero (Kirk Douglas), who has refused to throw a fight, is stalked and beaten by hoods. *The Set-Up* opened to glowing reviews, and that fall it won Wise the FIPRESCI critics' prize at the Cannes

---

*The scene was shot at Ocean Park Arena in Santa Monica.

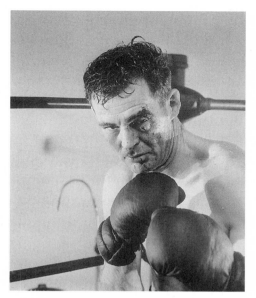

"This is so true it makes me sick," one former prizefighter told Ryan during production of *The Set-Up* (1949). The boxing classic would become a primary inspiration for Martin Scorsese's *Raging Bull* (1980). *Franklin Jarlett Collection*

Stoker Thompson, cornered by Little Boy and his thugs, at the climax of *The Set-Up* (1949). "It had none of the usual mawkish glamour that is falsely attached to prizefight stories," Ryan observed. "It's not a glamorous business." *Film Noir Foundation*

Film Festival. But it would be snubbed at Oscar time, possibly because Hughes had rankled so many industry people by going after UA. *Champion,* however, was nominated for five Oscars, including Douglas as best actor.

There were compensations. One night, after a preview screening at the studio, Ryan was approached on the street by Cary Grant. "You're Robert Ryan," Grant said, offering his hand. "My name's Cary Grant." The self-introduction was almost comical: Grant was one of the most famous movie stars in the world, and Ryan had admired him for years. "I want you to know that I just saw *The Set-Up,*" Grant went on, "and I thought your performance was one of the best I've ever seen."[28] Ryan never forgot the experience.

WHAT SPARE TIME RYAN HAD during *The Set-Up* went into the 1948 presidential campaign. President Truman was running against Thomas Dewey, the Republican governor of New York, but also was being challenged on the right by Strom Thurmond, who had led a walkout of Southern Democrats from the convention over the party's new civil rights plank, and on the left by Progressive Party candidate Henry Wallace, whom Truman had fired from his cabinet two years earlier. Wallace wanted to give equal rights to women and racial minorities, abolish the Un-American Activities Committee, and dismantle America's nuclear arsenal, all attractive positions to Ryan. Yet he was going with Truman. Years later, in notes for a magazine article, Jessica Ryan would remember her husband's insistence that votes for Wallace would only throw the presidency to the Republicans. "Through those years, he repeated again and again the dogma he had been raised on, Vote the Party, not the Man."[29]

Wallace's man in Hollywood was John Huston, director of *The Maltese Falcon, The Treasure of the Sierra Madre,* and *Key Largo.* Philip Dunne, who had formed the Committee for the First Amendment with Huston, recalled that "when John took on the job, the only people who were really supporting Wallace out here were the Hollywood Ten. They were all going around with big 'Wallace in '48' buttons on. But nobody was supporting Truman very much, either. Bob Ryan and Dore Schary and [screenwriters] Lenny Spiegelgass, Allen Rivkin, and I were about the only liberals who were doing anything for Truman."[30] Ultimately, Wallace's candidacy generated more excitement in Hollywood; Jessica would remember a banquet for Truman that failed to attract any more star power than her husband and Alan Ladd, "while Henry Wallace was wreathed in beauty glamor and fame."[31] But in the end Truman won, carrying Los Angeles and the State of California and dominating the electoral map against Dewey in a stunning upset.

The campaign impressed upon Jessica how hardheaded her husband's politics were. When she had met him in the late '30s, he had been full of colorful stories about Chicago ward heelers, though at that point he seemed disengaged from it all, more focused on acting and the theater. "But when he came to a broader political consciousness during the war and afterward, he came to it with an infinitely greater sophistication and sense of reality than the intellectual and artistic liberals we met in Hollywood had.... He approached the issues, always, with an insistence on what was possible, what would work . . . with a degree of frustration and often contempt for the vagaries of the liberals who spent immense amounts of energy talking endlessly about things that ought to be done, but obviously could not be done in the framework of *how* things *got* done. I think that neither one of us were ever liberals in that sense of the word."[32]

After *The Set-Up* wrapped in mid-November, Ryan found himself without a pending assignment for the first time in nearly two years. Production at RKO was proceeding at a snail's pace under Hughes, who managed to appease the studio's distributors by doling out the fifteen completed pictures Schary had left behind. One of these was *The Boy with Green Hair*, which had finished shooting eight months earlier but sat in limbo as Hughes tried to turn its pacifist philosophy inside out. Director Joseph Losey remembered an endless succession of notes from Hughes, written in pencil on yellow scrap paper, with orders for recutting the picture, but Losey had shot so little excess footage that not much could be done without reshoots.[33] When the strange boy in the forest admonishes Dean Stockwell that war is harmful to children, Hughes wanted Stockwell to reply, "And that's why we must have the greatest army, the greatest navy and the greatest air force in the world."[34] The twelve-year-old actor refused.

Three months and $150,000 later, RKO executives and board members screened the new version, which was so bad they persuaded Hughes to bite the bullet and release *The Boy with Green Hair* in something close to its original form.[35] Losey stated later that only a few lines of offscreen dialogue were struck, though as he recalled, all the publicity "sort of militated against it because it made it appear to be a more important film than it was."[36] Reviewing the picture in the *New York Times,* Bosley Crowther called it "a novel and noble endeavor" but also "banal" and "weakly motivated."[37] Still, it was warmly received in liberal quarters, not least the Ryans' dinner table. "For some reason *The Boy with Green Hair* was a movie that had a big presence when I was a kid," Cheyney Ryan remembers.[38]

By the time *The Boy with Green Hair* finally opened nationwide in January 1949, the man who had initiated the project, Adrian Scott, was persona non grata in Hollywood. The Ten were still fighting their contempt citations in the court system, an ongoing financial challenge, and while the screenwriters among the group began to find work under assumed names, Scott and Dmytryk didn't have that option. Shortly after RKO fired them, they had launched their own independent production company and tried to secure funding for *Albert Sears,* a drama about a black family moving into a white neighborhood, but they got nowhere with the project. Dmytryk found work directing two pictures in England and was soon followed there by Scott and his family.

Act of Violence had opened in December to strong reviews; *Caught* followed in February, was savaged by critics, and flopped miserably, though by that time Enterprise Studio had already folded. Ryan had high hopes for himself professionally once *The Set-Up* opened in March. But one assignment weighed heavily on him as he puttered around his new home in the Valley, sleeping late, working out in the shed behind the house, and playing with his little boys. Of all the pictures on RKO's new production slate, none was dearer to Howard Hughes than *I Married a Communist,* a Red-Scare melodrama that he hoped would establish the studio's patriotic credentials under his leadership. As one of the few male stars still employed by RKO, Ryan was a prime candidate for the lead, but to star in something like this would be a slap in the face to his colleagues who were losing their careers.

I Married a Communist was a title in search of a script, and it quickly became the picture nobody at RKO wanted to make. It gained a reputation as a political litmus test, a way for Hughes to weed out suspected communists at the studio. Joe Losey, the first director to pass on it, recalled Hughes threatening to keep him idle for the full duration of his seven-year contract,[39] though eventually he was fired. "Howard Hughes dropped my option when I refused to work on *I Married a Communist,*" remembered Daniel Mainwaring, who had written *Out of the Past* for RKO. "He used that project to get rid of a lot of writers, directors, and actors. If you turned it down, out you went."[40]

John Cromwell, the left-wing director first announced for the project, confirmed this story but said he took the job figuring that the god-awful script, something about a San Francisco shipping executive being blackmailed by the party for his past membership, could never be salvaged.[41] Hughes dropped Cromwell anyway (after a fifteen-year career at RKO) to avoid paying him a scheduled salary increase. The picture's dire reputation couldn't have been much help in recruiting stars. RKO's shrinking list of contract players included only two suitable actors, Ryan and Mitchum—and Mitchum was currently serving a fifty-day jail term for drug possession, not exactly the credential Hughes needed for his patriotic picture. Hughes had indulged Ryan with *Caught* and *The Set-Up* and must have felt he was owed a favor. Ryan talked long and hard about it with Jessica, and in the end he capitulated; *Variety* announced on February 23 that he would star in *I Married a Communist*.

By that time Hughes had finally collared a director: Robert Stevenson, an Englishman whose most respected picture was a Fox adapation of *Jane Eyre* starring Joan Fontaine and Orson Welles. Script and casting problems delayed principal photography of *I Married a Communist* until April, when Ryan was joined on the set by Laraine Day, John Agar, and Thomas Gomez, the portly and commanding actor who had competed with Ryan for the Oscar a year earlier and was haunted professionally by his attendance at two Communist Party meetings back in the '30s.[42] Now he was doing penance as the sinister party boss, who summons Ryan's compromised hero to the docks one night and lets him watch as two thugs tie up a recalcitrant member and throw him into the ocean to drown.

Once the picture was shot, Hughes began his usual tinkering. He tended to fixate on odd details; during production of *The Outlaw* he had dispatched detailed memos on the proper presentation of Jane Russell's breasts, and on *I Married a Communist* he decided that Ryan and supporting actor William Talman each needed to be taught how to handle a gun. Before retakes commenced in June, RKO executive Jack Gross sent a memo to producer Sid Rogell informing him that Hughes wanted Ryan and Talman "taken out to a target range and taught to shoot, particularly how to draw, shoot, and not flinch when shooting."[43] Hughes further insisted that the instruction be followed by a screen test of their progress, to be delivered to him personally.

In later years Ryan could barely bring himself to mention the picture. When a teenaged Cheyney remonstrated with his mother over his father's decision, arguing that his father should have stood his ground, Jessica replied, "Let's have this conversation when you have a career yourself, and see how you feel about it."[44]

seven

Learning by Doing

In March 1949 the Ryans decided to celebrate their tenth wedding anniversary with a big blowout at their new home. Everyone they knew in Hollywood was invited, including their classmates from the Reinhardt School who had attended the ceremony a decade earlier. For the most part, though, they preferred small dinner parties with their more educated, writerly, serious-minded friends. "We don't ask actors home," Jessica later wrote. "We haven't, Robert or I, much to say to them privately. Nor do they have much to say to us. We aren't interested in the same things."[1]

Her own creative life was in flux. After publication of her second mystery, *Exit Harlequin,* she decided to try her hand at a romance novel, but it was tough going. She wrote in the morning, as Tim, now three years old and the image of his father, roamed around the house and Cheyney entertained himself in his playpen. (Writing to Dido and Jean Renoir, she predicted needing "an eight-foot steel fence to contain these two men.")[2] No one expected her, the wife of a movie star, to do anything but care for him and his children, but being a mother wasn't enough. She devoted her spare time to the American Friends Service Committee, a Quaker-affiliated organization that ministered to Japanese-American interns during the war and now mobilized support for refugees in Europe and Asia. A native of freethinking Berkeley, she studied yoga with Indra Devi, a Russian-Swedish immigrant who had arrived in LA two years earlier, and experimented with homeopathic remedies prescribed to her by Devi's friend (and eventual husband) Siegfried Knauer, a physician on Sunset Strip whom Jessica referred to as "the Witch Doctor."[3]

She had given up on tennis, given up on acting, and now might fail as a writer. She was prone to anxiety, and nothing stoked it more than the women who threw themselves at Robert. "There was a time when a lot of silly girls wanted my autograph," Ryan would recall a decade later. "Today my wife remembers that period as the most unbearable part of our . . . years together."[4] Especially after *The Set-Up*, Ryan had become a beefcake idol to bobby-soxers; fans often requested photos of him bare chested, and photographers asked him to strip for the camera. "Heck, I'm no Tarzan," Ryan told the *Hollywood Citizen-News* that summer. "But if that's what they want, I'll give it to them."[5]

Despite his exhibitionism, Ryan struck most people as a good husband. Laraine Day, who costarred with Ryan in *I Married a Communist*, would describe him years later as "such a gentleman. It was a pleasure to work with him. And especially because he was so devoted to his wife. It was wonderful to listen to him talk about her and their life together, because you felt there was real devotion."[6]

After moving to North Hollywood, the Ryans made another positive change to their lives by hiring Solomon and Williana Smith, a black couple in their early fifties, as household help. Born in Waterproof, Louisiana, a delta town on the Mississippi state line, Solomon had run a radio repair shop in New Orleans, where he married Williana in 1925. During the war, as part of the great migration, they had moved to Vallejo, California, where Solomon worked at the Mare Island Naval Shipyard, and since then they had come to Los Angeles, buying a house in the Mid-City neighborhood. They had no children. "Smith," as everyone called him, tended to the Ryans' house and garden, chauffeured Bob back and forth to the studio, and took Jessica on errands (she hated driving). Willie cooked, cleaned, and minded the children. "Smith was one of these guys that knew how to do everything," Cheyney Ryan recalls. "They were people who had an enormous amount of practical intelligence."[7] During the week the Smiths stayed in a guest room the Ryans had added to the house, and before long they became part of the family.

A month after completing *I Married a Communist*, Ryan began shooting a romance with Joan Fontaine called *Bed of Roses*. This would be his first women's picture since *Tender Comrade* six years earlier; Jessica had urged him to take it, fearing he was in danger of becoming typecast as a heavy. "I spend a lot more time now posing for romantic stills," he told fan-magazine writers Reba and Bonnie Churchill. "All the photos the studio had on file were shots of me snarling at the camera."[8]

Williana and Solomon Smith worked for the Ryan family from 1948 through the early 1960s, stabilizing a household that was buffeted by the demands of a movie star's career. *Robert Ryan Family*

No less than seven screenwriters and five directors had labored over this adaptation of a 1928 romance novel called *All Kneeling,* to which Fontaine owned the rights.[9] When Hughes assigned Nicholas Ray to direct, Ray and writer Arthur Schnee took yet another crack at the script, working more feverishly perhaps than the material required. Producer Robert Sparks advised Ray not to get so wrapped up in this star vehicle, but Ray was adamant: "This picture shows the turmoil inside a woman's heart." Sparks replied, "The only turmoil inside Joan Fontaine's heart is whether her dressing room is heated in the morning."[10]

Born in 1911, Ray had grown up in LaCrosse, Wisconsin (also the hometown of Joseph Losey), and in the early '30s studied under playwright Thornton Wilder at the University of Chicago. Through Wilder he won a fellowship to the experimental arts community created by Frank Lloyd Wright at his Taliesin estate near Spring Green, Wisconsin. After moving to New York City in 1934, the young man acted in and directed left-wing political theater for the ragtag Theatre of Action company, during which time he joined the

Communist Party. Eventually the Theatre of Action was absorbed into the Federal Theatre Project, and before long Ray was staging community-based theater in the rural Southeast. During the war years, John Houseman had hired Ray to direct radio programs for the Voice of America, and eventually launched him as a Hollywood director.

Ryan was struck by Ray, who summoned the five lead actors for an initial table reading of the script before shooting commenced, something that rarely happened at RKO.[11] Ray had fought to get Ryan on the picture, having admired his low-key charm in *The Boy with Green Hair,* and the two men connected, though Ryan was a little frustrated to be working with Ray on such a weak story. Christabel Scott (Fontaine), the beautiful schemer at the center of *Bed of Roses,* climbs the ladder of high society by marrying a millionaire (oily, mustachioed Zachary Scott) but then cheats on him with a mischievous, razor-sharp novelist (Ryan). Ray's dialogue was witty, and at the very least he concocted a meet-cute that ranked as one of Ryan's few genuinely comic moments on-screen. Staying with friends, Christabel thinks she's alone in the house, but her phone call is interrupted by a man's voice ordering her to get off the line. She races back into the kitchen, where the other phone handset is located, and Ryan's grinning face pops up from behind an open refrigerator door.

Ray and Ryan would make two more pictures together in fairly quick succession before the director left RKO; one of the enduring mysteries of the blacklist period is why Hughes protected Ray, a former party member. Earlier in Ray's career, Hughes had tried to force *I Married a Communist* on him; after Ray asked his agents to free him from the project, he received a Christmas Eve summons to meet with Hughes at the Goldwyn studios (where he found the boss watching *Caught*).[12] Somehow Ray managed to wriggle out of the assignment without losing his job.

All spring and summer there had been worrying headlines from Berlin and mainland China. Following the massive Berlin airlift, which had thwarted Joseph Stalin's blockade of the city, the United States had established the German Federal Republic and the Soviets began constituting the German Democratic Republic. In the East, Mao Zedong's Communist forces had captured Nanjing, capital of the Republic of China, and driven Chiang Kai-chek's nationalist government south to Canton, hastening the end of the decades-long civil war. Then, on September 23, President Truman grimly announced "evidence that in recent weeks an atomic explosion occurred in the USSR." The atomic monopoly of the United States was over.

Domestically the news itself had the force of a blast, and the confluence of international developments only fed the flames of anticommunism in Washington. A week after Truman's fateful announcement, Mao Zedong declared the People's Republic of China; a week after that, *I Married a Communist* test screened in Los Angeles and San Francisco. Audience response was dismal. After the blacklist hit, several studios had defensively launched anticommunist dramas, but the ones that had opened—MGM's *Conspirator,* with Elizabeth Taylor; Republic's *The Red Menace*—had bombed. Now people were confronted with the possibility of nuclear annihilation on American soil; in the era of the bomb shelter and the unspeakable end, who wanted to relax at the movies with a picture about scheming communists?

RKO executives pleaded with Hughes to tone down the politics and change the title; he was incredulous, considering the title "one of the most valuable parts of the picture,"[13] but reluctantly agreed. *Variety* reported that *I Married a Communist* would open in January 1950 as *Where Danger Lives,*[14] but when it finally arrived in theaters six months later, collecting ho-hum reviews and expiring at the box office, it was titled *The Woman on Pier 13.*

The Secret Fury, which began shooting in October and continued through early December, looked to be even worse, a tepid mystery starring forty-six-year-old Claudette Colbert (*It Happened One Night*) as a classical pianist who may be suffering from amnesia and Ryan, who turned forty during the shoot, as her concerned fiancé. After the holidays Ryan reported back to RKO for a series of retakes on *Bed of Roses;* Hughes wanted a new ending, but even this failed to mollify him, and four months later he was still dispatching instructions for reediting the picture.[15] Like *I Married a Communist,* the caustic romance would sit on the shelf for the better part of a year, come out under a different title (the saucier *Born to Be Bad*), and do lackluster business.

The glacial production pace at RKO had become par for the course under Hughes; all through 1949 the studio had been promising to ramp up the release schedule, but of thirty pictures announced, only a dozen were produced. One executive recalled, "Working for Hughes was like taking the ball in a football game and running four feet, only to find the coach was tackling you from behind."[16] RKO Radio Pictures had lost $5.2 million in 1948, the year Hughes took over, and hemorrhaged another $3.7 million in 1949. "I think he bought RKO as a tax liability," said director Joe Losey. "He wanted to run it into the ground so he could take a huge loss."[17]

Jean Renoir and Eddie Dmytryk were long gone. Losey, Bob Wise, and Jacques Tourneur had escaped to other studios. Given the dearth of directing talent at RKO, Ryan looked forward to his next project with Nicholas Ray. Ryan's friend John Houseman had approached him to star in a crime thriller he and Ray were trying to get off the ground at RKO, to be adapted from a 1946 British novel by Gerald Butler called *Mad with Much Heart*. Ray was fascinated by the book, in which a London police detective tracks a mentally disabled child murderer through the snowbound English countryside, but RKO had passed, and when Houseman sent the book to his friend Raymond Chandler, the writer replied with a withering critique. Ryan agreed to make the picture if he could approve the script, and Sid Rogell, head of production at RKO, relented. The film that finally emerged two years later, retitled *On Dangerous Ground,* would include one of Ryan's most indelible performances and become a key film in his screen persona. But first it had to get past Hughes.

MAD WITH MUCH HEART was an odd novel, a suspense story that evolved into a melancholy romance. In a quiet farming community, two little girls have been strangled, and one dies; the father of the other, Walter Bond, seethes with anger. "Why are such things allowed to happen?" he asks his wife. "Has the eye of the Lord left our village?"[18]

Shotgun in hand, Bond hopes to kill the culprit in the ensuing manhunt; holding him in check is James Wilson, a plainclothesman who has been dispatched from London to command the investigation. The two men follow the murderer by car in a blinding snowstorm and eventually spin out into a ditch; after Bond finds the suspect's deserted vehicle, he and Wilson trudge to the nearest house. Its occupant is a beautiful blind woman, Mary Maldon, who invites them in but acts suspiciously. Wilson guesses correctly that she's hiding something. The killer is her younger brother, whom she cares for; she says he's been missing for days, but Bond doesn't believe her and Wilson isn't sure if he should.

Packed with action, Butler's book was tailor-made for the screen, but what really fascinated Ray was a short passage at the midpoint, after the snowstorm forces Bond and Wilson to suspend the search until morning and the blind woman offers them shelter. Tucked into a chair before the fire, Wilson dwells on his unhappy life in the police force: "There was never anything clear and clean, never any gift without a hook in it, never a meeting without some undercover deceit.... You thought it was going to be a romantic life.... You didn't know you were simply putting your head into a world that stinks from top to bottom. You didn't know you were choosing the life of a garbage man, digging and prodding and letting the smell out from human dregs."[19]

Ray wanted to relocate the story to the United States and envisioned a prefatory sequence showing Wilson as a cop driven to savagery by the ugliness and venality all around him. To adapt *Mad with Much Heart* he recruited screenwriter A. I. Bezzerides—"Buzz" to his friends—a Greek-Armenian immigrant who had grown up in Fresno, California, and published a hardboiled novel about truckers, *They Drive by Night,** that was adapted to the screen for George Raft and Humphrey Bogart. Since then Buzz had become a screenwriter himself and adapted his novel *Thieves' Highway* for director Jules Dassin. Ray sold him on the idea of riding with big-city cops to learn what their daily lives were like; Bezzerides spent a few nights with the LAPD, and Ray, visiting the East Coast, rode with Irish cops in Boston. In New York, Ray saw Sidney Kingsley's new play *Detective Story,* which also dealt with a brutal cop in a big-city precinct.

"We start with the cop in the city being called up for his violence," Bezzerides remembered. "He's a vicious cop, vicious to criminals because he can rationalize it. Criminals are criminals to him, they're not people. So he's sent out of the city for his behavior, into the mountains."[20] The urban section, shot in Los Angeles, would take up the first half hour of an eighty-minute picture, and its tone was uniformly harsh, its city a nocturnal cesspool of drunks, hookers, and hustlers. The ostensible story line, a police procedural in which Jim Wilson and his two partners search for a cop killer, was simply dropped when the action moved out to the country; the real narrative was psychological, a series of encounters with urban lowlifes that exposed Wilson's disgust with humanity.

The bifurcated story made Houseman uneasy, but for Ray it was the key to the picture: he even wanted to heighten the contrast by shooting the city scenes in black and white and the natural scenes in color (an idea the studio quickly nixed). Ryan signed off on the script, and on Monday, March 27, he set

---

*Not to be confused with Ray's first feature, *They Live by Night* (1948).

off from Union Station in Los Angeles to Denver, Colorado, and from there to Granby, Colorado, in the Rocky Mountains. According to Ray biographer Bernard Eisenschitz, "Ryan was in a scene as soon as he arrived, at 4:30 in the afternoon."[21] Ida Lupino, a luminous actress (*High Sierra*) who had become one of the few women directors in Hollywood, was cast as Mary, and Ward Bond, a hard-line anticommunist active in the right-wing Motion Picture Alliance, would play Bond, renamed Walter Brent. For Danny, the frightened man-child on the run, Ray managed to sneak in his nephew, Sumner Williams (whose anguished, inarticulate performance hinted at the work Ray would coax from James Dean in *Rebel without a Cause*).

Staying at the El Monte Inn, the cast and crew got a warm reception from the townspeople of Granby and nearby Tabernash, some of whom appeared in the film. Ray would remember the Granby shoot as a wonderful experience, and Ryan was sufficiently at ease there to show up at the local high school, speak to the boxing club, and sign autographs. Heavy snowfall impeded the two-week shoot, and at one point the generators broke down and the camera tripods began to freeze up. But the fresh snows created a blinding whiteness for the chase scenes, and the mountain terrain was stirring, a stark backdrop for the contest between Wilson and Brent over whether Danny will be apprehended or executed.

Back in Los Angeles, the focus shifted to the interiors and later the city locations, where Ray and Ryan really began digging into their embittered hero. The picture was ahead of its time in noting how cops are isolated and worn down not only by the repellent characters they deal with every day, but also by the fear and contempt of law-abiding citizens. Prowling the streets, Wilson and his two partners think they've spotted their man, and Wilson runs him down; a crowd gathers, but the guy is clean. "Dumb cops!" he blurts out angrily. "I was only running." Wilson has to be held back from clocking the guy, and the policemen retreat to more snide comments from the crowd. Shortly after this altercation the trio stop at a drugstore, where Wilson sits at the soda fountain and flirts with the counter girl. When someone teases her about her boyfriend, she replies, "That's all he'd need to know—me going out with a *cop.*" Wounded, Wilson spins around on his stool to hide his face, and his mouth tightens in resignation.

The night is full of users. At a dive bar Wilson is trailed by Lucky (Gus Schilling), an alcoholic trembling for his next drink, and gets hit on by an underage B-girl (Nita Talbot). At a side table a balding, bespectacled, obscenely grinning man (played by Bezzerides) tries to force some money on Wilson. Searching for a suspect named Bernie Tucker, Wilson pays a visit to Myrna (Cleo Moore), a slatternly platinum blond who shows him the bruises Tucker left on her and insinuates that he can leave a couple of his own if he likes. "The dissolve at the end of [the scene] will be played in such a way as to avoid the direct impression that Jim is about to indulge in a sex affair with Myrna," Joseph Breen, head of the Production Code Administration, had instructed Harold Melniker of RKO.[22] Ray cross-fades to a shot of Wilson coming down the stairs of the apartment building alone, but the sexual implication hangs in the air.

Breen was even more concerned about the graphic scene in Bernie Tucker's apartment, where Wilson corners the suspect. Bernie, a grinning slimeball, dares Wilson to hit him, but his smile fades when he realizes he's taunted the wrong man. "Why do you make me do it?" Wilson sputters, his voice rising in desperation. "Why do you make me do it? *You* know you're gonna talk. I'm gonna *make* you talk! I *always* make you punks talk! Why do you do it? *Why? Why?*" In an era when studio releases were subjected to additional censorship from local boards, Breen pointed out that the ensuing beat-down "would unquestionably subject the picture to extensive cutting and possibly even rejection, especially in the many municipalities where censor control is exercised by the police department."[23] In the release version Ray fades out as Wilson comes down on Bernie, but no on-screen punch could be as unnerving as his twisted reasoning: *Why do you make me do it?*

The picture supplied Ryan with not only his most demented on-screen moment but also, ironically, the most moving love scenes he had ever shot. Ryan liked Lupino; as the blind Mary, she invested what might have been a mawkish character with an arresting combination of strength and empathy. When Mary asks Wilson what it's like being a cop, he confesses, "You get so you don't trust anybody." Mary replies, "You're lucky. You don't have to trust anyone. I do. I have to trust everybody." Lupino disliked the downbeat ending, which showed Mary alone and weeping after Wilson returns to the city, and Ray was sufficiently swayed to let her and Ryan improvise a new one in which Wilson turns around and comes back, and the characters are reunited.

Ray had elicited mesmerizing performances from both his leads. To hear Ryan tell it, Ray never gave him explicit instructions, which was fine with him.

Ida Lupino and Ryan in *On Dangerous Ground* (1952). His role as an angry, despairing cop supplied him with not only his most demented screen moment but also the most moving love scenes he had ever shot. *Film Noir Foundation*

"I hate film-makers who want long discussions with actors over a scene," he explained. "An actor who doesn't know what a scene he's going to play is all about is in the wrong profession. Nick had, I think, great respect for me. Right from the start of our collaboration, he only offered me a few suggestions." [24] Mostly Ray would tell Ryan about the Irish Catholic cops he had ridden with in Boston and how they had behaved in certain situations, and then let him take it from there.

In Wilson's apartment, the dresser is decorated with high school athletic trophies and a crucifix, evidence of the personal route Ryan was taking into his damned character. He had long since left the church, but the church had never left him; raised by Jesuits, he had come to manhood believing in the horrible stain of original sin, the sin of Adam, which had corrupted mankind forever. Lamont Johnson would remember commiserating with Ryan over "the hangovers that we both shared as ex-Catholics." These involved "a hell of a lot of residual anger that I have, and I could sense that that was part of what there was with Bob. . . . I mean, we all had other things too, you can't blame it all on the Catholic Church, but it was certainly a considerable portion of it, and you would see Bob just retreating into a cynical, cold, and conceivably dangerous guy in some moods. [He] was by no means the great, good-hearted Herbert that a lot of people think."[25] Whatever repressed rage Ryan may have been carrying around came bursting out in *Mad with Much Heart.* Then, like any other job, it was over, and he went home to his wife and kids.

FOUNDED IN 1947 on the University of California campus in San Diego, the La Jolla Playhouse had become a magnet for movie actors looking to get back onstage. Ryan had appeared there in the romantic farce *Petticoat Fever* in summer 1949, and on July 4, 1950, he returned to play the low-rent tycoon Harry Brock in a six-day run of Garson Kanin's comedy *Born Yesterday.*

At one performance Jessica met Irene Selznick, the wife of producer David O. Selznick and daughter of MGM lion Louis B. Mayer, and over a drink in the Valencia Hotel, the two women started talking about their children and the chronic school overcrowding in California. Since the war began, the state population had swelled by 3.5 million, and there was an ongoing shortage of teachers and classrooms. Schools in Los Angeles County were operating on double shifts, with students receiving only a half day of instruction; one school had four kindergarten sessions stacked up from morning to late afternoon.[26] The US birth rate had spiked in 1946, increasing nearly 6 percent, and a year from now those children—including Tim Ryan—would all be old enough for kindergarten.

Jessica mentioned that her pediatrician, Siegfried Knauer, had suggested she start her own school, and to her surprise, Selznick explained that during the war she had done just that: "You get together some children and find a place. Then you get a teacher to run it."[27]

Years later, in a memoir about the founding of the Oakwood School, Jessica would trace her interest in starting a school to her own insecurity. "My hang-up was a simple one: I felt I had not had enough education. Meaning college. With the passing of time this want had become, family and friends tell me, something of an obsession."[28] Robert had to drive out to Kenab, Utah, in August to shoot locations for an RKO western called *Best of the Badmen,* but not long after his return, Jessica talked him into meeting with Tim's nursery school teacher to discuss the idea. The teacher referred them to Sidney and Elizabeth Harmon, similar-minded parents who lived in nearby Studio City

Cheyney, Jessica, and Timothy Ryan (circa 1951). *Robert Ryan Family*

and had four children, and the two couples got together for cocktails.

"Lizzie was a small, pretty woman with a breathless manner and childlike eyes that gazed with some bewilderment on the world," wrote Jessica. Sid Harmon "wore horn-rimmed glasses on myopic brown eyes that looked warmly upon all the people he liked which, together with a fondness for talking, often made him resemble a benign rabbi." In fact, Harmon was a producer—in the early '30s, he had mounted a Pulitzer Prize-winning production of Sidney Kingsley's *Men in White* with the Group Theatre, and a few years later he had come out to California to break into the picture business.* Lizzie had attended the private Ethical Culture Fieldston School in New York City, whereas Sid,

---

*Harmon was nominated for an Oscar for the original story of George Stevens's *The Talk of the Town* (1942), starring Cary Grant and Jean Arthur.

like the Ryans, had gotten his primary education at public schools. The two couples agreed to host an open meeting for interested parents at the nursery school where Tim was enrolled with Andy Harmon.

Through director Joe Losey, the Ryans met producer Frank Taylor and his wife, who had started the Westland School near Beverly Hills; they sent the Ryans to meet its director, Lori Titelman. "Her advice was refreshingly uncluttered and to the point," wrote Jessica. "In starting a school we must make up our minds to call a spade a spade—meaning, calling progressive *progressive,* even though the word had lately become suspect in both its educational and political context." [29]

Progressive was a code word for *communist,* yet progressive education was actually rooted in the philosophy of John Dewey, embracing the notion that children learn better when engaged with the world around them. When the parents' meeting at the nursery school took place, drawing in about fifty people,[30] someone asked Ryan if he was proposing a progressive school. Winging it, he replied, "Modified progressive." Harmon expressed the idea that the school would be open to all races and religions, to which someone commented, "Sounds pinko to me."[31] That first meeting did flush out one more interested couple: Ross Cabeen, a ruddy-faced petroleum engineer and rock-ribbed Republican, and his wife, Wendy. Cabeen "was out to make a great deal of money," Jessica recalled. "But he was bugged by a conscience (partly his wife) telling him that he should do more."[32]

A second parents' meeting was called, with Lori Titelman as guest speaker, but her left-leaning philosophy and the idea of opening a racially integrated school seemed to scare off many of those attending. By this time loyalty oaths had become part of civic life in California, required of municipal and county employees as well as faculty and staff at state universities; that fall the Regents of the University of California had fired twenty-six tenured professors who refused to sign. The Levering Act, which passed the California legislature weeks later, barred state employees from collecting their checks unless they signed a statement denying membership in any organization deemed subversive by the US attorney general.[33]

Communism had become a hot issue in the 1950 midterm elections, especially after North Korean forces crossed the thirty-eighth parallel into South Korea in late June. In California, Democratic Congresswoman Helen Gahagan Douglas—a former actress married to movie star Melvyn Douglas—was running for an open Senate seat against Republican Congressman Richard M. Nixon. As a member of the House Un-American Activities Committee, Nixon had come to prominence investigating whether former US State Department official Alger Hiss had passed secrets to the Soviet Union, and his work had led to Hiss being convicted of perjury. Nixon decided to make his anticommunist credentials central to his campaign, one so cunning in its attempts to smear Douglas that it would forever saddle him with the nickname Tricky Dick. The masterstroke was a flyer, printed on pink paper, that compared her voting record with that of New York Congressman Vito Marcantonio, widely thought to be a communist. A half million copies of this "Pink Sheet" were distributed across Southern California.

Ryan stumped for Douglas and contributed two hundred dollars to her campaign,[34] but for the most part the Hollywood community shied away from her. Nixon, grasping the power of television, finished out the election cycle with a flood of commercials in which he accused Douglas of being soft on communism. A whispering campaign against her husband insinuated that he had changed his name from Melvyn Hesselberg to conceal his father's Jewish roots in Russia. In the end Nixon clobbered Douglas, winning 59 percent of the popular vote. "There, in that murderous character assassination campaign," wrote Jessica, "we saw that the horror of what had been going on in Hollywood with the rise of the blacklist was not a particular attack on the movie business by HUAC but had entered the state and national scene . . . *and* was winning."[35] The Republicans picked up twenty-eight seats in the House and five in the Senate, and like the Eightieth Congress, elected four years earlier, the Eighty-Second would bring a blast of red-baiting.

SYMPATHY FOR DOUGLAS was in short supply on the set of Ryan's latest picture, a big-budget war movie teaming him with John Wayne. *Flying Leathernecks* chronicled the exploits of a Marine aviation unit in the Battle of Guadalcanal, allowing Howard Hughes to indulge two of his great passions—aerial heroics and knee-jerk patriotism. Wayne was currently president of the Motion Picture Alliance for the Preservation of American Ideals. Producer Edmund Grainger and screenwriter James Edward Grant, who had created Wayne's giant hit *Sands of Iwo Jima* (1949), were active in the Alliance as well. Crusty character actor Jay C. Flippen and on-set screenwriter Rodney Amateau were staunch conservatives. Cornered on the left were Ryan and director Nick Ray. "We often asked ourselves what we were doing on a film like this," Ryan would recall. "I hate war films."[36]

By this time Wayne had been in pictures for twenty years, but in the last few he had really caught fire, giving iconic performances in *Fort Apache* (1948), *Red River* (1948), *She Wore a Yellow Ribbon* (1949), and *Rio Grande* (1950). In *Flying Leathernecks* he played Major Dan Kirby, who arrives in Oahu, Hawaii, to take command of the VMF 247 Wildcats unit but prefers not to get too close to men he may have to sacrifice. Ryan was his philosophical antagonist, Captain Carl Griffin, beloved by the men but passed over for promotion. "I cast [Ryan] opposite Wayne because I knew that Ryan was the only actor in Hollywood who could kick the shit out of Wayne," Ray wrote in a memoir. "That conflict was going to be real, so I'd have two naturals."[37]

Ryan wasn't inclined to kick the shit out of anyone, though his skill with his fists always guaranteed him a wide margin of respect from Wayne, who admired not only his strength but his education and intellect. In any case Wayne was in no position to question Ryan's patriotism, given his own lack of World War II service; unwilling to let his career languish, Wayne had passed up numerous opportunities to serve with his friend and director John Ford in the US Navy's photographic unit, which earned him Ford's eternal scorn. The day after Thanksgiving, principal photography for *Flying Leathernecks* commenced at Camp Pendleton, where Wayne had shot *Sands of Iwo Jima* but Ryan actually had drilled recruits during the war.

Flying Leathernecks had been blessed by the military, and the Marines came across with men and materiél; production files show Grainger requesting more than three dozen fighter planes (F6F Hellcats and F4U Corsairs) for aerial photography, another twelve planes for set decoration at Henderson Field, a long list of ground equipment, and the services of one hundred marines. As usual with Hughes's projects, the story was a mess. Ray actually was working from three different scripts, shooting elements he liked from each, and he hired Amateau to collate them into a single narrative. The result was so disjointed and generic that, by default, the conflict between Kirby and Griffin, over how much empathy to show the men, became the picture's most interesting story element. Ray was right about the two stars: both men were 6' 4" and they filled the frame, Ryan often hovering silently behind Wayne and stealing scenes with his sidelong glances. "It's all in the eyes," he would tell his son Tim about the art of acting. "That's where you do most of your work."[38]

Ray purposely staged their big showdown inside a tent, "using the space for tension, so you could expect that the moment Duke dropped his right, Ryan would stiffen, and pretty soon they'd bring the tent down around them."[39] Unfortunately, the dialogue didn't live up to the staging. "You just can't bring yourself to point your finger at a guy and say, 'Go get killed!'" Kirby says. "You've gotta tear your guts out worrying about his flight record, or because some dame back in the States is giving him the brush-off!" Ryan does his best with Griffin's overripe response: "Four hundred years ago a poet put it better than I ever could: 'No man is an island.' When the funeral bell rings, it isn't just for the dead guy. It's a little bit for all of us." He was glad to get the whole thing behind him.

With the new year, the Ryans, Harmons, and Cabeens pushed forward with their school. Harmon suggested that they relocate their meetings to the Country Schools, a nursery school and summer day camp in the area, and the group circulated a letter, signed "Robert Ryan, Chairman, The Oakwood School," inviting people to get involved:

> For the past eight months a group of parents in the San Fernando Valley has been working to lay the groundwork for an Independent Elementary School . . . which would be dedicated to the principles of the best in modern education.
>
> We plan a non-sectarian, non-profit school with a serious program of parent participation.
>
> We plan a school
>
> where—The children are encouraged to work, play and learn together as responsible parts of a group and a community.
> where—The teacher guides the child to achieve learning not by rote but through his curiosity and activity.
> where—The classes are smaller, and closer individual attention is possible than in the overcrowded public schools.
> where—The school belongs to the child and the parents as well as to the Professional Teaching Staff.[40]

Parents at the Country Schools proved more receptive to these ideals. "The word *progressive* could be used without fear of it reflecting upon one's loyalty to one's country," Jessica wrote in her memoir about the school. "Certain common goals became clear: the school certainly should be open to all children regardless of race, color or creed. In fact, we should make every effort to assure a broad democratic base.... Scholarships should be made available to children of working-class parents."[41]

The Ryans had begun immersing themselves in the philosophy of education, especially the writings of John Dewey. "I believe that the only true education comes through the stimulation of the child's powers by the demands of the social situations in which he finds himself," Dewey wrote in 1897. "Through these demands he is stimulated to act as a member of a unity, to emerge from his original narrowness of action and feeling and to conceive of himself from the standpoint of the welfare of the group to which he belongs."[42] *Sounds pinko to me,* parents at their early meetings might have commented. But for Ryan, who had championed motion pictures as a tool for enlightenment four years earlier, the idea of reaching people at a more impressionable age must have been enticing—in any case, more enticing than *The Secret Fury, Best of the Badmen,* or anything else RKO might have in store for him.

THE NEW CONGRESS was sworn in on January 3, 1951, and two months later the House Un-American Activities Committee returned to Hollywood with a vengeance. By this time the original Hollywood Ten had all gone to prison for contempt of Congress, and those who had been paroled found themselves unemployable under their own names. The sole exception was Edward Dmytryk, the RKO director whose career had been so intertwined with Ryan's; in September 1950, from inside a federal prison in Mill Point, West Virginia, Dmytryk released a statement affirming his loyalty to the United States and swearing he was no longer a Communist Party member or sympathizer. He was paroled two months later, and in mid-April 1951, as a second wave of congressional subpoenas rolled through the studios, Dmytryk testified before the committee as a friendly witness and named names. This time there wasn't a whisper of protest from the Hollywood Left. Of the 110 people called to testify, more than half would recant their radical beliefs and inform on their past associates.

Interviewed more than thirty years later, Dmytryk would reveal that he quit the Communist Party of America after cell leaders began pressuring him and Adrian Scott to alter the story of *Crossfire* (he gave no details). To hear him tell it, he stuck with the Ten in 1947 because their Fifth Amendment strategy required solidarity, but he couldn't tolerate being linked with some of his fellow defendants. "The first day the unfriendly witnesses hit the stand, I knew I was not with them," said Dmytryk. "The question from then on and for the next two and a half years or more, 1947–1950, was how do I do it? When do I do it as gracefully as possible?"[43] Dmytryk would be reviled by some, but he returned to Hollywood and within a year scored a four-picture deal with liberal producer Stanley Kramer.

Dmytryk had plenty of company: writers Clifford Odets and Budd Schulberg, directors Elia Kazan and Robert Rossen, and actors Edward G. Robinson, Lee J. Cobb, Sterling Hayden, and Lucille Ball all prostrated themselves before the committee and were spared. Other industry people, such as actor Lloyd Bridges, were allowed to testify secretly.* As the panic took hold, a whole cottage industry of red-baiting organizations sprang up around the entertainment industry, companies such as American Business Consultants, which published the infamous *Red Channels* index of alleged communists and contracted with the studios to help "clear" employees with suspect activities or associations. Compared to the blacklist, which banned specific people from working at the studios, the "graylist" of independent pamphlets and newsletters was even more insidious, a creeping mist of rumor and innuendo.

While this inquisition played out, much of the nation was also mesmerized by the hearings of the Kefauver Crime Committee, established by the US Senate in May 1950 to investigate organized crime in America. Chairman Estes Kefauver was a liberal Tennessee Democrat determined to eradicate crime syndicates in America, and over the next fifteen months he and his four-member committee traveled across the country to hear testimony from local mobsters. Sessions in New Orleans, Detroit, and New York City were broadcast on live television and drew rapt audiences; for many Americans, this was their first exposure to the Mafia. Mobster Frank Costello refused to show his face on camera, and a close-up showed his twitching hands as he spoke.

Watching all this unfold, Howard Hughes decided he had the perfect topical hook for a remake of his silent 1928 gangster drama *The Racket*. Adapted from a play by Bartlett Cormack, it told the story of an NYPD captain, Tom McQuigg, trying to get the goods on a fearsome crime boss, Nick Scanlon (the role had made Edward G. Robinson a Broadway star in 1927). Report-

---

*Although Howard Hughes had the connections to make this happen for Ryan, no evidence has ever emerged that he did.

er-turned-screenwriter Samuel Fuller was tapped to update the story, but Hughes rejected Fuller's florid script in favor of a more prosaic draft hammered out by William Wister Haynes and hard-boiled novelist W. R. Burnett (author of *Little Caesar, High Sierra,* and *The Asphalt Jungle*). Their main innovation in the wake of the Kefauver hearings was to saddle the old-school gangster Scanlon with a new, nationwide syndicate of smooth corporate operators who considered his bare-knuckled style embarrassingly passé.

The Racket was Ryan's first picture with Robert Mitchum since *Crossfire* four years earlier (Hughes preferred to parcel out the few stars still on his payroll), though the two actors and their pal Jane Russell sometimes drank together in Mitchum's trailer on the RKO lot. As in *Crossfire,* Mitchum sauntered through the picture as the police captain, letting Ryan tear it up as the ruthless thug. Whenever the two of them squared off, the picture crackled: newly assigned to the district, McQuigg barges into Scanlon's office to put him on notice, and the gangster emerges from a side room eating an apple. For Ryan the apple was a typical bit of business that helped him define the character: Scanlon talks with his mouth full, stops short of taking a bite in reaction to something McQuigg has told him, and, when McQuigg pushes him too far, angrily flings the half-eaten fruit aside.

Fuller, who would later direct Ryan in *House of Bamboo,* thought he had a "charismatic gift for making you like the bastard he played, because he understood what made that bastard tick—and he made the audience understand it."[44] What makes Scanlon tick is Joe, the younger brother he's been grooming for a more respectable life than his own. To Scanlon's dismay, he learns that Joe has proposed to a two-bit cabaret singer (Lizabeth Scott), and for a moment McQuigg becomes his unlikely confidante. "You'd never guess what I've done for that kid," Scanlon fumes, pacing around his office with his hands jammed in his trouser pockets. "Made a gentleman out of him. Sent him to four colleges. *Four!* And the last one, I had to buy a *chair.*" Scanlon kicks a nearby armchair. "Not like that! An endowment, they call it."

Amid the interest generated by the Country Schools meetings, the parents in North Hollywood decided to move forward and find a school supervisor. David Walden, finance secretary for the American Friends Service Committee, referred them to a Quaker educator named Lloyd Nixon, who was skeptical of actors but soon recruited a promising candidate for the job. Bryson Gerard, a teacher at Pacific Ackworth Friends School in far-off Temple City, California,

impressed them with his notion of a school rich in the humanities, respon-
sive to the parents, and inspired by the democratic principles of the Quaker
meeting. Jessica, who by that time was quite pregnant with her third child,
talked Robert and the others into funding the school. Classes would begin
in September, around the time she was due to give birth.

Right after Independence Day, Ryan began rehearsing a low-budget thriller
with Ida Lupino called *Day without End,* about a woman held captive in
her home by a violent schizophrenic. Mel Dinelli's story had been through
several incarnations already: it debuted in January 1945 as an episode of the
CBS radio anthology *Suspense,* starring Agnes Moorehead and Frank Sinatra, and since then Dinelli had turned it into a short story and a successful
play. Lupino had bought the screen rights for her production company, The
Filmmakers; Hughes agreed to loan Ryan out for the picture, which would
be shot in three weeks, mostly on one set, and to distribute the result through
RKO. Lupino, despite her own résumé as a director, handed this project over
to Harry Horner, an Oscar-winning production designer.

Like *On Dangerous Ground,* the new picture relied heavily on the strange
chemistry between Lupino, playing a similarly benign and ethereal character,
and Ryan, cast again as a dangerously volatile, physically intimidating man.
"I know what it is to be lonely too," her character tells his, in a distinct echo
of the blind woman and the cop from the earlier picture. This time, however,
beauty fails to tame the beast. The opening scene finds Ryan's character, Howard Wilton, tending to his handyman chores in a woman's home, calling out
for his employer, and then swinging open a door to discover her dead body
sprawled on the floor. (In a close-up of Ryan's hand, his fingers jump with
fright.) Howard doesn't remember having killed her, but he flees anyway,
hopping a freight train and landing in a new town where he hires on with
Helen Gordon (Lupino), a recent war widow. (For some reason the action
is set in 1918.)

Howard seems like a model employee at first, gentle and courteous, but
Helen is soon alarmed by his moodiness and paranoia. Once again Ryan shows
his talent for startling physical movement; after Howard has fallen to the floor
of the parlor in anguish, he grabs his forehead, pulls himself to his feet, and
lurches unexpectedly into the foreground of the shot, where he collides with
a little Christmas tree. During another such spell Howard lightly bumps a
table lamp, setting the crystal decorations that hang from the shade tinkling

like his own disordered mind. "Scenes, like life itself, are mostly a matter of feeling and action," he once said. "Hardly anyone ever thinks of what he wants to say—almost everyone thinks about what he wants to do."[45] The role gave Ryan a chance to essay a variety of moods: at one moment Howard is quiet and humble, at another he accuses Helen of conspiring against him, his voice shaking with rage. It was a real tour de force, though the premise, so effective in a half-hour radio play, was stretched too thin for a feature-length film.

Less than a week after they finished the picture (whose title would be changed to *Beware, My Lovely*), Ryan flew into Chicago on TWA—the boss's airline—with producer Edmund Grainger and actress Janis Carter to attend the gala premiere of *Flying Leathernecks*. "A spectacular aerial exhibition by a squadron of Marine Corsairs, piloted by Korean War aces, was staged over Lake Michigan [Sunday] night," press materials reported. "The Marine air-devils, as climax to their stunts, released flares spelling in the skies at high altitude 'FLYING LEATHERNECKS,' which was visible as far west as Aurora."[46] The premiere on Monday, August 14, brought even more pomp, including a three-mile parade down Michigan Avenue with Marine bands, color guards, and fife-and-drum corps. Ryan rode in a car with Grainger, Carter, and Radio-Keith-Orpheum president Ned Depinet (who was nearing the end of his rope with Hughes and would soon resign). In Washington, Richard Nixon caught an advance screening of *Flying Leathernecks* and commended Grainger on the floor of the Senate.[47]

All that summer the parents had scouted North Hollywood and Studio City for a suitable classroom facility, as Jessica struggled with the minutiae of health and fire-code regulations. "The job of starting a school," she remarked, "often seemed entirely to do with fires and toilets. . . . Meanwhile what you taught in the school, who taught it, and how it was taught, was of no interest to anybody." Originally, they had hoped to find a vacant house, but such properties were in short supply. Following the example of Westland School, they began inquiring at places of worship, which often owned multiple buildings, and settled on one belonging to Temple Beth Hillel. It was located near Magnolia Boulevard at the end of a dirt road, near a giant flood control project; as Jessica recalled, its concrete channels "were of such unreasonable width and depth they got a rumor going that they were really secret military highways to be used in case of atomic attack."[48]

Ryan's business manager, Henry Bamberger, had advised him and Jessica to form a nonprofit corporation; according to Jessica's memoir, she and Robert hosted the other two couples one evening to come up with a name for the institution. "As the evening progressed (and the liquor flowed)," wrote Jessica, "we went from ideas like San Fernando Elementary School and North Hollywood Elementary School to things like Ryan-Harmon-Cabeen's Folly, Disturbed Children's Lyceum, Blacklisted Writers' Refuge, and The Little Red School House by the Flood Control Project. And laughed and laughed."[49] Despite her recollection, the project had been announced months earlier as the Oakwood School, after a Quaker school by that name that Sid Harmon recalled in his native Poughkeepsie, New York. The name stuck.

Ryan was named president, Harmon vice president, and Ross Cabeen secretary-treasurer. Tuition was set at fifty dollars, with some thirty-two parents enrolling thirty-five students.[50] In the weeks before the school opened, the parents all pitched in to clean up the building, scrubbing the floors and the desks. One conspicuous absentee was Jessica, who had gone into labor and given birth to a baby girl on September 10. The Ryans named their new child Lisa—after Lisa Sokoloff, wife of their old acting coach, Vladimir Sokoloff. Ryan was proud of the child, proud of his wife, and proud of the classes starting up across town, which had been all her idea. The harmony of Jessica giving birth as Oakwood opened its doors was lost on no one, though of the two offspring, Lisa Ryan would prove much less troublesome.

eight

The Whiz Kids

Nearly a decade had passed since Ryan signed with RKO. In that time he had made more than twenty pictures for the studio, but gems such as *The Set-Up* and *On Dangerous Ground* were few and far between. Max Reinhardt would have been disappointed to see him squandering his talent on potboilers like *Flying Leathernecks* and *Beware, My Lovely*. "He could have written his own ticket after the war, on the strength of *Crossfire,*" observed columnist Louis Berg earlier that year in the *Los Angeles Times*. "He let the golden opportunity dangle. 'I'm doing fine,' is his invariable reply. 'I've got time.'"[1] Ryan must have been stung by the observation that his career had crested, but Berg was right. Beholden to Hughes for his political protection, Ryan took what he could get at the studio. Too many people were depending on his paycheck—not just a wife and three children, but a private school now as well.

Luckily for Ryan, the fall of 1951 brought an intriguing new assignment. Earlier that year the talented Warner Bros. producer Jerry Wald (*Mildred Pierce, Johnny Belinda, Key Largo*) and comedy screenwriter Norman Krasna had formed the independent Wald-Krasna Productions (whose acronym earned them the industry tag the Whiz Kids) and struck a deal with Hughes to release sixty features over six years. Now Wald wanted to film *Clash by Night,* the Clifford Odets flop that Ryan had performed ten years earlier on Broadway with Tallulah Bankhead and Lee J. Cobb. The screen rights had been parked at RKO for years. Wald sold Hughes on the idea of relocating it from Staten Island to Monterey, California, and stripping away its outdated social commentary to focus on the adulterous love triangle.

Barbara Stanwyck signed to play Mae, the smothered wife, and Paul Douglas was cast as her simple, devoted husband, Jerry. Ryan took third billing as Jerry's malignant friend Earl, the part Joseph Schildkraut had performed back in 1941, and Keith Andes inherited Ryan's original role as Jerry's younger brother, Joe. To play Joe's fiancée, Peggy, Wald cut a deal with Twentieth Century Fox to borrow twenty-five-year-old starlet Marilyn Monroe. At Stanwyck's urging, Fritz Lang was hired to direct; his brilliant career in the German cinema (*Metropolis, M*) was now two decades behind him, but he had eked out a second act in Hollywood that included such haunting dramas as *Fury* (1936), *The Woman in the Window* (1944), and *Scarlet Street* (1945). Wald indulged Lang by sending him and cinematographer Nick Musuraca up to Monterey to shoot extensive footage of fishermen and canners at work, with Monroe and Douglas in tow; after three days they came back with ten thousand feet of footage that Wald had edited into a documentary-type preface for the beginning of the picture.

"It was the first time I could convince any producer that we should have rehearsals, as is done for the stage," recalled Lang. "Because it dealt mainly with three people, you could, in a certain way, rehearse the main scenes. . . . We marked the exact positions of the camera, its movements and so on. It was wonderful to work with all three: Barbara Stanwyck, Bob Ryan and Paul Douglas."[2] Ryan ranked the director alongside Jean Renoir and Max Ophuls in his ability to recognize and heighten an actor's best qualities, though in contrast to Renoir, who made everything feel spontaneous, Lang wanted complete control over every aspect of a scene. "He leaves nothing to chance," Ryan explained. "He plans everything in advance."[3]

The one element Lang couldn't control was Monroe, whose chronic inability to remember her lines began to slow down production almost as soon as shooting commenced in October 1951. She was terrified of Lang, who tried to banish her trusted acting coach, Natasha Lytess, from the set; sometimes the pressure brought out red splotches on Monroe's skin. Lang watched from behind the camera, fuming, as Stanwyck tried to pull off a complicated stretch of dialogue while hanging clothes on a line and Monroe wrecked the scene again and again. Stanwyck never complained, but Lang took to berating Monroe. At some point Ryan intervened, taking the director aside and urging him to lay off. Ryan took a dim view of colleagues who were unprofessional, but clearly the girl was trying, and haranguing her would only exacerbate the situation. Besides: *look* at her!

Earl Pfeiffer (Ryan) gets tanked up with Peggy (Marilyn Monroe) in *Clash by Night* (1952). Ryan took Monroe's side against director Fritz Lang, and she never forgot it. *Franklin Jarlett Collection*

Something about *Clash by Night* brought out the worst in people, and Ryan watched in dismay as the cast, like that of the Broadway production, was riven by professional jealousy. A rumor began circulating around town that Monroe was the young woman posing nude in a new girlie calendar (according to one account, the information was leaked by RKO's publicity man in the hope of drumming up interest in the new picture).[4] Reporters flocked to the set, ignoring the forty-four-year-old Stanwyck as well as Douglas and Ryan. Monroe had sat for the photo back in 1949, when she was still unknown and needed the fifty dollars for a car payment. "The calendar business was no secret in Hollywood, but the public didn't know about it," recalled Ryan. "One of the reporters asked me, 'Where's the babe with the big tits?' He didn't even know her name."[5] At one point Wald received an anonymous call from someone demanding $15,000 to keep quiet about Monroe's deep, dark secret; instead the producer wanted to put her name above the title with those of the other three stars.

Earl (Ryan) moves in on Mae Doyle (Barbara Stanwyck), his best friend's wife, in *Clash by Night* (1952). *Franklin Jarlett Collection*

Lang remembered their reaction when they heard the news. "Douglas said, 'I will never give my permission, never! Who is she? A newcomer! She will never make the top grade.' Ryan didn't say anything, but Barbara said, 'What do you want—she's an upcoming star.'"[6] Monroe got her above-the-title billing, fourth after Ryan. Douglas was furious; on the set, after Monroe referred to him in passing as "Paul," he ordered her to address him as "Mr. Paul Douglas."[7] According to Keith Andes, Stanwyck eventually grew frustrated with Monroe, who would "always come in late and all f_____ up. Stanwyck finally said, 'Look, unless she's working, keep her off the set. I don't want her around.' After all, Barbara was a good-humored woman but she was also a professional."[8] After Monroe's death, Stanwyck would remember that she "drove Bob Ryan, Paul Douglas and myself out of our minds . . . but she didn't do it viciously, and there was a sort of magic about her which we all recognized at once."[9]

Ryan tried to stay above the fray, just as he had with Lee Cobb and Tallulah

Bankhead. He had a much better part this time, though Earl Pfeiffer would be his third heavy in a row after *The Racket* and *Beware, My Lovely.* A projectionist at the local movie house, Earl despises his wife, a burlesque performer who is constantly on the road. "Someday I'm going to stick her full of pins, just to see if blood runs out," he tells Mae. Earl can be an embarrassment—at a restaurant, as a joke, he pulls his eyes into slits and jabbers obnoxiously in mock Chinese—but Mae is attracted to his hard body and cynical talk, and tired of the dully unimaginative Jerry. When Mae and Earl go into a clinch, Mae hungrily reaches up under the back of his wife-beater, a sharply sexual moment probably inspired by the recent release *A Streetcar Named Desire.* Lisa Ryan would remember her mother always getting angry when Stanwyck's name came up.[10]

To produce *Clash by Night,* Wald and Krasna had chosen Harriet Parsons, one of very few women in the business and the daughter of gossip columnist Louella Parsons. Harriet persuaded her mother to write a column on Ryan, her first since the 1948 profile in which she had hinted at his affair with Merle Oberon. This time around Louella was squarely in his corner: "With all this talk of divorce and scandal in Hollywood, Robert Ryan is almost too good to be true. None of these evils has ever touched him, and I'm going to put my neck out a mile and say I'm sure none ever will." Louella visited the set to watch Ryan play a scene as Earl, and according to the column, Ryan asked her afterward, "How did you like me as a home wrecker?" The complex social transaction was completed when Ryan credited Harriet for having persuaded him to take the role. "When Howard Hughes first sent word that I was to play this dubious gentleman for Wald and Krasna, I had plenty of reservations. I had never been a no-good character who steals another man's wife."[11]

Production wrapped in early December, leaving Ryan with a two-month interim before his next job. When the story about Monroe's nude photos finally broke the next year, the young actress made a frank statement about it that disarmed critics, and as Wald and Krasna had hoped, the publicity drove ticket sales for *Clash by Night,* which connected at the box office and drew good reviews as well. Seven years later, when Ryan was shooting *Lonelyhearts* at Samuel Goldwyn Studio, he would take his son Cheyney over to meet Monroe as she filmed *Some Like It Hot* on a neighboring soundstage, and the boy would be surprised by how warmly she received his dad.[12] Word had gotten back to Monroe that Ryan took her side with Lang, and she never forgot it. "Poor kid, she was so bewildered," Ryan said after her death. "Right after the picture was finished she sent me a big box of candy with a very touching note."[13]

Once 1952 arrived, the Ryans grew busy again with the Oakwood School. After searching fruitlessly for a better facility than the temple building, Ryan and Ross Cabeen decided to buy land and put up a building themselves. The parcel they chose was on Moorpark Street in North Hollywood, a few miles southwest of the Ryans' home. "Circling the property on two sides was a dry wash as yet unreclaimed by the Flood Control System; it still presented a sandy bottom lined with scrub willows," wrote Jessica in her memoir. "The property itself consisted of close to three acres of ground with a magnificent stand of eucalyptus trees down one side bordering the wash."[14]

The two men bought the property for $6,500 and went before the parents' group proposing that everyone contribute toward a building fund. According to Jessica, this idea met with controversy because the parents, now numbering about thirty-five, would neither own the property nor have any legal power over the buildings' disposition—only Ryan, Cabeen, and Sid Harmon had incorporated the school. With or without the parents' participation, Ryan and Cabeen resolved to go ahead and construct two classroom buildings on the lot.

Their first hurdle was to win a zoning variance from the city, which meant collecting signatures from all the neighbors. Whenever Ryan had a day off from work, he and Cabeen spent the afternoon making the rounds with their petition. One tough customer, wrote Jessica, told them he didn't like actors, children, or Jews, but after several visits they caught him after a few drinks, listened politely as he recalled his days as a Klansman back in Illinois, and finally won his signature by promising to "keep *them* out."[15] A building fund of $14,000 was established, heavily endowed by the Ryans, Harmons, and Cabeens, and construction began in April. Instead of laying a cornerstone, the parents staged a little ceremony in which each child at the school laid a concrete block on one row of a wall.

With production at RKO slowing to a crawl again, Hughes loaned Ryan out to Universal-International for a two-picture deal: the first, *Horizons West*, began shooting in February 1952, and the second, *City Beneath the Sea*, followed soon afterward, keeping him busy through early May. The deal must have seemed like a good move: he would get top billing in both films, which would be shot in Technicolor and directed by the capable Budd Boetticher. In *Horizons West* he plays a former Confederate soldier who returns to his native

Jessica plants a tree at the Oakwood School in North Hollywood as Tim and Bob look on. "More than anyone else, she was responsible for Oakwood's survival," wrote the school's director, Marie Spottswood. *Robert Ryan Family*

Austin, Texas, and, frustrated in his plans to establish himself in business, turns to horse rustling and amasses a small fortune; Rock Hudson is his brother, whose new job as sheriff of Austin puts them on a collision course. ("He's not getting married again soon," Ryan would remark whenever Hudson's name came up.)[16] *City Beneath the Sea* teamed him with Anthony Quinn in a tale about deep-sea divers. Universal was a lesser major studio, carried by the tireless Abbott and Costello, yet it was in better shape than RKO.

The first time RKO had loaned Ryan out—to MGM for *Act of Violence*—all hell had broken loose in his absence, and the same thing happened again as he was shooting at Universal. *Variety* reported in February that both Edmund Grainger Productions and Wald-Krasna Productions were at wits' end, waiting endlessly for Hughes to approve their scripts.[17] Then, two months later, as the American Legion and other right-wing groups massed for another anticommunist assault on the entertainment industry—not just movies this time but also TV, radio, and theater—Hughes shut down production on the Gower Street lot for a second time, announcing that he would conduct a systematic purge of communists and their sympathizers from the studio ranks. Industry observers wondered if this were just a prelude to Hughes selling his interest in the studio; the president of the Screen Writers Guild, which had been feuding with Hughes over giving screen credit to blacklisted writer Paul Jarrico, argued that Hughes had "thrown a mantle of Americanism over his own ragged production record."[18]

As part of this crusade, Hughes established a new security office at RKO to screen all employees for suspect activities or associations. Many were suspended, and at some point Hughes must have made up his mind that Robert Ryan would have to go. Publishing in *The Worker,* launching this bohemian school out in the Valley, stumping for the Progressive Citizens of America, American Civil Liberties Union, and United World Federalists—now that Hughes had to put up or shut up, he may have decided Ryan was too far over the line to be defended. Before long the actor had a new contract with RKO stipulating only that he make one picture a year. For the first time since signing with the studio in 1942, Ryan was a free agent.

THE BREAK WITH RKO opened up a world of possibilities for Ryan—he could return to Broadway, even play Shakespeare—but more immediately he needed to land a good picture, just to prove he was still bankable. Once he found himself on the open market, he gravitated immediately toward Dore Schary, the liberal producer who had cast him in *Crossfire* five years earlier. Since fleeing the Hughes regime at RKO, Schary had returned to his previous employer, MGM, where he kept up the good fight with such stark, serious-minded dramas as *Battleground* (1949) and *The Red Badge of Courage* (1951). In a studio shake-up he had recently replaced the aging Louis B. Mayer as president, and now he came through for Ryan with a plum assignment, supporting James Stewart and Janet Leigh in Anthony Mann's harsh psychological western *The Naked Spur.*

Ryan had never cared much for westerns, and they were hell to make, with remote locations and strenuous action shots. But the *Naked Spur* script, by first-timers Sam Rolfe and Harold Jack Bloom, read like a chamber drama; aside from a brief shootout with some Blackfoot Indians, the action was restricted to only five characters, all locked together in a treacherous mountain journey. Bounty hunter Howard Kemp (Stewart) has arrived in the Rocky Mountains searching for Ben Vandergroat (Ryan), who's accused of murdering a marshal in Abilene, Kansas. Aided by an elderly prospector, Jesse Tate (Millard Mitchell), and a disgraced cavalryman, Roy Anderson (Ralph Meeker), Kemp manages to capture the outlaw and his unwitting young accomplice, Lina (Leigh), but as they cross the mountains on horseback to collect the reward, Vandergroat begins sowing discord among the three men.

The role had originally been earmarked for Richard Widmark, and Ryan was happy to have aced him out: here was a smart, layered character who threatened to turn the pat morality of most westerns on its head. Ryan played him as a cracker-barrel philosopher, his homespun wisdom dispensed in a mirthless chuckle. When a frustrated Kemp offers to shoot Vandergroat on the spot, the outlaw peers up at him, his brow lined with the years, and replies, "Choosin' a way to die, what's the difference? Choosin' a way to *live*—that's the hard part." Ryan tosses off this Will Rogers dialogue with ease, yet it masks an ugly soul. Near the end of *The Naked Spur,* Vandergroat succeeds in peeling away the old prospector, Tate, with the promise of a gold mine, then wrestles away his rifle and coldly murders him. "Look at him, lyin' there peaceful in the sun," he tells the horrified Lina, slipping back into his gentle drawl. "Ain't never gonna be hungry again, want anything he can't have."

Four years earlier Ryan and Leigh had shared an electric scene together in *Act of Violence; The Naked Spur* gave them much more screen time, and they worked well together. The ambiguous relationship between the outlaw and his young charge turns out to be the most troubling aspect of *The Naked Spur.* Vandergroat presents himself as the only family Lina has left, and they're tenderly affectionate with each other. Bound at the wrists, he drapes his arms over Lina's head, even brushing her forehead with a kiss; plagued by a sore back, he periodically calls on her to "do me," and she faithfully massages his shoulders. At the same time he's not above exploiting her sexually, especially after he realizes that both Kemp and the low-rent Anderson are taken with her. "The more they look at you, the less they'll be lookin' at me!" he whispers to her in a quiet moment.

The entire film was shot on location in the San Juan Mountains, near Durango, Colorado, from late May to early July. The cast was lodged about fifteen miles from town in a group of cabins at El Rancho Encantado. "It was a congenial, pleasant, cheerful group, and I believe everyone thoroughly enjoyed themselves," Leigh recalled.[19] Jimmy Stewart and his wife, Gloria, threw an anniversary party for Leigh and Tony Curtis, during which Curtis buttonholed Ryan for a program in which they would visit with underprivileged kids in East Los Angeles. Ryan was joined by Jessica and the children; the boys got to watch stunt work being filmed, and one evening the family drove into town and caught an early show of *Best of the Badmen* at a drive-in theater. It was the first time the children ever saw their father on-screen.[20]

Ryan loved working with Stewart—a class act who, on one occasion, finished his own shots early but stuck around all afternoon feeding lines to Ryan and Leigh from behind the camera. But the best professional relationship Ryan would carry away from *The Naked Spur* was with director Tony Mann. "What made Mann so brilliant," remembered Ralph Meeker, "was his ability to pick a backdrop that might be green and lush or barren and stark, or a rushing river, and he could put his actors against these backdrops, and it all became *one.*"[21] Mann's camera sense was superb; he knew not only how to tell a story in pictures but how to tell it in landscapes. He liked vertiginous overhead shots and put his actors through quite a gauntlet as they rode and climbed, using doubles only when absolutely necessary. Leigh would recall the tall rock above a roaring river where she, Ryan, and Stewart filmed the climax: "The ultimate panic was being on top and peering down down down at the angry water and rocks below. With no guard rails, with no nothin'! . . . The fear we registered was genuine."[22]

Tall and athletic like Ryan, Mann had grown up in San Diego and bounced around RKO and the low-rent Republic Studio before distinguishing himself with some dynamic crime pictures (*Raw Deal, Border Incident, Side Street*) and Stewart's hit western *Winchester '73*. No one could ever get a word out of the guy, though Ryan liked this. "I understand that for certain people it became very difficult to work with him," he later said. "For young people especially, since they love to talk about their character for hours. . . . There are certain actors who, to light a cigarette, need to create a back story. Me, I prefer not to talk."[23] He and Mann would make three pictures together, all of them excellent, and Ryan would rank his performance in *The Naked Spur* as one of his best. It gave him just what he needed at this career juncture: a chance to shine as an actor, working alongside the best in the business.

By August the two school buildings on Moorpark Street had been completed, but they were only unfinished concrete shells: the parents would have to finish the buildings and construct a school grounds around them. Chuck Haas—who, with his wife Emilie, became such a devoted backer of the school that Oakwood would later credit them equally with the three founding families—supervised the carpentry work. Bryson Gerard took charge of laying a concrete walk, and Ryan paired off with Sid Harmon to erect a rickety fence around a small yard for the kindergarten. Mothers painted; fathers built furniture. Even then Oakwood was strapped for space; word of the school had spread and enrollment had risen. The school acquired a substantial loan for more building construction, but in the meantime, Gerard suggested that the older children, second through fifth grade, be quietly relocated to parents' homes.

For several months the fourth- and fifth-grade teacher took up residence in Ryan's Refuge out in the backyard, while Ryan found refuge elsewhere. Children would come into the house to use the bathroom, Jessica remembered, and afterward might talk to Smith as he gardened or play in the yard with little Lisa trailing after. "Often, having been to the toilet, they would stay inside the house playing with our boys' things or just wandering around," she wrote. "It was disconcerting sometimes if one was trying to take a bath or get dressed when one or another unfrustrated child would walk blithely in."[24] This surreptitious home schooling continued until a third building was erected on the Moorpark lot.

THAT SUMMER the Democratic Party, convening at the International Amphitheatre in Chicago, nominated the liberal, well-spoken Governor Adlai Stevenson of Illinois for president. The Ryans watched on the TV set in their den as Stevenson was chosen on the third draft, beating out Estes Kefauver and Senator Richard Russell of Georgia. "Robert let out a whoop of joy—a whoop repeated that day, I have no doubt, in thousands, no, millions of Democrat homes, ranch-style or otherwise," wrote Jessica in a later magazine piece that would never see publication.[25]

In accepting the nomination, Stevenson promised to "talk sense to the American people," and he made good on that promise in late August when he attacked red-baiting in a speech to the American Legion convention in New York. "True patriotism, it seems to me, is based on tolerance and a large measure of humility," Stevenson declared, denouncing those who would exploit patriotic feeling to oppress minority groups or silence minority opinions. "The tragedy of our day is the climate of fear in which we live, and fear breeds repression. Too often sinister threats to the Bill of Rights, to freedom of the mind, are concealed under the patriotic cloak of anticommunism."[26]

Ryan was itching to get involved in the campaign, though as Jessica would observe, many actors still were skittish about supporting liberal candidates; to the self-appointed cops who published red-baiting pamphlets, the merest hint of involvement in the Progressive Party or Henry Wallace's 1948 presidential bid was considered subversive. A Hollywood for Stevenson committee was formed, and Dore Schary hosted a glamorous launch party at his home in Brentwood; though Jessica noticed a heavy star quotient, she attributed that to Schary more than Stevenson: "When the head of MGM called, you went!"[27] She and Robert shook hands with Stevenson and had their picture taken with him and Schary. Then in mid-October, Ryan got a call from screenwriter Allen Rivkin, head of Hollywood for Stevenson. Rivkin was having trouble finding stars to take part in a rally on Wednesday, October 15, at the Cow Palace in San Francisco, so the Ryans made the trip, joining Mercedes McCambridge, Lauren Bacall, and Humphrey Bogart.

Despite his gangster image, Bogart was a cultured man who had grown up in New York City as a child of privilege just like Ryan. The two men got along well; Ryan especially appreciated the fact that Bogart always turned up on time. "Bogey is the only other man in town with a punctuality complex," he once joked to a fan magazine. "He's a great comfort to me and the hours we've spent waiting for parties to start have allowed us to become intimately acquainted."[28] Appearing at the Cow Palace without his toupee, Bogart did a little comedy routine in his familiar tough-guy persona, ordering the audience to vote for Stevenson or else; Ryan spoke extemporaneously, giving what Jessica considered "a short, articulate, knowledgeable and sometimes funny speech."[29] Ryan claimed he had spoken off the top of his head, and though Jessica knew he had prepared carefully, she still was floored by his poise.

Soon after this the Ryans traveled out to the East Coast to campaign for Stevenson in the final week before Election Day, and during the trip they traveled with Bogart and Bacall. The couples had adjoining rooms at the Statler Hotel in Boston, where the three stars appeared at a rally at Mechanics Hall. "Robert did his extempore thing, but it was strikingly changed from the Cow Palace," wrote Jessica. "He had familiars before him, Irish city machine politicians, and the blood of Old Tim rose; he almost talked with a brogue, not a new experience for me."

Back at the hotel Ryan and Bogart invited their driver up for a drink, though Ryan made "a slightly slurring remark" to Jessica that the little Irishman was "a typical ward heeler."[30] The man had no interest in the Stevenson campaign, only the local races that affected patronage hiring. "Bogart and Betty listened with distress and horror, Bogart particularly," Jessica observed. Ryan enjoyed the experience, always amused to see Hollywood liberals confronted by the sort of down-and-dirty machine politics he had known as a child in Chicago.

The next day began with a breakfast for Governor Stevenson that was being hosted by Governor Paul Dever of Massachusetts at a Cambridge hotel. Out in the hall, Ryan was approached for directions to the breakfast by the young Congressman John Kennedy, who was running for the US Senate against the moderate Republican Henry Cabot Lodge Jr.—and whose father, Joseph, had formed RKO back in 1928. When Ryan introduced himself, Kennedy replied, "I know who *you* are."[31]

After breakfast the Ryans and Bogarts joined a daylong motorcade through the southeast suburbs of Boston. As they neared each stop and the caravan slowed to a crawl, gawkers would move down the line of cars looking for celebrities and waving and yelling at Ryan and the Bogarts. When they peered in at Jessica, though, their faces darkened. "It wasn't the first time I'd experienced this strange hostility from people who had come to see movie stars and suddenly were cheated by people who weren't anybody being there too," she wrote in her notes.[32] Bogart won her heart by yelling at fans through the window glass that she was Rosalind Russell, which some of them seemed to buy. Jessica had always swooned for Bogart in the movies, and in person she found him "a bright, gentle, warm, human being. . . . Sure, there had always been crazy stories about him in Hollywood. He drank a lot and fought with various wives . . . that's what they said. It was nothing to me. Bogart was a gentleman."[33] Also a comedian: at one point, when he and Ryan had been signing autographs, Bogart observed, "I notice that your fans are younger than mine, and I don't like that."[34]

There followed a whistle-stop tour from Boston to New York City, where Stevenson addressed a late-night rally in Harlem. Walking down 125th Street toward the Hotel Theresa, Jessica got separated from the group, and Ryan was mobbed in the lobby of the hotel until none other than boxer Joe Louis pulled him out of the crowd to safety. "Respect from the champ," Jessica wrote. "R has always had respect from them. They recognized in the fight pictures he made that he really knew how to box. They all value him for making *The Set-Up*."[35] Louis took Ryan out a back exit and enlisted a friend to drive the actor back to his own hotel.

New York City was the final stop on the campaign swing, with a giant rally at Madison Square Garden on Wednesday, October 29. Broadcast live on TV, the program opened with a chorus singing "Stevenson for President" (updated from the old Gershwin tune "Wintergreen for President"). Ryan was supposed to speak first, but through some miscommunication he missed his cue. When he heard himself announced over the loudspeakers, he had to race for the stage. On-screen there was an awkward moment of dead air before a singer launched back into the song and the other performers shifted around nervously; more than a minute passed before the star appeared to recite his piece. Ryan was angry and embarrassed about the incident, though it seemed to be par for the course in the chronically unorganized campaign.

Election night brought heartache when General Dwight D. Eisenhower handily defeated Stevenson with 55 percent of the popular vote. Ryan was devastated; he generally took a live-and-let-live attitude toward Republicans, but he despised Eisenhower. "My father's hatred of Eisenhower was over the top," said his son Cheyney. "And it would always come out as, 'You can't let the military do anything. You can't let a general do anything. Generals and officers just screw it up.' "[36] Not only did the Eisenhower victory usher in four years of Republican supremacy, with functional majorities in the House and Senate, it elevated Richard Nixon to the vice presidency, only two years after he had destroyed Helen Gahagan Douglas. At one point during the campaign swing, Jessica was amused when some idiot thought Ryan was Dick Nixon. "It was many long years before I ever told Ryan that someone had taken him for Nixon," she wrote. "But even that many years after the fact he still got furious."[37]

BY THE END OF 1952 about seventeen million homes in the United States had TV sets; the figure had doubled in just two years. The Hollywood studios, scrambling to meet this new assault on their viewership, embraced a strategy of playing up technological innovations that couldn't be reproduced by a cathode-ray tube. At Twentieth Century Fox, Darryl F. Zanuck had placed a large bet on CinemaScope, mounting the widescreen biblical epic *The Robe,* but while that was in preproduction, the independent Arch Oboler Productions made a small fortune with the first 3-D feature, a low-rent jungle adventure called *Bwana Devil.* Eager to jump on this bandwagon, Zanuck decided that *The Waterhole,* a desert survival drama to be directed by Englishman Roy Ward Baker, would be shot in 3-D.

Baker had made two pictures for Fox already (the second a creepy thriller with Richard Widmark and Marilyn Monroe called *Don't Bother to Knock*), and he was fascinated by the long stretches of action in Francis Cockrell's short story "The Waterhole," about a spoiled millionaire stranded in the Mojave Desert by his scheming wife and her lover. "I had always had an ambition to make a picture in which the leading character spends long periods alone on the screen, where the interest would be in what he does, rather than what he says," Baker wrote.[38] To handle the complicated process of shooting in 3-D, Baker recruited cinematographer Lucien Ballard, who had worked with him on *Don't Bother to Knock.*

Ryan couldn't have been pleased to hear that Ballard was on the picture, having slept with his wife throughout production of *Berlin Express,* but apparently the shoot passed without incident. Merle Oberon had left Ballard in 1948, shortly after her affair with Ryan, taking up with an Italian shipping magnate. Ironically, an adulterous affair lay at the center of the new picture (later retitled *Inferno*), yet that element of the story was confined almost entirely to William Lundigan and redheaded Rhonda Fleming as the conniving lovers. Ryan's scenes as the beleaguered millionaire, shot in the Mojave near Apple Valley, California, were almost entirely wordless (though a superfluous internal monologue would be dubbed in later). Ryan always rose to a creative challenge, and he loved Baker's idea of shooting a modern silent picture; in fact, the idea of a man trapped in a hellish desert terrain recalled the climax of one of the great silent features, Eric von Stroheim's *Greed* (1925).

Stereoscopic images had been around since the early nineteenth century, and the anaglyph process, which split the image into red and green and recombined them with polaroid glasses, dated back to the 1939 New York World's Fair. Over the years people had tried to release stereoscopic films, but the big studios had never gotten involved until now: *Inferno* would join a surge of 3-D releases that year, including MGM's *Kiss Me Kate,* Warner Bros.' *House of Wax,* and Universal's *It Came from Outer Space*. Baker described the contraption he and Ballard were using: "Two cameras were bolted onto a large plate at right angles to each other and mounted on the usual dolly. A polar screen was placed in front of the lens of each camera and the two screens were set in opposition to each other. A two-way mirror was set in front of both cameras at 45 degrees: the right-hand camera shot straight through the mirror and the left-hand camera received the mirror image, which was then [flipped] in the processing so as to present it the right way round. . . . The cameras were interlocked and run in synch. Thus we had two matching films, left eye and right eye."[39]

This setup was so unobtrusive that Fleming didn't even realize until later that the picture was being shot in 3-D.[40] Baker mainly avoided the gimmickry of objects flying toward the camera; he was more interested in the way 3-D allowed him to place his actors in front of mountain ranges and capture the skyline in all its wondrous depth.

Four years earlier Ryan had played a fictionalized version of Howard Hughes in *Caught,* and now he had been cast as another capricious millionaire wrestling with the limits of his wealth. Like Hughes, Donald W. Carsons II disappears on people; his secretary refers to his desk as "the bottleneck," and his second-in-command at the mining firm is paralyzed waiting for the boss's signature. "I think he's always had the fear that without his money he'd be nothing, helpless," the executive remarks at one point. Meanwhile in the desert, Carsons is discovering the exact opposite: stranded on a mountainside with a broken leg, he manages to straighten the leg, bind himself with splints, lower himself down the rocks to the ground, find a water hole under the surface of the sand, and kill a deer for food. The rock-climbing sequences rival those in *The Naked Spur,* particularly the tense moment when Carsons lowers himself past a rattler coiling on a rock ledge.

The picture ended with Carsons being rescued, his wife returning guiltily to his side, and her lover, Duncan, fleeing for Mexico. But when Zanuck saw this cut, he decided the picture needed a slam-bang ending that would deliver on the promise of 3-D action. Assisted by fight choreographer Dick Talmadge, Baker staged a scene in which Duncan trails Carsons to a little shack where he's being sheltered by a local desert rat (Henry Hull); the antagonists go after each other, a flung oil lamp ignites the shack, and Carsons is pulled to safety while the flaming roof caves in on Duncan (in a hair-raising point-of-view shot, to make Zanuck happy).

Retitled *Inferno,* the picture opened in London, New York, Chicago, and Los Angeles, but so few theaters in the United States were equipped for 3-D projection that it never got a wide release and soon disappeared, despite strong reviews that singled out Ryan's work. The picture's failure was disappointing to him; interviewed in the early '70s, Ryan would list his best screen work as *Crossfire, The Set-Up, God's Little Acre,* and "a picture nobody ever heard of called *Inferno* which I made for Fox."[41]

THAT SUMMER the Ryans rented a beach house in Malibu. The children—seven-year-old Tim, five-year-old Cheyney, and little Lisa, coming up on her second birthday—frolicked in the waves as their parents read or had drinks with Joan and John Houseman, who had a house nearby. Ryan was shooting *Alaska Seas,* a romantic drama with Jan Sterling and Brian Keith, as part of a two-picture deal with Paramount. The studio that had given him bit parts and then dropped him in 1940 was now paying him $125,000 per picture. The Ryans lived modestly out in the Valley, and the summer rental was something they could easily afford. Besides movies, Ryan moonlighted on radio and TV, and a few years earlier he had signed a lucrative deal as a pitchman for Chesterfield cigarettes. His business manager, Henry Bamberger, advised him to invest in real estate, and Ryan had bought several apartment buildings, as well as a shopping mall in Beverly Hills. Then there was the school, which would cost the Ryans some $40,000 by the end of the decade.[42]

Houseman, who understood that Ryan was "trying to shed the stigma of playing only brutal and violent parts,"[43] recruited him for *Her Twelve Men,* a women's picture he was producing at MGM with Greer Garson. The British actress had been at MGM since *Goodbye, Mr. Chips* (1939), but at forty-eight she was nearing the end of her tenure at the studio; shot in color, this last picture evoked *Mr. Chips* with its story of a beloved teacher at a tony boarding school for boys, coincidentally named the Oaks. Ryan played another teacher at the school and, eventually, Garson's love interest, but the script was weak. Shortly after the cameras began rolling in August, Houseman disappeared, busy with the editing of *Julius Caesar* and the preproduction for *Executive Suite,* and Ryan fended for himself with director Robert Z. Leonard, a long-time MGM hack who had been making pictures since Ryan was in short pants.

The tweedy, upper-class world of the Oaks stood in ironic contrast to the Oakwood School, which seemed to be spinning out of control. The founding parents had launched the school with no clear vision for how it should operate; that had come mainly from Bryson Gerard, who modeled the parent-teacher partnership after Quaker meetings with their vigorous debate and eventual consensus. This proved unworkable: a like-minded congregation might arrive at this "sense of the meeting," but the Oakwood parents more often fell prey to bickering, backbiting, and political point scoring. The group had split into two factions: a radical wing that kept trying to use the school as a political arena, and the more responsible parents who had sunk their own money into the project. According to Jessica's memoir, one father, a blacklisted writer, refused to admit a student whose father had informed on him to HUAC; this angered oilman Ross Cabeen, who thought they should keep their politics out of the school.

Gerard had arrived with plenty of ideas about hands-on learning, his curriculum "built around hand-crafts, bug, tree, rock, and bird studies, cookouts, animal husbandry, and camping trips," as Jessica reported. The children sang, danced, and acted in plays. But two years in, parents were beginning to complain that their children couldn't read. When Jessica conferred with Tim's teacher about his slow progress in reading and writing, the teacher blamed Gerard for failing to provide the proper teaching materials. Mothers were getting back to her with reports that the staff couldn't get a curriculum or any supervision from him. Rumors were circulating that he had been avoiding parents, and Wendy Cabeen wanted him out.

Jessica called a meeting to clear the air, and the parents unloaded on Gerard, their grievances seeming to come from all directions. As she recalled it, the radical wing argued that Oakwood should be "making a contribution to the community" by "having a series of lectures and discussion groups—child psychology, adult psychology, ceramics, noted psychoanalysts, political experts." It should "take political action in terms of the reactionary forces in the public school system, fighting for higher salaries, smaller classes, and integration."[44] This provoked Ryan, who had clocked so many hours with his conservative friend Ross Cabeen trying to build up the school. Chuck Haas was absent from the meeting, but he received a report from Sid Harmon: "Bob stood up and said, 'Look, I agree with your position, but this is not the place for it. If that's how you feel, goodbye.' "[45]

Whenever the going got tough, the founders would retreat to the core of families that seemed to share their commitment and good sense. "It was a small group of us who knew exactly what we wanted and that's what we got," Haas remembered.[46] The Quaker-meeting model, they decided, was too unwieldy, and what the school needed was a board of directors. According to Jessica's account, a long discussion over Gerard's future was capped off by her husband, who voiced what no one else would: "It looks as though maybe he will have to go."[47] Gerard was asked to leave at the end of the school year; and according to Haas, the three original founders—Ryan, Sid Harmon, and Ross Cabeen—went to their attorney and drafted by-laws "setting them up as general members perpetually, with the ability to take over the school if necessary, and setting up a board of directors which ... would run the school instead of the town meeting."[48]

RYAN'S CONCERN about being typecast as a thug was well-founded: in the past two years alone, as Hughes finally coughed up some long-delayed projects at RKO, moviegoers had seen Ryan play nasty, sometimes violent characters in *The Racket; On Dangerous Ground; Clash by Night; Beware, My Lovely;* and *The Naked Spur.* He hoped the just-completed *Alaska Seas* and *Her Twelve Men* would help reverse this trend, and as the second picture of his deal with Paramount, he would play a quiet, bookish gentleman closer to his actual personality than any other character he had taken on. Adapted from a novel by Vina Delmar, *About Mrs. Leslie* starred Shirley Booth as a lonely New Yorker and Ryan as a wealthy married man who falls in love with her and funds their annual rendezvous at a little cottage along the Pacific coast. A respected stage actress, Booth had just won an Oscar for her feature film debut in *Come Back, Little Sheba,* costarring Burt Lancaster; now that picture's producer, Hal Wallis, and director, Daniel Mann, had sold her on *About Mrs. Leslie* as a suitable follow-up.

Bringing Delmar's book to the screen required a fair amount of narrative convolution; the Production Code Administration, undaunted after all these years, wouldn't permit a story in which adultery was glamorized, so the screenwriters contrived to make the love relationship between George Leslie and Vivien Keeler completely chaste. When Vivien meets George on a Los Angeles airfield and drives with him to his beach home, she doesn't know he's married, and there's a conspicuous scene in which he shows her to a separate bedroom. They meet again the next year before Vivien, back in New York, learns from a newsreel that he is George Leslie Hendersall, an aviation giant vital to the Allied war effort, with a wife and two grown boys.

Shirley Booth and Ryan in *About Mrs. Leslie* (1954). His role as a quiet, bookish gentleman was closer to his actual personality than any other character he played on-screen. *Franklin Jarlett Collection*

Ryan would remember Shirley Booth as "uncomfortable working in pictures." Off-screen she was even more meek than her character. "I picked her up in my car about a quarter of a mile from the studio on three consecutive days, and on the third day I finally asked her why she walked. She said she parked her car where she did because it was the only parking lot she could find—and she paid $3 a day to do it. So I informed her that, as the star of the picture, she had the right to park on Paramount's lot."[49] Daniel Mann brought a warm, nicely melancholy tone to the picture, but *About Mrs. Leslie* flopped at the box office and, like *Inferno,* disappeared completely from circulation, an unjust fate for such a gentle, heartfelt drama.

That fall John Houseman, a little guilty over having abandoned Ryan during *Her Twelve Men,* approached him with a head-turning offer: he wanted Ryan to star in an off-Broadway production of Shakespeare's *Coriolanus.* Ryan liked to tell people he'd perform in the men's room at Grand Central Station if he could do Shakespeare,[50] and this would be considerably better: the 1,100-seat Phoenix Theatre on Second Avenue and Twelfth Street, whose new owners wanted to present challenging plays at reasonable ticket prices and had solicited Houseman to direct their second production.

Ryan and Houseman got together to discuss the project, and Houseman was frank with his old friend: this would be a real challenge for an actor who had never performed blank verse and lacked the vocal training of a Shakespearean actor. Ryan's voice, Houseman later wrote, "was pitched rather higher than it should have been in a man of his size, and his speech—though that of an educated man—had the ineradicable nasality of his Chicago origin."[51] The New York critics might murder him. Ryan understood, but there was no way he could turn this down. Curled up inside him was the solitary teenager who had memorized *Hamlet*.

nine

Rum, Rebellion, and Ryan

Among Shakespeare's plays, *Coriolanus* had the distinction of being both highly regarded and rarely staged. T. S. Eliot called it the Bard's greatest tragedy, yet the proud protagonist, Caius Martius Coriolanus, is a hard man for audiences to like. A military hero in Rome, he runs for consul of the senate, but his aristocratic contempt for the popular will gets him banished from the city, and he takes up arms against his own people. Houseman understood that the play tended to refract the politics of the day, and three years after President Truman had relieved General Douglas MacArthur of his command in Korea, civilian control of the military was still a provocative issue. "De Gaulle and Churchill (and to a lesser degree Eisenhower) had raised the question of the wartime hero as political leader," wrote Houseman. "Inevitably, as I edited and prepared the play for production, I found myself emphasizing its political aspects."[1] Ryan, with his long-standing antipathy for generals, couldn't have been more sympathetic to Houseman's conception of the play.

Coriolanus takes place in the fifth century B C, when Rome is a republic but not yet a democracy, and Shakespeare is notably ambivalent about the wisdom of popular rule. Coriolanus can barely restrain his frustration with the people: "He that trusts to you, / Where he should find you lions, finds you hares; / Where foxes, geese. . . . With every minute you do change a mind / And call him noble that was now your hate, / Him vile that was your garland."[2] His controlling mother, Volumnia, persuades him to take up politics, and the senate welcomes him, but street protests organized by his political enemies send him into a rage. Coriolanus reminds the senators that commoners were the downfall of ancient Greece and argues that catering to them will only "break ope the locks o' the senate and bring in / The crows to peck the eagles."[3] As Houseman noted, *Coriolanus* had gained a new currency in the 1930s as Hitler and Mussolini took power. Yet its tragic hero was a timeless figure: the warrior with no place in a civil society.

Ryan had links to several of the cast members. Aufidius, the enemy commander, was played by John Emery, who had been married to Tallulah Bankhead when Ryan was appearing with her in *Clash by Night*. ("I never understood how an essentially gentle man like him could get mixed up with a dreadnought like Tallulah," Ryan later remarked.)[4] Lauri March, cast as Coriolanus's wife, Virgilia, was the daughter of poet Joseph Moncure March, author of *The Set-Up*. (Her father disliked the movie version because it had turned his black fighter into a white one.) The players were first-rate: Mildred Natwick as Volumnia, Alan Napier as the wise patrician Menenius, and, providing comic relief as a trio of servants, the young actors Jack Klugman, Jerry Stiller, and Gene Saks (the first two would become TV stars, the third a successful director). Houseman also made the nervy decision to cast Will Geer as Sicinius, one of Coriolanus's rabble-rousing antagonists. Blacklisted in Hollywood, Geer had been reduced to working as a gardener in LA (for Sidney Harmon, among others), and Houseman would catch hell at MGM for having hired him.

With this largely American cast, Houseman decided the best vocal strategy for Ryan was to stick with his plain midwestern accent rather than strive for a classical delivery. "Shakespeare can be enjoyed—and understood—just as well if actors perform it in modern theatrical style," Ryan told a columnist. "Many performers have a tendency to over-act when they get their teeth into a Shakespearean passage—not only with their bodies, but with their voices. The result can quite often be unintelligible."[5] Whatever his vocal limitations, Ryan was a commanding presence onstage. Houseman brought in a judo expert to choreograph Ryan and Emery in hand-to-hand combat, though these rough-and-tumble sequences proved too bruising on the stage's hardwood floor. Most important, the director understood Ryan's dark appeal as a performer, the "disturbing mixture of anger and tenderness," as Houseman phrased it, that had powered *On Dangerous Ground*.[6]

The Ryans decided to move their children to New York for the six-week run, and the boys got to see two rehearsals and three performances of *Coriolanus*. They watched their father applying his makeup, and Cheyney took home one of his putty noses. "This was wonderful for me," Ryan said. "Movie making is hard to explain to children.... But the theater was different. They could see and feel and understand what I was doing."[7] While he was working, Jessica filled the children's days with museums and other cultural activities. Having grown up in the San Fernando Valley, the children were a little overwhelmed by the city, where their father's fame was more of an issue. On one occasion Jessica took them ice skating in Central Park and their father chanced to join them; before long a crowd gathered, and the children were frightened by the crush of bodies. Eventually police had to wade into the crowd, form a protective cordon around them, and remove them to safety.

Coriolanus opened on January 19, 1954, to positive reviews, with much credit going to Houseman for his incisive framing of the play's politics. Ryan's delivery was faulted by George Shea of the *Wall Street Journal* ("His voice was not always under control, and it quickly became obvious that he is not yet sufficiently accustomed in the verse form")[8] but excused by Brooks Atkinson of the *New York Times,* who liked Ryan's conception of the Roman general as "an attractive, well-bred son of the upper classes who despises the people more out of intellectual sluggishness than malice.... This is a refreshing interpretation of the massive personality of Coriolanus. Mr. Ryan plays it with warmth, candor, grace, and a kind of artless sincerity."[9] The play enjoyed a successful run of forty-eight performances before closing on February 28 to accommodate the next production in the series. Ryan loved the experience, and he and Houseman made vague plans to collaborate on another Shakespeare play. This would never happen, but as the family returned to Los Angeles, Ryan could take heart in knowing he had grown substantially as an actor.

Back in North Hollywood, the Oakwood School was unraveling again. After Bryson Gerard was let go, the parents launched a national search committee to find a new school director, but it was badly organized and failed to produce a suitable candidate. In desperation the founders hired Mary Bernick, who had studied school administration at City College and been recommended by one of the teachers at Oakwood. According to Jessica's account, Bernick became a polarizing figure, finding common cause with the more radical parents and communicating to the staff that "the reason the children were not learning any more than they had before was because it was impossible to teach the spoiled children of the rich."[10]

Bernick was let go at the end of the school year after the volunteer bookkeeper, Marvin Brown, announced a $12,000 deficit. Frustrated and confused, the founders debated throwing in the towel and giving the school away. Ryan and Ross Cabeen appeared before the Country Schools' board of directors to offer them the school—land, buildings, and all—but the board wasn't interested. The couples discussed simply liquidating the corporation's assets and giving the money to the United Jewish Appeal. But Sid Harmon insisted on making one last stand and suggested that his wife, Liz, search for a new director while she was visiting her mother in New York City. Liz was still there in late June when Ryan flew out to promote *About Mrs. Leslie,* and she urged him to meet with a woman who might be the ideal candidate: fifty-seven-year-old Marie Spottswood.

Unlike Bryson Gerard or Mary Bernick, Spottswood was a seasoned educator with a sophisticated understanding of progressive thought. Born in Mobile, Alabama, she had graduated from Randolph-Macon College in Virginia and studied at Tulane University and the University of Chicago before earning a graduate degree from Columbia University. Since 1929 she had been at Ethical Culture Fieldston School in New York, Liz's alma mater, though she had recently resigned as principal of the Lower School and was considering job prospects in Chicago, Vermont, and Massachusetts. According to Jessica's account, Ryan came to her office wearing gray gloves and a hat, the sort of patrician clothing George Leslie Hendersall might have worn. Spottswood, a white-haired woman with a fondness for cats, didn't know him from the movies, but Ryan could always present himself as an urbane, intelligent man, and did. Attracted by the idea of a warmer climate, she accepted an invitation to come visit the Ryans in North Hollywood.

Jessica liked her immediately. Spottswood had "prematurely white hair brushed back from a strong-featured face—a handsome woman and sometimes beautiful, even awe-inspiring, when the visionary gleam appeared in her eyes. One sensed the presence of a passion in her, put to the service of education and cats."[11]

Ryan had promised Spottswood complete control over the educational policy, and she began outlining her plans for a curriculum based on social studies, with a particular focus on California's early Spanish and Indian cultures. In addition to this, heavy emphasis on the arts would engage the students creatively. But Spottswood also understood that reading instruction at Oakwood was seriously deficient, and she wanted to recruit her friend Mary

Davidson, a phonetic reading specialist at Fieldston Lower, to join the staff. The Ryans held a buffet dinner for Spottswood and the parents, at which she was offered, and accepted, the job. That fall, when she took over at Oakwood, the parents began to realize that they had finally turned the corner.

DORE SCHARY LOVED BEING FIRST: no one had ever made a picture about anti-Semitic violence in America before *Crossfire,* and now MGM would make the first picture about the attacks on Japanese-Americans during World War II. Howard Breslin's short story "Bad Time at Honda," about a southwestern town covering up the lynching of a Nisei (second-generation) farmer, had appeared in the January 1947 issue of *American* magazine, but seven years later it was still controversial for the movies. Having bought the rights, Schary requisitioned an in-house report on violence against Japanese-Americans and read of numerous incidents (mainly arson and dynamite attacks, but also shootings) cited in *Life,* the *Saturday Evening Post,* and other publications. He assigned Millard Kaufman to adapt the Breslin story, and for the lead role he set his sights on Spencer Tracy.

Despite the desert setting, "Bad Time at Honda" was more of a mystery than a western. Honda, located between a bluff and a rail line, is so isolated that the Silverliner train screaming westward every morning has become "an event to Honda, a glimpse of the sleekness and wealth, the silver-chromium speed, that belong to other places." One morning, to the townspeople's shock, the train slows to a halt and disgorges Mr. George Macreedy of Chicago, who checks in to a local hotel but deflects questions about his business. He hires a young woman, Liz Brooks, to drive him out to a place in the desert called Adobe Wells, where he finds a small complex of burned-out buildings. Someone fires a warning shot at them, and when they return to town, everyone is watching Macreedy. In the hotel he's confronted by a trio of local ranchers, the leader of whom, Coogan Trimble, alludes to the lynching but warns Macreedy that he'll never prove anything. "Other places . . . settled it other ways," Trimble remarks. "Camps. Things like that. We only had the one. We ran him out. Burned him out. That's all."[12]

Macreedy knows he's licked, and as he waits for his train out of town, everyone in Honda celebrates at the local watering hole. But before he leaves, Macreedy barges into the tavern. Someone silences the jukebox, and they all stare. " 'Now, listen,' said Macreedy. 'All of you know I came here to find Old

Man Kamotka. You know what happened to him. So do I—now.' He could hear the breathing in the room, and he went on: 'This is why I came. There was a kid named Jimmy Kamotka. He left here years ago. He never wrote his father. The old man couldn't read. I met Jimmy in the Army. In Italy. He asked me to look in here. . . . Jimmy Kamotka was killed in Italy. I think maybe this town should know that. And remember it.' "[13]

Kaufman made a number of changes to the story, the most significant of which was turning the mob violence into a smaller, more focused attack. In "Bad Time at Honda" Kamotka dies of a heart attack while fleeing the crowd; in the movie, retitled *Bad Day at Black Rock,* Komoko has been shot to death by the town's fearsome boss man, Reno Smith (which sounded more menacing than "Coogan Trimble"). The conflict between Smith and Macreedy generated more of a showdown, and Kaufman's elongated story line borrowed significantly from *High Noon,* with Macreedy boxed in by the uncooperative townspeople. When Tracy read the script, he complained that Macreedy wasn't dimensional enough, so Schary, salvaging a story idea from an abandoned project, suggested that Macreedy have a paralyzed arm, which satisfied Tracy. He would play the part in a baggy suit with his left sleeve tucked into its pocket.

Bad Day at Black Rock quickly became a sticking point between Schary and Nicholas Schenck, the seventy-two-year-old president of Loews, Inc. (MGM's parent company). Early in the development, when Schary was at home recovering from a kidney stone, Schenck dropped in on him to insist he cancel the picture. A shouting match ensued, Schary prevailed, and when none of his producers expressed interest in the script, he took on the project himself. A month before production commenced, an interoffice memo notified him that a State Department official had informally complained to the studio about the damage the picture might do to the United States overseas. "Historically there never was a lynching of this kind," MGM's Kenneth MacKenna wrote to Schary, "and the whole issue of Asiatic-American relationships is such a touchy matter that such an un-historical incident might be used by our enemies to stir up further misunderstandings."[14] Schary had been through all this before with *Crossfire,* which turned out to be a huge success, so he simply plowed ahead.

Given the similarity between the two pictures, Ryan was a natural choice to play the bigoted Reno Smith, and whatever reservations he may have harbored about the role, which was rather thinly written, they paled before the opportunity to make an A picture with Tracy. Ryan trusted Schary, who demonstrated once again his skill at assembling a superb cast. Ernest Borgnine, the brutal sergeant in *From Here to Eternity,* would play Reno Smith's hot-tempered strong man, Coley, and lean, mean Lee Marvin, who had given bare-knuckle performances in *The Big Heat* and *The Wild One,* was cast as the coolly bullying Hector. Walter Brennan, a three-time Oscar winner, signed on as Doc Velie, the local undertaker who becomes Macreedy's sole ally and the town's conscience. The story was a welcome corrective to *Behind the Rising Sun,* the anti-Japanese propaganda picture that had become Ryan's calling card in the Marines.

Production began on Monday, July 19, in Lone Pine, California, about two hundred miles north of LA in the Owens Valley. "The temperature was about a hundred degrees," recalled Anne Francis, who had been cast as Liz. "And in those days, they used klieg lights to offset the sun. So, *with* those lights, we were working in 115, 120 degrees. We all lost a tremendous amount of weight; I mean, at the end of the day, who was hungry? Spencer Tracy had a *very* hard time. They had to coax him more than once to please, *please* see it through, because it was terribly draining for him."[15] In fact, Tracy had tried to drop out of the picture the week before shooting began, but Schary reminded him that his pay-or-play clause would obligate him to reimburse MGM for nearly half a million dollars. Tracy caved, and to mollify the star, Schary promised to visit the set and suffer in the heat with the rest of them, which he did on one occasion.

"When I was starting out in Hollywood, I would spend any day off I had or any free time on the set watching Spencer Tracy, who was one of the great masters," Ryan recalled. In getting to know the actor, he was gratified to learn that Tracy had been the same way. "When he was a young man in New York, he would wait outside a certain theater at a certain time just to see Lionel Barrymore leave. He couldn't afford to see him act on the stage but at least he could watch and see him walk out of the theater. I think this is terribly important."[16] Tracy, a political conservative, seemed unsure of what to make of Ryan. Anne Francis recalled that after she and Ryan borrowed Tracy's car to get dinner, "I got the silent treatment because he felt Bob and I were having an affair, which we weren't."[17] After shooting one of Macreedy's confrontations with Reno Smith, Tracy asked Millard Kaufman, "Does Ryan scare you?"

Kaufman replied, "No, I've known Bob Ryan for years. He's a fine man." Tracy replied, "Well, he scares the hell out of me.' "[18]

Ryan got a chance to hold his own against Tracy at the picture's midpoint, when Macreedy, trapped in Black Rock until the next day's train, sits outside a gas station and Smith fills up his wagon. Shooting in CinemaScope, director John Sturges placed Tracy at the left of the frame in his dark suit and hat and Ryan at right, flanked by a pair of ten-foot gas pumps painted bright red, the vast blue sky behind him. "Somebody's always looking for something in this part of the west," Smith tells Macreedy. "For the historian it's the Old West, to the book writer it's the Wild West, to the businessman it's the un-developed west.... But to us, this place is *our* west, and I wish they'd leave us alone!" The scene ran more than five minutes and was filled with dialogue; as Tracy sat immobile, Ryan kneeled down to face him and paced back and forth. Watching them work, Borgnine thought at first that Ryan was stealing the scene but then realized his gaze had been fixed on Tracy the whole time. When they finished the scene and Sturges asked for a second take, Tracy refused.

Movie publicists routinely fabricated stories about actors doing their own stunts, but in fact Ryan liked the physical part of his job and would take a crack at something if it didn't look too dangerous. On *Bad Day at Black Rock,* though, he gambled and lost. The picture climaxes with a night scene in which Macreedy, pinned down by Smith's rifle fire, improvises a Molotov cocktail and sets the rancher ablaze. A long shot of a stunt man wearing an asbestos suit resulted in the man scorching his lungs and being taken to the hospital. Ryan completed the sequence with a less risky shot in which Smith, now partially extinguished, flops to the ground with flames still clinging to his left side. "There was a hole in his asbestos suit, so he actually got burned doing that," said Cheyney Ryan. "That was one of the few times that anything like that had ever happened."[19]

Years later twelve-year-old Lisa Ryan phoned her father during a sleepover at a friend's house to tell him that *Bad Day at Black Rock* was playing on the late show. Ryan always disliked the idea of his children seeing him injured or killed on-screen, and he forbade Lisa to watch the movie. "So of course I had to watch it," Lisa recalled. "And he gets set on fire at the end.... I was so traumatized by that scene that I called him, and I said, 'Are you all right?' He said, 'I *told* you not to watch that movie!' "[20]

TALKING TO COLUMNIST ERSKINE JOHNSON of the *Los Angeles Daily News,* Ryan disparaged fan-magazine stories about life with the Ryans: "They come rushing over for home layouts and photograph me with my children. And they've got their stories already written before they even see me."[21] But an "as-told-to" piece he published in *Parents* magazine in September 1954 turned out to be unusually reflective and revealing. With all his reading on early childhood development, Ryan had a lot on his mind, not least his own three children: "Tim, the older, is extremely sensitive. I was so much like Tim as a boy that—and I say it in all humility—I truly believe that I have a deep understanding of him through my own past. I too was a completely nonaggressive youngster. . . . Cheyney gives evidence of being of a totally different mold. He has, we think, just the right amount of aggressiveness. Not so much that he needs his ears pinned back by either parents or playmates, but enough to stand solidly on his rights. . . . As for Lisa—well, she's not three yet and we haven't taken a shot at cataloguing her. . . . She fits into family life in her own way and altogether is very much the fair-haired girl any father of two sons dreams about."[22]

Ryan took advantage of the piece to plug the Oakwood School, crediting Jessica for her initiative and reporting that the present enrollment had hit sixty-five. The month the story appeared, Marie Spottswood began her first semester as director of the school, and the change was dramatic. To address the reading crisis, she divided all the students into "readiness groups" regardless of grade, and Mary Davidson, the reading specialist newly arrived from Fieldston Lower, began working with the groups individually, using the phonics-based approach advocated by educator and psychologist Anna Gillingham in her book *Remedial Training for Children with Specific Disability in Reading, Spelling and Penmanship.* By the end of the school year, wrote Jessica, every student was reading at his or her grade level.

A new board was voted in, with Jessica as president and Marvin Brown, who had uncovered the gaping budget deficit, as treasurer. He set about collecting tuition from deadbeat parents, and the board announced that, for the survival of the school, tuition would have to be hiked from fifty dollars a month to seven hundred annually. Even after that the school would continue to run an annual deficit of about five thousand dollars, which the Ryans and others would cover. That included a scholarship program for minority students, something the founding parents considered crucial. With Spottswood in place, the Oakwood School seemed like a much worthier cause, and the Ryans took pride in what they had managed to accomplish. Ultimately, they wanted to expand the school to include the seventh and eighth grades.

That fall Ryan reteamed with Barbara Stanwyck for *Escape to Burma,* a ridiculous jungle adventure that RKO was distributing for the independent Filmcrest Productions. His character, an American businessman, goes on the run after being framed for the murder of his partner, the Burmese prince, and hides out with Stanwyck's character, who owns a teak plantation. At one point they welcome some locals into her courtyard with a trained baby elephant that does tricks and performs a little dance routine, kicking its back legs in the air. The picture fulfilled Ryan's one-a-year obligation to Howard Hughes, who had recently cemented his control over the studio by purchasing all the outstanding stock of Radio-Keith-Orpheum for $23 million. But after an experience like *Bad Day at Black Rock,* the new picture was a pitiful reminder of how erratic Ryan's career had grown. It was enough to drive a man to drink.

And it did. Alcohol had been an integral part of Ryan's life since his Dartmouth days, when he ran for class marshal on the slogan "Rum, Rebellion, and Ryan." He and Jessica bonded over drinks, and cocktails were central to their little social scene. In her memoir about Oakwood, Jessica remembers going out with Ryan and Sid Harmon to discuss some vexing problem and winding up at a family place called Fatso's Mile High Ice Cream Cones, where Ryan tried to order scotch and soda, and then beer, to no avail. Harmon asked for an ice cream soda; her husband "ordered two coffees and sat back in a state of shock."[23]

He was a big man who could hold his liquor, and in the booze-soaked '50s that was good enough. "He told me that when they were doing movies out in the desert, he was drinking about two fifths of whiskey a day, just to get through the day," said actor James Naughton, who worked with Ryan years later. "That didn't count wine with dinner, or beer and so on. Because making movies out there in the desert was about the most boring thing anybody could do."[24]

A drink made him more genial and charming, but he could also slip into angry silences that pulled him away from the family and into his little refuge out back (now that he had reclaimed it from the fourth and fifth grades). Everyone knew not to bother Daddy when he was in one of his Black Irish moods. "He had difficulty speaking about personal things," his friend Millard

Lampell explained. "It just wasn't in his past, it wasn't in his tradition."[25] Later in life Ryan would confess that he had always been haunted by the death of his brother, Jack, so many years earlier. There was unfinished business with his father, another man of dramatic mood swings. There was the nagging sense that the success he had chased all his life was hollow. And there was the world going to hell all around him.

"When my father got depressed, it was usually about Richard Nixon, it wasn't about his life," observed Cheyney Ryan. "It would be more about what was happening in the world."[26] Ryan was increasingly distressed by the threat of nuclear weapons. Earlier that year the US military had detonated a hydrogen bomb on the Bikini Atoll in the Marshall Islands; the fifteen-megaton blast, the most powerful in human history, was supposed to be a secret, but news of it had spread around the world after the wind carried radioactive fallout to neighboring islands, which had to be evacuated, and infected the crew of a Japanese fishing boat, killing one man. The fallout had spread as far as Southern California. If that didn't kill Ryan, he'd damn well do it himself. "Cancer by the Carton," a story in the December 1952 *Reader's Digest,* had revealed that cigarettes almost certainly caused lung cancer: "Above the age of 45 the risk of developing the disease increases in simple proportion with the amount smoked."[27] Ryan smoked two packs a day.

Bad Day at Black Rock opened the first week of January 1955 to stellar reviews. "This is one of the finest pictures ever made," raved John O'Hara in *Collier's;*[28] a more measured assessment from Robert Hatch in the *Nation* lauded it as "a tight, economical work, directed and acted with conviction" that "enlarges the stature of everyone in connection with it."[29] The State Department's concerns notwithstanding, *Bad Day at Black Rock* was released overseas in March and collected even more superlatives from critics. That year it represented the United States in the Cannes Film Festival (along with Elia Kazan's *East of Eden*), and the following year brought Oscar nominations for Spencer Tracy, John Sturges, and Millard Kaufman. Ticket sales were less impressive: after a year and a half in release the picture had posted a profit of only $600,000.

Shortly after Ryan hit movie screens as the murderer of a Nisei farmer, he flew to Tokyo to shoot a big-budget crime thriller for Twentieth Century Fox. *House of Bamboo* was an A remake of an old B movie, *The Street with No Name* (1948), in which an FBI agent tracks an organized crime operation;

Darryl Zanuck, eager to make the first Hollywood feature shot in Japan, had screenwriter Harry Klein write a new version set in Tokyo, where an army investigator going under the name Eddie Spanier (Robert Stack) infiltrates a gang of American ex-G.I.s led by the dapper, calculating Sandy Dawson (Ryan).

The cigar-chomping director, Samuel Fuller, had worked as a crime reporter and served as an infantryman in the "Big Red One," experiences that informed his gripping Korean war drama, *The Steel Helmet* (1951), and his nineteenth-century period picture about newspapermen, *Park Row* (1952). Having scored at Fox with the itchy crime picture *Pickup on South Street* (1953), he was looking to move up, and *House of Bamboo* was a classy project in color and CinemaScope, with exotic locations and a big star. "Robert became a true friend," Fuller would write. "He was well read and balanced, a kindhearted man with grand democratic ideals."[30]

Fuller had a few twists of his own to add to *House of Bamboo*. "I moved the entire shebang to Tokyo," he would later write, ignoring Klein's contribution, "added stuff about Japanese contemporary life, threw in some sexual exploitation and interracial romance, and then, for some unexpected pizzazz, wrote a violent love scene between two hardened criminals. . . . Zanuck loved it, even the homoerotic scene with the two gangsters."[31] As conceived by Fuller, *House of Bamboo* included a male love triangle: Sandy Dawson is intimate with his second-in-command, Griff (Cameron Mitchell), but then falls for the new man, Spanier, and elevates him to Griff's role. To slip this romantic subtext past the Production Code Administration would require skillful underplaying, and Ryan embraced the challenge. "I like Sam, he's crazy!" he told an interviewer in the early '70s. "We were very much in agreement during the filming of *House of Bamboo*."[32]

Sometimes Fuller seemed like a character in one of his own movies. "He liked to keep a gun strapped to his hip while we were shooting in Japan—he looked like General Patton," wrote Stack. "And instead of saying 'Action!' to start a scene, he would take a .45 out of the holster and shoot it in the air—*Boom!* And people all around would run and scurry and hide."[33] As Stack remembered it, Fuller didn't seem to comprehend how the conquered Japanese would feel about an American firing a pistol for emphasis. Still, people stayed out of his way.

Soon after they arrived in Tokyo, Fuller needed to shoot a simple scene

Ryan and director Samuel Fuller agreed privately that Sandy Dawson (Ryan), the menacing crime lord in *House of Bamboo* (1955), would be a closeted man lusting for undercover cop Eddie Kenner (Robert Stack). *Franklin Jarlett Collection*

in which Ryan would drive up to a curb and get out, but when the company arrived at the location, they were greeted by anti-American protesters. The director told his cinematographer, Joe MacDonald, to film the people who had gathered, and as soon as the camera was turned on them, the crowd dispersed.

Fuller already had shot one picture in CinemaScope (the submarine adventure *Hell and High Water*), and he took advantage of its extremely long aspect ratio—1 to 2.55—to suggest on-screen what he couldn't get past the censors in typescript. For the interior scenes with Dawson's gang, he created a series of elegant tableaux showing male bodies in repose, with Ryan bisecting the group and often elevated in the frame to stress his tall, lanky physique. Dawson doesn't appear until nearly twenty minutes into the picture, but when he does, Fuller employs a startling shift in perspective. Griff finds Spanier trying to shake down a club owner and punches him out; Spanier crashes through a paper screen into a private room, and the tear left by his body frames Dawson, cool and lean as he sits atop a table, surrounded by his boys. From *Caught,* Ryan recycled the business in which his character banks a cue ball around a billiard table as he holds forth, and as in the earlier picture, the ball's movement traces a triangle.

What Fuller described as a "violent love scene between two hardened criminals" was not really a love scene but an execution: Dawson decides that Griff has ratted him out to the cops and arrives at Griff's home to find him bathing in a wooden tub. The gang leader steps into the room and pumps eight shots into his underling, the bathwater squirting out of the tub through the entrance holes. "You didn't know what you were doing," Dawson tells his dead lover, cradling his head tenderly. "I could see you had no control of yourself, absolutely none. And I knew, Griff. I knew when you started blowing your buttons for no reason whatsoever. Griff, I wish I hadn't been right. But I was, Griff. Like always." Fuller loved this psychotic moment: "Sandy is gentle for the first time, almost sensual," Fuller later wrote. "Except the object of his affection is his dead victim, showing just how insane the sonofabitch has really become!"[34]

While shooting in the streets of Tokyo, Fuller found the perfect location for Dawson's violent end: a twenty-story building anchored by a department store that operated a children's nursery on the roof. Carnival rides had been erected on one side, including a little carousel in the shape of Saturn; a gold half-sphere spun clockwise as a ring of seats turned counterclockwise. In the climactic sequence the bad guy is cornered high above ground, like Bogart in *High Sierra* (1942) or Cagney in *White Heat* (1949). Stack would recall his unease as he and Ryan filmed their showdown on the contraption, high above the street; the carousel was rusty and the gigantic CinemaScope camera unbalanced it. But the results were spectacular, a yawning vista of Tokyo behind them as Sandy Dawson is shot to death. A subsequent reverse angle shows Spanier stepping off the carousel and Dawson's body draped over the edge of the ring as it continues its slow rotation.

RYAN'S STEADY WORK SCHEDULE always prevented him and Jessica from vacationing at length; they might pack up the kids for a quick trip to La Jolla, Santa Barbara, or the Ojai Valley, and the previous year they had all gone to New York while Ryan was performing *Coriolanus.* But in April, Jessica wrote to Dido and Jean Renoir to announce, "We are coming to France! It seems quite astonishing that we actually have definite plans to make such a trip but it is true—and all for vacation and no work."[35] She and Robert, along with the children and Williana Smith, would set off from New York in early July on the steamship *Independence,* arrive in Cannes eight days later, and spend the next six weeks "vagabonding" around France and Italy by auto before departing from Naples on September 4. Robert was about to leave for Durango, Mexico, to costar with Clark Gable in a big-budget western for Fox called *The Tall Men,* but after that he was free and clear.

Raoul Walsh, director of *The Tall Men,* was another grand old man of the movie business, his career stretching back to the Silent Era and encompassing such hard-charging talkies as *The Roaring Twenties, High Sierra, They Died with Their Boots On,* and *White Heat.* He had made more than a hundred features, and *The Tall Men* was just another of them, with a weak script about antagonistic ranchers that was mainly an excuse to stage an epic cattle drive in CinemaScope. Jane Russell is Gable's love interest, and their dialogue scenes are excruciating. Walsh was still working on the script as the cameras began rolling in mid-April, the first order of business being the big, expensive cattle-drive sequences that had brought them to Mexico (no US location offered a sufficient number of cattle).

First Tokyo, now dusty Durango. Hoping to pull people away from their TV sets, the big studios turned increasingly to dramatic location photography, which meant Ryan was spending more and more time away from the family. In Durango he shared a bungalow with costar Cameron Mitchell, whom he had known since the days of the Millpond Playhouse on Long Island; Russell was lodged in a nearby hacienda, and Gable and Walsh shared another. "I went through the location in a haze," Ryan later said. "I've hardly any recollection of Durango—Gable and Jane and I would sit around getting swacked! I can't even remember where I lived!"[36]

A generation after *It Happened One Night* (1934), Gable was a craggy fifty-four and humbly resigned to playing himself in picture after picture. Ryan found him to be an uncommonly gracious and decent guy; one time, when Ryan ran out of his brand of cigarettes, Gable got up early and drove into town to fetch him a few cartons. Walsh was great company too, and Ryan pumped him for stories about his hero Douglas Fairbanks, whom Walsh had directed in *The Thief of Bagdad* (1924).

These pleasant moments notwithstanding, *The Tall Men* was a tough shoot. According to Walsh, four hundred people in the cast and crew contracted dysentery. Then, after years of heavy drinking, Ryan came down with alcoholic hepatitis. Shipped back to Los Angeles for treatment, he learned he was also suffering from cirrhosis of the liver. The trip to France, which Jessica had so looked forward to, was canceled. "He didn't go to the hospital, but he was in bed for quite a long time because of that," Cheyney Ryan recalled. "I think [he] cut back on alcohol because he realized he was going to die."[37] Ryan's doctors told him he couldn't touch any booze for a year. "I damn near died when I heard that," he told a reporter years later. "But I got through the first two weeks, and I never had the same urge again."[38] Eventually he would fall off the wagon, holding himself to a couple Löwenbräus every night. But in the immediate aftermath of his illness, at least, Ryan got a chance to look at the world sober for the first time in decades.

ten

The Gates of War

Recovering from his illness, Ryan had plenty of time to take stock of his career. Since parting ways with RKO, he had landed some nice deals, first with Paramount and then with Fox, that had given him starring roles in A pictures. Dore Schary came to him with good supporting roles at MGM. He had shared the screen with James Stewart, Spencer Tracy, and Clark Gable. Around town he was known as a consummate professional, quietly cooperative and reliably inspired. Yet somehow he always got shut out of the big parts. Early in 1954 he had eaten his guts out as Gregory Peck landed the role of Ahab in John Huston's lavish adaptation of *Moby Dick;* Ryan still read the novel once a year, and watching the part slip away was like seeing the great white whale disappear into the blue waters.

His reclusiveness didn't help. "I don't want any identification between my personal life and my acting life," he once said. "An actor's private life should be very private. The public should see nothing but what they see on the screen."[1] Jessica had grown to loathe photo sessions. "Asking her to pick up a coffee pot and have her pour coffee while I grin over her shoulder for a photographer is murder."[2] Their home out in the Valley had pulled him away from the movie business, and getting so involved in the Oakwood School had sapped all his free time. All around him stars were making their way outside the studio system, cutting profit-participation deals or even forming their own production companies. Ryan didn't want to produce or direct—that would mean even more time away from home—but there had to be a way of finding projects that were more engaging and ambitious.

An intriguing possibility emerged that fall when his friend Sidney Harmon landed a three-picture financing and distribution deal with United Artists for his independent production company, Security Pictures, Inc. The first picture, *Variety* reported, would be *Men in War,* set during the Korean conflict and based on Van Van Praag's 1949 novel *Combat.* Soon after came news that Harmon and his partner, screenwriter Philip Yordan, would produce a screen adaptation of Erskine Caldwell's best-selling, notoriously salacious novel *God's Little Acre,* with Anthony Mann directing. Ryan trusted Harmon from their many years in the trenches at Oakwood, and through him had gotten to know Yordan, a Chicago native and a voracious reader. "We used to socialize quite a bit," remembered Yordan, "and by socialize I mean just come over [to] the house and sit down, and smoke and drink beer."[3] Quite naturally the three men had kicked around the idea of working together, and now they had financing.

Yordan would earn a reputation as a classic Hollywood hustler.* Originally an attorney and entrepreneur, he had come to Hollywood in the late '30s and written such hard-boiled pictures as *Dillinger, House of Strangers,* and *Detective Story.* But he also served as a front for blacklisted writers, passing their work off as his own and giving them a percentage. Harmon had sent several people his way. "Sidney, in a sense, was my conscience," recalled Yordan, who was so apolitical he claimed he never read a newspaper until he was fifty. "He says, 'Phil, you've got so much money, you've got a play on Broadway, you're making $5,000 a week, and these guys are starving to death. Give them some work, for chrissakes.'"[4] Ben Maddow, who hadn't written under his own name in Hollywood since 1952, remembered Yordan fronting for him on *Men in War* and several other scripts; Yordan offered him a 50 percent cut, though as Maddow noted, "I was never sure of what percentage it actually was."[5]

Maddow watched in amazement one afternoon as Yordan tried to parlay a western script Maddow had written into a novel and a picture deal. As Maddow related to writer Patrick McGilligan, Yordan phoned Simon and Schuster and asked if they were interested in publishing a novel that Warner Bros. was adapting to the screen. Then he called Warners and asked if they were interested in adapting a novel that Simon and Schuster was publishing. To clinch the deal, Yordan contacted a "minor executive" at Warners and offered to retire the man's $14,000 gambling debt if he would pimp the script to studio head Jack Warner, claiming he had picked it up by accident and

---

*For a definitive account of Yordan's storied career , see Alan K. Rode's "'First Is First and Second Is Nobody': The Philip Yordan Story," *Noir City Sentinel,* November/December 2009.

been bowled over when he read it.[6] Maddow was then dispatched to write the nonexistent novel, though the picture was never made; when he later saw the book in print in Europe, he said, Yordan had attached his own byline.

In December 1955, Ryan returned to work, playing Abraham Lincoln in a half-hour TV play called *Lincoln's Doctor's Dog*.* Lincoln spends most of this little fable laid up in bed, the human cost of the war weighing heavily on his mind. His friend and physician, Robert K. Stone (Charles Bickford of *The Woman on the Beach*) examines him, taking his pulse from his ankle as his feet stick out from the covers, and insists that he get at least twenty-four hours of rest. The extended scene between them is beautifully written and gently played; at one point Lincoln pages through *Henry IV,* part 2, and takes a solemn pass at one of Prince Hal's soliloquies: "O polish'd perturbation! golden care! / That keep'st the ports of slumber open wide / To many a watchful night!" Unfortunately, this gives way to a sappy resolution in which the doctor cheers Abe by getting him a puppy.

The new year brought two more mediocre pictures whose sole consolation was top billing. *The Proud Ones,* another CinemaScope western for Fox, costarred Virginia Mayo and Jeffrey Hunter, with location work in Nogales, Arizona. *Back from Eternity,* a jungle survival drama, was being shot—thank God—at RKO Pathe Studios, with a $300,000 tropical set and sixty exotic birds. Ryan plays an alcoholic airline pilot who tries to save his passengers after their plane goes down somewhere in South America; among them are Swedish bombshell Anita Ekberg and the tightly wound Rod Steiger. By this time Howard Hughes had severed his ties with RKO Radio Pictures, selling his share to General Tire and Rubber Company for a $6.5 million profit. His bizarre stewardship of RKO would be remembered as the most baroque episode in the era of the great movie moguls, an era that was now, clearly and irrevocably, coming to a close. When Harmon and Yordan approached Ryan with a profit-participation deal to star in their first picture, *Men in War,* he grabbed it.

RYAN HADN'T MADE A PICTURE about ground combat since he and Pat O'Brien starred in the trite *Marine Raiders* back in 1943. *Men in War* took

---

*This homespun tale was part of the NBC anthology series *Screen Directors Playhouse,* which showcased the small-screen work of veteran Hollywood filmmakers (in this case, H. C. Potter).

Sergeant Riordan (Phillip Pine) and Lieutenant Benson (Ryan) in *Men in War* (1957). "The battalion doesn't exist," Benson tells Riordan. "The regiment doesn't exist. Command headquarters doesn't exist, the USA doesn't exist. . . . We'll never see 'em again." *Wisconsin Center for Film and Theater Research*

a much darker view of its subject: the story of an army patrol stranded behind enemy lines in the early days of the Korean conflict, it had no romantic subplot, no flag-waving speeches, no moral compass. Since the end of World War II, Hollywood war movies had grown more adult, ambivalent, and even philosophical, but *Men in War* was downright existential, focused like a telescope on the wild terrain and the men's desperate, improvised tactics against an encroaching but unseen enemy. "The battalion doesn't exist," the despairing Lieutenant Benson (Ryan) tells his loyal radioman, Sergeant Riordan (Phillip Pine). "The regiment doesn't exist. Command headquarters doesn't exist, the USA doesn't exist. They don't exist, Riordan. We'll never see 'em again." The picture ended with a bitter scene in which Benson, Riordan, and Sergeant Montana (Aldo Ray) toss a dead officer's silver stars into the brush as they read off the names of all the men they've lost.

The entire story transpired out in the field, which made Tony Mann an inspired choice to direct: all he needed to create drama was good actors and a good location. Yordan had known Mann for years, and Ryan was eager to work with him again after *The Naked Spur.* According to Yordan, Mann read the 150-page script and cut it down to 82 pages, stripping out nearly all the dialogue. "Of course, I put all of the dialogue back in to get Aldo Ray and Robert Ryan to play it," remembered Yordan. "I said to [Mann], 'What am I going to do if you send them this script? They won't show up!'"[7]

Fortunately, they did show up, to a hilly, overgrown area of Thousand Oaks, California, thirty-five miles northwest of Los Angeles in the Conejo Valley, where shooting began in July 1956. Harmon had rounded up a sharp supporting cast, including Vic Morrow, L. Q. Jones, Nehemiah Persoff, and James Edwards (who had played the black fighter Luther Hawkins in *The Set-Up*). Aside from the players, Mann had little at his disposal but a few old jeeps and some explosive charges, but that didn't matter—his muses were the open sky, the billowing smoke, and the tall, bleached grass that seemed to stretch in every direction, enveloping the men and concealing the enemy.

This bare-bones approach lay at the opposite end of the spectrum from something such as *Flying Leathernecks,* with its fleet of fighter planes supplied by the Marine Corps, but shooting on the cheap bought the filmmakers some artistic freedom. *Flying Leathernecks* features a corny scene in which John Wayne struggles to write a condolence letter to the parents of a fallen marine under his command; its corollary in *Men in War* is a grim, wordless shot in which Lieutenant Benson cuts a dog tag off a dead G.I. and adds it to a thick stack he keeps on a key ring. The entire division has retreated under a tank assault from the North Koreans, who are advancing to Pusan, and Benson is responsible for leading his men to safety. He's a good commander, cool-headed and resolute, but his mission is complicated when the patrol collides with Sergeant Montana (Ray), the chauffeur and self-appointed caretaker of a mute, shell-shocked colonel (Robert Keith). From Ryan's perspective, nothing could have symbolized the military command structure better than a catatonic officer strapped into a jeep and staring blankly into space.

"Tell me the story of the foot soldier and I will tell you the story of all wars," declares an opening title, signaling not only the picture's antiwar leanings but also Mann's minimalist approach. The men here are vividly human—scared, confused, fiercely devoted to one another—but there are no reminiscences about girlfriends back home or dreamy soliloquies outlining plans for the future. Forced to fill in the blanks, Ryan drew on his own life, adding a rare personal touch that would become the picture's sole reminder of an outside world: when the lieutenant takes off his helmet, nestled inside is a snapshot of Jessica, Tim, Cheyney, and Lisa. Ryan didn't often lose track of himself in a character, but during *Men in War* he began to feel he *was* Benson. "With each day I felt dirtier, grimier, lousier and more forsaken," he told one reporter. "It became more and more difficult to sleep in my clean bed at night. I found it finally, impossible. I had to sleep on the floor."[8]

Shooting close to home was a blessing; Ryan could commute to the location, and there were frequent visits from Jessica, the kids, and the Harmon family. Tim and Andy Harmon, good friends at Oakwood, latched onto a copy of the screenplay and wrote their own digested version of *Men in War,* which they rehearsed with Cheyney and some of their classmates and performed for their fathers. Back then the empty lot just west of Oakwood on Moorpark Street was a sandy wash with overgrown bushes and dried-out drainage canals that were perfect for playing war. "Tim and Andy were always writing a movie," recalled Toya Harrison, daughter of Chuck Haas. "Tim was always the star, and the girls in the class, me included, we were always the nurses. . . . Tim and Andy were fantastic at persuading us all that these movies were gonna be made and we had to rehearse them. . . . I remember Tim as being a very gentle soul, really quiet-spoken. A lot like Bob, really."[9]

That summer the Democrats nominated Adlai Stevenson to run again for president. He faced an even tougher race than he had in 1952: the Korean conflict had ended, the economy was booming, and polls showed widespread support for President Eisenhower. Stevenson staked out courageous positions supporting a nuclear test ban, an issue dear to Ryan's heart, and proposing an end to the military draft. In the final weeks of the race Ryan flew out to Washington to appear at a $100-a-plate Stevenson dinner, which was being carried by closed-circuit TV to thirty-three other locations around the country. Henry Fonda, Frank Sinatra, Bette Davis, Marlon Brando, Harry Belafonte, Geraldine Fitzgerald, and Lauren Bacall were among his costars; sorely missed was Humphrey Bogart, who was battling cancer and had only months to live. Ryan got to introduce President Truman, who lambasted Eisenhower and Nixon and promised, "The day of liberation for the city of Washington is close at hand."[10] Stevenson carried only seven states on election day, but he would always be a hero to the Ryans. "Till the day they died they had a picture of Adlai Stevenson over the mantelpiece," Cheyney recalled.[11]

Robert and Tim Ryan during location shooting for *Men in War* (1957). That summer Tim and his brother, Cheyney, got their hands on a script and staged scenes with their playmates on the grounds of the Oakwood School. *Robert Ryan Family*

After *Men in War* wrapped, Ryan didn't work for the rest of the year. By this time Universal, Paramount, and Fox all had tried him out as a leading man, with decent but unspectacular financial returns, and Nicholas Schenck had finally canned Dore Schary as president of MGM, leaving Ryan without a connection at that studio. He was forty-six and looked it, in a business whose hottest new star was twenty-one-year-old Elvis Presley. Hollywood legends such as Clark Gable, Gary Cooper, and Cary Grant were still playing romantic leads well into their 50s, but Ryan was hardly in that league; the more lined his face, the more menacing he looked. The Dartmouth alumni magazine reported in December that he was trying for the lead in a Jack Dempsey biopic, though nothing came of this.[12] He could have gotten more television gigs, but that was a step down from pictures.

Near the end of the year Ryan got an irresistible offer when theatrical pro-ducer-director Harold J. Kennedy asked him to appear in a local production of Jean Giraudoux's antiwar satire *Tiger at the Gates*. First staged in Paris in 1935, as the Nazi threat gathered in Europe, *Tiger at the Gates* was a mod-ern-language take on the *Iliad*, though in contrast to Homer's epic poem, set near the end of the ten-year Trojan War, the French play takes place on the eve of that conflict. Hector, the Trojan commander whom Kennedy wanted Ryan to play, has just returned from battle and craves peace; reunited with his loving wife, Andromache, he plans to march into the city's courtyard and close the Gates of War forever. But in his absence another conflict has been brewing: his brother Paris has kidnapped Helen, the beautiful queen of Sparta. "Those poor gates," observes Andromache's caustic friend Cassandra. "They need more oil to shut them than to open them."[13]

Ryan loved the play, particularly the elegant translation by Christopher Fry. Hector was like a well-spoken version of the weary Lieutenant Benson: confiding in Andromache, the Trojan warrior remembers the precise moment when his sense of glory deserted him, just as he was preparing to slay an opponent. "Up to that time, a man I was going to kill had always seemed my direct opposite," he says. "This time I was kneeling on a mirror, the death I was going to give was a kind of suicide."[14] He and Andromache plead with the people of Troy to surrender Helen, but their fellow citizens, unacquainted with battle, all have their own agendas. In protest Hector refuses to make the expected oration for the men slain in the last conflict. "An Oration for the Dead of a war is a hypocritical speech in defense of the living, a plea for acquittal," he declares. "I am not so sure of my innocence."[15]

Witty and flamboyant, Kennedy had won a Tony in the mid-1940s performing his own play *A Goose for the Gander* on Broadway before he branched out as a director on the West Coast. Ryan first met him in 1951, when Kennedy invited him to Lucey's Restaurant, across the street from the RKO lot, and asked him to play the brutal cop in an LA production of Sidney Kingsley's *Detective Story*. Having just played a similar character in *On Dangerous Ground,* Ryan politely declined, telling Kennedy, "If I'm going to work in the theater, and for no money, I have to have a chance to do something I would never be allowed to do in films, and that probably would never be done in films."[16] *Tiger at the Gates* certainly fit that description, and Ryan agreed to play Hector for Actors Equity scale, which was fifty dollars a week. A one-week tryout was scheduled in mid-January 1957 at the Sombrero Playhouse in Phoenix, followed by a two-week run at the four-hundred-seat Ivar Theatre in Los Angeles.

A Republican stronghold, Phoenix was hardly the ideal town for a pacifist play, only two months after the Soviets had crushed the Hungarian Revolution. According to Kennedy, opening night was a fiasco, as patrons "stormed out in droves during the first act and fled to the bar, which set a new liquor record for the night."[17] The next morning Ryan came to his hotel room, perspiring heavily—"flop sweat," he explained. (This was a common physical reaction on his part; Jessica recalled him dripping with sweat at the giant Stevenson rally in San Francisco in 1952.) Kennedy assured Ryan that the play would be more warmly received in Los Angeles, and he was right. Buoyed by positive reviews, *Tiger at the Gates* sold out in its final week and set a new box office record for small venues in LA. Unable to secure seats, Howard Hughes sent his chauffeur to buy four tickets from waiting patrons at fifty dollars each, and experienced Ryan in the full flower of his liberal pacifism.

A certain amount of offstage drama attended the run. During the final week, Ryan's seventy-three-year-old mother, Mabel, was hit by a car on her way to the theater, sustaining cuts, bruises, and a five-inch laceration on her head.[18] She asked police not to notify anyone until the performance was over, and given the fact that Old Tim had died of complications from being struck by an auto, the news must have upset Ryan when he got it. According to Kennedy, Ryan also stepped out on his wife during a drunken cast party, disappearing with a young actress in the cast who was enthralled by him. Early the next morning, Kennedy wrote, Ryan showed up at his house, sat down in the living room, and told him, "I've been on this couch all night." After Kennedy agreed to stick with this fiction, Ryan remarked, "I wish I had been."[19] Kennedy waited for a phone call from Jessica Ryan, but it never came.

TIGER AT THE GATES might have played well past its scheduled two-week run, but Ryan had committed to joining Aldo Ray on a two-week promotional tour for *Men in War,* and Kennedy considered Ryan so essential that he decided to close the show rather than replace him. With a financial stake in the new picture, Ryan had promised Harmon and Yordan an intensive publicity push; according to another item in his alumni magazine, he lost thirteen pounds on the road. The effort must have paid off, because *Men in War* turned out to be a critics' favorite. "*Men in War* ranks with the great war pictures," raved the *Washington Post,* praising its "commanding use of silence, detail and accent on the crude monotony of warfare."[20] Writing in the *Los Angeles Times,* Philip Scheuer noted the picture's documentary feel: "It has something of the on-the-spot reportage of, say, John Huston's memorable

San Pietro, made on the Italian front in World War II."[21] For relatively little money, Security Pictures had made a daringly modern war movie, though its box office performance left something to be desired.

That May the Oakwood School held a groundbreaking ceremony for its new classroom expansion, which would add two classrooms, an instructors' room, and a conference room for the board, and allow Oakwood to expand its enrollment from sixty-five to ninety-seven students.[22] The school continued to operate at a deficit every year, but where Oakwood was involved, Ryan never seemed to reach the bottom of his pocket. Nor was he averse to using his Hollywood connections to help out the school; Lamont Johnson, an Oakwood parent from the beginning, remembered stage-managing one benefit that included Frank Sinatra, Sammy Davis Jr., Peggy Lee, Peter Ustinov, Dean Martin, and Jerry Lewis.

"Marie Spottswood, who was absolutely brilliant, and Bob and Jessica were the soul and the spine of the whole thing," said Johnson.[23] Jessica was still deeply involved in Oakwood, but on a less conspicuous level than her husband, working with Spottswood to create teaching materials for the social studies curriculum. When Spottswood lamented the lack of any suitable children's books about the Spanish in early California, Jessica wrote one, called *Mañana,* and followed it with a book about the Aztecs, *Teca and the Plumed Serpent.* "We needed all sorts of unavailable illustrative material," Spottswood later wrote, "such as charts of Norse runes, Egyptian hieroglyphics, Chinese calligraphy. No problem: she would do the job. Soon the children were using her beautiful handiwork."[24] The two women grew close. Jessica would portray Spottswood as devoted only to her students and cats, but according to the Ryans' old friend Robert Wallsten, the older woman "went into an absolute flutter any time Ryan came her way. It wasn't all education she had in her mind or at least it was another kind of education. And I'm not sure how conscious she was of it. I'm sure Jessica was aware of it."[25]

With *Men in War* in release, Harmon and Yordan turned to *God's Little Acre,* an even more ambitious project with serious literary credentials. Published in 1933, this story of a poor, hard-lusting family in rural Georgia had become the center of a landmark First Amendment case when the New York Society for the Suppression of Vice sued the publisher, Viking Press, for violating a state statute against disseminating pornography. The judge in the case ruled for Viking, establishing two important legal precedents: first,

Ryan, Marvin Brown, and Marie Spottswood break ground for a classroom expansion at Oakwood School. It continued to operate at a deficit every year, but where Oakwood was involved, Ryan never seemed to reach the bottom of his pockets. *Robert Ryan Family*

the work was judged in its entirety, not on the basis of selected passages, and second, the court considered the opinions of other writers in evaluating the work's merit (a committee organized to defend Caldwell had included Sinclair Lewis, H. L. Mencken, Sherwood Anderson, Dorothy Parker, and Alexander Woollcott). The publicity from the trial, and from censorship efforts in other localities, stoked the sales of *God's Little Acre;* by the time Security Pictures got hold of the book in December 1955, it had sold eight million copies.

Ben Maddow would later claim authorship of the screenplay, which Yordan flatly disputed; one can understand why either man would want credit for the elegant adaptation, which highlighted the book's humor and humanity while deleting or toning down its randier episodes. Even after a quarter decade, *God's Little Acre* was too hot for the screen, with open infidelity and crudely sexual talk. Ty Ty Walden, the cracked patriarch at the center of the story, is widowed and celibate, but he cheerfully praises his daughter-in-law's "rising beauties" in front of his grown children: "They're that pretty it makes me feel sometime like getting right down on my hands and knees like these old hound dogs you see chasing after a flowing bitch. You just ache to get down and lick something. That's the way, and it's God's own truth as He would tell it Himself if He could talk like the rest of us."[26] The picture was a little more decorous: "If the good Lord seen fit to put a beauty like you in our house, I'm gonna take my fill of lookin' while I can." Harmon and Yordan told *Variety* they were going to bypass the Production Code Administration and seek independent distribution,[27] but ultimately they submitted to the usual negotiations with the Breen office.

Ryan's representative at the William Morris Agency begged him not to accept the role of Ty Ty; the character was seventy years old, and if Ryan pulled it off, he might find himself typecast as an old man. But Ty Ty was too juicy to pass up, a grand, earthy, philosophical fool. The Waldens live in cotton country, but for the past fifteen years Ty Ty has been gripped with gold fever, digging gigantic holes on his land in search of a treasure chest described to him by his dying grandpappy. A good Christian man, Ty Ty reserves one acre of his farm for the Lord, giving everything grown on it to the church; he keeps moving its location around, though, because he needs new places to dig and can't stand the thought of his preacher getting all the gold. As scripted, the role ranged from raucous physical comedy to quiet drama, with the sort of poignant moments that seldom came Ryan's way. This was the sort of big, rich part the studios never offered him. According to Yordan, Ryan "just went over his agent's head, and he did it."[28]

Harmon, Yordan, and Mann did their best to reunite the company that had collaborated so well on *Men in War:* cinematographer Ernest Haller, composer Elmer Bernstein, actors Vic Morrow and Aldo Ray. Tall, curvaceous Tina Louise, a Broadway actress who had appeared in the musical *Li'l Abner,* would make her screen debut as Ty Ty's daughter-in-law, Griselda, and rotund comedian Buddy Hackett signed on to play Pluto Swint, the hapless political candidate who's too busy sniffing around Ty Ty's youngest, Darling Jill, to canvas for votes. As with *Men in War,* Aldo Ray shared top billing with Ryan, holding down another story line as Will, the striking millworker married to Ty Ty's elder daughter, Rosamond. Locked out of work for eighteen months, Will has begun scheming with his fellow strikers to seize the mill and start it up again; this situation added yet another wrinkle to the picture's release, since it might be attacked as subversive.

The producers had scouted locations in Georgia, but the book's reputation preceded it, and pressure from business and civic leaders in Atlanta prompted them to look closer to home; in early September, principal photography began in Stockton, California, five hours north of Los Angeles in the San Joaquin Valley. Tina Louise remembered Ryan as distant; she gravitated toward Aldo Ray and Jack Lord, who played her husband, Buck. Ryan preferred the company of Hackett, who could make him laugh until his sides hurt. "He adored Buddy Hackett," remembered Lisa Ryan. "I think my dad felt more comfortable being around people like Buddy Hackett than people who were more like my dad, who made him nervous."[29] Ryan and Hackett shared some memorably funny scenes together; after learning of Ty Ty's quest, Pluto persuades him that what he needs is an albino, because these white-skinned people have a special power for divining gold. Ryan's expression widens in wonder as Ty Ty considers this, and before long the old coot has kidnapped a swamp-dwelling albino named Dave (played by young Michael Landon) and brought him back to the farm.

The character's saving grace was his humility, which allowed his ludicrously comic moments to coexist with his sincere religiosity. When Dave the albino follows his quivering dowser wand right to the makeshift cross that marks God's little acre, Ty Ty uproots it once again and ultimately moves it out to the river's edge. "Now God, I don't aim to cheat you none, I swear I don't," prays Ty Ty, as Bernstein's score swells. "But what with this unseasonable weather and all, I believe you'd admire to have your acre in a cooler spot. If you don't like this, if you don't approve of what I'm doing, Lord, then strike me down dead right here where I stand." Ty Ty shuts his eyes to wait for the lightning, then opens one eye and grins with satisfaction. "Thank you, Lord, Glory be. Amen."

Ryan must have known they had something good here, though in a quick note to the president of the Dartmouth boxing club, he was typically self-deprecating. "[Erskine] Caldwell came up to watch us shoot," he reported, "and is either the quietest man ever born or was stunned at the awfulness of what we were doing to his little epic. It has sold second only to the Bible but as one of our actors said, they do not come as a set."[30]

WHILE RYAN WAS SHOOTING *God's Little Acre,* an organization that would become his political focus for the next few years was taking shape in New

Ty Ty Walden (Ryan) succumbs to gold fever in *God's Little Acre* (1958). Erskine Caldwell's salacious novel, Ryan noted, "has sold second only to the Bible, but as one of our actors said, they do not come as a set." *Wisconsin Center for Film and Theater Research*

York City. Earlier that year the revered theologian Albert Schweitzer had issued a "Declaration of Conscience" that explained how radioactive fallout from nuclear test explosions was infiltrating the water and food supply. "That radioactive elements created by us are found in nature is an astounding event in the history of the earth and of the human race," Schweitzer wrote. "To fail to consider its importance and its consequences would be a folly for which humanity would have to pay a terrible price."[31] Published in the *Saturday Review,* this statement ignited a fierce debate over nuclear testing in the United States, where stories about milk tainted with the radioactive isotope Strontium-90 had been cropping up in the news for the past year. That summer the crusading editor of the *Review,* Norman Cousins, and two prominent figures in the American Friends Service Committee, Lawrence Scott and Clarence Pickett, summoned various civic leaders to discuss the issue, and from this gathering emerged the National Committee for a Sane Nuclear Policy.

The new organization, nicknamed SANE, met again that fall and published a full-page ad in the *New York Times,* asking readers to press President Eisenhower for an international test ban, to be enforced by the United Nations, and new powers for the U.N. to monitor all missiles and satellites worldwide and to pool all world science for the purpose of space exploration. The public response was overwhelming, and what began as a small group of intellectual elites broadened into a mass movement with 25,000 members in about 130 chapters nationwide. Ryan was already affiliated with the United World Federalists (UWF) and the American Friends Service Committee, and he threw in with the new group as well, participating in rallies at Madison Square Garden and the Manhattan Center on Thirty-fourth Street, and in smaller public meetings convened to raise awareness of the issue.

Cousins liked Ryan a great deal, finding him not only passionate but also smart, informed, and pragmatic. "He had obviously done the proper homework on these issues," Cousins recalled, though their discussions focused less on the science and more on political strategy—how to combat the Eisenhower administration's arguments for nuclear readiness, how to address the Atomic Energy Commission's promotion of nuclear power, how to counter the pronuclear lectures being delivered across the country by physicist Edward Teller, father of the H-bomb. Ryan, Cousins discovered, had a shrewd sense of how to put ideas across to the public. "What should a program be, how do we stage them to appeal to people, these were the operational questions. Here, he had a very searching knowledge of the people involved, and could tell you who could do what, and not much time was wasted."[32] Actors involved in political issues could be egotistical and uninformed, Cousins learned, but Ryan was just the opposite, more interested in results than in scoring points.

Though the public support for SANE was encouraging, both Ryan and Cousins knew from bitter experience just how easily pacifist movements could be derailed by assaults from the right and bad news from overseas. As members of the United World Federalists, they had seen the organization swell to a membership of fifty thousand in 1949 and then shrivel after the Korean conflict erupted in June 1950. Protecting its right flank, the UWF supported President Truman's decision to send US troops to the Korean peninsula, which put the group in the untenable position of seeking world peace even as it endorsed armed conflict. Still the attacks came: in 1951 the Senate Appropriations Committee voted to prohibit funding of groups that promoted world government, and by 1953 government employees were being asked if they had ever belonged to the UWF, regarded now as a communist front organization. By the end of the decade Ryan was serving as president of the Southern California chapter, though the fact that the nation's third largest metropolitan center sustained just one chapter only highlighted the uwf's diminishing relevance.*

Ryan had plenty of time for activism, because his picture offers were drying up. After *God's Little Acre* he decided to take some television work, appearing simultaneously in three different anthology series during the 1957–58 season. Both *Goodyear Theatre* and *Alcoa Theatre* were broadcast Monday nights on NBC and aspired to quality drama, though the half-hour playlets Ryan appeared in sometimes fell short of the mark. He also appeared on an episode of the western anthology *Zane Grey Theater,* with two more to follow in the 1958–59 season. But no movie star had ever forged a TV career appearing in drama anthologies. Many of Ryan's young costars in *God's Little Acre* would become household names on TV over the next decade, but all in continuing series that identified them with single characters: Vic Morrow as a foot soldier on *Combat!,* Tina Louise as the starlet on *Gilligan's Island,* Michael Landon as the junior brother on *Bonanza,* Jack Lord as a detective on *Hawaii Five-O.*

A more enticing TV project came up in summer 1958 when Ryan landed the title role in a *Playhouse 90* adaptation of *The Great Gatsby.* Ryan had always cherished the book. "I was a child of the 1920s—a dream world," he recalled. "Life was a ball: two Cadillacs, the trip to Hawaii, lots of fun, no problems—and everyone was going to make a million. That's why Scott Fitzgerald is the best; he got it down the way we lived it."[33] His long history of playing strong, confident men with secret vulnerabilities made him a natural for Jay Gatsby, the wealthy bootlegger pining for his lost love.

Unfortunately, the broadcast would fail to capture the novel's mystery and only emphasized Ryan's advancing age. Fitzgerald describes Gatsby as being about thirty-two years old; Ryan was visibly forty-eight. Rod Taylor, as the story's narrator, Nick Carraway, and Jeanne Crain, as Gatsby's coveted Daisy Buchanan, were much closer to their characters' ages. Ryan shone in the scenes where Gatsby, having contrived a meeting with Daisy at his palatial home in West Egg, frets and fusses prior to her arrival, then relaxes into himself when they finally meet. As an adaptation of Fitzgerald, the script was functional but

---

*For a biting history of the UWF, see John A. Yoder's "The United World Federalists: Liberals for Law and Order" in *Peace Movements in America* (New York: Schocken Books, 1973), 95–115.

uninspired, and the broadcast, recorded and edited on the new technology of magnetic videotape, suffered from Franklin Schaffner's clunky direction.

The challenge of adapting classic literature to the movies hit home even harder in the weeks after the broadcast, when Ryan reported for work on a screen adaptation of Nathanael West's corrosive 1933 novel *Miss Lonelyhearts*. Fired from MGM, Dore Schary had gone back East to produce a play he had written about Franklin Roosevelt, *Sunrise at Campobello,* which became a Broadway hit; while in New York he had seen a stage version of *Miss Lonelyhearts* and bought the rights, then tossed out Howard Teichmann's script and wrote his own version of West's story. Financed by United Artists for a modest $750,000 (about the same as *God's Little Acre*), the project heralded Schary's triumphant return to Hollywood as an independent producer, and he filled the cast with old friends: Montgomery Clift as the tormented advice columnist, Ryan as his cynical editor, Myrna Loy as the editor's unloved and unhappy wife. Vincent Donehue, who had directed *Sunrise at Campobello,* was brought out West to make his screen directing debut and signaled his stage inclinations immediately by calling for two weeks of rehearsal prior to shooting.

Unfortunately, no amount of rehearsal could compensate for Schary's script, which suffered from a playwright's verbosity and a Jewish writer's indifference to a deeply Catholic work. West's protagonist, a newspaper writer assigned to his paper's lovelorn column, has become a connoisseur of human misery: a severely deformed girl who pines for a boyfriend, a woman who fears her eighth pregnancy will kill her, and a deaf girl who has been sexually assaulted are only a few of the anguished souls introducing themselves in the letters that cross his desk. Shrike, his jaundiced boss, has written a little prayer mocking his sense of having taken on the world's troubles: "Soul of Miss L, glorify me / Body of Miss L, nourish me / Blood of Miss L, intoxicate me / Tears of Miss L, wash me."[34] Schary updated the story to the '50s and got rid of all the Jesus talk; in place of the novel's dark ending, when Miss Lonelyhearts finally wins the crucifixion he's been seeking, he wrote a sunny-side-up conclusion in which the hero—renamed Adam in Old Testament fashion—lives happily ever after with his sweetheart, and even the rancid old Shrike learns to be a little nicer to his woman.

"The picture was a misfire—a compromise," Ryan would later say. "It would have been much more interesting, and equally commercial, if they had made it really like the book."[35] He admired Nathanael West and must have related to the novel's eerie mingling of Catholic mysticism and grotesque black humor; as a lapsed Catholic, Ryan was drawn more to the Passion than the Resurrection. "He only went to church once a year; he'd go on Good Friday," remembered Lisa Ryan. "I went with him a couple of times. Talk about the most depressing service you could go to!"[36]

Montgomery Clift, doing the picture for a mere $25,000 as a favor to Schary, thought the script was horrendous. It was full of overripe dialogue, and Ryan had more than his share, his arch delivery only emphasizing its stiffness: "Love and kindness. Man is good. Well listen, Little Boy Blue. You'd better take a bath and wash off the eau de cologne—it stinks." The hero's Christ complex was watered down to something more revealing of Dore Schary, that tireless supporter of causes and charities: "Is it a sin to feel?" asks Adam. "Is do-gooder a dirty name? Why should it be?" Clift thought the whole thing read like an Andy Hardy movie.[37]

Perpetually drunk and whacked out on pills, Clift struggled to get through the picture. "He would start to cry in the middle of scenes and they'd have to stop the film," recalled Cheyney Ryan, who visited the set. "One time he literally lay down and got into a fetal position in the middle of a scene and started crying and rolling around, and everyone's sitting around waiting for this to end."[38] Some of the crew and minor players began to get fed up with Clift's behavior, and the situation came to a head during a barroom scene in which Adam punches a colleague at the paper. The punch was choreographed as a right cross, but in the take Clift twisted and around and clocked actor Mike Kellin with his left. Kellin cursed him out and Clift was taken away, after which Robert Ryan donned Clift's shirt and jacket and stood in for a close-up of the punch that was inserted to rescue the botched take. "I've always wanted to work with you," Ryan told Loy during the production, "and now that I am, I hardly see you. You're too busy taking care of Monty."[39]

Lonelyhearts, as Schary had titled the picture, was Ryan's first screen work in nine months. He had quit smoking and put on weight. A vague sheen of perspiration—the old flop sweat—clung to him as he tried to put across the turgid dialogue. When the picture was released at the end of the year, critics were merciless. "The play had at least tried to capture some of the book's agony, but in the film everything is munched down into pablum," wrote Stanley Kauffmann in the *New Republic.*[40] In *Esquire,* Dwight Macdonald published a feature story on Schary's return to Hollywood, labeling *Lonelyhearts* "the apotheosis of the adult soap opera" and observing, "Robert Ryan, a self-conscious and wooden actor who depends for his effectiveness on a sinister cast of countenance, plays Shrike like a Western bad man coached by Noel Coward, nor is he more successful than Clift in making contact with his opposite number, Myrna Loy, who plays Mrs. Shrike in a world-weary manner more suitable to the Oriental vamps she used to do in the Twenties."[41] Macdonald's piece ended with Schary admitting that he and his wife had felt like outsiders in Hollywood; he would produce only two more pictures before his movie career petered out five years later.

Ryan wound up as the highest paid performer in *Lonelyhearts,* taking home $75,000. But the job must have put him in an awkward position with his old friend Pat O'Brien, who had played Shrike in the Broadway production but been passed over by Schary for the screen role. Unloaded from RKO in 1949, O'Brien had fallen on hard times in LA, scratching around for B movies and TV guest shots and wondering why every door in town seemed to be shutting on him. In his 1964 autobiography he would write of being blackballed by liberal studio executives who considered him part of the anticommunist right. Schary had a reputation for getting even with red-baiters—John Wayne liked to say that the only blacklist in Hollywood was the one Schary ran at MGM—and O'Brien would recall Spencer Tracy threatening to quit MGM's *The People vs. O'Hara* unless Schary gave O'Brien a role. "I was against communists, I was against the methods and the procedures by which they and fellow travelers had, it was reported, infiltrated the studios," wrote O'Brien. "But I hadn't made a full-time crusade of it."[42] Ironically, Joseph Losey would remember O'Brien, whom he directed in *The Boy with Green Hair,* as one of the few people who came to his aid when he was blacklisted.

"SOME ACTORS think they're businessmen," Ryan told *Variety* earlier that year, "but few of them are. Most of them are going through the motions of playing executives. I'd rather let somebody else take care of the production details. If you are your own producer, you might start making concessions. You can't do a good acting job and be a producer at the same time." Most actors didn't know how to judge a script, he observed, and as producers, "they all wind up making westerns."[43]

He preferred the kind of profit-participation deals he had cut with Security Pictures. In his words they constituted "income roulette," and the promotional tours were grueling: two or three weeks, city after city, each day beginning with press interviews at breakfast and continuing on to nightfall or even midnight screenings. Yet as Ryan explained to one reporter, "The odds are generally in your favor if you get enough of these deals and one comes through to tip the scales."[44] *God's Little Acre* had been that picture—according to Phil Yordan, Ryan pocketed a quarter million dollars for it. When Yordan and Sid Harmon offered Ryan another participation deal for their last United Artists release, he readily accepted.

Of course, it was a western, adapted from a novel by Lee Wells called *Day of the Outlaw*. Director André De Toth had directed six westerns with Randolph Scott, making the occasional detour into crime (*Pitfall*) or horror (the 3-D release *House of Wax*). Harmon and Yordan brought back Tina Louise to play Ryan's love interest and recruited another cast of talented character actors: William Schallert, Nememiah Persoff, and Elisha Cook Jr. Yet *Men in War* and *God's Little Acre* had been happy experiences; *Day of the Outlaw* turned into a nightmare.

Yordan's script was intriguing, a chamber drama set in a snowy western outpost, with the balance of power shifting radically at different points. Rancher Blaise Starrett (Ryan) rides into Bitter, a frontier town in the Wyoming Territory, itching to kill a local farmer who has married Starrett's true love (Louise). But just as this conflict comes to a head, the town is invaded by a renegade army officer (the immense, gravel-voiced folksinger Burl Ives) and his band of violent derelicts. Hunted by a cavalry outfit, they take over the town and threaten to rape the four women. Starrett, once a gunslinger, is forced back into his old role as the town's protector, though this time he succeeds through cunning: with the cavalry nearing the town, he persuades the outlaws to follow him to safety on a secret path through the snowy mountains, and leads them into the face of a deadly blizzard.

De Toth loved the idea of the fearsome gang "terrorizing a small Western village, and then, by a quirk of nature, becoming equally the prisoners of the white silence in the middle of nowhere." Harmon and Yordan, he would later argue, "didn't understand where I was heading—a sphere I had been exploring for some time: is it worse being the jailer, instead of the prisoner?" The producers wanted him to shoot in color, on a soundstage; De Toth insisted on black and white, to make the blizzard sequences as stark as possible, and persuaded them to erect an exterior set of half a dozen building fronts on Dutchman Flat, located southwest of Bend, Oregon, in full view of the Cascade Range. He wanted the buildings up by the fall, so that they would be properly weathered and snow-encrusted when shooting commenced in mid-November. Ryan backed De Toth on this point, and the set construction began. "He was a gentleman, a sincere human being—and what an actor," remembered De Toth. "He was with me all the way. Without him, I would've been laid out in the snow and counted out quickly."[45]

The relationship between Harmon, Yordan, and De Toth deteriorated further when the director discovered that the art director had ignored his compass coordinates for the set and built it facing in the wrong direction, which ruined his plans for taking advantage of available light and keeping the snow in the background pristine and untouched. The producers, who had spent most of their UA money on the last two pictures and budgeted this one for a measly $400,000, considered simply firing De Toth, but Ryan stuck by him and the production went forward. "[Ryan] was a loyal man, which is very uncommon in Hollywood," Yordan said, "in fact it's very rare in the business world."[46] The set was rebuilt just before the cast and crew arrived, and De Toth shot a few scenes there before taking off for Mount Bachelor, twenty-two miles west, to shoot the blizzard sequences.

The work was punishing, as Ryan, Ives, and the actors playing his henchmen rode on horseback through three-foot snowdrifts. After a few days Ryan was diagnosed with pneumonia; a week was lost before he was well enough to return to work. Snowstorms pushed the production even further behind schedule, and according to Yordan, the location shoot was finally shut down and the cast and crew brought back to Hollywood for interior scenes that would be needed to patch up the story.

Yordan was proud of his script and bitterly disappointed with how the picture turned out: "It could have been a real winner," he argued.[47] The picture's reputation would grow steadily in the decades ahead, as people began to appreciate its novel plot structure and brutal naturalism. But when *Day of the Outlaw* opened in July 1959, it bored critics and tanked at the box office, bringing Ryan's relationship with Security Pictures to an ignominious close. The next time he worked with Phil Yordan and Sid Harmon, he would need them more than they needed him.

eleven

Beautiful Creatures

Andy Harmon often came over to the Ryans' house on Kling Street to play with Tim. He liked the atmosphere there, so cool and quiet compared to his own home. "I thought the Ryans were the height of elegance," he recalled. "It certainly seemed to me like they never argued, whereas we always argued." The Ryans had dinner every night at 6:30; Jessica said a Quaker grace, and they would talk about politics or current events at the table. But Jessica could be distant, and at times the children were admonished to be quiet around her. "There would be this mysterious thing where one of [the parents] would be in bed for a long time in the mornings, which I didn't understand, 'cause my dad was literally out of bed and in his tie and jacket at 7:30 in the morning."[1] Like any child, Andy could only puzzle out what was going on in the grown-up world, but Bob and Jessica Ryan seemed even more private than most parents.

As the decade wore on, Jessica grew increasingly troubled, until she suffered a breakdown sometime in 1958. "I don't think she was hospitalized," said Cheyney Ryan. "But you certainly had the sense that there was something wrong with her. I remember this in part because we were all supposed to go to Palm Springs and we didn't do that, and then there was some plan to take a cruise somewhere, we didn't do that. So things were being canceled because of this, and she went into psychoanalysis." Jessica had long been an avid student of Jungian psychology, and she became a patient of therapist Max Zeller, a founder of the C. G. Jung Institute of Los Angeles. "What she said about it afterwards was that . . . she didn't want to be just a regular housewife, and people were telling her that she should be."[2]

Years later, in the introduction to a scholarly manuscript, Jessica would identify herself as "a middle-aged American woman, wife, and mother of three children, wondering if I can find a better answer than I have yet had, to why I am the way I am, to why I have had an uneasy life with men and them with me." All around her she saw women who "feel that they were promised something, even if they have no notion of what, or by whom, or when or why; the promise unfulfilled, they continue to resent and rage, while they play the roles they feel have been assigned to them. But underneath, it is as if they suffer a feeling of some great disappointment."[3]

And so she withdrew—from the Oakwood School, from her friends, and, to some extent, from her children. She stopped attending school functions and no longer accompanied her husband to political or charity events, not to mention movie promotions or Hollywood parties. She shut herself up in the house and buried herself in books, searching for an intellectual answer to a problem that, as some of her children would later suppose, might have been addressed more effectively with less booze, more exercise, and a mild antidepressant. She wrote incessantly, filling up page after page in longhand. (Despite her feelings of having been squashed professionally, her career wasn't going badly; her novel *City of Angels* had been published in France, and she had recently placed a children's mystery, *The Malibu Monster,* with Bobbs-Merrill.) Jessica always had been the center of the family, and now her husband and children rallied around her. "There was this kind of thing happened in the family, that Mom was fragile," said Cheyney. "When you have someone like that, the whole family thinks it's their role to prop her up."[4]

The Ryans drew a cloak of privacy over Jessica's condition. Cheyney would wonder if his parents were ever physically intimate again after his mother's breakdown, but there was no doubt of their mutual love and respect. "I never remember their being sarcastic with each other," he marveled. "I never remember their raising their voices with each other. I never remember them ever acting in any way that suggested that they weren't taking each other's views about whatever the issue was with complete seriousness."[5] Ryan may not have understood how women felt in a world dominated by men, or what Jessica experienced as the wife of a movie star, or how his occasional, guilty infidelities had damaged their relationship. But he valued his family, and now his family was in trouble. In any case, he was so reclusive himself that Jessica's growing agoraphobia seldom presented much of a practical issue.

Regardless of what transpired at home, Ryan was still the breadwinner, so in February 1959 he flew off to New York City to begin shooting a crime thriller with Harry Belafonte called *Odds against Tomorrow.* At that point Belafonte was one of the biggest recording stars in the world: in the new age of the long-playing record, he had shot to the top of the *Billboard* album chart with a self-titled LP in early 1956 and four months later followed it with *Calypso,* which spent a staggering thirty-one weeks at number one and another year on the chart after that. He had started out in show business as an actor in New York, but he was unhappy with the screen roles that had come his way and decided to start his own production company, HarBel, to release through United Artists. Adapted from a novel by William P. McGivern, *Odds against Tomorrow* combined a heist plot with tense racial drama, as Johnny Ingram, a Harlem musician in debt to gamblers, agrees to stage a daring bank stickup with Earl Slater, a bigoted white Oklahoman. Belafonte hired Robert Wise to direct, and they agreed that the man to play Slater was Robert Ryan.

Ryan didn't agree at first—when they had sent him the script the previous fall he passed, explaining that he didn't want to go down that road again. "A great many people realize that the characters they see on the screen are fictional or created but there is a substantial group that does not make that distinction," he later wrote in a self-exculpatory piece for *Ebony,* reminiscent of the things he had published when *Crossfire* was released twelve years earlier. "I changed my mind about playing Slater after re-reading the script and appreciating its excellent qualities. . . . *Odds against Tomorrow* says something . . . of significance and says it well, dramatically, without preaching. The drama strongly suggests that bigotry is based on fear and envy and that the most important thing that keeps a bigot operating is the feeling that he is better than another man."[6]

He also liked the script's evenhandedness: unlike the quietly suffering role models Sidney Poitier often played, Belafonte's character was embittered by racism and ultimately pulled down to Slater's level. And here was a chance to work again with Bob Wise, who had done a spectacular job directing *The Set-Up* and since moved on to such highly regarded dramas as *The Day the Earth Stood Still* (1951), *Executive Suite* (1954), and *I Want to Live!* (1958).

Belafonte had admired Ryan's work for years, and their paths had crossed during the Stevenson campaign in 1956, but they had never met properly before shooting the picture. "What really surprised me was that, in many of the films that he did, he had always played a heavy villain," Belafonte recalled, "and to meet the man in person, to find out that his whole persona, and his way of life, and his thinking and his philosophy, was so the opposite. . . . The contrast was so glaringly evident." Earl Slater would complete Ryan's big trinity of intolerance, along with Monty in *Crossfire* and Reno Smith in *Bad Day at Black Rock*—"I'm either killing a Jew, a Jap, or a Negro," he would lament to one reporter."[7]

Yet Belafonte came to realize that Ryan's acceptance of these roles, and the penetrating intelligence and empathy he brought to them, was a kind of activism in itself. "I think he took them because he really believed that he was making a contribution to people's overall sense of what it was to be a minority or to be discriminated against."[8] Ryan, in turn, was impressed by Belafonte's humanity and political commitment; he would maintain an affectionate friendship with the younger man for the rest of his life.

Ten years had passed since Ryan and Wise had collaborated on *The Set-Up;* in the interim, that postwar cycle of shadowy, morally conflicted crime dramas had petered out at the box office, even as French critics dubbed it *film noir* and, breaking into the movie business themselves, began to draw on its realism and immediacy. Ryan had appeared in numerous pictures now regarded as part of the noir canon—not only *Crossfire* and *The Set-Up* but also *Act of Violence, The Woman on Pier 13, On Dangerous Ground, The Racket,* and *Beware, My Lovely.* Wise would consciously revisit the genre with *Odds against Tomorrow;* along with Ryan, the cast included such noir veterans as slimy Ed Begley (*On Dangerous Ground*) and saucy Gloria Grahame (*Crossfire*). For the climactic bank robbery sequence, shot on location in the small town of Hudson, New York, Wise would recycle a prominent visual motif from *The Set-Up,* a street scene with a public clock marking the time.

Belafonte first gave the book to John Oliver Killens, a talented black novelist and a cofounder of the Harlem Writers Guild. But Killens had never written a screenplay; when his effort proved unsatisfactory, Belafonte turned to veteran screenwriter Abraham Polonsky (*Body and Soul, Force of Evil*), who had been blacklisted since the second HUAC investigation in 1951. Killens gladly agreed to front for Polonsky, and Belafonte approached both Wise and Ryan to explain what was going on. Ryan "threw his lot in with us and said, absolutely, he'd take a stand, and he thanked me for informing him that it was Abe Polonsky. He and Abe became very good friends after that."[9] The script was expertly structured, and Polonsky was an old hand at the cynical poetry

Ryan with Harry Belafonte on the set of *Odds against Tomorrow* (1959). The younger man awakened his interest in the civil rights movement and would introduce him to Martin Luther King Jr. *Franklin Jarlett Collection*

Ryan initially turned down the role of Earl Slater, the bigoted criminal in *Odds against Tomorrow* (1959). "A great many people realize that the characters they see on the screen are fictional or created," he wrote in *Ebony*, "but there is a substantial group that does not make that distinction." *Franklin Jarlett Collection*

of film noir. When Ingram learns about the bank job from seedy Dave Burke (Begley), the disgraced cop masterminding the operation, his first response is, "I did all my dreaming on my mama's knee."

"You didn't say nothin' about the third man bein' a nigger!" Slater complains to Burke as the two men case the bank from a hotel room across the street, and Wise accents this declaration of theme with one of the oldest noir tricks in the book, using venetian blinds to cast horizontal stripes across Ryan's face. Ryan always felt for the soft spot in his most despicable characters, and he would note how Slater was "peculiarly provoked by the kind of Negro he finds himself involved with. It just so happens that this young Negro is better looking, better dressed, more intelligent; is, in fact, everything that Slater would like to be but isn't. . . . Slater, therefore, is a many-sided character and this made the problem of projection a lot more difficult."[10] Initially, it also had discouraged him from taking the role; as with Monty and Reno Smith, there was the danger of making this heel a little too sympathetic.

McGivern's novel ended with Slater and Ingram learning to trust one another, but that denouement was too reminiscent of Stanley Kramer's recent hit *The Defiant Ones,* another tale of a black man and a white man yoked together, so Belafonte and Polonsky agreed on something darker. The carefully planned robbery falls apart after Slater, unwilling to leave Ingram with the keys to the getaway car, gives them to Burke, who is shot down by police outside the bank. Slater and Ingram fire angrily on each other even as they flee the cops, and Ingram chases Slater across the giant tanks of a nearby oil refinery. An errant bullet ignites one of the tanks, and—shades of James Cagney in *White Heat*—the antagonists are blown to kingdom come; when their bodies are carted off by the police, the black man and the white man are indistinguishable. The finishing touch would be an edgy symphonic score by John Lewis of the Modern Jazz Quartet.

The shoot was mostly uneventful, though actress Shelley Winters, who played Slater's blowsy girlfriend, was coming unglued over her rocky marriage to actor Tony Franciosa. "My God, we had to nurse her through that sometimes, and Bob was a big help on that," said Wise. "Bob was very, very patient with her and worked with her and helped her and didn't get out of sorts, which some actors might have."[11] For his trouble, Ryan would turn up in one of the kiss-and-tell memoirs Winters published in the 1980s, which detailed her affairs with Errol Flynn, William Holden, Sterling Hayden, Burt

Lancaster, and Sean Connery. According to Winters, she and Ryan had known each other "not-so-casually" after being introduced by Marilyn Monroe on the set of *Clash by Night* back in 1951. Reunited for *Odds against Tomorrow,* she wrote, they spent a good deal of time together between takes, talking about "the theater, organic farming, where Hollywood was going in this age of television, anything but what we were really thinking about."[12]

Ryan had more on his mind than Winters might have imagined: he and Jessica had decided to sell the ranch house in North Hollywood and move out of the San Fernando Valley, back to the movie colony in Los Angeles. Numerous factors influenced their decision: Only a block south of Kling Street, construction had begun for the Ventura Freeway, which the Ryans were certain would spoil the quiet little neighborhood. Jessica wanted some physical distance from the Oakwood School, and Ryan hoped a big house might raise his professional profile. After he returned from New York, they settled on a beautiful Georgian Colonial residence in Holmby Hills, just east of the UCLA campus.

The family moved that summer, and the children all started at public schools in the fall, Tim and Cheyney at Emerson in West Los Angeles and Lisa at Warner Avenue Elementary in Holmby Hills. They couldn't understand why they were being uprooted and moved into this fancy new home, though Cheyney would later attribute the decision to his mother's unhappiness: "The kind of thing my parents would do is move when there was a problem."[13] His remark echoed Ryan's recollection of his own parents pulling up stakes after his brother, Jack, died back in 1917: "We had to move and we did."[14]

"WHEN WE MOVED TO HOLMBY HILLS, it was like living in a fortress," said Lisa Ryan.[15] The old neighborhood in North Hollywood was built on a street grid, but Holmby Hills discouraged outsiders with its maze of hilly, winding streets, and all the homes were protected by high walls. The one at 301 N. Carolwood Drive had been built in 1937 for Joan Bennett, Ryan's costar in *The Woman on the Beach,* by noted architect Wallace Neff, an originator of the California style. Walt Disney lived nearby. The house was luxurious by the Ryans' standards, backed up by a large patio that gave way to a lawn and then a swimming pool with beach houses on either side. For the first time each of the boys had his own room, but the streets were too steep for bicycle riding and the grounds too landscaped for playing catch. "If you missed the ball, you'd have to spend twenty minutes trying to find it in some thicket or something," Cheyney Ryan recalled.[16] In North Hollywood they could walk a few blocks to the drugstore, but here they had to get in the car and drive out the security gate that cordoned them off from the rest of the world.

The move baffled many of the Ryans' friends, who had never considered them materialistic despite their comfortable lifestyle. Lamont Johnson thought he understood: "There was a part of [Ryan] that was sort of lace-curtain Irish, that loved not only keeping up with the Joneses but beating the shit out of them."[17] Interviewed at length by columnist Sidney Skolsky, Ryan presented the move as a simple matter of needing more space. "When the children were babies, it was fine; we were all close together, and we had a nice yard and a wonderful life there; but my children are getting quite large now, and we found that we were all bumping into each other. Also, there didn't seem to be room enough for anything, and I had about exhausted the expansion possibilities of the house we had, having built on it six times already." The new house, he pointed out, had "a huge playroom downstairs where the kids can go down and turn on the TV full blast, which is the only way they seem to enjoy it. None of us can hear it upstairs. That I think is the outstanding feature."[18]

Saddled now with a hefty new mortgage, Ryan took off in August for Petersburg, Alaska, to begin location shooting for *Ice Palace,* his very first picture for Warner Bros. and the first in three years that he had made for his straight salary of $125,000. A big-budget melodrama spanning almost fifty years, *Ice Palace* was adapted from a fat best seller by Edna Ferber, author of *Giant;* when Ryan got a look at the Mendenhall Glacier, which figured in the story, he joked that the picture should be retitled "Giant-on-the-Rocks."[19] He and Richard Burton starred as young entrepreneurs who build a fishing and canning empire together but then grow apart, Burton's character lusting for wealth and Ryan's becoming a political crusader for Alaskan statehood and environmental protection; of course, they both love the same woman.

The picture was junk, but at least it presented Ryan as a sympathetic figure. "I think it's good for business to be liked by the audience every few years," he told Skolsky. "This particular part involved portraying what you might call a practical saint, and this is a very unusual experience for me."[20] The role also required him to age forty-seven years over the course of the story. "It took me two hours to make up for the twenty-eight-year-old," he would crack, "and about fifteen minutes for the man of seventy-five."[21] Three weeks later

Ryan was back in Los Angeles shooting interiors for the picture, and work continued through December (the final cut would clock in at nearly two-and-a-half hours).

His free time during this period was largely consumed by politics; he and late-night comedian Steve Allen were trying to launch a new chapter of the National Committee for a Sane Nuclear Policy, to be called Hollywood for SANE. The inaugural event, a buffet dinner at the Beverly Hills Hotel on September 26, drew about two hundred industry professionals, a healthy turnout by Hollywood standards, and the cochairs announced a drive to raise $50,000 from the entertainment community by the end of the year. Three weeks later, on Saturday, October 17, the Ryans hosted a second meeting at their new home on Carolwood Drive, with Norman Cousins as the guest of honor. "An executive present at both meetings said that film writers were the most prominent industry figures at the initial dinner," reported the *New York Times*. "At Mr. Ryan's house, many more actors and directors attended."[22]

This was significant: writers could hide behind fronts, but the large contingent of actors—Rod Steiger, David Niven, James Whitmore, Mercedes McCambridge, Keenan Wynn—suggested that for Hollywood liberals the frost was beginning to thaw. Three months later, director Otto Preminger would announce that Dalton Trumbo, one of the Hollywood Ten, was the screenwriter of his forthcoming United Artists release *Exodus*, and even before that picture came out, Kirk Douglas credited Trumbo on-screen as the author of *Spartacus*. After twelve years the blacklist was unraveling. "People in Hollywood are finally ready to speak out for something besides mother love," Ryan declared after the second Hollywood for SANE gathering.[23] Cousins seemed to share his optimism: "The long silence is over," he observed. "Hollywood is again putting itself on the line for public issues."[24]

Ryan's continuing commitment to *Ice Palace* prevented him from doing a publicity tour for *Odds against Tomorrow,* which opened in November, but whenever he got time away from the set, he sat down with press people to talk about the picture and the problem of race prejudice in America. Doing the picture, he wrote in *Ebony,* had forced him to reexamine his own attitudes and increase his own commitment to ending bigotry. Unfortunately, even as the magazine was hitting newsstands, Ryan committed a cringe-worthy racial gaffe on network TV. After completing his day's work on *Ice Palace,* he rushed over to the NBC studios, the fake gray still in his hair, to appear on a prime-time game show called *It Could Be You,* a hidden camera catching him out in the hall as he got his shoes shined. As part of the show, Ryan surprised the owner of the shoeshine stand, O. C. Jones, by bringing him in front of the studio audience to accept a $200 tip. Ryan towered over Jones, and as he was exiting, he impulsively rubbed the man's head as if he were a dog.

One benefit of the Ryans' new house in Holmby Hills was its proximity to UCLA, where Ryan had helped found a fledgling experimental theater company earlier that year as part of the extension program. Along with Sidney Harmon and theatrical producer Eddie Cook, Ryan proposed the idea to Abbott Kaplan, head of the UCLA Extension, who allowed them to use the university's conference center at Lake Arrowhead for a brainstorming session. Lee Strasberg addressed this gathering of about eighty people, and a subsequent meeting on campus drew such big names as Paul Newman, Joanne Woodward, Anthony Quinn, and Eva Marie Saint. That summer the newly christened Professional Theatre Group of the UCLA Extension presented three staged readings—Dylan Thomas's *Under Milkwood,* Bertolt Brecht's *Mother Courage,* and Nikos Kazantzakis's *Sodom and Gomorrah*—that nearly sold out their six-day runs. Emboldened by this response, Kaplan hired John Houseman as artistic director, and for the first full production, in January 1960, Houseman asked Ryan to play Thomas Beckett, the martyred Archbishop of Canterbury, in T. S. Eliot's *Murder in the Cathedral.*

Remembering the production in one of his memoirs, Houseman was typically rigorous in his assessment of Ryan. "Though he had done some work on his voice since *Coriolanus,* it remained flat and unresonant," Houseman wrote, "but, as in *Coriolanus,* his vocal weakness was offset by his physical presence, his intelligence and his personal experience . . . of the emotional problems of this profoundly Catholic play."[25]

As it opens, Beckett is returning to England in 1170 after seven years in exile, having offended King Henry II by proclaiming his primary allegiance to the Pope; the faithful celebrate the archbishop's return, but the king dispatches four knights to assassinate him. Beckett is visited by a succession of tempters, each of whom offers him some compromise that will save his life, but he rejects them all and waits in the peace of God for the end to come. After the knights arrive and hack him to death, each offers his justification to the crowd, and the last of them argues with some force that Beckett was no martyr at all but "a monster of egotism."[26] Eliot's aim, then, was not simply to celebrate Beckett's spiritual devotion but to note how even the most perfect devotion can be corrupted by the sin of pride.

Murder in the Cathedral opened on January 18 at UCLA's Schoenberg Hall, a 526-seat classical music venue whose hydraulic orchestra pit enabled Houseman to create various levels in the action as Beckett was addressed by the tempters and a chorus of the faithful. Writing in the *Los Angeles Times,* Philip Scheuer praised the production but faulted the casting of Ryan, who "appears to have bent over backward to emphasize the turn-the-other-cheek side of this dedicated priest."[27] The review pinpointed what a stretch this passive, contemplative character was for Ryan, who had played so many angry, dynamic men. In the Christmas sermon that bisects the play, Beckett explains: "A martyrdom is always the design of God, for His love of men, to warn them and to lead them, to bring them back to his ways. It is never the design of man; for the true martyr is he who has become the instrument of God, who has lost his will in the will of God, and who no longer desires anything for himself, not even the glory of being a martyr."[28]

The two-week run was well attended, and the Theatre Group would continue on the campus for eight seasons, staging forty-one productions before it moved to the Mark Taper Forum in 1966. Houseman's insistence on casting big names from movies and television led to some friction between the company and the university's theater department, but the Theatre Group became a source of great cultural excitement in Los Angeles. "Going to the plays had the feeling of attending a private party," wrote critic Cecil Smith in 1981. "You ran into friends there, people of like interests. Intermissions were alive with spirited discussions."[29] Ryan's founding role in all this would go largely overlooked, and he would never get another chance to perform with the group.

After the play closed, Ryan hosted *A Call from . . . ,** a star-studded, hour-long TV special, produced by his friend Marsha Hunt, about the United Nations' yearlong campaign to address the humanitarian crisis of some fifteen million refugees worldwide. Over the past decade Ryan had developed a reputation in Hollywood as someone who never said no to a good cause—the ACLU, the NAACP, the United World Federalists, the American Friends Ser-

---

*The special was restored in 2009 as *A Call from the Stars.*

vice Committee, and so on. "Everyone would like to do things for others," he told one reporter. "Let's just say that between acting assignments, I have time to do them."[30]

He had an especially hard time turning down Hunt, a probing and articulate woman who had been blacklisted after her name appeared in *Red Channels*. Her professional hardship hardly had dented her social commitment; she may have been the only liberal in Hollywood capable of exhausting Ryan. At one point she called asking him to appear on a program and heard a sigh on the other end of the line. "Marsha, you know I'm with you, and all of the things that we're working toward," Ryan replied. "I think maybe it is someone else's turn for a while." Hunt would chuckle at the memory: "He put it so kindly and so gently, but he was perfectly right."[31]

Always on the lookout for literate scripts, Ryan agreed to fly to New York in mid-March to appear in a TV adaptation of Ernest Hemingway's "The Snows of Kilimanjaro" for CBS. Sponsored by General Motors, *Buick-Electra Playhouse* was a series of four 90-minute Hemingway specials scheduled throughout the 1959–60 season, the first two of which—an adaptation of "The Killers" starring boxer Ingemar Johansson and a production of *The Fifth Column*, Hemingway's only play, with Richard Burton and Maximilian Schell—had aired the previous fall. *The Snows of Kilimanjaro,* scheduled for broadcast on the evening of Friday, March 25, was to be shot and edited on videotape by thirty-year-old John Frankenheimer, one of the most talented and innovative of the young directors then coming up through TV. The strong supporting cast included Mary Astor, James Gregory, Brock Peters, and Liliane Montevecchi. But Ryan would be the lynchpin: as Harry Walters, the washed-up writer dying of gangrene on safari in Africa, he appeared in almost every scene, with flashback sequences that followed him to Paris and New York.

Hemingway famously had disliked the 1952 movie version starring Gregory Peck, which replaced the protagonist's death and spiritual deliverance with a happy ending in which a rescue plane arrives with penicillin just in the nick of time. The TV version promised to be much better: writer A. E. Hotchner had done several Hemingway adaptations, and he made liberal use of Harry's haunting interior narration, turning it into dialogue or voice-over. He had certainly nailed the character, whose regrets eat away at him even worse than the gangrene. Once a promising artist, Harry has squandered his talent doing mediocre work he thinks will sell, something Ryan might have identified with after *Ice Palace*. Given the actor's envy of Peck, he must have relished the opportunity to give a better performance in the same role.

But when Ryan arrived in New York a week before the broadcast, Frankenheimer came to him with bad news: someone at CBS had learned that taping the program would constitute a copyright infringement on the Fox release, so the teleplay would have to be performed live. Ryan, who had never done live TV, asked Frankenheimer what this would mean in terms of staging. "What it means is that you're gonna be in for the ride of your life," Frankenheimer replied.[32] He was still trying to figure out how on earth they would make the transitions from the jungle set, where Harry is tended by his wife and their African guides, to the flashbacks, which showed his life leading up to the fateful safari.

Brainstorming with art director Burr Schmidt, Frankenheimer came up with a novel solution: their elaborate jungle set would remain, but the bed on which Harry lay dying would be placed on a large turntable unseen by the viewer, and a camera would be mounted on the turntable as well, at the foot of the bed. Whenever Harry slipped into one of his reveries, the camera would zoom in tight on his face, grips would push the turntable counterclockwise into the flashback setting, the camera would zoom out again, and Ryan would simply climb out of bed and walk into the next scene. To make this elaborate floor plan more manageable, Schmidt painted some of the flashback settings on giant sheets of paper that could be drawn behind the action like a curtain, and his impressionistic imagery would heighten the sense of a fevered memory play, turning a problem into a creative advantage. Frankenheimer thought their scheme would work, but the fact that his star had never done live TV was worrisome, to say the least.

To execute this high-wire act, CBS moved the production to Los Angeles, where Frankenheimer could take advantage of the network's giant Television City complex. The day he began blocking the program, CBS executives brought in the legendary Warner Bros. director Michael Curtiz (*Captain Blood, The Adventures of Robin Hood, Yankee Doodle Dandy, Casablanca, Mildred Pierce*) to watch him work. Curtiz, whose career had declined in the '50s, was considering a move into TV, but this was hardly the best introduction.

"The madness of trying to block this thing, I mean, I cannot describe it to you," Frankenheimer told a seminar audience years later. "Cameras would come crashing through and just missing people . . . and booms coming and going through the paper, and we'd knock [the paper sets] down and put 'em up again.... We did kind of a stagger-through of this thing—you couldn't call it a run-through, because it was just insane."[33] At one point Frankenheimer glanced over to the control room and saw the elderly, well-dressed Curtiz with his collar open and sweat running down his face. The old man watched for an hour and then fled, telling Frankenheimer, "You are crazy! This whole business is crazy!"[34] He would never work in television.

The pressure of doing a live drama for network television was incredible; many actors vomited from nerves. As Frankenheimer would recall, the hour between dress rehearsal and airtime was the scariest: "You were sitting there, most of the time, with your own thoughts. And it was a very private time, because going on the air with one of these things—it really wound your watch, let's put it that way."[35] Ryan always had sought to challenge himself as an actor, but this time he had his work cut out for him: barely leaving the screen for ninety minutes, he would have to turn on a dime from the African scenes, where Harry is swept into delirium by his advancing illness, to flashbacks that took place years earlier, played in a variety of moods. Twenty years into his career, Ryan never had so much riding on a single performance, and at 5:30 PM,* when an assistant director counted down the seconds to air and then cued the action, the actor would draw on everything he had ever learned onstage or in front of a camera.

Not only did Ryan pull off the live broadcast, but he also delivered one of his best screen performances. The extreme close-ups of Harry in his sickbed, closing his eyes and slipping away into the past, showed Ryan's great subtlety of expression, every thought registering in his strong features as the bed slowly spun beneath him (a faint grinding could be heard at one point, but otherwise the turntable worked like a charm). The flashbacks, by contrast, took advantage of his physical agility: when Harry gets into a fistfight with a British soldier in Paris, Frankenheimer concocted an elaborate ground-level shot in which the triangle formed by a woman's legs frames a silhouette of the men beating each other, cast in shadow against a brick wall.

The shot would have been difficult even for a movie, and there were plenty more like it. Yet aside from a bit of fumbled dialogue in the first act, Ryan

---

*The program was performed live for the Eastern and Central time zones, and videotaped for broadcast later that evening in the Mountain and Pacific zones.

negotiated it all with ease, giving an assured, impressively rich interpretation of the Hemingway character. "For anybody to do something like this, it was fabulous," Frankenheimer said. "For him to do it, never having done live television, was unbelievable."[36] Then, at 7 PM, the performance was over, and few ever saw it again.*

RYAN LIKED TO TELL PEOPLE that when his agent phoned to offer him a part in *King of Kings,* a biblical epic being shot in Madrid, he turned to Jessica and said, "Here we go again—Judas."[37] But, in fact, his old friends Phil Yordan and Nicholas Ray, who were making the picture for producer Samuel Bronston, wanted him to play John the Baptist. The salary was $50,000, well below his usual fee, but his scenes would take only a week and then he could go home. From their perspective, attaching Ryan's name to *King of Kings* provided some much-needed credibility, given that the *New York Times* had just published a story about the picture's shaky financing.

The diminutive Bronston embodied the new breed of international film hustler: born in Bessarabia, then part of Russia, he had made a few pictures in Hollywood during the war but resurfaced more recently as a producer of historical spectaculars in Franco's Spain, where dirt-cheap labor and favorable banking policies allowed a producer to put a lot on-screen for very little money.** By this time Ray had peaked commercially with *Rebel without a Cause* (1955), which crystallized the emerging youth culture in America; his masterful *Bigger Than Life* (1956) and *Bitter Victory* (1957) both had underperformed at the box office, and a pair of out-and-out flops (*Wind across the Everglades, Party Girl*) had ended his career in Hollywood. He looked on this Spanish adventure as a chance to get his career back on track.

Attacking the project with his usual vigor, Ray immersed himself in the historical Jesus, fascinated by the political conflicts swirling around this so-called king of Judea. He hired Yordan to crank out a new screenplay presenting Jesus as a radical humanist, and Yordan hit on the plot gimmick of playing up Jesus' relationship to the criminal Barabbas, portrayed in his script as a violent rev-

---

The Snows of Kilimanjaro has never been released to home video, though it can be viewed by request at the New York or Los Angeles facilities of the Paley Center for Media.

**His first such effort, the flag-waving flop *John Paul Jones* (1959), was bankrolled by Pierre du Pont III, an heir to his family's fortune.

olutionary. Script in hand, Ray, Yordan, and Bronston managed to secure $5.5 million in financing from MGM, which hired Yordan to supervise production.

Ryan, having just played a "practical saint" in *Ice Palace* and a genuine saint in *Murder in the Cathedral,* now took a crack at John the Prophet, portrayed as a muscular evangelist in animal skins, a bushy wig, and a long beard. After Ryan arrived in Madrid, the company drove out to the countryside to shoot John's baptism of Jesus in the River Jordan. (Ryan would recall being chauffeured to the location in costume with costar Jeffrey Hunter, who played Jesus, and the two of them startling onlookers when they got out of their stalled car to give it a push.)[38] There were a few more scenes, shot on a local soundstage, where John is imprisoned by Herod in a lonely dungeon. When Jesus appears at the window of John's cell, reaching a hand through the bars to comfort him, John scrambles up the stone incline to the window and manages to clasp his hand. "For the first time in my life," reported film editor Renee Lichtig, "I saw technicians weeping when silent rushes were screened."[39]

Ryan was intrigued by the Spanish movie industry. Cinema was still the national entertainment there, and movie production was a more freewheeling affair than in Hollywood. Bronston burned through MGM's money at an astonishing rate; a story in *Family Weekly* described a Sermon on the Mount featuring seven thousand extras "costumed in hand-woven desert fabrics scoured from every corner of the Mediterranean world. . . . Camels from the Canary Islands mingled with uncounted horses and burros. The sequence is so vast it had to be planned like a military operation."[40] Originally budgeted at $5.5 million, the movie would top out at $8 million; talking to reporters upon its release, Ryan would hasten to point out that his $50,000 salary was for only a week's labor.

Back home from Madrid, Ryan looked forward to a blissful summer: Katharine Hepburn had asked him to costar with her in *Antony and Cleopatra* at the American Shakespeare Festival Theatre in Stratford, Connecticut, and the family was coming along for a three-month stay. The 1,500-seat Festival Theatre was located on a lovely stretch of land that ended at the Housatonic River, and the Ryans had a house overlooking the water, only a hundred yards from the theater. Hepburn had been heavily involved with the festival from its inception, performing in three productions there since the theater opened in 1955. She adored Ryan personally and thought him a marvelous talent, and once they arrived she immediately befriended his family, bonding

Cheyney, Jessica, Tim, Robert, and Lisa Ryan in Stratford, Connecticut. "The family struck me as a rather private group," remembered Mike Metzger, who worked for the Ryans while studying at UCLA. "They were quiet and contemplative." *Robert Ryan Family*

Bob and Jessica in Stratford, Connecticut. "He was dependent on her for her critical attitudes," director Arvin Brown observed. "He admired a great deal what she had to say about him in performances, and he took her very seriously." *Robert Ryan Family*

especially with his two sons and taking them on sailing expeditions. Eight-year-old Lisa, who often peeled off from the boys, spent many long afternoons watching in fascination as the company rehearsed. "When I first showed up, Katharine Hepburn was angry that there was a child sitting in the audience, and demanding to know why I was there. And my father said, 'Well, that's my daughter. She'll be quiet.' I'd just sit there all day."[41]

Performing Shakespeare and relaxing with his wife and kids—for Ryan, show business didn't get any better than this, and as he sat in the nearby Fagan's-in-Stratford pub, having steak and a beer with a reporter from *Cue* magazine, he was unusually frank about his career. "The junk I've played!" he exclaimed. "An actor spends years on junk. And then comes a chance to do something better—by the greatest dramatist that ever lived. . . . Just the effort to master the master increases the stature of any actor. I think that's why so many Shakespearean actors get better as they grow older. They grow greater with greater understanding of him."[42] He admitted that his 1954 run as Coriolanus left something to be desired and that he would play the role again, given the chance.

Cleopatra was one of Shakespeare's strongest female characters, so the play naturally favored Hepburn, but in Ryan she had selected as her stage lover an actor whose power and virility projected to the back row. Writing about Ryan for the *Dartmouth Varsity,* fellow alumnus Raymond Buck noted that teenage girls lined the hall outside his dressing room and swooned when he opened the door to admit Hepburn, who had come to introduce her father.[43]

The critics were considerably less gaga: "Mr. Ryan's Roman clumps about in what seems to be a perpetual hangover, more stumblebum than fallen hero," wrote Judith Crist in the *New York Herald Tribune.* "We see no flashes of past greatness in his meeting with Lepidus and Caesar; he gives no impression of strength beyond the physical. True, he is besotted, but his monotone and single-keyed performance fails to evoke a past image or a present sympathy."[44] Ryan always made a show of laughing off bad reviews, but when it came to Shakespeare, they cut deeper.

The family returned home after Labor Day, and the kids went back to school, though their parents, who knew a thing or two about educating children, had decided they didn't like the public schools in West Los Angeles. Lisa, who had been miserable at Warner Avenue Elementary, returned to Oakwood, while Tim and Cheyney were enrolled at the Harvard School for Boys, a military academy on Coldwater Canyon Drive in Studio City. Beginning that fall, Solomon Smith began driving them out to the Valley in the morning and picking them up in the afternoon. Lisa was overjoyed to be back at Oakwood, but the boys despised the Harvard School. Their parents were impressed by the school's academic reputation, though given their politics, the decision to send the boys to a military academy was surprising. "The problem with the school was not just the military side," Cheyney explained. "It was drawing on a kind of a conservative LA business element that was very racist, anti-Semitic, believe it or not. I don't think they understood that that was what they were getting into with the school."[45]

With the kids squared away, Ryan took off for Cypress Hills, Saskatchewan, to shoot *The Canadians,* a British adventure about the Royal Mounted Police that would be released in the United States by Fox. It had an interesting historical angle — the Mounties must deal with Sioux populations that have been driven north into Canada following the Battle of the Little Bighorn in 1876 — but the picture would die at the box office. ("Ryan, expressionless as his horse, gives a stolid performance," noted *Variety.*)[46] The assignment precluded him from doing anything in the 1960 presidential campaign, though he contributed enough to Democratic nominee John F. Kennedy to be invited to the inauguration the following year (he did not attend). Jessica disliked Kennedy for his philandering, which was an open secret around Hollywood, and decided to vote for Eric Hass, the Socialist Labor candidate.[47]

As a prominent member of SANE, Ryan was concerned chiefly with the nuclear test ban treaty being negotiated between the United States and the USSR in Geneva. The Soviets had unilaterally suspended atmospheric testing in March 1958, to be followed by the United States in August, but since then the talks had stalled. In January 1960, Ryan and Philip Dunne had written an open letter from Hollywood for SANE to the likely presidential candidates, asking them to express their support for the test ban, and the following month Ryan signed and helped pay for a full-page SANE advertisement in the *Washington Post* and other papers nationwide. "Agenda for Geneva" suggested incremental steps toward disarmament that included dismantling all missile bases and suspending production of all nuclear, chemical, and biological weapons.

The letter to candidates notwithstanding, Hollywood for SANE concerned itself mainly with raising funds and corralling celebrities to take part in public-awareness campaigns. A series of radio spots had been recorded and distributed to some 650 disc jockeys and SANE chapters, featuring not only Ryan, Steve Allen, and Allen's wife, Jayne Meadows, but also such stars as Janet Leigh, Tony Curtis, Jack Lemmon, Anthony Quinn, Keenan Wynn, and Mercedes McCambridge. The two chapter presidents, Ryan and Allen, spoke at civic organizations around the Los Angeles area, along with James Whitmore and Ryan's friend Lee Marvin. Hollywood for SANE answered letters addressed to the many celebrities on its letterhead and distributed informational audiotapes to schools, universities, and discussion groups (one featured a panel with noted atomic scientists, recorded after the premiere of Stanley Kramer's postapocalyptic drama *On the Beach*). SANE chairman Norman Cousins would remember Ryan as a tireless advocate: "I can't think of an affair for the Federalists or for SANE that he didn't accept."[48]

Earlier that year SANE had suffered the sort of internal convulsion that Cousins always dreaded. A giant rally was planned for Madison Square Garden in May 1960, to be followed by a Harry Belafonte concert at the Shrine Auditorium in Los Angeles. But in the days leading up to the rally, Democratic Senator Thomas J. Dodd of Connecticut—a vocal critic of the test ban—charged that the rally's chief organizer, Henry Abrams, was a member of the Communist Party of America. Abrams, a cochairman of SANE's West Side New York chapter, was summoned to appear before Dodd's Senate subcommittee on internal security, and when asked about his political association, he invoked his Fifth Amendment rights. Cousins asked Abrams to come clean with the SANE board, but Abrams refused. Faced with the prospect of SANE going down in flames, Cousins fired Abrams, and the national board instituted a new rule requiring chapters to screen out members of the CPA. A wrenching internal debate followed, and a quarter of the organization's local chapters, all located in the New York area, were ejected for noncompliance.

Cousins would be pilloried for his decision, yet he knew SANE could never achieve its goal of marshaling public opinion if it were tarred as a front for communists. The skittishness of the Hollywood chapter played no small part in this calculation; as Steve Allen would explain, SANE owed its unusually large star contingent to the fact that it was a squarely liberal organization, "a center to coalesce around that was not extremist, not considered hopelessly idealistic, not denominational, not unrealistically radical . . . an organization to whose center flocked respectable people of all sorts."[49] Allen served as master of ceremonies that October when SANE met for its annual conference in Chicago; the attendees voted to endorse the new membership standards, but the organization was severely wounded by the whole episode.

After the new year nothing of interest materialized for Ryan. He slept late and puttered around his vast new home, enjoying the quiet while the kids were in school. Since the family's move to Holmby Hills, Jessica had begun work on a new novel and hired young Priscilla Ulene, a student at UCLA, to type up her longhand drafts, help with the shopping, and pick up the kids from school. She was followed in early 1961 by Mike Metzger, another UCLA student, who took over the same duties. Metzger came from a show business family—his grandfather was the great entertainer Eddie Cantor—and he grew chummy with the kids, introducing Tim to the finger-style guitar playing that would become his lifelong passion. Hammering away at the typewriter in Ryan's office, Metzger got a firsthand look at the household. "The family struck me as a rather private group," he said. "They weren't real social. There weren't a lot of people hanging around. They kind of went off and did their thing, whatever that was. They were quiet and contemplative."

Metzger knew Ryan from the movies, but in real life he was a different guy, always deep in thought. One afternoon Metzger was typing away in the office, a TV playing silently in the corner. Passing by the open door, Ryan glanced at the screen and saw one of his old black-and-white RKO pictures playing. "Oh my God, that thing," he remarked to Metzger. They watched it for a few seconds, then Ryan grunted and walked off. "Two minutes later he doubled back, came back, sat transfixed, turned the sound up, and watched the whole film, with great interest," Metzger recalled. "And he would make comments like, 'Ah, Christ!' as though he were reliving the making of that film. I probably said, 'Was that a particularly memorable film?' 'Nah!' You know, that kind of thing. But he was definitely interested."

Ryan always struck Metzger as "a giant animal in a small cage.... He seemed to me like a person who was really born to be out in the woods." Often Ryan would disappear to go hiking, either in the ravine behind the house or, as Cheyney recalled, up in the Hollywood Hills, around the reservoir where Hollis Mulwray's body would be recovered in the movie *Chinatown*. After one of his hikes out back, Ryan came into the office carrying something in a rag and invited Metzger to take a look. "Here was this dead hawk, and it was in perfect condition. He was amazed by it. He said, 'Look at this thing! It's beautiful.' He spread the wings and he said, 'There isn't a mark on this thing. Must have just died naturally. This is a beautiful creature.'" He was going to have it stuffed. Ryan walked off with his prize, and Metzger forgot about it.

A week later, Ryan was sitting in his armchair reading as Metzger worked, and from the basement they heard a shriek: Williana Smith had gone into the freezer looking for a package and discovered the dead hawk stowed there. "He jumped out of his chair. I mean, this guy is six-foot-six or something. And she's four-foot-eleven.... He did one of those, it was almost like a silent-movie take, where he went, 'Oh, *shit!*' And he made it through the French doors out into the yard.... She comes storming into the den, screaming, with this hawk in her hands.... 'Where is he? Where is he? I'm gonna skin him alive!' If you can picture seeing this huge man sneaking past the glass windows back and forth, trying to dodge her."[50]

WHEN RYAN HEARD that British actor and director Peter Ustinov was developing a screen adaptation of Herman Melville's seafaring story *Billy Budd,* he leapt into action, calling Ustinov personally to lobby for a role in the picture. Melville had left this Christian allegory unfinished when he died;

published in 1924, it fueled the giant resurgence of interest in his work that had engulfed Ryan in his college years. The story opens in 1797, when the Revolutionary French Republic is flexing its muscles on the high seas and the Royal Navy is struggling to maintain order after major mutinies aboard two of its warships. Captain Edward Fairfax Vere, commander of the HMS *Bellipotent*, fears that the rebellion may spread to his own vessel, and John Claggart, his black-hearted master-of-arms, carefully monitors the crew for any hint of conspiracy. Ryan must have known he would be offered the role of Claggart, but his love of Melville ran so deep that in this instance playing the villain didn't bother him.

As it turned out, he was a perfect fit for the project: Ustinov needed a Hollywood star to bolster the picture's commercial prospects in the United States and, as he later wrote, thought Ryan "a massive and wicked presence on the screen."[51] Making Claggart an American actually was consistent with the story, in which he is rumored to be a foreigner—possibly a criminal—serving in a lowly rank with the British Royal Navy. Ustinov gave Ryan top billing but reserved for himself the more sympathetic role of Captain Vere; the title character, an angelic teenage sailor whom Claggart sets out to crush, would be played by a twenty-two-year-old theater actor from London named Terence Stamp, making his screen debut.

Ryan had played some sinister men in his day, but none so cold as Claggart, whose evil, Melville notes, is "not engendered by vicious training or corrupting books or licentious living, but born with him and innate, in short 'a depravity according to nature.'"[52] Perceptive and intelligent, Claggart recognizes in Billy a sort of divinity: "If askance he eyed the good looks, cheery health, and frank enjoyment of young life in Billy Budd, it was because these went along with a nature that, as Claggart magnetically felt, had in its simplicity never willed malice or experienced the reactionary bite of that serpent. . . . One person excepted, the master-at-arms was perhaps the only man in the ship intellectually capable of adequately appreciating the moral phenomenon presented in Billy Budd."[53]

Melville's story was hardly cluttered with incident—barely anything happens in its first half—but Ustinov and coscreenwriter DeWitt Bodeen had at their disposal an excellent stage version by Louis O. Coxe and Robert Chapman, who had first presented it at New York's Experimental Theatre in 1949 under the title *Uniform of Flesh*. From their version came the scene

Ryan and Peter Ustinov shooting *Billy Budd* (1962) off the coast of Alicante, Spain. For Ryan, starring in a screen adaptation of Herman Melville was a dream come true. *Franklin Jarlett Collection*

in which Billy approaches Claggart on deck one moonlit night and tries to reach him emotionally. When Billy notes the sea's calm, Claggart replies, "The sea's deceitful, boy: calm above, and underneath, a world of gliding monsters preying on their fellows. Murderers, all of them. Only the sharpest teeth survive." When Billy offers to keep Claggart company during his watches, the older man softens but then recoils: "No! Charm me too, would you? Get away!"[54] Ustinov drew heavily on the play's structure and scenic development, steadfastly ignoring the homoerotic subtext of Melville's story; he would have enough trouble selling this as a family picture with its multiple lashings and its climactic scene of the hero being hanged.

Billy Budd began shooting June 1 off the coast of Alicante, Spain, where Ustinov had expended much of his $1.4 million budget hiring two ships, one to play the *Bellipotent* (here renamed the *Avenger*) and another to double as both the *Rights-of-Man*, from which Billy is impressed, and a French warship that later attacks the British. A solid lineup of English character actors—John Neville, Cyril Luckham, John Meillon, Robert Brown—was embellished by handsome David McCallum (soon to become an American TV star on *The Man from U.N.C.L.E.*) and Melvyn Douglas, whose wife Helen had been pulverized by Nixon in the 1950 Senate race. Terence Stamp, who was tying himself in knots worrying about his performance, found Ryan distant on the set: "He never said two words to me. And it wasn't really until after the movie that I realized what a great favor he'd done for me, because the big scene, the pivotal scene between Claggart and Billy, was really difficult and really subtle. . . . He was a wonderful actor, and I think he sort of anticipated that. And he kept me at arm's length."[55]

The company were met with a terrible storm the first day of shooting but continued undeterred for six weeks, shooting six days a week from dawn. Interviewed by *Variety,* Ryan said his experiences aboard the *City of New York* in the early '30s had steeled him against seasickness. Many of the cast and crew were dosed with Dramamine, and the cameras were equipped with a stabilizer to balance out the swelling and ebbing seas. When the exteriors were completed, the company took a short break, and Ryan traveled to County Tipperary in Ireland to search for his family's roots. Production resumed at British Elstree Studios in Hertfordshire, England, and continued through August; by the time he returned home in September, another school year had started.

"John the Baptist and Claggart mark a new epoch," Ryan observed. "I used to feel like a plumber in most of my past movies."[56] *Billy Budd* collected glowing reviews in the United Kingdom and United States when it opened more than a year later, bolstering the independent Allied Artists. Ryan was delighted with the picture and proud of his performance, a remarkably detailed piece of work reaching deeper into a malignant soul than any other he had given. He dominated almost every scene, finding his match only in Ustinov. His most incisive moment may have been the one in which Claggart, counting off the lashes of a man's corporal punishment, reaches his proscribed limit, and the grim pleasure in his face gives way to weakness and even need as he is denied any more. In one of the subtle movements that were Ryan's stock in trade, Claggart turns away, unconsciously swatting his leg with a swagger stick to deliver the additional strokes. No matter how many saints Ryan might play, he would always be more intimately acquainted with the serpents.

twelve

The Longest Day

While Ryan was in England finishing *Billy Budd,* he saw a newspaper story about himself whose headline noted he had been married for twenty-two years. "They seemed to be more impressed with this fact than what I did as an actor," he later joked.[1] Yet filming this last picture had kept him away from the family for three long months, during which time he could only monitor by phone and letter the condition of Solomon Smith, their longtime handyman, who was dying of lung cancer.

Smith was more than a servant; after more than twelve years around the house, he had become a surrogate father to Ryan's children—especially Lisa, who liked to eat dinner in the kitchen with the Smiths while her parents and brothers were yacking about politics in the dining room. "If I was afraid in the middle of the night, I would go and climb into bed with Willie and Smith," she explained. "They were the people that I would go to before I would go to my parents. I don't know why exactly, but they were much more accessible. And they were around a lot more than my dad was."[2] Ryan went to visit Smith on his deathbed, where the big man had shriveled to about a hundred pounds, and came home badly shaken.[3] Smith died on November 26, 1961, at age sixty-three.

His passing left a hole in the family that Christmas season, and only a few weeks later Ryan departed again, heading this time to France to shoot a few scenes for Darryl Zanuck's star-studded war epic *The Longest Day.* Based on a gripping nonfiction book by Cornelius Ryan, the picture chronicled the Allied invasion of Normandy on June 6, 1944, and featured a giant international cast, though few of the actors had much more screen time than Ryan.

As General "Jumpin' Jim" Gavin, who commanded the parachute assaults of the Eighty-Second Airborne Division (and who now served as a technical advisor on the picture), Ryan shared his only major scene with John Wayne, playing paratrooper Lieutenant Colonel Benjamin Vandervoort. They enjoyed each other's company during the shoot, though Ryan never had considered Wayne to be the sharpest knife in the drawer. Wayne was appalled by SANE and all it represented. "He probably wonders why I think the way I do," said Ryan. "He figures I ought to wear horn-rimmed glasses and be five-foot-four. He's fairly conservative and I'm fairly liberal—whatever that means."[4]

In practical terms it meant a good deal. On Monday, February 5, 1962, Ryan received a long-distance call from Jessica: the previous evening, someone had phoned the house on Carolwood Drive and promised Williana Smith that a bomb attack would follow if Ryan took part in a scheduled radio program about the archconservative John Birch Society. Listener-supported KPFK-FM in Los Angeles had produced a weeklong series, to begin Monday night, that combined panel discussion with recordings of Hollywood stars reading from the society's "Blue Book."

The previous week, bombers had struck the homes of two local ministers, John G. Simmons of North Hollywood and Brooks Walker of Canoga Park, as they took part in a public discussion about the radical right. Ryan's friend Marsha Hunt participated in that same event and remembered leaving the synagogue where it was held to find every car in the parking lot with a leaflet pinned to its windshield: "It had on it the communist hammer and sickle, the Jewish Star of David, and the United Nations wreath of peace, all concentric . . . and three words across the bottom: *Know Your Enemy*."[5]

KPFK had received three bomb threats as well; one caller warned, "You commies are next."[6] Jessica instructed the station to broadcast her husband's taped reading as planned, and though Ryan wanted to drop everything and come home, she persuaded him to stay put. He arranged for a security company to guard the house and escort the children to school, which excited Lisa and embarrassed the boys, but there wasn't much else he could do from across the Atlantic. "I have talked to Mr. Ryan in France and he was quite disturbed," Leonard Kaufman, a family friend, told the *Hollywood Citizen-News*.[7]

Wayne was furious when he heard the news and volunteered to fly back with Ryan and be photographed guarding the family's home personally, an offer that touched Ryan and later morphed into one of his Irish stories. As

Philip Dunne repeated it in his autobiography, Bob and Jessica arrived home one night and "spotted a man armed with a rifle standing at their front door. Bob slammed on the brakes, and was starting to back out, when the intruder waved and stepped forward into the glare of the headlights. It was dedicated right-winger Wayne, on sentry duty to protect his friend and colleague, liberal or not."[8] According to the Ryan children, this episode was pure fantasy.

Despite Jessica's firm response to the incident, the couple was spooked; and after Ryan returned home from France, they decided to vacate the house in Holmby Hills temporarily and relocate to Ojai, California, an hour and a half northwest of Los Angeles. At first Tim and Cheyney were told they would be boarding at their school, which set Cheyney to wondering, "What can I ingest that will make me so sick that I can't board at Harvard Military School?"[9] But a week later his parents changed their minds and announced that all three children would be accompanying them and transferring to new schools; Willie, still grieving for her late husband, would remain in Los Angeles. At first they rented a cabin at the Ojai Valley Inn and Country Club, a posh resort where Spencer Tracy and Katharine Hepburn had shot their beloved comedy *Pat and Mike* (1952), then they sublet a home in the area. Tim and Cheyney, whose school routine had included drilling in uniform, now enrolled in a school run by the Krotona Institute of Theosophy, which was even freakier than the Oakwood School with its curriculum steeped in Eastern mysticism.

The kids had been told they would return to LA after things cooled down, but after three or four months their parents dropped another bombshell on them: now the family was moving, at least temporarily, to New York, where their father hoped to jump-start his ailing career by starring in a new Broadway musical called *Mr. President.* "You don't mean to tell me that people are going to pay money to hear you sing?" asked fourteen-year-old Cheyney when he heard the news.[10] But Ryan was much taken with the idea: Rex Harrison didn't have much of a voice either, yet he had transformed his career in 1956 with *My Fair Lady,* and Robert Preston had pulled off the same trick the following year with *The Music Man.** Jessica considered the Broadway show a wonderful idea and couldn't wait to get out of California; after Ryan headed East in July to start working on the show, she began arranging the move to New York.

Mr. President looked like a good bet: producer Leland Hayward, director

---

*Preston costarred with Ryan in the RKO western *Best of the Badmen* (1951).

Joshua Logan, and the writing team of Howard Lindsay and Russel Crouse had already collaborated, in various combinations, on such classics as *State of the Union, Mister Roberts, South Pacific,* and *The Sound of Music.* Most impressive of all, the songs for *Mr. President* would be penned by the great Irving Berlin, returning to the theater at age seventy-four after a decade in retirement. Katharine Hepburn, knowing of Ryan's secret ambition to try musical comedy, had recommended him to her friend Howard Lindsay for the title role, and Ryan had flown out to audition in June, singing Kurt Weill's "September Song" and Berlin's "Always" for the composer and Leland Hayward. According to Ryan, Berlin told him, "That last note was great," and a half hour later he was signing a contract.[11] Nanette Fabray, his old friend from the Reinhardt School, would costar as the long-suffering First Lady. After seven weeks on the road in Boston and Washington, DC, *Mr. President* would open in New York on October 20, at the seventeen-hundred-seat St. James Theatre on West Forty-Fourth Street.

As promising as all this seemed from a distance, Ryan realized once rehearsals began that the show was in deep trouble. Howard Lindsay was suffering from the early effects of leukemia, and Russel Crouse had just undergone surgery to remove a blood clot; in their weakened conditions they couldn't assemble a decent script by the time rehearsals commenced, and as Logan remembered, they resisted any revisions.[12] Ryan later described the show's genesis as "a dogfight, and one unhappy experience after another. In the first two weeks, the dance director wasn't speaking to the composer, and the feuds just grew after that."[13] Logan and Crouse clashed over the length of the show and Logan's desire to underscore some of the dialogue with music. Berlin's songs were good, and his enthusiasm drove the production along, but Ryan braced himself for the worst as the show lurched toward its Boston opening. Once the curtain rose, he would be at the center of this whole thing, with his homely baritone and negligible dance skills, and at this rate it might crumble around him.

The hype surrounding *Mr. President* only increased the pressure on everyone involved: news of Berlin's comeback, combined with the sterling reputations of the producer, director, and writers, had driven advance ticket sales to an astounding $2.5 million. At the same time, rumors swirled that *Mr. President* would satirize the Kennedy family, when in fact, Lindsay and Crouse had written a rather melancholy story about a lame-duck president, Stephen Decatur Henderson, preparing to leave office, move back to the Midwest, and resume life as a private citizen (only Berlin's participation had turned the play into a musical). Talking to the press, Ryan did his best to deflate the Kennedy rumor, which might prove fatal once people discovered how apolitical and distinctly old-fashioned the show was. He must have kicked himself for committing to the project without having read the script, but almost everyone else had made the same mistake.

As usual, Ryan kept his head down and worked hard, worrying most about his singing. Berlin had given him some good numbers: "In Our Hide-Away" was a loping, eminently hummable tune in which he held down the melody while the more skilled Fabray snaked around him providing harmony, and the husky ballad "It Gets Lonely in the White House" considered the solitary burden of the presidency, concluding, "The White House is the loneliest place in town." But the book refused to come to life; in the age of the Cuban Revolution and the Berlin Wall, it seemed irrelevant even for musical theater. *Mr. President* was savaged by the Boston critics, as well as *Time* and *Newsweek;* in late September the cast and crew moved on to the National Theatre in Washington, where the opening performance, a benefit for the Kennedy Foundation, was attended by Jacqueline Kennedy. "There was literally no laughter at all," Logan wrote. "Every time a joke was launched from the stage, the audience, like an audience at a tennis match, looked to the First Lady to see if she was laughing, and then turned back to the play, stony-faced."[14]

The president, preoccupied with top-secret reports of Soviet missile silos in Cuba, missed most of the performance, though he came backstage afterward and, to Ryan's surprise, brought up their momentary encounter ten years earlier in Boston, during the first Stevenson campaign. A gala party followed at the British embassy, heavily attended by the Kennedy family, administration figures, and the diplomatic corps. *Variety* reported that the show was being revised throughout its Washington run, as Logan pumped up the production numbers to compensate for the lifeless script. The flag-waving finale, wrote Les Carpenter, could have been topped only by having Ryan "rip off his shirt to display the US Constitution tattooed on his chest."[15]

By the time *Mr. President* arrived on Broadway it was already damaged goods. "It is always painful when a man you admire introduces you to his awkward, charmless fiancée," wrote Walter Kerr in the *New York Herald Tribune,* encapsulating the sense of disappointment that surrounded the show.[16] Two days after the New York opening, President Kennedy addressed the nation to reveal the presence of Soviet missiles in Cuba, and Americans held their breath, wondering if nuclear annihilation was at hand, until Premier Khrushchev announced on October 28 that the missiles would be removed. Jessica would remember her eldest, Tim, observing that the crisis must be worse for her generation than for his: "We have always sort of taken it for granted that sooner or later they'd blow up the world. But you can remember a time when it couldn't be done. So it must be harder for you to get used to the idea that it may happen tonight. Or tomorrow."[17]

Ever the good soldier, Ryan always talked up his projects in the press—when *King of Kings* had opened to scathing reviews a year earlier, he assured one reporter that it would clean up at the Academy Awards (it failed to receive a single nomination). Now he would go to bat for *Mr. President* too. "Perhaps our mistake was in opening in New York after the critics had been torn to pieces by 'Who's Afraid of Virginia Woolf?' which is not at all like 'Mr. President,'" he said. "But the old people like it and I think we should make the old people happy." Privately he conceded the show was a dud and, according to Harry Belafonte, discouraged his friends from seeing it.[18]

Unfortunately for Ryan, the advance sales guaranteed *Mr. President* a long run despite its dim critical reception, and it held out for 265 performances, closing in June 1963. For days, weeks, and then months, Ryan tried to give his best to a show that refused to die despite the fact that nobody seemed to like it much. The loneliest place in town, it turned out, was center stage at the St. James Theatre.

INSTEAD OF MOVING TO MANHATTAN, which seemed too wild for the kids, the Ryans decided to find a place in Westchester County, close enough for Bob to commute into the city every day. Sunday was his only day off from rehearsals, and with Jessica and the children arriving soon, he quickly rented a house in the wealthy village of Bronxville. "The furnishings aren't very fancy," he explained, "but it was the *only* house for rent in Bronxville, and we wanted to live in Bronxville because the public schools here are very good."[19] The children thought they would be returning to Los Angeles after the show closed—whenever that was—but privately their parents had more or less decided to stay on the East Coast for good. For financial reasons, more and more American movies were being shot in Europe now; living near New York would lessen Bob's travel time and even enable him to come home occasionally during long shoots. The house on Carolwood Drive was put on the market, where it would stay for some time, owing to a recent dip in demand for luxury properties, before finally selling to writer George Axelrod.

The move was rough on Tim, Cheyney, and Lisa—by this time they had changed schools four times in three years—and though Bronxville might have struck Ryan as the sort of quiet bedroom community the family had enjoyed in North Hollywood, they soon discovered that their neighbors were nothing like the ones they had known in the San Fernando Valley. Bronxville was a lily-white suburb, hostile to blacks and Jews and not terribly fond of Catholics either, especially if they were in show business. "I was so shocked, because I'd grown up in this completely Jewish environment," remembered Lisa Ryan. "I couldn't understand it. And racist—I mean, it was just awful."[20]

Williana Smith had come along with the family but found the experience so dismal that she returned to Los Angeles after a few weeks, ending her employment with the Ryans after fourteen years (the children would keep in touch with her until her death in 1988). Clearly Bronxville was a mistake, but they had signed a lease, and doing *Mr. President* six days a week was so grueling that for the time being they would just have to stick it out. The bitterly cold winter took the children by surprise, and everyone in the family came down with chicken pox.

Though *Mr. President* kept Ryan at home, his schedule barely overlapped with the children's. He slept late and sat around in his pajamas and robe until late afternoon, then showered, dressed, and drove down to the theater off Times Square, returning home around midnight and going to bed a couple of hours later. During the run he granted a long and fascinating interview to *Holiday* magazine writer Joe McCarthy, who paid him a visit in Bronxville and noted that, in contrast to the Cadillacs and Jaguars parked at other houses in the neighborhood, the Ryan fleet consisted of a Falcon station wagon and a black Buick sedan.

During the interview (which would never run), Ryan reflected on the new experience of doing musical comedy onstage. "There are certain things about acting in a musical comedy that I'll never learn," he admitted. "Did you ever notice that a good musical comedy performer, like Bert Lahr or Ethel Merman, or Nanette Fabray in our show, doesn't speak the lines to the other actors in the scene? They turn and speak to the audience, like the comedians in the old-time burlesque shows. I can't do that."[21]

Bronxville aside, Ryan quite liked being back in New York, where he had lived first as a young man out of college and later as a newlywed husband hitting the straw-hat circuit with his fine young wife. The Ryans had good friends here: Robert Wallsten, who had acted alongside them at the Millpond Playhouse, and his wife Cynthia; married screenwriters Frances Goodrich and Albert Hackett, whose track record included *The Thin Man* (1934), *It's a Wonderful Life* (1946), *Easter Parade* (1948), and *Father of the Bride* (1950); and Millard Lampell, who had met Ryan through director Dick Brooks back in the late '40s, before Lampell was listed in *Red Channels* and his screenwriting career ended. Starring in a Broadway show gave Ryan a good opportunity to renew old acquaintances; he looked forward to the time when he and Jessica could move the family into the city, as they ought to have done all along.

Unwilling to relocate to the East Coast, Mabel Bushnell Ryan had remained behind in Los Angeles, and in March 1963 her son received word that she had died of a heart attack at her home in North Hollywood, at age seventy-nine. "I never saw him so distraught," said Wallsten, who came over to the house in Bronxville and found Ryan in his bathrobe. "When he burst into tears I was very surprised that he was that moved, although these things are always more important to people than they let on. I remember him putting his arm around my shoulder and squeezing so hard that it hurt as he wept."[22] The family traveled by train to Chicago, and Mabel was buried in Calvary Cemetery beside her son Jack, who would have been fifty-one now, and Old Tim, dead for twenty-seven years. Ryan was the last survivor of the little family in Uptown, yet he couldn't conceive of being laid to rest anywhere but beside Jessica.

Once the lease in Bronxville expired, the Ryans wasted no time in getting out. That summer they stayed at a place in Westport, Connecticut, and in the fall they moved into a spacious apartment on the top floor of the Brentmore, located at 88 Central Park West and facing the park at the corner of Sixty-ninth Street. "Frances and Albert Hackett lived there," said Cheyney, "and I remember that was important to Dad because he felt that people he knew lived there."[23]

Ryan was entering a scary new period in his career: apparently the stink of *Mr. President* clung to him, because he couldn't get a movie to save his life. *The Canadians* had sunk without a trace in the United States, and *King of Kings* had been ridiculed in the press (with Jeffrey Hunter tagged the "teenage Jesus"). Ryan's performance in *Billy Budd* had won glowing reviews, but the picture was poorly marketed in the United States and failed to have the impact he had hoped for; Terence Stamp won an Oscar nomination for best supporting actor, but the picture had been eclipsed by another maritime drama, MGM's remake of *Mutiny on the Bounty* with Marlon Brando. Ryan had abandoned Hollywood to become a Broadway sensation, and now Hollywood had abandoned him.

He kept busy as best he could. Millard Lampell had written a documentary feature called *The Inheritance,* about immigrant labor and the union movement, and Ryan offered to supply the narration for a token fee of one thousand dollars. Before getting into pictures, Lampell had performed in the Almanac Singers with Woody Guthrie, Pete Seeger, and Lee Hays, and the documentary reflected his folk roots; over one section Ryan recites:

> Layin' down track for the west-bound train
> Stackin' up timber in the State of Maine
> Diggin' out coal in the West Virginia hills
> Hammerin' steel in the Pittsburgh mills. . . .
> Six-day week and a 12-hour day
> And it's welcome boys to the USA

That November Ryan also managed to pick up a starring role in an hour-long TV drama for NBC's *Kraft Suspense Theatre.* "Are There Any More Out There Like You?" was an interesting little piece about a wealthy man whose collegiate daughter, played by young Katharine Ross, is arrested after she and her friends drunkenly run over a pedestrian. The rest of the time Ryan loafed around the house playing pool on his new, regulation-size table in the apartment, or at some of the old billiard parlors on Broadway. By now he was smoking again, and his daily diet of a couple Löwenbräus had given way to a couple glasses of J&B Scotch.

Ryan especially liked slipping out for a game of pool late at night, at some of the old halls where legendary players might turn up. But going out in public could turn sour at a moment's notice. One evening Ryan took Cheyney with him to shoot some pool, and a crowd gathered around them as they played. "What a nightmare that was," Cheyney recalled. "These guys were big admirers of the war movies and stuff. *Odds against Tomorrow* apparently had been on television within the last week, and there's a scene where Dad is supposed to throw some keys to Harry Belafonte and he doesn't do it 'cause he's a racist. We're trying to play pool and this guy keeps yelling at us, 'Hey Bob, why didn't you throw Harry the keys?' Over and over again, and then laughing. Even if he'd been inclined to do dad things with his son, you'd go out and weird shit like that happens."[24]

Now that Ryan lived in New York, he spent more time with Belafonte, getting together for the occasional dinner or game of pool but also becoming more involved in the civil rights movement, which hadn't reached the same level of intensity on the West Coast as it had in the South and the northern industrial cities. Belafonte had a sixteen-millimeter projector in his home and sometimes hosted movie nights for his friend Martin Luther King Jr., who loved movies but seldom went out to theaters. On one occasion, Belafonte invited Ryan, Anthony Quinn, and other friends to meet the minister, and they watched *Come Back, Africa* (1959), Lionel Rogosin's striking drama about apartheid in South Africa, which had introduced the United States to singer Miriam Makeba. Like Ryan, King was a longtime SANE sponsor, and the two men seemed to connect. Ryan "was quite enamored of Dr. King and quite humbled by the experience," Belafonte remembered.[25]

Ryan signed and bankrolled advertisements supporting the Southern Christian Leadership Conference, and at Belafonte's behest he took part in several civil rights forums around town. In August 1963, he and Belafonte flew to DC for the March on Washington, joining a large contingent of Hollywood celebrities that included Sidney Poitier, Marlon Brando, Burt Lancaster, Tony Curtis, Sammy Davis Jr., Tony Bennett, Lena Horne, and Charlton Heston. At the Washington Monument, Lancaster delivered a scroll brought from Paris with the signatures of some fifteen hundred French artists expressing their support, and the entertainers joined the march to the Lincoln Memorial, where King captured the nation's imagination with his historic speech. Tim Ryan attended the march on his own and was startled to see his father onstage. A few months later Ryan would help bankroll an ambitious production slate by the Free Southern Theatre in Jackson, Mississippi, an independent black company that mounted plays by Langston Hughes, James Baldwin, Ossie Davis, and John O. Killens.[26]

Upon returning to New York, Ryan had also reengaged with SANE, serving as emcee for a program at New York Town Hall in spring 1963, and on November 15 the organization celebrated its fifth anniversary with a dinner honoring Steve Allen at the Biltmore Hotel. SANE had reason to celebrate. After the United States and the USSR had resumed atmospheric testing in March 1962, the organization mounted a vigorous campaign to restart the Geneva talks, including a highly influential advertisement that featured the trusted pediatrician and author Benjamin Spock. In the wake of the Cuban missile crisis, Norman Cousins had served as a secret envoy from President Kennedy to Premier Khrushchev, and subsequently the two superpowers managed to agree on a partial ban that would permit tests underground but prohibit them in the atmosphere. The Senate's ratification of the ban in September 1963 gave new hope for détente and disarmament.

A week after the dinner, Kennedy was assassinated in Dallas. "I remember walking to the window, and cars were going through red lights and driving rather aimlessly," Ryan recalled. "The whole city seemed to be in shock at that moment, and it stayed that way, all that day and the next."[27] Schools let out early, and Ryan drove across town to pick up Lisa. "I could have just gotten home by myself, but he made a point of coming and getting me," she said. "He was crying."[28] Like the rest of the country, the Ryans spent the weekend clustered in front of the TV, trying to make sense of what had happened and recoiling in shock as the suspect, Lee Harvey Oswald, was murdered on camera by another mysterious assailant. "Dad was beside himself," said Cheyney. "I think he felt the whole country was just falling apart, and God knows what was gonna happen next. He didn't put on his clothes for three days. . . . I remember him ranting about Texas and how stupid they were down there, and these idiots with their ten-gallon hats."[29]

In early 1964, Ryan turned to TV, doing guest spots on dramatic series and hosting *The Bell Telephone Hour;* the latter gave him a chance to perform the recitative for an orchestral performance of Aaron Copland's *Lincoln Portrait* as Matthew Brady photos of Lincoln filled the screen. It was pretty square stuff compared to *The Ed Sullivan Show* two nights previous, which had introduced America to the Beatles, but in fact Ryan often characterized himself as a square. Millard Lampell's documentary, *The Inheritance,* opened in May at the Carnegie Hall Cinema, and Ryan took part in the premiere, which included folk music by Judy Collins and Pete Seeger. His intelligent handling of the picture's narration was much noted and led to more voice-over and spoken-word gigs, the honorable piecework of the fading movie star. Later that year CBS hired him to perform the words of Abraham Lincoln for a one-hour special, *The Presidency: A Splendid Misery,* and to narrate an ambitious eleven-hour series, *World War I: The Complete Story.*

That summer Ryan finally managed to score a picture, dodgy as it may have seemed, when Argo Film Production, a British independent, cast him alongside English actor Stewart Granger in *The Crooked Road,* an international intrigue to be shot in Zagreb, Yugoslavia. "When they first discussed this project with me they inquired what my demands might be," Ryan told the *Los Angeles Times.* "Only two, I told them—a good script and my salary in advance. I got both."[30] The script wasn't bad at that; adapted from a novel by Morris L. West, it critiqued the United States' support of corrupt governments abroad, though its more serious intentions were undercut by a far-fetched love triangle. Richard Ashley (Ryan), an American journalist in a fictional Balkan nation, comes into possession of some letters proving that its silver-haired leader, the Duke of Orgagnia (Granger), has been lining his own and his backers' pockets with economic aid from the United States. Ashley's pursuit of the story throws him back into the arms of a former lover, Cosima (Romanian actress Nadia Gray), who is now married to the duke but disgusted by the venality of his rule.

Ryan must have been drawn to the script's realpolitik angle. "You, my dear Ashley, are a man of a new world, America," the duke points out. "A great country, a great people, but sometimes so naïve. . . . Your country invested millions and millions of dollars here for one reason, to prevent a communist government. Is there a communist government? No! Well then, why are you so outraged at some of the methods we adopt to reach that end?"

Of course, Yugoslavia had a communist government, one whose leader, Josip Broz Tito, loved Hollywood movies (his favorite stars were John Wayne and Kirk Douglas). Shortly after the Federal People's Republic of Yugoslavia was declared in 1945, a government order established the Central Film Studio in Belgrade; originally, it operated in partnership with the venerable Soviet studio Mosfilm, but after Tito broke with Stalin in 1948, the Yugoslavian outfit, better known as Avala Film, began courting international co-productions. Studio boss Ratso Drazevic, formerly with the state security apparatus, knew how to move money around, and production funds from Western partners had a way of migrating to other state projects.*

---

*For an eye-opening, if somewhat sentimental, history of Avala Film, see Mila Turajlic's 2012 Serbian documentary *Cinema Komunisto.*

"For the filmmaker, the conditions are close to ideal," Ryan told the *Los Angeles Times*. "They have Westrex sound, all brand-new equipment. The technicians are a little slow, but excellent. The producer has his choice of the finest classical actors in Europe. They speak a myriad of languages and sometimes the set sounds like Babel, but it doesn't matter." The dialogue, he explained, was usually postdubbed, though in the case of *The Crooked Road,* direct sound was recorded and "everyone spoke English, sort of. I imagine there will be considerable rerecording prior to release."[31] Visiting movie stars were treated like royalty in Belgrade, lodging at the lavish Hotel Metropol, and the countryside was stunning; the picture's big action sequence, with Ryan and Gray tooling down the highway in a Mercedes convertible, was shot along the Dalmatian coast.

The job forced him to miss a big "Stars for SANE" event, which was a bit embarrassing given that he still cochaired Hollywood for SANE. "I am now in Split, Yugoslavia, trying to start a SANE branch to be known as Split for SANE," he wrote in a letter to the attendees. "Of secondary importance is the fact that I am also here trying to make a movie and a living." Ryan took advantage of the opportunity to pay tribute to JFK: "The Test Ban Treaty, for which our late President will indeed be remembered, is the first step of a long trip. We still have the atom and we always will; we still have the bomb and the ever dwindling time before it falls into possibly maniacal and homicidal hands. We must, therefore, work unceasingly to extend and enrich the period of grace in which we now live."[32]

Back in New York, Ryan tried to get used to the idea that his children were growing up. Tim had graduated the previous spring from the Collegiate School on the Upper West Side and spent the ensuing year with the American Friends Service Committee, caring for disabled children at a rehabilitation center in New Hampshire and helping an Episcopal priest dispense social services to the poor in Jersey City. That summer he had returned to Los Angeles, working for an American Friends day camp in Watts prior to his enrollment that fall at Pomona College in Claremont, California. Cheyney, now sixteen, had pulled himself out of an academic rough patch and become a star student at the Collegiate School; he was spending the summer in rural Kentucky, teaching literacy for the American Friends. The tumult of moving to New York, combined with the usual stresses of adolescence, had put some distance between the boys and their father; once they grew old enough to converse on his level, they began to understand what a sealed envelope he was. Friends would recall Ryan's enormous pride when he spoke about his children, but around them he kept his feelings to himself.

That fall the family moved again, but only three blocks, to a grand twelve-room apartment at the Dakota on Central Park West and Seventy-Second Street. Built in the 1880s, the seven-story, Gothic-style apartment building featured an interior courtyard with an entrance on Seventy-Second; the Ryans' unit had a large living room facing east and overlooking the park below, while the dining room and kitchen were at the west end of the unit, overlooking the courtyard. "It was an elegant apartment, but he and Jessica didn't spend any money fixing it up, or making it lavish," said Millard Lampell. "The old, worn furniture that they had from the California days did them perfectly fine; they weren't interested in impressing anybody, and although it was a big apartment, it was somehow probably the only apartment in the Dakota that I was ever in that felt kind of homey and comfortable."[33] Lauren Bacall lived in the Dakota with her second husband, Jason Robards; among the other tenants were designer Ward Bennett, author Betty Friedan, and actress Judy Holliday (whose kitchen window was across the courtyard from the Ryans').

Ryan took on more TV work, shooting a pilot episode for *Indictment,* a legal drama to debut the next year on NBC. Produced by Universal-TV and shot in color, it featured Ryan as a crusading assistant DA, with Robert Duvall of *To Kill a Mockingbird* and Richard Beymer of *West Side Story* as attorneys on his staff (the series never got picked up). Ryan also guest-starred on episodes of *Wagon Train* and a new CBS series called *The Reporter,* starring Harry Guardino.

Years later, Cheyney met Jerome Weidman, who had created the series and invited Ryan to appear, and Weidman recounted Ryan's on-set clash with Guardino. Production of TV series was tightly scheduled, and on the first day of shooting Guardino didn't show up until the afternoon, letting the cast and crew cool their heels. When this happened again the second day, said Weidman, Ryan strode up to Guardino and told him off in front of everybody: "If you pull this again, I'm gonna punch your lights out. Because we're professionals here, and this is unacceptable."[34] After that, Guardino showed up on time.

"I'm available," Ryan told the *Los Angeles Times.* "All I want is a good script.

Here at home I won't require my salary in advance."[35] Even this abject plea failed to elicit a good offer from the studios, so after the holidays Ryan flew off to West Germany to appear in another international co-production, a spy thriller called *The Secret Agents*. The picture would be shot by four different directors in Berlin, Paris, and Rome, and Ryan would be the character linking these episodes, a US intelligence officer who negotiates with the Soviets for the exchange of captured spies. Henry Fonda had been signed for the Berlin segment, playing an American operative who returns from the German Democratic Republic; the other principals were Italian actor Vittorio Gassman (*Big Deal on Madonna Street*) and French actress Annie Girardot (*Rocco and His Brothers*). All three were billed above Ryan, but he liked his world-weary character, and the picture had been conceived as a TV pilot, which might mean a full-time job later. "What I'd really like," he told one reporter, "is to get a TV series in New York so I could stay home all the time."[36]

Berlin was much changed from the ruined city he had visited in August 1947, when he and Merle Oberon were sneaking around behind her husband's back during location shooting for *Berlin Express*. Oddly, both pictures ended the same way, with a friendly encounter between an American and a Russian at the border between East and West. In *The Secret Agents* two cars meet on a suspension bridge, and Ryan's general makes an exchange of prisoners with his Soviet counterpart, played by Wolfgang Lukschy. Their business concluded, the men share a smoke; the American promises to have a carton of the cigarettes delivered to the middle of the bridge, and the Russian tells him there will be some caviar waiting. As they're returning to their cars, Ryan concludes in voice-over, "Hell of a way to make a living, isn't it?" Unfortunately, *The Secret Agents* was distributed in the United States by American International Pictures, the cheapo outfit that had given the world *Beach Party* and *I Was a Teenage Frankenstein;* chopped down from two hours to ninety minutes, furnished with a cheesy organ score, and retitled *The Dirty Game,* it quickly disappeared from theaters.

Back in the States, Ryan played Abraham Lincoln for the fourth and last time when Dore Schary asked him to come to Washington and perform in costume as the sixteenth president on the east steps of the Capitol. Schary was re-creating Lincoln's second inaugural exactly one hundred years later, on March 4, 1965, and for this kind of oratory, at least, Ryan's flat, midwestern voice worked to his advantage. Captured on film for later broadcast on

TV, the event drew some thirty thousand people, the largest live audience of Ryan's career.

"Robert waited for work to come to him, he didn't go out and seek it," Millard Lampell observed.[37] But when Ryan heard that Sid Harmon and Phil Yordan had cut a deal with Warner Bros. to shoot a Cinerama epic about the Battle of the Bulge, he phoned them and asked if they could find him a part. They did more than that: according to Yordan, when he went to Jack Warner to propose Ryan for the cameo role of General Grey—whose subordinates would be played by Henry Fonda, Robert Shaw, and Dana Andrews—he persuaded the studio chief to pay Ryan his top salary of $125,000. "He would have worked for short money to come back," Yordan said, "but then it would have been a hard road coming back because everybody watches the salaries. When he came back he worked for his full salary, and from then on he made more money than he ever made in his life."[38] Ryan departed for Spain in March and soon completed his scenes, the best of which paired him with Fonda. The two men became friends and even talked about doing theater work together; Fonda had long wanted to start a company on the East Coast and develop work for the New York stage.

Cheyney returned to Kentucky that summer to continue his literacy work, while the others—including Tim, who had finished his first year at Pomona—stayed in a rented home on Martha's Vineyard. Ryan had heard about the place for years, and he looked forward to seeing the Hacketts and Jim Cagney, a quiet and reclusive man who had retired from the screen four years earlier and now spent all his time painting. Millard Lampell and his wife, Elizabeth, visited the Ryans one weekend, though Millard recently had fallen in love with another woman. He and Ryan opened up to one another as they strolled along the beach together, or so Lampell thought. "That was the time I really found out that Robert had never been unfaithful to Jessica," Millard later said. "He told me about a couple of passes that had been made at him, one by Joan Crawford and one by Rita Hayworth, and some other actresses that I don't remember . . . he seemed about women a mixture of naivete and boyishness."[39]

Battle of the Bulge wouldn't be released until December, but already the news of Ryan's well-paid cameo brought dividends. That summer his old friend Dick Brooks, author of *The Brick Foxhole,* offered him a starring role in a new western he was writing and directing for Columbia Pictures called *The*

Professionals. Based on Frank O'Rourke's potboiler *A Mule for the Marquesa,* the picture would star Burt Lancaster, Lee Marvin, Woody Strode, and Ryan as soldiers of fortune hired by a millionaire to rescue his kidnapped wife from a Mexican revolutionary. Ryan's part wasn't as flashy as Marvin's or Lancaster's, but at this point both Marvin and Lancaster were Hollywood A-listers, and just working alongside them would restore some of Ryan's luster. Brooks knew how to write a movie—he had won an Oscar in 1961 for adapting Sinclair Lewis's *Elmer Gantry* to the screen—and his script for *The Professionals* was both punchy and philosophical. After two years of forgettable TV shows and half-assed international thrillers, Ryan set out for the West Coast in October to shoot the picture that would become his biggest hit since *Crossfire.* All he had to do was survive six weeks in Las Vegas with Lee Marvin.

thirteen

One of the Boys

The Professionals takes place mostly in Mexico, but shooting there would have required Richard Brooks to submit his script for government approval and transport cast and crew across great distances to get the locations he needed. Instead he stayed in the United States, filming along a rail line in Indio, California, and in Death Valley before moving the cast and crew to Las Vegas for more location work at nearby Lake Mead and Valley of Fire State Park. Woody Strode would remember the trip from Death Valley to Vegas: "Robert Ryan, Lee Marvin, and I made the ride in a limousine. I was riding in the jump seat, and I mixed martinis for 250 miles. By the time we arrived in Las Vegas, we were falling down drunk."[1] (They must have been, because the drive from Death Valley to Las Vegas is less than 120 miles.)

The party rolled on at the Mint Hotel, where the cast lodged for six weeks; Marvin remembered it having "seven bars, twenty-seven hours a day gambling, anything you wanted, twenty-one topless Watusi girls in the basement."[2] Their second night at the hotel, Strode—whose character in the picture was an expert archer—crawled out the window of his room onto a ledge and shot an arrow at Vegas Vic, the giant, waving cowboy that decorated the Fremont Hotel across the street. When the arrow connected, the whole statue shorted out. Strode and a drinking buddy raced upstairs to Marvin's room and asked him to hide the bow before the police arrived. "Well, that crazy son of a bitch got so excited he fired a shotgun out of his window," Strode wrote. "The cops came and found the bow in his room. Lee was so proud; it got to be the biggest joke in town."[3] Ryan wasn't inclined to this sort of mischief—for him the highlight of the stay was a visit from Tim, now a sophomore at Pomona—but when you hung around with Marvin, you were bound to hoist a few.

Theirs was a complicated friendship. Both men had served in the Marines during the war, though Marvin, fifteen years younger, had seen action, narrowly surviving the bloody Battle of Saipan in the summer of 1944. As a young supporting player on *Bad Day at Black Rock*, he had looked up to Ryan, and his combat experience made him a highly credible spokesman for SANE. But the last few years had reversed their status in the Hollywood pecking order: Ryan's professional decline had been noted around town, whereas Marvin had just turned in a star-making performance in the western comedy *Cat Ballou*, with Jane Fonda. They both could put away the whiskey, but as Phil Yordan once explained, Ryan was "a sober drinker. He drank by himself; he never gave anybody any trouble."[4] Marvin was trouble personified, a loud, sometimes belligerent drunk who infuriated Burt Lancaster by showing up blasted one Friday for a scene atop a twenty-five-foot rock and had to be straightened out by Brooks over the weekend. Lancaster, a serious and highly professional man, much preferred the dependable Ryan (and would recruit him for two more pictures down the road).

In keeping with the popular heist movies of the '50s, Brooks gave each of his four heroes a specialty: Fardan (Marvin) is an automatic weapons instructor, Dolworth (Lancaster) a dynamite expert, Sharp (Strode) a peerless scout and tracker, and Hans Ehrengard (Ryan) an experienced horseman. Described as an "ex-cavalry man, cattle boss, wrangler, bullwhacker, pack master," Ehrengard is the group's senior member and sole bleeding heart: Brooks introduces him on his ranch, where he catches a hired man brutalizing a wild horse and punches the guy out.

Once these four have set off on their mission to rescue the kidnapped Maria (Italian sex symbol Claudia Cardinale) from the formidable Jesus Raza (Jack Palance), Ehrengard emerges as the weak link in the unit, too old to handle the brutal heat and too merciful to be trusted in such a cutthroat operation. After the professionals fend off an attack by Raza's men, killing all ten, Ehrengard persuades Fardan to set loose the men's horses rather than shoot them, which tips off their enemies and results in another attack. As the mission winds on, Dolworth and Ehrengard become moral antagonists, though Brooks comes down time and again with the strong and pitiless. At least two of Ryan's professional pals, screenwriter Philip Dunne and director Michael Winner, thought his character sadly underwritten.[5]

Protesting, Ryan would joke with Winner that he had the most important line in the picture—"If it isn't hot, it's cold. If it isn't cold, it's raining"—because it explained away the seesawing weather conditions as the company tried to complete an ambitiously long action story shot almost entirely outdoors. Brooks recalled temperatures as high as 115 degrees Fahrenheit during the Death Valley sequences (the heat so overwhelms Ehrengard that he collapses, telling Dolworth, "I hate the desert. It's got no . . . pity"). After the company moved on to Valley of Fire State Park, they were pelted with rain, sleet, and even snow. As Lancaster biographer Gary Fishgall reported, "On December 13 a flash flood swept through the area, trapping cast and crew in a box canyon until workers with the requisite road grader and shovel loader could rescue them."[6]

Ryan must have been relieved to wrap the picture and get back to New York, but his time on *The Professionals* was well spent. Released the following November, it would collect strong reviews from *Life*, *Newsweek*, and the *New York Times* and go on to become Columbia's highest grossing picture of 1966. Almost as important for Ryan, its modern take on the western would prove influential over the next few years, and a younger generation of filmmakers, such as Winner and Sam Peckinpah, would make similar use of Ryan as they tried to reinvent the genre themselves. In their pictures he would also figure as the odd man out, an outsider among outsiders. He had always been drawn to the offbeat roles anyway; the conventional machismo of westerns and war movies never had appealed to him. In a sense, though, his casting in this new breed of action pictures also reflected how the industry had begun to perceive him; having gone his own way for so long, Ryan now was considered rather an eccentric character himself.

"HE WAS A WONDERFUL MAN, and it was a privilege knowing him," Ryan had told a reporter after Adlai Stevenson died of a heart attack in July 1965. "He always wanted to be called governor, rather than ambassador. He considered that his greatest honor."[7] Now, with Kennedy and Stevenson gone, the face of the Democratic Party was President Johnson. "I remember getting into some rant about Lyndon Johnson," recalled Lisa Ryan, "and my father defending Johnson and saying, 'Listen, you don't know what you're talking about. He's done a lot of good.' He was always trying to point out the humanity in everybody."[8]

Ryan admired LBJ for pushing through the Civil Rights Act, the Voting Rights Act, and new educational initiatives such as the Head Start Program, but Vietnam was going to pull him down. SANE had come out against the war in early 1965 as the troop numbers escalated and Johnson began bombing North Vietnam. That November SANE staged a march on Washington, with Ryan as one of its sponsors, and drew an orderly, responsible crowd of thirty-five thousand people, countering the media myth of a peace movement dominated by angry radicals.[9]

Though born and raised in the Democratic Party, Ryan was beginning to waver. When liberal Republican Congressman John Lindsay—a key vote on Johnson's civil rights legislation—ran for mayor of New York in fall 1965, in a three-way race against conservative writer William F. Buckley Jr. and Democratic machine politician Abraham Beame, Ryan finally broke ranks and voted for Lindsay. "By then the dyke of any rational political system—two-party system—had cracked and the waters of chaos were beginning to rush in," Jessica Ryan observed.[10]

They lifted the boat of Hollywood song-and-dance man George Murphy, who mounted a successful campaign against JFK confidante Pierre Salinger that fall for California's open US Senate seat. Ryan would tell one reporter that he himself was approached to run against Murphy: "So help me God, I was. A very powerful Democrat urged me to consider running for the nomination. I didn't consider it for a second. I want to make a contribution. I would not like to make an ass of myself. Nor would I want to be a front man for the politicians backstage."[11]

Television was turning politics into show business, which gave any skilled performer the edge. Ryan had become an occasional guest on TV talk shows, especially in the local New York media, where his facility with political issues tended to blur the line between him and the real thing. "Not long ago, Robert was on a TV panel show with a well-known and distinguished United States senator," Jessica wrote around this time. "After the show, R. got a number of letters from [viewers] that said, not only did he seem to know all about politics, but he looked more like a senator ought. Therefore, they thought he should be the senator."[12]

Director Robert Aldrich reinforced the notion of Ryan as a marginalized figure when he and producer Kenneth Hyman signed him for *The Dirty Dozen*, a big-budget World War II epic they were shooting for MGM in England in April 1966. Lee Marvin, fresh from a triumphant Oscar win for *Cat Ballou*, starred as John Reisman, a pugnacious army major handed the assignment of staging a suicide mission against the Germans with a motley crew of military convicts (among them Charles Bronson, Jim Brown, John Cassavetes, Telly Savalas, and Donald Sutherland). To Ryan fell the thankless task of playing Marvin's nemesis in the first of the picture's three acts, a prim, vainglorious West Point man with the pedigreed name of Colonel Everett Dasher Breed. Commander of the parachute school for the 101st Airborne Division, Breed bristles when Reisman shows up with his men to train for their top-secret mission, and eventually Reisman's crew are forced to prove themselves to the shrewd General Worden (Ernest Borgnine) by going up against Breed's company in a war games operation.

By 1966 there were 400,000 American troops in South Vietnam, and *The Dirty Dozen,* with its jaundiced take on the military, would connect with a generation of kids questioning the war and the draft. Yet the picture, adapted by veteran screenwriter Nunnally Johnson (*The Grapes of Wrath*) from a best-selling novel by E. M. Nathanson, was antiauthoritarian without really being antiwar; opening someone's throat was okay, it suggested, as long as you were doing it for your own purposes and not getting suckered by the brass. In this context Breed was a priggish heavy, ramrod straight and devoted to the chain of command. By now Ryan had played quite a few career soldiers—in *The Longest Day, The Secret Agents,* and *Battle of the Bulge*—but as Colonel Breed he's the butt of every joke, scowling impressively as he absorbs one insult to his dignity after another. Ryan shouldered the challenge with his usual skill and resolve, turning in a spirited comic performance amid a rogue's gallery of posturing tough guys.

Ryan's standout scene comes when Reisman first arrives with his truck full of reprobates, and Breed, instructed by the higher-ups that a general will command the hush-hush operation, welcomes the truck with a military band and troop inspection. Trim and handsome in his dress uniform, sunglasses, and leather gloves, Breed glows with excitement as the party rolls in. Reisman hasn't brought any general, however, so he drags the grubby, unshaven goofball Vernon Pinkley (Sutherland) from the back of the truck to impersonate one. This charade reduces his fellow convicts to hysterics, and Breed gives Reisman a tongue-lashing. In the sort of comeuppance that was Ryan's lot for the picture, Reisman silences him with the barbed implication that he's a bit of a swish: "I owe you an apology, colonel. I always thought that you were a cold, unimaginative, tight-lipped officer. But you're really . . . quite *emotional,* aren't you?"

Colonel Everett Dasher Breed, the vain martinet of *The Dirty Dozen* (1967). In the westerns and war movies of the late 1960s, Ryan increasingly would figure as the odd man out, an outsider among outsiders. *Franklin Jarlett Collection*

Despite the large male ensemble, *The Dirty Dozen* was Marvin's picture, just as *Bad Day at Black Rock* had been Spencer Tracy's. But Ryan was used to that. The job paid well, and the picture would be an even bigger hit than *The Professionals,* solidifying his comeback as a graying character actor. He always enjoyed England. Lisa, now fifteen, flew in from New York with a girlfriend to visit him and was hanging around the set one day when a soused Lee Marvin reeled into her orbit and began hitting on her. Starstruck, she talked to him for a while until her father spotted them. "The next thing I remember is my dad came marching over and said, 'Lee! That's my daughter!' . . . [Marvin] literally jumped backwards. I mean it really was like he got zapped with a cattle prod or something."[13]

AFTER RETURNING HOME FROM THE UK, Ryan flew out to Hollywood to costar with TV comedian Sid Caesar in a mystery spoof adapted from Donald Westlake's novel *The Busy Body.* Ryan may have treasured the great works of literature—he gave Lisa a copy of *Ulysses* when she was only fourteen—but he also loved farce; among the few TV shows he could be bothered with were *Get Smart,* starring Don Adams as a bumbling secret agent, and the campy *Batman,* whose inane, monosyllabic theme song his daughter heard him singing around the house.[14]

The Busy Body had a funny plot: Ryan is a Chicago mob boss and Caesar his wacky lieutenant, who makes the funeral arrangements for one of their men but accidentally buries him in a jacket lined with a million dollars. Unfortunately, the two stars were severely mismatched, Caesar mugging as Ryan turned in his usual meticulously detailed performance. Producer-director William Castle, best known for gimmicky horror movies such as *The Tingler* and *House on Haunted Hill*, proved the old showbiz adage that death is easy but comedy is hard, squandering a lively young cast that included Dom DeLuise, Godfrey Cambridge, Bill Dana, and Richard Pryor (he and Ryan shared no scenes).

From Los Angeles, Ryan then flew to Torreón, Mexico, to costar with his Dakota neighbor Jason Robards and James Garner in an MGM western about the gunfight at the O.K. Corral. Director John Sturges had worked with Ryan on *Bad Day at Black Rock* and since directed two action classics, *The Magnificent Seven* (1960) and *The Great Escape* (1963). He had already made one picture about the famous shootout—*Gunfight at the O.K. Corral* (1957), with Burt Lancaster and Kirk Douglas—but that one climaxed with the gun battle, whereas this one would open with it. Carefully researched by screenwriter Edward Anhalt, *The Law and Tombstone* followed the repercussions of the gunfight as Wyatt Earp and the Clanton gang fight for political control of the town. Garner played the legendary marshal, Robards the hard-drinking Doc Holliday, and Ryan the ruthless cattle rustler Ike Clanton, who skips out on the gunfight but then mounts a legal and public-opinion crusade against the two lawmen.

"It's a very good part, a very interesting part," Ryan told a German radio reporter on the set, "because [Clanton] pretends to be a very substantial citizen, a very fine man, but actually he's using all these killers to do his work."[15] Anhalt had written a sober, thoughtful script, pondering the issues of civil authority that were implicit in the famous tale. After Earp and Holliday kill Clanton's nineteen-year-old brother, Billy, and two other outlaws, Ike has the corpses displayed for the people of Tombstone in a storefront window and leads a memorial procession through town to protest the killings, glowering at the two lawmen as he passes. Ryan's interest in the picture must have been stoked by the fact that his wife's grandfather, George Washington Cheyney, had held a prominent position as superintendent of the Tombstone Mill and Mining Company when the gunfight took place in October 1881.

Torreón was another of those soul-killing Mexican towns that hosted one Hollywood western after another, and Ryan took advantage of the shoot to get to know Robards, another heavy drinker with a love for Eugene O'Neill. Born in Chicago but raised in LA, the raspy-voiced actor had delivered some extraordinary performances in O'Neill plays: he had made his Broadway debut in 1956 as James Tyrone Jr., the dissolute elder brother, in the original production of *Long Day's Journey into Night,* and given what many considered a definitive portrayal of Hickey, the dream-weaving salesman, when Sidney Lumet directed a two-part TV version of *The Iceman Cometh* for public television in 1960. Two years later Robards had reprised his role as Jamie Tyrone when Lumet directed the heralded screen version of *Long Day's Journey,* starring Ralph Richardson, Katharine Hepburn, and twenty-five-year-old Dean Stockwell (*The Boy with Green Hair*). Ryan's conversations with Robards must have set him to thinking, because four months later he would star in his own version of the play, tackling the role of the bitter patriarch, James Tyrone Sr.

That November, to Ryan's dismay, Ronald Reagan completed his metamorphosis from movie star to president of the Screen Actors Guild (where he helped enforce the Hollywood blacklist) to TV pitch man for General Electric (one of the nation's top defense contractors) to governor of California. "Ronnie's a pleasant guy, but I don't believe the man has any degree of knowledge of what he's talking about, and I don't believe he has any strong convictions," said Ryan on the eve of Reagan's victory. Most actors, he pointed out, were introverts, but Reagan was "the most gregarious man you ever met.... Ronnie loves campaigning and meeting people and giving speeches."[16] Talking to the Dartmouth College paper a few months later, Ryan found the perfect line for Reagan: "There aren't any series around, so I might as well be governor."[17]

A clause in Ryan's contract guaranteed him time off for Christmas, and back in New York he attended to Jessica, who was grieving over her mother's death earlier that month at age eighty-one. ("While it was a blessed release from what had become a meaningless existence, it was difficult," she wrote to Jean Renoir. "As I guess these things are, regardless of how well-prepared you think you are."[18]) Jessica was always encouraging Ryan to return to the theater, and now that he had four successive Hollywood pictures under his belt, he decided to take her advice and also cheer her up with a trip to Europe. Shooting *The Dirty Dozen* in the UK, he had crossed paths with actor Paul Rogers, one of the sailors in *Billy Budd,* and through Rogers got back in touch with their old cast mate John Neville, now artistic director of the Nottingham Repertory Theatre in the East Midlands. In March 1967, Ryan flew to England and met with Neville to discuss a residency at the theater that coming fall; announced in the trades a month later, the deal called for Ryan to play the title role in *Othello* and the father in *Long Day's Journey into Night*. His pay would be $150 a week.

With this engagement in place, Ryan also picked up cameo roles in three pictures that were shooting in Europe that summer; he set off for Italy in late May, and Jessica and Lisa followed in early June, spending the entire summer with him. None of the pictures threatened to set the world on fire: *The Prodigal Gun*, released in the United States as *A Minute to Pray, A Second to Die*, was a cheapo spaghetti western with Alex Cord as a storied gunslinger and Ryan as governor of the New Mexico Territory, who has created a volatile situation by declaring an amnesty for local outlaws. *Anzio* was another thundering World War II epic, this one from Columbia Pictures, that reunited Ryan with his old RKO collaborators Bob Mitchum and Eddie Dmytryk. The picture chronicled the botched amphibious landings at the title beach, with Ryan as an incompetent general based on real-life Allied Commander Mark W. Clark. Before Ryan even arrived, the conservative Mitchum, having just visited American troops in Vietnam, prevailed upon Dmytryk to lighten up on Clark in the script.

The Ryans stayed in Florence for six weeks, making a quick side trip to Madrid so that Robert could appear in *Custer of the West* for his friend Phil Yordan. Like *Battle of the Bulge*, it was being shot in Cinerama, an elaborate widescreen process that involved three synchronized cameras, and its intimate character study of the doomed general, played by Robert Shaw, alternated with screaming long shots that showcased the stunning countryside and hundreds of horses and extras. The role gave Ryan a chance to repay the great favor Yordan had done for him two years earlier, when he and Sid Harmon (with whom Yordan had since parted company) hired Ryan at his top salary for *Battle of the Bulge* and launched him on the comeback trail. "He told his agent that it was between he and I, and that he was going to do the picture for me for nothing," Yordan recalled. "That's when he was drawing about $150,000 a picture. It was a magnificent gesture. Even though it was an expensive picture, there was no money at that time, and I would have had to hire some character actor."[19]

As Sergeant Patrick Mulligan, a jolly deserter whom Custer sends to the firing squad, Ryan had only three scenes, his little episode taking up ten minutes of a 143-minute release, but he injected more juice into them than Shaw could manage for the balance of the picture. Jessica and Lisa accompanied him to Madrid, and Lisa rarely had seen her father in higher spirits. "He seemed to be incredibly happy when he was making movies," she recalled. "No matter what the movie was."[20] The man striding around on set couldn't have been more different from the one she saw at home, lapsing into silent dejection for hours on end.

John Wayne happened to be in Madrid at the same time, and he, Ryan, and Yordan got together for dinner one night. Yordan saw a great many similarities between the two men, politics aside: both were quiet, modest, loyal to their friends, and highly cooperative on the set. "Once they signed to do a picture, you never heard a peep," Yordan recalled. As the evening progressed and the two actors threw back the drinks, Wayne couldn't help needling Ryan about some political issue. "Wayne had a real devilish sense of humor. . . . It got to the point where Ryan said, 'Okay, Duke, let's go outside and settle it.' Now, Duke's a big man, you know, but Ryan was bigger than Duke, and not only that, he was the heavyweight champion in college. Well, Duke had no intentions of going outside with Bob. He realized he had gone too far, and we both calmed him down."[21]

By early August the Ryans had fled the summer heat of Florence and settled in a London flat, where Ryan studied his lines for Nottingham and wrote his old friend Dore Schary to turn down a role in a play back home. "I am very concerned about what I may do (if ever) on the New York stage after the 'President' fiasco," he admitted. When the Nottingham engagement ended, he wrote, his next order of business would be getting another picture to build up their bank account. "As Bernard Shaw said, art is expensive."[22] The letter was illuminating: four years after *Mr. President* closed, Ryan still couldn't shake the humiliation of having to front a bad production night after night on the Great White Way, which might explain why his first stage performances since then would be tucked away in the English countryside. At the same time, he expressed little affection for contemporary American theater, telling one reporter, "It stinks."[23] Working with Max Reinhardt and John Houseman had inclined him toward adventurous work; the only recent play he really liked was Harold Pinter's *The Homecoming*.

Founded in 1948, the Nottingham Repertory Theatre had moved recently into a modern new building in Wellington Circus, designed by architect Peter Moro, whose circular auditorium accommodated 750 people and whose

highly functional performing space could be easily converted from a pro-
scenium to a thrust stage. Hired shortly thereafter, John Neville had revi-
talized the company, bringing in such fine young talents as Judi Dench and
Ian McKellen, and added a youth group, poetry readings, and a weekly jazz
night to the theater's offerings. Ryan's residency at the Playhouse was another
innovation: "There had never been a Hollywood star in regional theatre
before," said Neville.[24] *Othello* and *Long Day's Journey into Night* opened in
mid-September, shortly after Jessica took Lisa back to the United States to
begin the school year, and both productions drew big houses that welcomed
Ryan heartily. "The camera never gives you six curtain calls," he boasted to
the *New York Times*.[25]

The critics were less starstruck. "Mr. Ryan takes the stage with a brooding,
dignified presence, stiff in gait but noble in bearing," observed John Peter of
the *Times* in his review of *Othello*. The American's interpretation, he wrote,
lacked "the controlled animal impulsiveness that sets Othello apart from his
Venetian masters. Thus portrayed, he is not much of a prey for Iago, and John
Neville plays that part in splendid isolation."[26] When *Long Day's Journey into
Night* premiered a week later, Peter was more impressed, calling Ryan's performance as the aging matinee idol James Tyrone Sr. "a finely muted portrait of
glamour in decay."[27] Ryan had grown philosophical about his limitations as a
classical performer—"Shakespeare requires a dimension of acting I probably
never will attain," he confessed to *Variety*[28]—but he considered such work its
own reward. Playing O'Neill was gratifying too, though he felt his English
costars failed to grasp the Irish-American melancholy so central to the play.
Long Day's Journey, he thought, might be just the thing to revive his stage
career in New York.

A few weeks before returning to the United States, Ryan corresponded with
Lisa to inform her that he had met her "dreamboat," Albert Finney, who came
backstage and stuck his head through the shower curtain in Ryan's dressing
room to introduce himself. As the performance schedule wound down, Ryan
had gotten a chance to see two American pictures at the local cinema: *Bonnie
and Clyde,* which he disliked, and *Cat Ballou,* which he enjoyed only for "Lee
M. who was marvelous." To his relief, he had just played the last of the school
matinees offered by the Playhouse. "Shakespeare naturally is sacrosanct, so
6 yr. old moppets are allowed to watch a play about murder, sexual jealousy,
and foul conniving," he reported. "The results are what you might expect: last

week we played the big O to a constant storm of laughter which reached a crescendo in the bedroom scene. My killing of the lady was evidently funnier than the 3 Stooges. We did 6 of these horrendous things and I feel that I have paid for all my sins in this world."[29]

WHILE THE RYANS EXPLORED EUROPE, American opposition to the war in Vietnam continued to build, broadening from the loyal ranks of students, professors, and clergymen into a genuine middle-class movement. The father of two draft-age sons, Ryan had a personal stake in the issue; he had never supported the war, and that summer he took advantage of an interview with the *New York Sunday News* to make his opposition clear. "The thought of sending them off to a war we shouldn't be in is something that's awfully hard to live with," he said. Asked if he thought such statements would hurt his career, he replied, "During the McCarthy era, I had my say—and it didn't injure me at all. If I didn't keep my trap closed in those days, I'm certainly not going to remain quiet now."[30] His proud recollection didn't really square with the careful balancing act he had maintained all through the blacklist years; in fact, a more private concern for him now was how to encourage his sons in the pacifist principles they had been taught but discourage them from marginalizing themselves for the rest of their lives.

Both his sons had made clear that they weren't going to Vietnam. Tim had applied for conscientious objector status several years earlier but was denied; when he was called for his physical that year, he turned in his draft card in protest but was never prosecuted. Cheyney had been radicalized by his summer social work; once a neighbor of Walt Disney, he had suddenly found himself in the desolate strip-mining community of Hazard, Kentucky. Back in New York he had joined the Catholic Worker Movement, whose founder, Dorothy Day, left a deep impression on him; when his draft card arrived, he informed his parents that he intended to burn it. "My parents correctly said, 'Well, you haven't even gone to college yet, and you'll get yourself thrown in federal prison for doing something like this. I don't see [Dorothy Day] having to face going to jail for the Vietnam War.'"[31] When Cheyney won a student deferment and enrolled at Harvard (where he skipped a year and started as a sophomore) the issue subsided temporarily, but the draft wasn't going away. By the end of 1967 more than twenty thousand Americans had died in the conflict.

Once Ryan returned to the United States, he dove back into the roiling protest culture that had always been a key attraction of life in Manhattan. On a single weekend in January 1968 he participated in two high-profile benefit concerts that brought together some of the biggest stars in the country: on Saturday, January 20, he provided narration for matinee and evening performances of a show memorializing folk singer Woody Guthrie at Carnegie Hall, and the following night, at Philharmonic Hall, he performed in a "Broadway for Peace" concert to raise campaign funds for US congressmen who had taken stands against the war. With the presidential election less than eight months away, the hot topic that weekend was Senator Eugene McCarthy, a vocal opponent of the war who had declared himself a candidate for the Democratic nomination and said he intended to beat President Johnson in the New Hampshire primary that coming March.

"Bob was a great fan of folk music, and his kids were very involved with it," remembered Millard Lampell, "particularly Tim, who wanted nothing better than to be another Woody Guthrie."[32] The revered songwriter had died the previous October after a fifteen-year battle with Huntington's disease, and his former manager, folk impresario Harold Leventhal, had organized the Carnegie Hall shows to raise money for Huntington's research, enlisting Lampell (who had performed with Guthrie in the Almanac Singers) and Will Geer (who had helped care for Guthrie in his last years). Lampell wrote a narration drawn from Guthrie's writings, to be performed by Geer and Ryan; the singers on the bill included Seeger, Odetta, Judy Collins, Arlo Guthrie, and the little-known Richie Havens, whom Lampell had discovered playing in the East Village. The star attraction, however, would be Bob Dylan, out of the public eye now for twenty months following a much-publicized motorcycle accident. "Carnegie Hall was entirely sold out two hours after the tickets went on sale," remembered Lampell. "There was a kind of electric excitement and anticipation."[33]

Cheyney came home for the show, and Lampell recruited Lisa as a stage manager. Outside the concert hall, Seventh Avenue was mobbed with people trying to score tickets; inside, the performers gathered for a single rehearsal of the program. Dylan had brought his backup band, the Hawks, and when they launched into Guthrie's "The Grand Coulee Dam" that afternoon and evening, the house went wild. After the evening concert, the performers all were invited back to the Dakota for a party at the Ryans' apartment, which also drew Paul Simon, Art Garfunkel, and Allen Ginsberg. Lisa listened incredulously as her father—who loved to tease her with his Dylan impersonation—told the wild-haired singer how much he admired his music.[34] "Bob [Ryan] sat on the floor with his kids all around him," Lampell said, "and he listened to the singing, which lasted until two or three in the morning, and then a few of us stayed on rehashing what had gone on, and I had never seen Bob grin so much in my life."[35]

The concerts generated $7,500 for Huntington's research, a relatively meager amount compared to the $100,000 raised for antiwar candidates at Philharmonic Hall on Sunday. "Broadway for Peace" was more of a show-biz affair, with appearances by Ryan, Harry Belafonte, Paul Newman, Tony Randall, Barbra Streisand, Leonard Bernstein, Diahann Carroll, Joel Grey, Alan Arkin, and Carl Reiner. The proceeds all were earmarked for legislative candidates—Senator Wayne Morse of Oregon, Representative John Conyers of Michigan—who had voted against either the Gulf of Tonkin Resolution, which authorized President Johnson to prosecute the war, or the $700 million appropriations bill that followed in 1965.

Newman and Randall both liked Eugene McCarthy and planned to campaign for him as the March 12 primary approached. McCarthy was the sort of politician Ryan respected; he was Catholic and, like Stevenson, a man of learning and of principle. "When he was alone he acted bravely, and I was moved," Ryan later said.[36] On January 27 the national board of SANE cast its lot in a presidential race for the first time, endorsing McCarthy by a vote of thirty-six to zero.

To some degree the McCarthy endorsement was SANE's attempt to heal a terrible internal schism between energized radicals who wanted to end the war by any means available and conventional liberals who wanted to work inside the system. The leadership maintained a careful distance from communist or radical elements that might besmirch the group's reputation, even as the grassroots membership pushed for a broad coalition with antiwar groups across the political spectrum. The issue reached a boil in spring 1967 when SANE sat out the giant Spring Mobilization Conference in Washington, and boiled over in the fall when the organization declined to endorse the March on the Pentagon planned for October. Both Norman Cousins, who favored the more isolated approach, and Dr. Benjamin Spock, whose membership in other peace organizations had added to the friction, resigned from SANE. In the wake of this crisis, McCarthy offered SANE something most of its members could latch onto: a credible, articulate candidate who wanted a negotiated settlement between the United States and North Vietnam.

Whatever residual loyalty Ryan may have felt for Lyndon Johnson probably evaporated on January 30, the day he took part in the historic reopening of Ford's Theatre in Washington, DC. Following the Lincoln assassination, the building had stood dormant for nearly 103 years, but now John Houseman was directing an opening-night tribute to the Great Emancipator, to be broadcast live on CBS. Ryan shared the narration with Henry Fonda and Fredric March, the three men positioned at lecterns across the very stage where John Wilkes Booth had cried, "Sic semper tyrannis!" Odetta, Harry Belafonte, Andy Williams, Helen Hayes, Nina Foch, and Richard Crenna rounded out the cast, and the show was to begin with a statement from President Johnson. But that afternoon came reports that the Vietcong and North Vietnamese Army had launched a giant surprise attack on key tactical zones in South Vietnam; the Tet Offensive, so called because it violated a cease-fire set for the Vietnamese new year, severely undercut the administration's rosy statements about the situation on the ground. Vice President Hubert Humphrey appeared on the program in place of LBJ, delivering a stone-faced introduction on the Lincoln legacy.

Public support for the war crumbled. Later that month, more than five hundred Americans were reported killed in a single week, and the Selective Service System issued a new call for forty-eight thousand soldiers. Ryan's next picture, a Warner Bros. western called *The Wild Bunch,* didn't start shooting until just after the New Hampshire primary, so the month before the vote he made himself available to the McCarthy campaign for the sort of retail politics his father had always practiced. Cheyney had decided to back McCarthy as well and stayed with his father a few times.

Seymour Hersh, the campaign's thirty-year-old press secretary, had graduated from the University of Chicago and worked as a crime reporter for the City News Bureau. Later he would win a Pulitzer Prize for exposing the My Lai massacre, but at that point he was taking a break from journalism and, with some ambivalence, trying his hand at politics. He remembered eating dinner with Ryan at the Wayfarer Inn in Manchester, ordering a hamburger and slathering it with ketchup. "[Ryan] looked at me and he said, 'So, what part of Chicago are you from?' Very funny line." Ryan told him about his father's experiences as a Democratic committeeman, and they traded stories of civic corruption. Hersh was impressed by the depth of his affection for the city: "We talked about the fun of Chicago." With luck, they would be there in August for the convention, with McCarthy as the party's nominee.

"He was a bit mystified by his son," remembered Hersh, who lunched once with Ryan and Cheyney during the primary. "As I got to be a father, I could understand it. You know, they grow old, they separate. . . . There's this sort of mystery of why they're not eight anymore."[37] The campaign staff were all young, and college kids flocked to support McCarthy, losing their beards, long hair, and psychedelic threads in response to the campaign's edict that they go Clean for Gene. Yet a large quotient of McCarthy's financial support came from older, straighter New York liberals like Ryan, who had congregated around Stevenson. Paul Newman and Tony Randall turned up in New Hampshire, along with the poet Robert Lowell. The last weekend of the campaign, Ryan and Randall were "carefully juggled at shopping centers," according to one memoir,[38] while *Time* reported that "Paul Newman's appearances had to be circumscribed for fear of a riot among Hampshire women."[39]

Watching all this, Hersh would note how savvy Ryan was politically; Newman was always seeking advice on how to handle certain questions, but not Ryan. "He didn't have to be educated about what the best thing to say about the draft was. And there was never blowback on anything he said. Newman would sometimes be maladroit a little bit, but not really. He was smart enough to know what he didn't know. Ryan didn't have to be."[40] The Saturday night before the primary, Ryan took to the podium in a ballroom of the Sheraton Carpenter Hotel to introduce McCarthy as the next president of the United States.[41] That Tuesday, McCarthy won 42 percent of the Democratic vote, and Johnson only 49 percent. Exit polls suggested that McCarthy's strong showing may have been more of a generic no-vote against the president than a protest against the war, but that didn't matter: Johnson was wounded.

A week later Ryan was back in Torreón, Mexico, rehearsing *The Wild Bunch* with director Sam Peckinpah. Like *The Professionals,* it was a strenuous action picture with a tight shooting schedule of eighty days; for the first ten weeks they would be shooting in and around the sun-baked town of Parras, a hundred miles east of Torreón. "Sam takes you to the asshole of creation," explained crew member Gordon Dawson. "Everyone was worried about dying. You're rehearsing with full loads in the guns and horses that are skittish. When you're dealing with thirty or forty horses, a lot of things can go wrong. . . . Off the set, we spent our time drinking and trying to get good food."[42] Ryan had seen a lot of miserable locations, but this one was like a ghost town. Peckinpah had scouted it out with cinematographer Lucien Ballard, who was working with Ryan for the fifth and last time.

Scripted by Peckinpah and Walon Green, *The Wild Bunch* recalled *The Professionals* with its story of aging outlaws chafing against the modern age. The year is 1913: Pike Bishop (William Holden), Dutch Engstrom (Ernest Borgnine), and their gang ride into a Texas town, disguised as soldiers, to steal a silver shipment from a railroad office, not realizing that Bishop's old partner, Deke Thornton (Ryan), waits on the roof of a building across the street with a gang of bounty hunters. Meanwhile, Peckinpah follows the progress of a local temperance meeting as a sermon gives way to a march through town with a brass band. These three narratives intersect when the outlaws emerge from the office with their booty, the parade crosses in front of them, and a rifle fight erupts between the outlaws and Thornton's crew. The next four minutes were complete chaos, with bullets tearing not only into people but out of them, and blood everywhere. The Motion Picture Association of America, representing the major studios, was in the process of scrapping the old production code in favor of a new ratings system, and *The Wild Bunch* would put it to the test.

As in *The Professionals* and *The Dirty Dozen,* Ryan's character was isolated from the macho crew of the title. Thornton once rode with Pike Bishop, until he was captured and sent to prison; now he has been offered his freedom if he captures or kills his old pal. Harrigan (Albert Dekker), the money man behind the posse, tells him, "You're my Judas goat, Mr. Thornton." Thornton wrestles with this epithet, and a quick flashback shows him stripped to the waist and suffering under the lash.

Thornton and his band of grimy reprobates set off in pursuit of Bishop, though Thornton has more respect for his old partner than his new ones. "We're after *men,*" he tells the noxious Coffer (Strother Martin), "and I wish to God I was with them." By this time Bishop, Engstrom, their surviving gang members (Warren Oates, Ben Johnson, Jaime Sánchez), and the cackling desert rat Freddie Sykes (film noir veteran Edmund O'Brien) have ridden into Mexico, where they enjoy themselves in the small town of Agua Verde and get caught up in a train robbery scheme on behalf of General Mapache (Emilio Fernández), its debauched ruler. The picture climaxes with an epic gun

Deke Thornton, the conflicted bounty hunter in Sam Peckinpah's western classic *The Wild Bunch* (1969). The outcry over its graphic bloodshed put Ryan in a difficult position after his many years of peace activism. *Franklin Jarlett Collection*

battle in the town square between the outlaws and the *federales*, replete with explosives and machine-gun fire. Thornton watches from a distance through binoculars as this unfolds. By the end of the bravura five-minute sequence, 112 people are dead; the total body count for *The Wild Bunch* would be 145.[43]

With plenty of down time during the shoot, Ryan pored over American papers for political news. Four days after the New Hampshire upset, Senator Robert F. Kennedy of New York had declared his candidacy, angering the Mc-Carthy faithful. By the end of March, President Johnson had seen the writing on the wall and announced that he would not seek reelection. Four days after that, on April 4, Martin Luther King Jr. was gunned down on a motel balcony in Memphis; a single bullet from a Remington pump-action rifle broke his jaw and neck and severed his jugular vein. Riots erupted that night in several American cities, including Washington, Baltimore, and Chicago. In Ryan's hometown—nearly a half century after the 1919 race riots of his youth—a three-mile stretch of Madison Street on the West Side was consumed by fires and looting. Ryan had brushed shoulders with King not only at civil rights events but through SANE; production records show Ryan missing from the set after King was killed, and *Variety* mentioned him flying to New York. Two weeks later he was back in Parras, where actors were being outfitted with exploding squibs to mimic bullet entry and exit wounds.

The McCarthy campaign had been turned on its ear by Kennedy's late entry and President Johnson's stunning abdication; now the Minnesota senator faced not an embattled president but the young heir to Camelot. Vice President Hubert Humphrey was the party establishment's choice to succeed Johnson, and though he had entered the race too late to compete in the elective primaries, he had the edge in the ones that were still negotiated in smoke-filled rooms. McCarthy's uneasy relations with organized labor and the black community made him a problematic candidate to win in the fall, and the contest between him and Kennedy turned bitter as RFK took Indiana and Nebraska and McCarthy defeated him in Oregon. In late May the *Wild Bunch* company returned to Torreón, where news arrived the morning of June 6 that Kennedy, a decisive victor in the California primary, had been shot by Sirhan Sirhan in the kitchen of the Ambassador Hotel in Los Angeles. His assailant emptied a .22 revolver, sending one bullet into Kennedy's head, a second into his neck, and a third tearing through his chest. Kennedy died twenty-six hours later.

These horrible events could only have exacerbated the ongoing tension on the set. Peckinpah was a terrible hothead, and he liked to goad and bully his actors. Holden and Borgnine both had run-ins with him, and according to Holden biographer Bob Thomas, Ryan lost his temper with Peckinpah as well. After the company moved to Torreón, wrote Thomas, Ryan asked Peckinpah for a few days off so he could do some campaigning,* but the director turned him down. "For ten days, Ryan reported to the set in makeup and costume. He never played a scene. Finally he grabbed Peckinpah by the shirt front and growled, 'I'll do anything you ask me to do in front of the camera, because I'm a professional. But you open your mouth to me off the set, and I'll knock your teeth in.' "[44]

Peckinpah may have provoked Ryan, but he also coaxed a superb performance from him. Like Hans Ehrengard in *The Professionals,* Deke Thornton is peripheral to the main action, yet he takes center stage in the denouement, after the wild bunch are wiped out and the bounty hunters arrive at the stricken town. Thornton finds his old friend Pike Bishop bloodied and dead, his arm hanging from the handle of a machine gun, and pockets Bishop's revolver as a memento. As his crew of scalawags loots the bodies, Thornton seems to buckle under the weight of it all; for hours on end he sits at the town gate, his horse standing by, as the bodies are carted out by the townspeople. Finally, the old codger Sykes rides up with a couple of Mexicans and an invitation to head out with them on some unspecified adventure. "It ain't like the old days," chuckles Sykes, "but it'll do." Thornton laughs, mounts his horse, and rides off with them, into the past.

Ryan flew home at the end of June, and that summer he and Jessica stayed in the little town of Holderness, in central New Hampshire on Squam Lake. Campaigning in New Hampshire that winter had reawakened Ryan's love for the state, and the couple had a friend in Holderness—Harold Taylor, who had been president of Sarah Lawrence College and a human-rights advisor to Adlai Stevenson. That summer the film board at Dartmouth College programmed a Jean Renoir festival, and Ryan drove out to Hanover for a screening of *The Woman on the Beach.* "Most of what I said was about you," Ryan wrote to Renoir the next day, "how important it has been in my life to have worked with you and to call myself your friend."[45] By the end of the summer the Ryans

---

*Thomas incorrectly reports that Ryan wanted to campaign for Robert Kennedy, a candidate he never supported and who, on the basis of Thomas's chronology of events, already would have been dead. A more likely supposition is that Ryan wanted to campaign for McCarthy in the New York primary, which took place on June 16.

had bought a piece of land in the Shepard Hill neighborhood of Holderness and were planning to build a second home on it.

Before returning to New York, Ryan traveled to Chicago to serve as a McCarthy delegate at the Democratic National Convention. McCarthy had no path to the nomination: by the time the elective primaries wrapped up in New York on June 16, Humphrey had a commanding lead in the delegate count, and McCarthy was too diffident a character to woo uncommitted delegates to his side. Senator George McGovern of South Dakota had leapt into the race as well, which would probably divide the anti-Humphrey vote at the convention. Ryan went anyway, largely to please a friend who was the head of the New York delegation. In Chicago he shared a hotel room with his son Cheyney and tended to his duties at the International Amphitheatre, while the younger man demonstrated against the war in Grant Park.

Cheyney asked his father if he could get him into the convention hall, and Ryan sounded out the head of the New York delegation for a second pass, with no luck. "The convention was being run by Mayor Daley, who was a big Humphrey supporter," Cheyney recalled. "So he wasn't gonna give anything to the McCarthy people." While Ryan was on the floor of the convention, however, a representative of the Pepsi-Cola Company approached bringing good wishes from Joan Crawford, whose late husband, Alfred Steele, had been president of the company, and who now served on the board of directors. "Ten minutes later, we have a pass to the convention!" said Cheyney. "I always thought, 'Well, that's an interesting anecdote about who runs the world.'"

Tension filled the convention hall: TV screens showed Chicago police clashing with protesters on Michigan Avenue outside the Congress Hotel, where Humphrey was staying. "When you were in the convention they had TV coverage everywhere," said Cheyney. "And most of the time they weren't showing what was going on in the convention, they were showing all these battles going on.... I was kind of bouncing back and forth. There was one night when I was there when all the police stuff was going on. And I remember another night I was actually in the convention. So it was quite an experience."[46] Disgusted with the whole situation, his father decided to go home, leaving Cheyney with the hotel room for another few days. Ryan missed the climactic police riot on August 28, but it was all over TV, and as the protesters pointed out, the whole world was watching. Anyone with a grasp of electoral politics knew what all this meant: Richard Nixon was going to be president of the United States.

fourteen

My Good Bad Luck

Among Jessica Ryan's papers is a curious fifteen-page typed manuscript that may have been begun by her husband but was certainly finished by her. "My name is Robert Ryan," it opens. "The vital statistics? Born: Chicago, Illinois. Educated in a Jesuit academy and at Dartmouth College. Married—thirty years—to the same woman. Father of three children, two boys and a girl. (Well, in order not to offend women's lib—a girl and two boys.)" The next four pages meander, touching on the social upheaval of the '60s and the author's experience of being confused with the vicious characters he had played onscreen. By the fifth page, however, another writer clearly has taken over, and the piece becomes a scholarly consideration of movie westerns and the white, patriarchal society they champion. In the old silent westerns of William S. Hart, the author explains, "Women were dance hall girls (never openly identified as whores) or Innocent girls. When an innocent girl appeared, the good man's concern for her was to rescue her from the bad man. Not for himself, but to protect her virginity. In the end, of course, riding off into the sunset, alone."[1]

The piece was never published; Jessica must have recognized that this wasn't the proper approach to such a rich topic, and alongside the ghostwritten piece are two longer manuscripts under her own name (*Woman—The Mythless American* and *America—Dream or Nightmare?*) in which the same ideas are worked out in much greater detail. She wrote constantly, which encouraged and to some extent excused her cloistered existence. Bobbs-Merrill had published her second children's book, *The Mystery of Arroyo Seco,* in 1962, and for a long period afterward she had labored over another novel called *The Smoking*

Mountain, but it never saw print. By the end of the decade she had turned to nonfiction, cranking out not only the two scholarly manuscripts but *If School Keeps,* a 150-page account of starting the Oakwood School; *Recollections of a Pioneer Grandmother,* about the frontier women in her family line; and the memoir *Campaign–'52, or A Camera's-Eye View from Two Odd Birds.*

Writing under her husband's name, and then realizing that she had to take ownership of the ideas herself, must have been a telling experience. Jessica had read Betty Friedan's book *The Feminine Mystique* when it shot up the best-seller charts in 1964, and she was taken with its clearheaded diagnosis of "the problem with no name"—that vague but gnawing sense among American women that there must be more to life than marriage, children, and creature comforts. "Sometimes a woman would tell me that the feeling gets so strong she runs out of the house and walks through the streets," wrote Friedan. "Or she stays inside her house and cries. Or her children tell her a joke, and she doesn't laugh because she doesn't hear it. I talked to women who had spent years on the analyst's couch, working out their 'adjustment to the feminine role,' their blocks to 'fulfillment as a wife and mother.' "[2] Even a woman such as Jessica, who had published five books and launched one of the most re-spected private schools in Los Angeles, understood. To the world, she was still Mrs. Robert Ryan.

Since moving to New York, Jessica had become a patient of psychologist Rollo May, whose books had helped introduce the idea of existential anxiety into American psychotherapy. Interviewed by *Psychology Today,* May defined anxiety as "the awareness of death. . . . This comes out in the loss of love, which is a partial death, it comes out when you write a book that turns out not to be publishable or to be a success, when something is not as good as you hoped. All of these things are partial deaths that precede our ultimate death." From his perspective, some anxiety was a good thing, "the struggle of being against non-being."[3] May became a powerful influence on Jessica, who had wrestled with anxiety all her life, and some of his ideas and terminology would creep into her work.

When Jessica set out to write a feminist study of her own, she naturally gravitated toward her family history of strong, independent women, and to the Jungian scholarship that so fascinated her, with its emphasis on the psychological repercussions of cultural myths. Jessica opened *Woman—The Mythless American* by explaining that she had once taken part in a study of violence in America, doing an analysis of how it was fueled by national mythology. "In the course of the work, two things began to be apparent to me," she wrote. "One, American mythology is entirely for men—and for men at a pre-adolescent, gang-age stage of human development; two, *there are no myths for women, nor are there women of any significance in the myths of men.*" For her, this cultural mind-set posed a greater problem for women than the more practical matters of equal pay and career opportunities. "All the legislation in the world with respect to women can change nothing if the mythology, the cultural mores of the nation do not change."[4]

The manuscript dead-ends after fifty pages, before the writer can follow her idea from the tall tales of the nineteenth century into the Hollywood dream world of the twentieth; one wonders what Jessica might have said about Ryan's endless schedule of westerns and war movies. *The Professionals, The Dirty Dozen,* and *The Wild Bunch* are all male romances, arguably "for men at a pre-adolescent, gang-age stage of human development," and their treatment of women ranges from chauvinism to violent misogyny. In *The Professionals,* the Claudia Cardinale character is a big-breasted trophy, fought over by various macho factions. The only female characters intruding on the large-scale buddy romance of *The Dirty Dozen* are a band of whores imported by Lee Marvin to service his boys. *The Wild Bunch* is even worse: when one of the outlaws, Angel (Jaime Sánchez), catches his former lover in the arms of the sinister General Mapache, he pulls out his revolver and murders not the general but the woman.

Even in its incomplete form, Jessica's manuscript provides some offhand insights into her personal experience of "the woman problem." Her parents' generation, she wrote, came of age as the Victorian era faded away, leaving behind "an aggregation of thrashing about, dissatisfied, frustrated women, taking out their repressed rage, not only on their husbands, but on their children—over-demanding, over-exploitative, over-protective, over-rejecting, over-almost everything, out of a lack of any surety within themselves." Jessica knew Robert had given her more respect for her ideas than a woman of her mother's generation might have enjoyed, but he was old-fashioned in his attitudes. "Most women want to discover the truth of their existence within the reality of themselves as women," Jessica wrote. "They find it mysterious and infuriating when men react to their plea with disinterest, if not out-and-out anger; it is even more mysterious when the reaction comes from the kind of liberal, intellectual-type man who pays lip-service to the cause of women's rights, publicly supporting their desire for the freedom to assert their power, but who, when that assertion interferes with his own personal preoccupations, retreats in boredom from the engagement."[5]

Jessica found a more sympathetic ear in young Ramona Lampell, the second wife of their friend Millard. Born to a coal-mining family in West Virginia, Ramona had boarded a Greyhound bus for New York City in 1947, on the eve of her seventeenth birthday; and after attending the Barbizon School of Modeling, she got a job in the fur department at Bergdorf Goodman. Millard had met her at a Bloody Mary brunch in Redding, Connecticut, in 1965, shortly before he and his first wife, Elizabeth, visited the Ryans in Martha's Vineyard; by 1968, when Millard helped stage the Woody Guthrie shows, he had divorced Elizabeth and married Ramona. Jessica loved Millard and took a real shine to Ramona, especially given their shared past as working women modeling clothes in Manhattan. The younger woman was touched and grateful for her friendship. "She was really very sweet to me," Ramona recalled. "When I first met Millard, he was married previously, and they knew him first. And it was difficult for me to come into the relationship as 'the other woman.'"[6]

Ramona was captivated by Jessica, who introduced her to yoga and who stood on her head every day for fifteen minutes. Jessica struck her as enormously shrewd in sizing up interpersonal situations, and careful about whom she allowed into her orbit. "She was fun, she was funny," Ramona recalled. "She had a very intelligent sense of humor. . . . And she was beautiful to look at—she was tall and had beautiful skin, and she exercised and kept her weight down. . . . She was the first person that I met that made her own noodles. She bought a machine, and we had such fun going over there, and her cooking her specialties." Robert and Millard indulged all the talk of equal rights for women, but they were also strong-willed men. "Millard was very bright and very aware, and so was Robert. But walking the talk didn't happen. I think they tried, and they were somewhat sensitive to it, let's say. Intellectually."[7]

The Lampells became part of the Ryans' inner circle in New York (along with Robert Wallsten and the writers George Bradshaw and Robert Thomsen), which put them in a privileged position when Ryan, bowing to the wishes of his publicist, threw one of his semiannual showbiz parties at the Dakota. "Everything else would have to be arranged, usually by public relations firms, and even the guest list was sort of drawn up, about half of it with people Robert didn't care about, or really know well," Millard recalled. "It was in order to get mentions in columns, but he did that really with a kind of amused contempt for the whole prospect, and the best part of it would be afterwards when all the guests went home, and Jessica and Robert and Ramona and I would sit around and do a sort of sardonic take-off on the people who had been at the party."[8]

At least one of these parties threatened to turn unpleasant—when Millard ran into director Elia Kazan, who had named names before the House Un-American Activities Committee. Kazan had always portrayed his friendly testimony to HUAC as a matter of principle, but many in Hollywood never forgave him. "We went to a social thing in Connecticut once, and Kazan was there," Cheyney Ryan recalled. "All that my father talked about on the way there was about what a f___head he was, and how he turned in his friends. And of course, when we get there we're all very nice to each other."[9] Millard had been blacklisted for years before resuscitating his career in the early '60s; when he won an Emmy in 1966, he took advantage of the opportunity to note from the podium that he was a victim of the blacklist, and followed this up with a piece about his experience in the *New York Times.* After he gave Kazan the cold shoulder at the Dakota, the director followed Ramona around, trying to explain his position, while Ryan took Millard aside and assured him that he understood how he felt.[10]

Among the guests watching this play out were Robert Mitchum, John Houseman, and Henry Fonda, whose friendship with Ryan recently had blossomed into a theater collaboration. On location together for *Battle of the Bulge* and *The Dirty Game,* the two men had discussed starting a regional repertory company that would allow them to mount classic plays and even develop productions for New York. Now Fonda had drummed up some interest from actress Martha Scott, who had been hired by the Theatre Society of Long Island as artistic director for the local Mineola Theater. Renamed the Plumstead Playhouse, it would open in fall 1968 with stock performances of two chestnuts: Thornton Wilder's *Our Town,* with Fonda as the Stage Manager and Ryan in a minor part as small-town newspaper editor George Webb, and, two weeks later, Ben Hecht and Charles MacArthur's *The Front Page,* with Ryan as conniving big-city editor Walter Burns and Fonda in a small role as one of the reporters populating the press room at the Criminal Courts Building in Chicago.

The Front Page had been Ryan's suggestion, inspired perhaps by his recent visit to Mayor Daley's Chicago and his chats with former City News Bureau reporter Sy Hersh during the McCarthy campaign. The play was forty years old at this point, but its breathtaking cynicism kept it evergreen. Hildy Johnson, a burned-out city desk reporter for the *Chicago Herald Examiner,* has finally walked out on Burns, his roaring, exploitative boss; but after a condemned man escapes from jail, Burns manages to rope Hildy into covering one last story. Ryan's old friend Harold Kennedy, who had directed *Tiger at the Gates* back in 1957, petitioned him for the part of the effeminate reporter Bensinger, which he had played in a previous production, and according to Kennedy's account, Ryan strong-armed Scott and director Leo Brady into casting him.

Kennedy would recall his growing unease as the director and the supporting players, many of them drawn from Brady's classes at Catholic University, squandered day after day of valuable rehearsal time, waiting for Ryan and Fonda to open *Our Town* and then turn their attention to *The Front Page.* When Ryan arrived and apprehended the situation, he whispered to Kennedy, "What have these people been doing for ten days?"[11]

Ryan's anger mounted as he and Fonda—who were already performing *Our Town* at night—tried to get *The Front Page* moving and some of the students proved unprofessional. Particularly irritating to Ryan was one student who kept missing his entrance because he was in the basement watching the World Series on TV. "What does he want to be, an actor or a ballplayer?" Ryan asked Kennedy. "He could learn more watching Hank Fonda in rehearsal for half an hour than he could learn at the Actors Studio in twenty years."[12] When the student missed his entrance for the fifth time in a row, wrote Kennedy, Ryan walked up to the footlights and told Brady he would quit the production unless something changed. *The Front Page* opened October 9, drawing considerably less attention than *Our Town.* Ryan was doubly frustrated by the experience because the professional actors in the cast—Kennedy, Estelle Parsons, John McGiver, Anne Jackson—were so good.

Privately, Ryan began hatching a scheme to restage the play in New York City. Five days after *The Front Page* closed on Long Island, he invited Kennedy over to the Dakota and asked him to direct the new production, offering to do the play for nothing but insisting that they recruit a first-rate cast. "I want you and me to have complete artistic control," he said.[13] An experienced producer, Kennedy crunched the numbers and determined that *The Front Page,* with its twenty-four speaking parts, would be prohibitively expensive off Broadway and could turn a profit on Broadway only if they could persuade star players to work for the Actors Equity minimum of $167.50 a week. Ryan signed on immediately, his name serving as bait for other performers, and Kennedy found financial backing from Theatre 1969, a nonprofit founded by Edward Albee and Richard Barr, for a two-week tryout in Paramus, New Jersey, and a limited, four-week run at the Ethel Barrymore Theatre. Leaving Kennedy to assemble the production, Ryan shipped out for the UK in late November to play the title character in MGM's nautical fantasy *Captain Nemo and the Underwater City.*

Since Ryan's comeback three years earlier, his career had evolved into a schizoid cycle of low-paying theater work that gratified him creatively and high-paying pictures that he often preferred to forget. But his years in the desert had taught him a lesson: a movie actor could be so choosy about his scripts that he wound up backing out of the business. "It's important to continue working in films to keep your image warm," he told one reporter. "If you insist on turning down bad pictures, people are going to say: 'Whatever happened to Robert Ryan?'"[14] The fact was that he'd done most of his best screen work when he was making pictures back to back; taking more jobs simply increased the odds that once in a while something would turn out well.

But sometimes that logic deserted him. Lisa Ryan, now a senior at the Nightingale-Bamford School, came home to the Dakota one night and found her father sitting in the kitchen alone. He hadn't heard her come in, and as she neared the door she overheard him muttering incredulously to himself: "God! Captain Nemo!"[15]

BEN HECHT got his start in the newspaper business as a picture snatcher for the *Chicago Daily Journal,* using all manner of skullduggery to score sensational photos of crime and accident victims, before he was promoted to reporter and eventually moved over to the *Chicago Daily News* as a columnist. When he and Charles MacArthur, another veteran Chicago journalist, collaborated on *The Front Page* in New York in 1928, they drew on a shared reservoir of colorful characters and outrageous anecdotes. Many of the caustic reporters who clustered together playing cards in the play's rat-a-tat opening scene were not only based on but named after real-life counterparts from Chicago, who basked in their newfound glory after the play opened. Walter

Burns, the barking, scheming editor of the *Herald Examiner,* was based on Walter Howey, MacArthur's boss first at the *Chicago Tribune* and then at the *New York Mirror;* Hecht described him as "an invisible menace who sat in a Hearst tower, and with the aid of witches' brews, second sight, and other unethical trumperies, outwitted the town's honest news hounds."[16]

Ryan had played this sort of comic heavy already in *The Busy Body,* but that picture was stupid and *The Front Page* was one of the great literary works of the American stage, perfecting the sort of staccato dialogue that Hollywood would embrace in its early talkies (the play was rapturously received in LA, and Hecht became a top screenwriter). For the first half of *The Front Page,* Walter Burns never appears onstage; he's heard only through the earpiece of a telephone, ranting at his long-suffering reporter Hildy Johnson. Sick of the newspaper business, Hildy has turned in his resignation and plans to live happily ever after with his new wife, which invites a cascade of abuse from Burns: "You dirty double crossing Swede! . . . Walkin' out on me like a stinkin' yellow belly. . . . You two-faced bastard! . . . You goddamn tittering Swede moron—you lousy stewbum."[17] Olivier might do a better Othello, but this was the gutter poetry of Ryan's youth, and no one could deliver it like he could.

As soon as Ryan returned from shooting *Captain Nemo* in Britain, he got back to work with Kennedy on the new production. Kennedy's search for a suitable Hildy was impeded by the low wage they were offering as well as Ryan's insistence on top billing (he didn't often fuss about such things, but this was his own project and his Broadway comeback after *Mr. President*). Van Johnson, Peter Falk, George Segal, Jason Robards, and Richard Benjamin all had been approached but for one reason or another didn't work out; in the end Ryan and Kennedy went with young Bert Convy, who had appeared in the original productions of *Fiddler on the Roof* (1964) and *Cabaret* (1966). Kennedy reprised his role as Bensinger, and from the Plumstead cast they had snagged John McGiver as the mayor and Charles White as the Cook County sheriff. Peggy Cass played Mollie Malloy, the condemned man's girlfriend, and Katharine Houghton (who costarred with her aunt, Katharine Hepburn, in *Guess Who's Coming to Dinner*) was Hildy's love interest, Peggy Grant.

The Front Page opened at the Ethel Barrymore on May 10, slaying the critics and selling out its scheduled run. A few doors down, the Biltmore Theatre was presenting James Rado and Gerome Ragni's "tribal love-rock musical" *Hair,* and in the East Village, Kenneth Tynan was about to open his nude revue

Backstage at the Ethel Barrymore Theatre after performing *The Front Page*; at right are Lisa Ryan and Helen Hayes. The show's critical and commercial success marked a triumphant return to Broadway for Ryan after the humiliating *Mr. President* six years earlier. *Robert Ryan Family*

Oh! Calcutta! Compared to these much-talked-about shows, *The Front Page* might have seemed hopelessly retrograde, but as *New York Times* critic Walter Kerr pointed out, "Plays that perfectly represent their own times never have to worry about what time it is."[18] According to Ryan, his old *Born to Be Bad* costar Joan Fontaine came backstage after a performance and told him, "Oh, Bob, it's so good to see a real play again!"[19] There were plenty of New York theatergoers who felt the same way, and another four weeks were added to the run, extending *The Front Page* into early July. After that, Albee's nonprofit group had to bow out, but plans were made to reopen the show under a new producing partnership in October.

That summer *The Wild Bunch* was released, collecting both critical raves and harsh condemnation for its graphic killing; Ryan hadn't appeared in such a hotly debated picture since *Crossfire*. "Never have I seen such a bloody, violent, senseless, tasteless manifestation of what ails America as 'The Wild Bunch,'" wrote one *Times* reader. "When such violence is depicted on movie screens without eliciting a picket line of protest, it can only mean that our citizenry has become completely immune to mass killing."[20] According to one story, patrons at a Kansas City preview of the new western went out into the alley to puke.[21] "I feel sorry for those who saw 'The Wild Bunch' and were so repelled they vomited," read another letter to the editor. "I wonder if they vomit from the real violence that we live with every day. The youths who won't return home or the ones who return maimed for life."[22] The *Times* even published a column satirizing the controversy, in which a cosseted Hollywood director is praised by a colleague for his recent feature *Mangled Entrails*. "That close-up of the girl's open carotid artery! And the way the sheriff's face exploded when the hand grenade hit him! You've got a beautiful grasp of the medium, baby."[23]

Ryan was impressed by *The Wild Bunch,* though the outcry over the violence gave him pause. After two decades with the American Friends Service Committee, United World Federalists, and SANE, how was he supposed to sell a picture that climaxed with an orgy of murder, a so-called "blood ballet" whose slow-motion shots, as critic Vincent Canby observed, rendered the violence "beautiful, almost abstract"?[24] The contradiction between his politics and the pictures he made for a living had seldom seemed more acute. "I think it put Dad in a difficult situation, because he felt he needed to defend the violence in the movie, but I don't think he had a very good defense of it," said Cheyney Ryan. His father, he said, fell back on the canard that "Peckinpah wanted to make a movie that was so bloody that no one would ever want to make this kind of movie again."[25] Of course, Peckinpah made another one just like it, and another after that.

The debate over *The Wild Bunch* took place in the wider context of the racial rioting that had rocked American cities every summer since 1965 and the conservative backlash against it that had carried Richard Nixon into the White House. "It is time for some honest talk about order in the United States of America," Nixon had declared in a voice-over for one of his campaign commercials, as images of rioters and burned-out buildings filled the screen. "Dissent is a necessary ingredient of change. But in a system of government that provides for peaceful change there is no cause that justifies resort to violence."[26]

This sort of rhetoric incensed Jessica Ryan, who, in her unpublished essay *America—Dream or Nightmare?,* was quick to broaden the definition of violence: "Law and order, as the term is used by politicians and defenders of the status quo, in itself, represents an act of violence; it blunts awareness of who the victims of violence are: ten percent of the population denied full rights of citizenship; millions of Americans living in poverty and degradation; students demanding that the academies become more relevant to the times. . . . Law and order allows violence to be done to the dissenters while it frees the general public of the necessity to feel any personal or individual responsibility for the conditions that produced the dissent."[27]

Interviewed two years after the initial controversy, Ryan was more philosophical about *The Wild Bunch*. "Whether or not the portrayal of violence is a good or bad thing no one will ever really know. . . . I, frankly, don't much care for the amount of violence shown in pictures. I thought *The Wild Bunch* in some cases—although it had style and distinction—overstressed the bloodletting. . . . Violence, however, is an integral part of modern life. You can't blink at it. I just wish we could find another way."[28] Talking to another reporter, Ryan hastened to put the issue in its historical perspective: "For a good many decades we were the country that led the world in lynching. We almost exterminated the Indians. We treated the blacks in the shameful way we still do. . . . When we don't like somebody, we shoot them!"[29]

During his summer break from *The Front Page,* Ryan took part in an independent short film that explored man's violent nature more wisely and subtly than any of the political invective flying around. Written by Arthur Miller as a one-act play, but turned into a thirteen-minute short by the young filmmaker Paul Leaf, *The Reason Why* centers on a couple of old friends, Roger (Ryan) and Charles (Eli Wallach), relaxing one fine morning on Charles's farm. The only props of note are a pair of binoculars, which Roger has been admiring, and a rifle with a telescopic site. Through the binoculars Roger spies a woodchuck about 350 yards away, and Charles tells him how he used to pick off woodchucks with his rifle—dozens of them—because they kept destroying his vegetable garden. Eventually he gave up, though, because the bullets cost more than the vegetables were worth. "Seriously—it kept reminding me of a war," says Charles. "For what it costs to kill these days, we could put a tractor on every farm in the world and send all their kids to the University of Texas."[30]

The Reason Why must have struck a chord for Ryan, who had been sickened by his first hunting expedition with his father decades earlier. When Charles asks Roger if he's ever hunted, he replies, "Years ago. Birds. But I never really liked it. They're so beautiful, it breaks your heart."[31] Yet Roger is a combat veteran who has killed two men in battle. When Charles brings up Vietnam, Roger observes, "These goddamn wars—they make everything seem so senseless." Eventually Charles goes into the house to retrieve his rifle and sights the woodchuck as Roger watches through the binoculars. Charles fires, the woodchuck goes down, and the two men walk out to the corpse and examine it. Charles tells Roger to leave the woodchuck for the circling hawks. When Roger asks him why he killed the animal, Charles replies: "I don't know. I probably won't anymore, though."[32]

Ryan occupied an interesting position in popular culture at that moment: after twenty-five years as a movie tough guy, he had become a trusted face to a generation of middle Americans, someone who could articulate liberal values without scaring the hell out of people. Later that year Millard Lampell enlisted Ryan to help his friends Paul Simon and Art Garfunkel when their hour-long TV special, *Songs of America,* ran into trouble prior to its scheduled broadcast on CBS. The original sponsor, AT&T, withdrew after it saw the boldly political program, directed by actor Charles Grodin, in which the duo's songs accompanied news footage of urban rioting, chaos in Vietnam, Cesar Chavez, and the Poor People's March. CBS backed the singers, Alberto VO5 stepped in as sponsor, and Ryan taped a thirty-second introduction to explain, "These two young men have attracted a tremendous following among the youth of America with their lyrical interpretation of the world we live in. We think you will find the next hour both entertaining and stimulating." (It was stimulating, all right: according to Grodin, one million viewers had turned it off by the first commercial break.)[33]

Much of the cast of *The Front Page* carried over when the show reopened at the Ethel Barrymore in October, though a few actors had moved on and one small role—Mrs. Grant, Hildy Johnson's prospective mother-in-law—went to Helen Hayes, not only the first lady of the American theater but the widow of Charles MacArthur. During this third incarnation, Martha Scott of the Plumstead Playhouse produced a fourth for TV broadcast, sponsored by Xerox and starring Ryan and George Grizzard as Hildy. Ryan was proud of the stage production, and like his idol Tallulah Bankhead in *Clash by Night,* he had no understudy, playing every single performance himself. But as he liked to quote Shaw, art was expensive, and by February 1970, he had left *The Front Page* and flown out to Durango, Mexico, for another western with Burt Lancaster, *Lawman.*

Canadian screenwriter Gerald Wilson had conceived of *Lawman* as a commentary on the US political scene, particularly the recent drumbeat for civil order. After a crew of drunken cowpunchers (led by Robert Duvall) shoot up the town of Bannock, Marshal Jared Maddox (Lancaster) tracks them to the neighboring town of Sabbath, where the cowardly Marshal Ryan Cotten (Ryan) grovels to a local cattle baron. Once a respected lawman, Cotten has long since lost his nerve, tumbling from one bad assignment to the next; the people of Sabbath mock him as "Cotton Ryan." He covers his cowardice with cynicism: "If you're a lawman, you're a disease," he tells Maddox. "They want you but they hate you."

Ryan hadn't been in Durango since 1955, when he was stricken with alcoholic hepatitis during production of *The Tall Men*. ("The place hasn't changed much, though I don't remember it any too well," he told one reporter.)[34] *Lawman* turned out to be a positive experience: Lancaster ran a tight ship, and Michael Winner, the Englishman directing the picture for United Artists, knew his way around a camera. First-rate actors filled out the cast: Duvall, Albert Salmi, Sheree North, John Hillerman, Ralph Waite, John McGiver (as Sabbath's deaf mayor, following the action with a listening horn), and, as the powerful cattle baron, Lee J. Cobb, Ryan's cast mate in *Clash by Night* on Broadway almost three decades earlier.

"Robert Ryan was an actor I'd admired nearly all my life," remembered Michael Winner. "He was the sweetest man in the world. He came to my house in Durango to say good-bye when he was leaving. He started to cry. He said, 'Michael, you'll never know what you've done for me. I can't thank you enough.' Tears were rolling down his cheeks."[35] Winner was taken aback by this effusive display, but it began to make sense a few weeks later; after notifying Ryan's agent that he would need the star to rerecord some dialogue in New York, he received a nonsensical reply that Mr. Ryan had broken his leg and could not oblige, followed by a confidential call from Ryan himself explaining that he was getting radiation treatments for lymphoma. An actor had to keep something like this quiet if he ever wanted to work again, though Ryan assured Winner he could do the recording session. He didn't tell Winner what his doctors had told him: his chances of survival were less than fifty–fifty.

The cancer was inoperable, so for four months Ryan received cobalt radiation therapy at New York Hospital, suffering the usual side effect of crushing fatigue. The rest of the time he and Jessica retreated up north to their house in

Holderness, which had been completed now and offered the utmost privacy. Ryan always had been proud of his looks and his physique, and he refused to let anyone but his family see him this way. Harry Belafonte met with Ryan after he got sick, but not often. "He really went into a social retreat during that period," said Belafonte. "I think he was just so discomfited by the disintegration, and I think his capacity to maintain social engagement and interest began to wane."[36] Ryan's doctors had told him that, even if the cancer went into remission, they wouldn't know he was cured for another five years. Squirreled away in New Hampshire, the Ryans began to reckon with the fact that Robert might not be around much longer.

Jessica had seen many sides of her husband over the past thirty years. "I can almost guess, when we walk into a room full of strange people, which will be his persona for the evening," she wrote. "If the gathering is primarily one of WASPs or Jews, he immediately becomes Roman Catholic. And with certain non-Catholic, grand types—John Houseman, for instance—also the simple Irish boy, grandson of immigrants. . . . If we are at a party where there are uninformed R.C.s, he becomes the intellectual Catholic, giving accounts of the sophistication, the intellectualism and the historical conniving of the Church. . . . On the other hand, should intellectual Catholics be there, Ryan goes Protestant."[37]

There were Ryans she didn't know—according to her friend Robert Wallsten, she once recalled opening a letter addressed to her husband from the Los Angeles Health Department and learning that he had been exposed to syphilis.[38] But no one had more pieces of the puzzle than she did, and no one but she saw the Ryan who sat silently in the little A-frame house overlooking Squam Lake, contemplating the end.

During this period, another drama was playing out in Cambridge. The previous fall, Cheyney Ryan and other members of Students for a Democratic Society had occupied a dean's office at Harvard to demand better treatment of black service workers, and the school had expelled him. He was still in town that spring, working as a dishwasher at Massachusetts Institute of Technology, when revelations that President Nixon had widened the war to Laos and Cambodia sent the student antiwar movement off the rails. On Monday, May 4, the nation was shocked by images of students shot and killed by National Guardsmen on the campus of Kent State University. A week later, Cheyney, forbidden to set foot on the Harvard campus, showed up for a protest, and a few months after that he was arrested and charged with criminal trespass; convicted and sentenced to sixty days in jail, he would appeal and be given probation.

Tim had dropped out of school and was trying to launch a career as a folk singer, hitchhiking up and down the West Coast and often playing on the street. On May 15, he was part of the growing protests over the impending shutdown of People's Park, the free-speech area on the Berkley campus, when riot police waded into the crowd cracking heads and Governor Reagan called in the National Guard. Ryan told one interviewer that his eldest was "going through a great deal of self-searching and examination to find out what he wants to do."[39] Around the same time, in a letter to the alumni office at Dartmouth, Ryan confessed his doubts about the value of a higher education: "My oldest son dropped out of Pomona in his senior year. He didn't feel what he was doing had any relevance to his life or the world around him. My youngest son was suspended in his senior year for nonviolent political activity. In neither case was the subsequent alternative a life of drugs or blissful inactivity. My youngest son was headed (easily) for a magna cum and is intellectually voracious. Whether or not he gets his Harvard BA is no longer of interest to him. Why?"[40]

Amid all this youthful alienation, Ryan crossed paths again with Nicholas Ray, whose *Rebel without a Cause* was only a distant memory now. After *King of Kings* flopped, Ray collaborated with producer Samuel Bronston and screenwriter Phil Yordan on one more Spanish superproduction, *55 Days at Peking* (1963) with Charlton Heston and Ava Gardner, but like the earlier one it spun out of control and the alcoholic director broke down (or was fired, depending on whose story one believed). Subsequent projects had crashed and burned, most recently a documentary about the Chicago conspiracy trial. "Mom, who is that guy sleeping on our couch?" Lisa asked her mother after she found Ray conked out in their living room at the Dakota.[41] His shaggy hair had turned white, and a recent embolism had forced him to wear an eye patch. "There's a pirate here now," Lisa told Cheyney when he phoned.[42] According to Cheyney, his father tried without success to get Ray a teaching job at Brandeis University, though the director would eventually land a two-year gig at Harpur College in upstate New York.

By the fall Ryan's doctors had pronounced his cancer in remission and said he might return to work, though he was greatly weakened by his ordeal and spending months in the desert on a western location was out of the question. Jessica, knowing how happy *The Front Page* had made her husband, urged him to return to the stage (before his illness, he and Harold Kennedy had made plans to move their hit out to Los Angeles, and the Plumstead Playhouse had announced that Ryan would star in Archibald MacLeish's *J.B.*). But Ryan understood that his big problem now was proving to the movie industry that he could still be insured. His old friend Phil Yordan managed to land him a second-billed role as a TV executive in Columbia Pictures' *The Love Machine,* adapted from a trashy best seller by Jacqueline Susann (*Valley of the Dolls*). Before the deal was sealed, executive producer Irving Mansfield, who was married to Susann, paid Ryan a visit to inquire about his health. "Look, there is one thing about cancer: you don't die quickly," Ryan assured him. "I'll be able to make the picture."[43]

The script was putrid, and Ryan disliked costar Dyan Cannon, who played his cheating wife.[44] Before long the picture wrapped, though, and he was back in New York at the Dakota with Jessica and Lisa, now nineteen, who had quit school also and was driving a hansom cab in Central Park. Now that Ryan had overcome the professional stigma of cancer, Jessica had less trouble persuading him to consider a play, and a dream project materialized when Jay Fuchs, a producer on *The Front Page,* put together a deal for Ryan to star in *Long Day's Journey into Night* at the Promenade Theater at Broadway and Seventy-sixth. Ryan had been blown away by the first Broadway production in 1958, and his experience playing James Tyrone Sr. in Nottingham four years earlier had only whetted his appetite for a second staging, one that might better capture O'Neill's bleak vision of an Irish-American clan coming apart at the seams one day in 1912, at their shabby summer home. Ryan's doctors had advised him against doing the play, which ran nearly three hours, but he ignored them.

With Ryan on board, Fuchs and his partners took a chance on thirty-year-old director Arvin Brown, a Yale School of Drama graduate who had done good things at the Long Wharf Theatre in New Haven. Brown would recall his trepidation when he arrived at the Dakota to meet the star: "My impressions of him before I met him were from movies, and he scared the shit out of me." Ryan seemed aloof as he invited Brown in, which did nothing to settle the young man's nerves. But they connected quickly enough over the play, which Brown had directed at Long Wharf five years earlier (with Frank Langella as young Edmund). Ryan "began to get a little more comfortable, and I saw a man begin to emerge who was so the opposite of . . . his film persona, that I could hardly believe what I was seeing."[45] Here was a man with a deep emotional, religious, and cultural connection to the play; he still remembered the racial discrimination faced by his grandfather and father, and his own Black Irish moods had made him a connoisseur of O'Neill's melancholy.

Casting was critical: aside from a maid who appears briefly, *Long Day's Journey* has only four roles, all of them demanding. Tyrone, the rigid patriarch, is a mass of contradictions: he frets over the health of Mary, his wife of thirty-six years, and Edmund, the younger of his grown sons, but his own childhood of dire poverty has left him a skinflint who paces around the house extinguishing lightbulbs and skimps on the family's medical care. To play Jamie—the elder son, whose disillusionment has driven him to a life of whores and whisky—Brown chose twenty-nine-year-old Stacy Keach, another Yale alumnus and already an established Broadway actor. James Naughton, a handsome, twenty-five-year-old member of the Yale Repertory Theatre, leapt at the chance to play Edmund, who learns during the course of the play that he suffers from tuberculosis. For Mary Tyrone, who has slid back into morphine addiction after a brief period of recovery, Brown considered Kim Stanley but ultimately, at Ryan's urging, cast fifty-seven-year-old Geraldine Fitzgerald, who was Irish through and through.

O'Neill had drawn on memories of his family all through his writing career, but *Long Day's Journey into Night,* his last completed work, was so nakedly autobiographical that he never allowed it to be produced in his lifetime. His father, James O'Neill, had shown enormous promise as a young actor but then made a fortune playing the title character in *The Count of Monte Cristo* and stuck with the play until he was trapped in it for the rest of his career. In the fourth and final act, as Tyrone and Edmund sit alone in the parlor playing cards and waiting for Jamie to arrive home, the father opens up to his son, venting his disappointment in himself as he looks back over his career: "I loved Shakespeare. I would have acted in any of his plays for nothing, for the joy of being alive in his great poetry. And I acted well in him. I felt inspired by him. I could have been a great Shakespearean actor, if I'd kept on. . . . But a few years later my good bad luck made me find the big money-maker. . . . What the hell was it I wanted to buy, I wonder."[46]

The words might have come from Ryan's own lips as he considered his straitened career and untapped potential. Friends who saw him perform *Long*

Day's Journey would be struck and in some cases disturbed by the parallels to his own life: the famous father, the fragile mother, the angry, idealistic sons.

That long, searching conversation between Tyrone and Edmund—over forty minutes of stage time—was the heart of the play, and Brown watched carefully as Ryan rehearsed with Jim Naughton, who was making his New York debut. Looking irritated, Ryan asked to speak with Brown afterward, and the director feared that he would demand another actor. Instead Ryan remarked, "The kid is really good, this was a good choice. But I don't wanna tell him that 'cause he'll get a swelled head. So I think you should say that to him."[47] The incident revealed to Brown what a buttoned-down man Ryan was, though in fact the actor had taken this tack before with rising young talents, such as Terence Stamp in *Billy Budd*. From his perspective, egotism was the Achilles' heel of many a performer.

Ryan had more trouble acclimating himself to Fitzgerald, who liked to blurt out her character's thoughts in front of the other actors and whose interpretation of Mary Tyrone turned out to be radically different from the way previous actresses had played her. Researching the role, Fitzgerald had learned that, while morphine abuse reduces most people to dreamy indolence, it can drive others to shrieking fits, and in contrast to the shrinking violet essayed by Florence Eldridge and Katharine Hepburn, her Mary—in keeping with Tyrone's recollection that she once tried to throw herself off a dock—was forceful, even manic. "Ah, she's doing Medea tonight," Ryan cracked one evening as he and Naughton stood in the wings watching her carry on.[48] He made the necessary adjustment, but he often thought Fitzgerald was overacting, a cardinal sin for him. Asked about Ryan's technique, Brown observed, "Above all things, it was economical. I think he loathed extravagance or wasted gesture."[49] Fitzgerald's performance, however, added a strong feminine will to what always had been a male-oriented play, shifting the balance of power and creating a fresh dynamic.

Long Day's Journey into Night opened Wednesday, April 21, to rave reviews from the *New York Times* ("a towering achievement"), *New Yorker* ("a triumph"), *New York Post* ("a stunningly acted production"), Associated Press ("a production of searing splendor"), *Cue* ("one of the decade's most memorable theatrical events"), *Variety* ("best single legit offering off-Broadway this season"), *Newsday* ("one of the major events of this season"), and on and on. Ryan liked to claim that, following Katharine Hepburn's advice, he never read reviews until a show was over, but his colleagues knew better, and after getting slammed so often for his serious stage work, he must have been elated by the universal acclaim. As *Times* critic Walter Kerr noted, the key to Ryan's performance was his strength: "He silences [Edmund] by the steel in his eyes and the sores on his soul he is perfectly ready to expose. His very candor is kindness; he disembowels himself to show that he was made of good stuff.... In his cups, he has a grip on his psyche that no one can dislodge. He is character locked into itself, aware, obtuse, knowing and unalterable. The portrait, in its all-of-a-piece complexity, is beautifully composed, and Mr. Ryan explores the mea culpa in which no forgiveness is asked with admirable, leather-tough control."[50]

That strength may have been illusory; as director of the show, Brown understood better than the other actors how cancer treatment had weakened this vibrant, athletic man. "Compared to what he was used to in himself, I think it was a hard adjustment," said Brown. "Jessica told that to me privately, too, in the early times of our relationship. It had just not occurred to him that he would be seriously ill.... He had been hit harder by it in certain ways than she ever expected."[51] Brown had assembled and rehearsed a second company to perform the matinees, keeping Ryan down to six shows a week, though even this accommodation upset the actor. "We knew that the doctors had told him they didn't think he should be doing it now," remembered Naughton. "So his actions spoke very loudly to us, and set an example for me and for Stacy."[52]

Keach and Naughton both adored Ryan, who was generous with them onstage and never pulled rank. "He loved acting, he loved the challenge of a great part," said Keach, who had admired Ryan on-screen for years. "[He had] an appetite, a wonderful appetite that was very inspiring to me as a young actor because I felt that it was something that I shared." Once the play had opened, Ryan initiated a little ritual with the young men. "At the end of the night," Naughton remembered, "when we were all changing to go out into the evening, he'd say, 'Okay, boys.' And Stacy and I would go into his dressing room, and he had a bottle of bourbon and three glasses. And he'd pour a shot glass for each of us. We'd have a drink together, and then off we'd go into the darkness, until the next night."[53]

As Brown got to know the Ryans better, Bob began talking more openly about his and Jessica's alcoholism, which figured heavily in his regard for *Long Day's Journey*. "That seemed to be an area that, at least privately with me, he wanted to deal with, that he understood in the character and did not want to romanticize," said Brown.[54] Talking to reporters, Ryan always claimed his hard-drinking days were over, and all during *The Front Page* he had stuck to two beers a night as he dined with Harold Kennedy after every show. But the sixth member of the Ryan family had always been liquor. "I went to a Quaker weekend with my parents once, when I was in high school," said Lisa Ryan. "I remember very little of it except that they were unhappy because there was no alcohol there. [They] brought booze and they would go back to their room to drink so that they could then go back out and deal with these Quakers."[55]

Long Day's Journey into Night ran for three months, enough time for the quartet onstage to really take each other's measure. The polarity between Ryan and Fitzgerald persisted all through the run: she loved to improvise, throwing new notes into each performance, whereas Ryan hated surprises onstage. "He planned things, and thought it through," said Brown, "and needed to rehearse and rehearse and rehearse, and feel absolutely comfortable in what he was doing, so that his process was always this one of stripping away and making it more economical."[56]

One night, when an onstage altercation between the brothers got out of hand, Edmund's shirt was badly torn and Naughton, deciding it was a distraction, shed the garment. No one thought to tell Ryan about this; when he made his next entrance and found Naughton bare-chested, he was flummoxed and more than a little angry. But Ryan might fool around backstage: one night Fitzgerald and Naughton, gazing through a window and ostensibly watching James Tyrone out in the yard, saw Ryan, hidden from the audience, peering back at them in a cat's-face mask.

Cancer hadn't impaired his sense of humor. Sometime during the run, Ryan wrote a little prose poem, "The Next Time You Want to Do a Play," in which he noted the various ego punishments of the New York stage. Among its warnings:

> The bad notices will bother you more than the good notices will please you.
> Kind friends will not fail to say things like, "I was furious at what John Simon said about your performance."
> Every night at curtain call you will stand up and humbly solicit the approval of a gang of faceless ass-shifters who have spent most of the evening coughing and yawning.

Your days will be completely wrecked, spent in either doing the play or
dreading it.

You will be besieged to do "talk" shows which pay nothing and operate solely to
enhance the careers of the hosts. Your heart-warming reward will be a letter
to your wife from an aging aunt in Round Rock, Texas, who will say, "I saw
Robert on the Dick Cavett show." Her total comment.

Local tradesmen will say something like, "I saw your show last night. That
Keach fellow is some actor, isn't he?"[57]

Ryan wrote the piece at a time when he could afford to poke fun at himself: *Long Day's Journey* was a genuine triumph and the pinnacle of his stage
career. The following year, when the New York Critics' Poll was released, the
play took best director, best actress, best supporting actor (Keach), and most
promising new off-Broadway actor (Naughton). Even in this instance Ryan
had to settle for being an also-ran, placing third behind Jack MacGowran
and Harold Gould for best actor, but everyone knew he had left his mark on
one of the great roles.

Keach left the show in early June to star in the boxing picture *Fat City*, and
in mid-July, Ryan, Naughton, and Fitzgerald handed the show over to the
matinee cast. Jessica wanted Robert to keep working with Arvin Brown, and
the young man became an occasional guest at their second home up in Holderness. "They had some of their happiest times up there," Brown recalled. "The
family was very relaxed, and it was wonderful to see them all not kind of edgy
with each other. It was really open." At such close quarters, Brown began to
get a sense of the couple's history. "The marriage that I saw was a very devoted
marriage, which you felt had had its problems and traumas—you certainly felt
that, it was nothing easy about the marriage or the relationship—but it had
become very strong. . . . He was dependent on her for her critical attitudes,
he admired a great deal what she had to say about him in performances and
whatnot, and he took her very seriously."[58]

Ryan's next picture was a French crime drama with locations in Montreal
and interiors at Boulogne Billancourt Studios in Paris. Director René Clément
had made some distinguished films after World War II (*The Battle of the Rails,
The Walls of Malapaga*), but he had reached the tail end of his career, and the
script, adapted from David Goodis's pulp novel *Black Friday*, undercut its
rich characters with an obscure and illogical plot. Charley (Ryan), a career

criminal, is the patriarch of a little crime family that occupies a rural house on the water, including his common-law wife (Italian beauty Lea Massari), his thuggish enforcer Mattone (Aldo Ray), and a grown brother and sister whom Charley adopted when they were children. Jean-Louis Trintignant (*And God Created Woman*) took second billing as Tony, a New York crook being held captive by Charley and his clan because he knows the location of some cash Charley wants.

Ryan excelled in this claustrophobic stretch: there's a funny scene in which Tony manages to stack three cigarettes end to end, collecting ten dollars from Charley, and the older man, with a series of elegant hand flourishes and wrist flicks, tries to execute the stunt but can't get the third cigarette balanced without the cylinder crumpling. At the midpoint, though, the movie turns into a garbled heist adventure in which Tony bands together with Charley and his family to kidnap a government witness against an organized crime figure. In keeping with Clément's pretensions, the French release title was *La Course du lièvre à travers les champs* (The race of a hare through the fields), though in the United States the picture would open (and quickly close) as *And Hope to Die*.

Jessica accompanied Ryan to Paris, where the growing fascination with film noir had begun to elevate him to cult-hero status. While they were there, a local cinema held a weeklong retrospective of his films, and according to Lisa, her mother and father ran into a group of film students on the street who began kneeling to Ryan and calling out the names of his old crime pictures. He thought they were nuts.[59]

Back at the Dakota, Ryan took a breather and began looking into new projects. As United Artists produced a screen version of the Broadway musical *Man of La Mancha,* a small outfit called International Producing Associates, with offices in Churubusco, Mexico, announced that Ryan would play the title character in a nonmusical adaptation of *Don Quixote,* with Buddy Hackett as Sancho Panza.[60] That spring the Ryans laid down their marker in the 1972 presidential race by holding a party at the Dakota for the dovish Senator George McGovern, then considered a long shot for the Democratic nomination. *New York Post* columnist Pete Hamill attended, and remembered Ryan telling him, "Maybe this is the last chance we're going to have."[61] Ryan had received an interesting script from MGM called *The Lolly Madonna War,* about two feuding families in rural Tennessee, but the shooting schedule conflicted with a trip to Europe he and Jessica were planning, so he turned it down.

Jim Naughton had formed a close bond with Ryan, and as an avid pool player, he had an open invitation to drop in at the Dakota for a drink and a few games. One day in May 1972, he phoned Ryan to see if he was free, but Ryan begged off, explaining that Jessica was ill. Feeling unwell, she had gone into the hospital for some tests, and on Friday, May 12, her doctors came to Ryan with the grave news that she was dying, quickly and incurably, of liver cancer. Stunned, Ryan summoned the children and, at the doctors' urging, concealed the truth from Jessica. "I asked myself if I was a good enough actor to keep the news from her," Ryan recalled. "Somehow I did. But after a few days, she knew. 'You're all lying to me, aren't you?' she asked. I had to admit we were."[62]

The news got out, and friends telephoned asking to see Jessica, but they were gently turned away. "It was very hard for me, because I loved her so much," said Ramona Lampell. "I'd never known anyone like her. And I'd never had anyone care about me the way Jessica did."[63] But once the Ryan family closed ranks, that was it. According to Arvin Brown, Jessica spoke privately with her husband and each of her children before the end, and her dying request to Ryan was that he stick to the theater and stay true to himself as an artist. Ten days after her diagnosis, Jessica Cadwalader Ryan died at age fifty-seven.

Ryan was thunderstruck: after all these months worrying about his health, how could she be the one who had died? Nothing made sense anymore, but one grim certainty confronted him: like a western hero from the silent era, he would be riding off into the sunset alone.

fifteen

The Loneliest Place in Town

"Dido and I woke up this morning thinking of Jessica," Jean Renoir wrote his old friend Bob Ryan three days after her death. "It is only a moment of weakness: when we think of her, we know perfectly well that she is still with us. She won't abandon you: from now on, her spirit is around you."[1] Jessica's private memorial service was held at the Greenwich Village meeting house of the American Friends Service Committee, with prayers from family and friends and songs from Tim and Cheyney; her ashes were given to Ramona and Millard Lampell, to be mulched into the ground of the New Jersey farm where they had recently moved, and where Bob and Jessica had been guests.

Once the service was over, Tim returned to California and Cheyney to Boston University, where he was teaching and earning a master's degree in philosophy. Lisa was getting an undergraduate degree at the School of Visual Arts in Manhattan and had long since moved out of the Dakota and into her own place. Ryan came home to a twelve-room apartment that now seemed shockingly empty. Eager to get out, he phoned his agent to see if MGM still wanted him for *The Lolly Madonna War,* and a month after Jessica died he found himself in Knoxville, Tennessee, shooting out in the woods with director Richard Sarafian, costar Rod Steiger, and a fine ensemble of up-and-coming players that included Jeff Bridges, Scott Wilson, Gary Busey, Randy Quaid, Season Hubley, Ed Lauter, and Kiel Martin. "'One-Take Ryan,' that's what we call him," Sarafian told the *Los Angeles Times.* "When he came in he was great with the young actors, and they have almost adopted him as a father."[2]

Adapted from a novel by Sue Grafton (later a best-selling mystery writer),

The Lolly Madonna War harked back to the Hatfields and the McCoys but took place in the '70s: Pap Gutshall, the rustic farmer played by Ryan, tools around in a dilapidated station wagon. He and his neighbor, Leonard Feather (Steiger), have been enemies ever since a piece of Feather's land was put up for auction by the county to retire back taxes and Gutshall bought it. The men's grown sons have been pranking each other back and forth for months, but things get out of hand when a young stranger (Hubley) arrives in town, waiting for a connecting bus, and is kidnapped by Hawk Feather (Lauter) and his brother Thrush (Wilson), who have mistaken her for an accomplice in one of the Gutshalls' conspiracies. Bridges, who had already turned heads with his charismatic performance in *The Last Picture Show* (1971), played Zack Feather, sobered by the death of his young wife, who strikes up a romance with the captured woman.

"I discovered that the only possibility for now was work," Ryan wrote to the Renoirs in mid-July, "so I am sweating it out in this steaming place doing a not-bad picture. . . . Jessica loved both of you so and we talked about you so many, many times—always with love, affection and admiration. She was a very rare lady and I feel a little ashamed to mourn when I should really rejoice that I knew her and that we had so many wonderful years together."[3] The Renoirs were back in Hollywood at this point, and Ryan promised them a visit when he came west to shoot interiors for the picture. People knew him as a solitary man, but now he was desperate for company. With Jessica to confide in, solitude could be rich; without her, he was inconsolably lonely. Cheyney Ryan, who had been covering the Democratic National Convention in Miami for the magazine *World*, stopped off in Knoxville on his way back to Boston, but then he was gone. "Something very big is missing," Ryan told a reporter on the set, "and I don't know what to put in its place."[4]

There was always alcohol. Friends and family noticed immediately that Ryan had hit the bottle with a vengeance. Millard and Ramona Lampell were worried by his emotional state—what Millard described as a "black funk"—when Ryan came out to New Jersey to see the pear tree that was growing from his wife's ashes.[5] "He sat on that bench crying," remembered Ramona, "and [talked about] how much he missed her. And it was just so sad."[6] Sitting out in the country with them, Ryan went over and over Jessica's life, excoriating himself for the ways he had failed her. Friends saw him filled with regret for the months and years he had spent away from his family.

"What the hell did I make all that money for?"[7] he asked Philip Dunne, as James Tyrone in *Long Day's Journey into Night* had asked, "What the hell was it I wanted to buy, I wonder."

Millard saw Ryan as a pillar: "He was sort of big daddy to everyone around him; that was the way Jessica felt toward him, that was the way his friends felt toward him. If you were in trouble, you could go to Robert."[8] Yet Jessica always had been the emotional center of the family, and once she was gone Ryan and the children began to drift apart. Lisa saw her father the most; now that she was an adult, they could drink together, and as they stayed up late playing pool, he began to open up to her about his life in a way he never had. Cheyney kept tabs on his dad from Boston but was dismayed by what he saw. "I thought my father handled my mother's death very badly," he admitted, "and one of the reasons why it was such a traumatic event, I think for all of us, was because my father just did not deal with it. . . . He thought only of himself; he was drinking all the time. I never got the feeling once that he gave a thought to the impact of this on the three of us, and fairly soon into that year I just started to get sick of it, to feel that this was a completely dysfunctional situation."[9]

Ryan returned to New York resolved to move out of the Dakota and buy a smaller unit back at 88 Central Park West, where the family had lived in the mid-1960s. He put out feelers that he wanted to lease the Dakota apartment and almost immediately had two prospective tenants: John Lennon and Yoko Ono, who had been living in the St. Regis Hotel on Fifth Avenue since they moved from England to the United States a year earlier. Ryan took Lisa with him when he went to meet the former Beatle; to her astonishment Lennon was excited to be shaking hands with Robert Ryan. "I guess he liked American westerns," she recalled. "And I'm just sitting there with my mouth hanging open, 'cause I'm meeting John Lennon."[10] The two men chatted amiably about their family lines back in Ireland, and the deal went through. Lennon and Ono would move into the Ryans' old home in February 1973, and Ryan rented a unit down the street, where, according to Lisa, he re-created his late wife's room.

Around that time, Arvin Brown and his wife, Joyce, hosted Ryan at their oceanside home in Branford, Connecticut, and found him grateful for any company. He liked Joyce Brown and went out shopping with her around town. "In certain periods of his life, he had a funny kind of deference in his personality," said Arvin. "He would sort of go along with what everyone was doing, and just trot along. And it was always great fun, because he was a very famous man, and wherever he'd go and shop everyone would do double takes and whatnot, which he was always delighted by."[11] Ryan filled them in on his children, praising them in a way he never would to their faces. "He was proud of what he felt was their honesty, and their integrity with themselves," Brown remembered. "Whatever concerns that he might have shared about their direction in life had nothing to do with what he felt was their character."[12]

Late that year Ryan was invited to a dinner party and spent a pleasant evening talking to his old friend Maureen O'Sullivan. Born in County Roscommon, Ireland, and educated in a convent school, O'Sullivan was discovered by director Frank Borzage and became a star at MGM in the early 1930s, working steadily for ten years before she retired from show business in 1942 to concentrate on her family. With her husband, John Farrow (who had directed Ryan in the RKO potboiler *Back from Eternity*), she raised seven children; Mia Farrow had become a star in 1967 with *Rosemary's Baby* (which was filmed at the Dakota), and Ryan had recently worked with her younger sister Tisa, one of the crime kids in René Clément's *And Hope to Die*. O'Sullivan, who resumed her career in the '50s, was known around Hollywood as a good mother and a faithful wife, until Farrow died in 1963. She and Ryan crossed paths briefly in January 1970, when she joined the cast of *The Front Page* just as he was leaving it. After the dinner party, the two of them became an item, spotted together in restaurants and at the theater.

Coming so soon after Jessica's death, the relationship pained some of those closest to Ryan but warmed others; Robert Wallsten and Albert Hackett thought O'Sullivan a great tonic for their old friend. Few doubted her affection for Ryan, though some wondered if he returned it in equal measure or simply needed a woman's care. Cheyney, who wound up having more contact with O'Sullivan than his siblings, appreciated what his father saw in her and what she did for him: "I think he liked the fact that Maureen had this kind of Irish Catholic reputation about her," he recalled. O'Sullivan struck him as "a fairly reserved and a thoughtful person. . . . You know, my mother was [my father's] sole emotional connection to reality. He was the kind of guy that was gonna relate to those things through having a female partner."[13]

Ryan had never forgotten the experience of filming *Billy Budd* on the high seas, and before Christmas he traveled to Newport, Rhode Island, to shoot an ABC movie-of-the-week aboard a 1970 replica of the HMS *Rose,* which had fired on American fortifications during the Revolutionary War. Based on an

1863 story by Edward Everett Hale, *The Man without a Country* starred Cliff Robertson as army lieutenant Philip Nolan, charged with treason in 1807 for having conspired with former Vice President Aaron Burr to found a new nation in Texas and Mexico. "I wish I may never hear of the United States again!" Nolan shouts at his trial, prompting the judge to exile him for life.[14] Over the years he's transferred from one navy ship to another, never to set foot on US soil again, and his crewmates are forbidden to tell him what's going on in his native land. Beau Bridges costarred as the career officer who befriends Nolan, and Ryan breezed through his cameo as a navy veteran who narrates part of Nolan's story. Beautifully written, the movie had a special resonance in a time when some thirty thousand Americans, having evaded the draft by going to Canada, now faced prosecution at home.

Since Ryan's cancer diagnosis two years earlier, he had become preoccupied with building up an estate, which meant doing pictures; yet Jessica had implored him to pursue theater work. A lovely compromise presented itself near the end of the year when John Frankenheimer, who had directed Ryan in *The Snows of Kilimajaro* on CBS in 1960, offered him $25,000 (a sixth of what he now commanded, but a decent sum) to play the whiskey-soaked anarchist Larry Slade in a screen version of Eugene O'Neill's *The Iceman Cometh*. Since their experience doing live TV together, Frankenheimer had become a top movie director with smart, paranoid pictures such as *The Manchurian Candidate* (1962), *Seven Days in May* (1964), and *Seconds* (1968). *The Iceman Cometh* would be rehearsed for three weeks in LA and shot in sequence over seven weeks on the Fox lot, with a cast to include not only Lee Marvin and Jeff Bridges, but also Ryan's hero Fredric March. Ryan flew out to the coast the first week of January 1973, pleased with the new year.

"HAS THE ICEMAN COME YET?" a man calls upstairs to his wife. "No," she replies, "but he's breathing fast."[15] O'Neill alludes to this dirty joke several times during *The Iceman Cometh*—it's a favorite of his high-spirited traveling salesman, Hickey—but as the biblical conjugation of the title suggests, the iceman is also Death. Running four hours, the play is confined to Harry Hope's saloon, a Lower Manhattan dive where men come to drink themselves into an early grave. Hope owns the five-story building, an SRO hotel, and by drawing a curtain across the street-level bar he can turn the back section into a "hotel restaurant" and legally serve liquor at all hours. The play opens in early morning, as bartender Rocky (Tom Pedi) arrives and finds the usual assortment of drunks passed out on the tables. But Larry Slade, Ryan's character, is wide-awake and philosophically inclined. His dreams, he confesses to Rocky, "are all dead and buried behind me. What's before me is the comforting fact that death is a fine long sleep, and I'm damn tired, and it can't come too soon for me."[16]

The picture was being produced by the American Film Theatre, a high-toned experiment in which faithful screen adaptations of great theater works would be exhibited at local movie houses on Monday and Wednesday nights, with patrons buying subscriptions for an entire "season" through American Express. Producer Eli Landau had already begun or completed adaptations of Edward Albee's *A Delicate Balance* (with Katharine Hepburn), John Osborne's *Luther* (with Stacy Keach), and Harold Pinter's *The Homecoming* (with Cyril Cusack); *The Iceman Cometh* would open the first season. The novel exhibition approach made running time less of an issue than usual, and though Frankenheimer pruned the play down with an editor, so many actors came to him during production with good arguments for restoring deleted dialogue that he wound up shooting close to the entire text at a length of four hours. Landau urged Frankenheimer to alleviate the play's claustrophobia by moving a few scenes out onto the street, but the director refused, arguing that the sense of enclosure was critical to O'Neill's take on illusion and reality.

The Iceman Cometh offered a colorful ensemble of characters, the main antagonists being Larry, a former anarchist who's renounced politics, and Hickey, who drops in at the saloon every few months to dispense good cheer and free drinks. Frankenheimer quickly settled on Ryan as the perfect Larry: "He had a deep sadness inherent in most of these O'Neill characters."[17] Casting Hickey was more difficult: Jason Robards was strongly identified with the role but had played it so many times that Frankenheimer opted for someone new, offering the part to Marlon Brando (who declined, saying he would never be able to memorize the lengthy soliloquies) and considering Gene Hackman before going with Lee Marvin. Fredric March, who had retired in 1970 to battle prostate cancer, returned for one last screen performance in the relatively small role of Harry Hope. Richard Dreyfuss, Keith Carradine, and John Savage all read for the part of Don Parritt, the young radical who arrives at the saloon looking for Larry and reveals their shared past. Savage even shot a screen test, though the role ultimately went to an uncertain Jeff Bridges.

As Bridges recalled, the offer came along when he was worn out from shooting *The Last American Hero* with director Lamont Johnson (Ryan's old friend) and, more fundamentally, was unsure whether he wanted to keep acting or pursue a music career. Initially he turned down the role, but when Johnson heard that the young man had passed up the chance to work with Ryan, March, and Marvin, he phoned Bridges, called him a "stupid ass," and hung up on him.[18] Bridges reversed himself, and by his own admission, the experience of making *The Iceman Cometh* inspired him to take his craft much more seriously. He and Ryan had met the previous year, shooting *The Lolly Madonna War* (ultimately released as *Lolly-Madonna XXX*), but shared no scenes together; in *The Iceman Cometh* they went head to head in scenes that stretched out as long as nine minutes. "He was one of my favorite actors," said Bridges (who, like Stacy Keach, still remembered Ryan's chilling performance as Claggart in *Billy Budd*). "As an actor he stood alone for me."[19]

Frankenheimer strived to create a good artistic environment. The ensemble of fifteen actors included such talents as Moses Gunn, Bradford Dillman, Sorrell Booke, and Clifton James, and Frankenheimer gave them all plenty of screen time; copying the Dutch masters, he used deep-focus photography to compose gloomy frames in which various barflies, stiff with drink, listened and sometimes reacted to a central character's extended speech. Ryan, March, and Marvin showed up whether they had scenes or not, just to watch. Arvin Brown took several phone calls from Ryan during the shoot: "Every time he called me it was to tell me about some brilliant thing that Freddy March had done on the set."[20] March had been ill during rehearsals but showed up on the last day with his part down cold, and he delivered on camera. Evans Evans, who was married to Frankenheimer and played one of the three hookers who frequent the bar, recalled a collegial Friday-night dinner on the set that attracted not only the cast but the entire crew and that Ryan thoroughly enjoyed.[21]

"As rehearsals progressed we became closer and closer," Frankenheimer later wrote in a letter to Lisa Ryan. "Naturally he told me of his sickness and your mother's death. Then the problem became not to let him personalize the role too much. But he didn't—always the pro—knowing just when to pull away."[22]

According to Frankenheimer, Ryan mentored Bridges throughout the shoot, but just watching Ryan work could be a lesson in itself. One day he and Bridges were seated at a table together, waiting for the crew to set up one of their long and demanding dialogue scenes; these had to be played at their full length because Frankenheimer was shooting with two cameras,

Former anarchist Larry Slade (Ryan) confers with Don Parritt (Jeff Bridges) and Hugo Kalmar (Sorrell Booke) in *The Iceman Cometh* (1973). "As an actor he stood alone for me," Bridges said of Ryan. *Franklin Jarlett Collection*

one for each actor and each with its own cues for zooming in and out. Years earlier, Ryan had confessed to one reporter that, for some reason, nothing fazed him like having to play a scene seated at a table.[23] The assistant director announced they were ready, and Ryan lifted his palms from the table to reveal twin puddles of perspiration—the old flop sweat. When Bridges asked Ryan if he still got nervous after all these years, Ryan replied, "If I wasn't nervous, I'd be really nervous."[24] Yet on-screen, Bridges is the one who looks nervous, giving the role his all but often giving too much; Ryan, ever the minimalist, pared his performance down to the bare essentials but made every reaction count. Spencer Tracy had upstaged Ryan in much the same fashion nearly twenty years earlier, in *Bad Day at Black Rock*.

The evolving relationship between Larry and young Don Parritt was steeped in the anarchist politics of the 1910s but still relevant in the bitter era of the Black Panthers and the Weather Underground. O'Neill based Parritt on a real-life figure, Donald Vose, who betrayed his mother and her anarchist comrades to the police after the 1910 bombing of the *Los Angeles Times* building; in *The Iceman Cometh,* the guilt-ridden Parritt comes looking for Larry, his mother's old lover—and, possibly, his father—hoping to make an emotional connection that the older man steadfastly resists. Larry has given much of his life to the anarchist dream, but he can no longer maintain the fervor it demands. "I was born condemned to be one of those who has to see all sides of a question," he tells Parritt. "When you're damned like that, the questions multiply for you until in the end it's all question and no answer."[25]

Cheyney Ryan visited LA during the shoot and spent some time on the set; he and his dad were sharing a car, and none of Cheyney's friends got up before noon, so he would hang around the Fox lot in the morning and watch the company work. As he later told writer Dwayne Epstein, Marvin showed up one day at 8 AM with a case of beer and proceeded to get hammered. "He got into a thing about what a big star he was," Cheyney recalled. "It was really unpleasant. . . . He said, 'Your father's not a big star anymore. I'm a big star. He used to be a big star and now I'm the big star.' This went on and on and on."[26] Frankenheimer took Marvin aside later and read him the riot act about his drinking, just as Richard Brooks had on *The Professionals,* and Marvin—who confessed to Frankenheimer that he was terrified to be working with Fredric March—promised to straighten up. "Bob did an awful lot toward calming Lee down," said Frankenheimer, "because Lee had tremendous respect for Bob Ryan."[27]

Marvin may have been right about his and Ryan's relative stardom, but *The Iceman Cometh,* with its philosophical contest between Larry and Hickey, gave the two actors a parity lacking in any of their previous collaborations. Hickey arrives at Harry Hope's saloon swearing off booze (though he sets up the drinks for everyone else) and urging his old friends to cast off their illusions and face the world. Larry already has expressed his feelings on the subject: "As the history of the world proves, the truth has no bearing on anything," he tells Rocky. "The lie of a pipe dream is what gives life to the whole misbegotten mad lot of us, drunk or sober."[28] Marvin came into the project at a clear disadvantage: he hardly was known for his theatrical prowess, and he clearly was an offbeat choice to play such a seemingly cheery character. Ryan, however, had found in O'Neill the sort of weighty, tragic characters he had been chasing his entire career. When critic Charles Champlin visited the set, Ryan told him, "This is one I'll want to be remembered by."[29]

RYAN WAS BOOKED into the Beverly Wilshire Hotel, but most nights he stayed at Phil Yordan's house on Benedict Canyon Drive. "He didn't want to be alone," Yordan recalled. "He was a very lonely man."[30] As a houseguest, Ryan was quiet and undemanding: coffee in the morning, a ham sandwich and glass of milk at lunchtime. Yordan was in the process of negotiating a huge deal with Television Corporation of America for the sale of all his films and literary properties, as well as his half-interest in a forty-acre studio in Madrid; *Variety* reported that he would join the company as a producer and listed as one of his upcoming projects a drama called *Riche,* to be shot in Yugoslavia the following year with Ryan, Rod Taylor, and Claudia Cardinale.[31] After *Iceman* wrapped in early March, Ryan moved on to *The Outfit,* a crime drama for MGM with Robert Duvall (who had become a star with *The Godfather*), Karen Black, and Joe Don Baker. Ryan played a mob boss, the sort of thing he could do in his sleep. "At that point his wife was gone and all he was interested in was creating an estate for his children," observed Yordan.[32]

John Flynn, the forty-one-year-old director of *The Outfit,* had apprenticed with Robert Wise on *Odds Against Tomorrow* back in 1959, and like Wise he populated his story with familiar noir faces: Jane Greer, Marie Windsor, Timothy Carey, Elisha Cook Jr. An edgy score from Jerry Fielding accompanies the tense opening sequence, in which two mob assassins, disguised as a priest and his cab driver, arrive at the rural home of their target and wordlessly stalk him in his backyard, cutting him down with silencers on their pistols as a German shepherd fights to get off its chain. Paroled from prison, the victim's brother (Duvall) learns what happened from his girlfriend (Black) and rounds up an old pal (Baker) to get even with the mob kingpin responsible for the hit (Ryan).

Flynn had learned his lessons well: *The Outfit* harked back to Wise's early, low-budget classics (*The Set-Up, Born to Kill*) in its visual economy, inventive framing, and propulsive editing. All things considered, it was a more satisfying genre revival than René Clément's *And Hope to Die.* Joe Don Baker, a Texan who had learned his craft at the Actors Studio in New York, came to the project as a fan of Ryan's performances in *The Set-Up* and *Odds against Tomorrow.* He found the elderly actor to be a quiet, modest man; the scuttlebutt around the set was that he was dying of cancer.[33]

The private home doubling as the mobster's mansion was located on Sunset Boulevard, only a few blocks from the Ryans' old house in Holmby Hills. Ryan told *Variety* that he had sold the place to George Axelrod for $175,000 back in 1962, at the bottom of the market; Axelrod, he reported, had recently sold it to Barbra Streisand for four times that amount. On the last day of shooting, producer Carter DeHaven threw a party in Ryan's honor, and the City of Los Angeles awarded him a plaque celebrating the completion of his eightieth picture.* Jane Russell attended, and so did Burt Lancaster, who had lined up Ryan to costar with him in a hush-hush project about the Kennedy assassination called *Executive Action*. Ryan got a laugh when he accepted the award, thanking the city but conspicuously omitting conservative mayor Sam Yorty. "Eighty pictures," Ryan marveled to Charles Champlin during the party. "And 70 of them were dogs. I mean, *dogs*."[34]

Back in New York, Ryan made the rounds with Maureen O'Sullivan, who spent a good deal of time at his apartment at 88 Central Park West. "He felt that he should wait a decent length of time before he got married after his wife's death," remembered Albert Hackett. At one point Ryan and O'Sullivan paid him a visit, and Ryan did a little soft-shoe routine to a song playing on the phonograph. "I never saw him so well and so happy," said Hackett, "and I thought he was getting ready for the big moment when the year was up, and they were going to get married."[35] Ryan also was plotting his return to musical theater after more than ten years: the *Hollywood Reporter* soon would announce that he had signed to star in a musical version of the Jimmy Stewart drama *Shenandoah* (1965), as a Virginia farmer who wants to keep his sons out of the Civil War. The show was scheduled to open on Broadway in March 1974.[36]

Executive Action, a speculative account of US industrialists plotting to assassinate President Kennedy, originated with Donald Sutherland and attorney Mark Lane, whose 1966 best seller *Rush to Judgment* had raised serious questions about the Warren Report. Sutherland put Lane together with playwright Donald Freed to draft a screenplay, but when the actor failed to secure financing, the project was taken over by Edward Lewis, an executive producer on *The Iceman Cometh* and a veteran of left-leaning Hollywood cinema (*Spartacus, Lonely Are the Brave, Seven Days in May, Seconds*). Dalton Trumbo was brought in to rewrite the script, and though he professed skepticism initially, he was converted after seeing the uncut Abraham Zapruder film of the assassination, which had never been broadcast, and concluding that it showed the president being fired upon from two different locations.

---

*Someone had miscounted, because *The Outfit* was only his seventy-first theatrical feature.

With a paltry budget of about \$500,000, Lewis persuaded Burt Lancaster to make the film for scale, and Lancaster sold Ryan on doing the same. Cheyney Ryan remembered his father praising the script, which at first he didn't know had been written by his old colleague Trumbo.[37] "I originally bought the lone assassin theory because it's been American history, at least as far as we know," said Ryan when he was interviewed on the set for a making-of documentary. "But when I read the script, the machinery of the conspiracy was so convincing that I began to change my mind. I don't mean I have the answer, but the script itself made me want to do the picture."[38] He always had an eye out for political provocations (for years he had wanted to make a picture about John Brown, the abolitionist who tried to launch a slave insurrection before the Civil War). *Executive Action* also offered the comfort of familiar faces—not just Lancaster but Will Geer, whose association with Ryan stretched back twenty years to John Houseman's production of *Coriolanus,* and who had recently gotten the last laugh on HUAC when he became a beloved figure on the hit CBS drama *The Waltons.*

Publicity materials would quote director David Miller saying that Ryan likened his *Executive Action* character—Robert Foster, a Texas millionaire scheming to kill the president—to Montgomery, the murderous bigot in *Crossfire.* Both men are closet fascists, the millionaire couching his race hatred in the cool, clean arguments of social Darwinism. Strolling around the grounds of his estate with James Farrington (Lancaster), a shadowy paramilitary type, Foster sketches out a dystopian future of exploding minority populations clamoring for limited resources. That's why victory in Vietnam is crucial: "An all-out effort there will give us control of South Asia for years to come. And with proper planning, we can reduce the population to 550 million by the end of the century. . . . Not only will the nations affected be better off, but the techniques developed there can be used to reduce our own excess population: Puerto Ricans, Mexican Americans, poverty-prone whites, and so forth." One last time Ryan breathed life into an incendiary political picture by embracing the thing he loathed.

Unfortunately any parallels to *Crossfire* end there, because *Executive Action* is clumsy and inert, more like an illustrated lecture than a story. Trumbo opens in early June 1963, as the genteel Foster hosts a little conference of powerful right-wingers on his estate. Geer, clad in a cream-colored suit, plays Harold Ferguson, a folksy oil tycoon whom the others need to back their covert action

Ryan gives his final performance, in *Executive Action* (1973), as the right-wing oil man Robert Foster. Victory in Vietnam, Foster insists, "will give us control of South Asia for years to come. And with proper planning, we can reduce the population to 550 million by the end of the century." *Franklin Jarlett Collection*

against JFK (the reason for this is never really explained). The bespectacled Paulitz (Gilbert Green) predicts that in the next few months the president will back civil rights, endorse a nuclear test ban treaty, and begin a retreat from Vietnam. Farrington presents a slide show detailing past presidential assassination attempts and argues that their best chance of success is triangulated sniper fire during a presidential motorcade; a later slide show acquaints them with their chosen patsy, Lee Harvey Oswald.

These endless lecture sequences are interrupted periodically by desert scenes in which three snipers (commanded by bald, hawk-nosed Ed Lauter of *Lolly-Madonna XXX*) practice firing on a moving target. Miller incorporates archival footage to show Paulitz's predictions coming true: Kennedy makes his famous speech at American University in June 1963 supporting a test ban treaty, states the moral imperative for a civil rights bill in a speech from the Oval Office that same month, and tells a reporter at a press conference that he hopes to have a thousand US advisors out of Vietnam by the end of the year. An obviously phony newscast hammers home the point that Kennedy intends to pull out of Indochina—still a matter of historical debate—and the report so incenses Harry Ferguson that he finally gives the kill order on JFK.

Despite the conspiracy theory, Ryan was fascinated most by the plush train car being used as a set for *Executive Action*. It must have brought back memories of the New England whistle-stop campaign for Stevenson twenty years earlier. One could rent a furnished train car and travel across the country by connecting with various lines, and Ryan had decided that he and Maureen O'Sullivan would collect family and friends and travel by rail through the mountain country of Tennessee and West Virginia.

In Los Angeles, he visited Philip and Amanda Dunne, and one day he turned up at the doorstep of John and Evans Frankenheimer's house in Malibu. They invited him to stay over, and before long he was spending every weekend with them. "A lot of it was great reminiscing, just very relaxed," said Evans. "We would have lunch and then he would read, and then later he would wander off."[39] He drank heavily, talking about Jessica, though otherwise his health appeared to be holding. "He honestly thought he had the cancer licked," said John Frankenheimer. "He never got over the fact that here he had the cancer and his wife nursed him through it, and after he was somewhat cured, then she came down with it. He couldn't understand it. He deeply, deeply missed his wife."[40]

Onscreen Ryan looked pasty and tired, and after he began complaining of back pains, Miller hastened to complete his scenes so he could return to New York and look after himself. Larry Goebel, a cinema student at the University of Southern California, would write a letter to the *Los Angeles Times* remembering his visit to the rail yard in Vernon, California, on the day Ryan shot his last scene with Burt Lancaster. When they were done, "the train's porter served martinis to the two stars. After one sip, Ryan went into one of the funniest drunk routines ever witnessed.... The entire crew was convulsed for five minutes. Shortly afterwards, he shook hands with everyone and left to catch a plane for New York."[41] Against all odds, Ryan's last performance was pure comedy.

On Tuesday, July 3, Ryan was admitted to New York Hospital. Maureen O'Sullivan informed Cheyney, who drove in from Boston to assess the situation. Along the way he stopped off in Newport, Rhode Island, to visit Mia Farrow, who was shooting *The Great Gatsby* with Robert Redford, and his sister, Lisa, who had accepted Farrow's invitation to be an extra in a party scene. When Cheyney arrived in Manhattan the next day, the information on his father was sketchy; he spent a few afternoons in the hospital with Ryan, watching sports on TV, and more time than he would have liked on the phone with John Lennon's people, trying to retrieve some air conditioners from the Dakota that his father wanted back. Ryan's mood was dark; at one point he told Cheyney, "I don't want to live anymore."[42]

Ryan and Burt Lancaster on location for *Executive Action* (1973). After completing their last scenes together, Ryan took one sip of a martini, performed a riotous drunk act for the crew's amusement, shook hands with everyone, and flew home to look after his health. *Franklin Jarlett Collection*

The following week the doctors came to Cheyney and O'Sullivan with grim news: the cancer had returned and spread to Ryan's lungs. Tim and Lisa were telephoned and began heading for New York, where they all were to confer with the doctors about the next phase of their father's treatment. Lisa and Cheyney visited Ryan on the morning of Wednesday, July 11. That afternoon his lungs hemorrhaged and he began to choke, but the staff managed to stabilize him. O'Sullivan arrived at 88 Central Park West that evening, distraught over Ryan's condition and unhappy with the care he was getting. Tim flew in from California that night; before he could see his father, though, the hospital phoned to notify them that Ryan had suffered another breathing attack and choked to death.

"I'VE HAD A GOOD SHOT AT LIFE," Ryan told a *Los Angeles Times* reporter the previous summer, reflecting on his earlier cancer scare. "So what the hell do I have to complain about. My brother died when he was six, and I've thought about it my whole life. He never even got started. I've been lucky as hell with my career and my family. We were always close. Still are. How many men can say that?"[43]

Tim, Cheyney, and Lisa were so shell-shocked that Millard and Ramona Lampell took care of the funeral arrangements. A private service was held on Monday, July 16, at Blessed Sacrament Church on Seventy-First Street, and descended into black comedy when the priest celebrating the funeral mass—a relative of Ryan's from Chicago—became confused by the English text, having performed the mass only in Latin, and made a mess of things. Jason Robards, Myrna Loy, Dore Schary, and John McGiver attended the service,[44] and the guests were welcomed back to 88 Central Park West afterward for what Millard described as "a regular Irish, old-fashioned wake."[45] He and Robards shot a few games of pool. The *Hollywood Reporter* had reported that Ryan would be buried in Chicago,[46] but in fact he was cremated and his ashes taken by the Lampells to be mixed with Jessica's on the grounds of their farm. His estate, estimated in the press at half a million dollars, was divided equally among the children.[47]

The tributes that followed praised Ryan's personal qualities as much as his acting. "There should be a poem of farewell for Robert Ryan, who was a good man in a bad time," wrote Pete Hamill in the *New York Post.* Hamill reminded readers of Ryan's long years in the liberal trenches, founding Hollywood for SANE amid the Red Scare, but also pointed out Ryan's "refusal to make his life a performance. He saved his private life for himself, and his children, and his wife, Jessica. He took no punches at photographers. There were no drunken car wrecks. There were no messy divorces."[48] In the *Los Angeles Times,* Charles Champlin connected this same modesty to his onscreen brilliance: "He did what he did with a caring, self-effacing professionalism which illuminated the character rather than his private persona, and he did it so well that the art was, in its paradoxical way, invisible."[49]

Newsweek writer Paul Zimmerman would fashion Ryan's cultural epitaph when he wrote that the actor left behind "a lifetime of roles too small for his talent."[50] This wasn't entirely accurate—Ryan had tackled great roles onstage and fallen short (*Othello, Antony and Cleopatra*)—but the consensus view among critics was that he had never gotten his due. For several years he had served on the board of governors for the Motion Picture Academy, yet aside from *Crossfire,* Oscar never had taken the least notice of his finest portrayals, not Stoker Thompson in *The Set-Up,* nor Jim Wilson in *On Dangerous Ground,* nor Ben Vandergroat in *The Naked Spur,* nor Ty Ty Walden in *God's Little Acre,* nor John Claggart in *Billy Budd,* nor Deke Thornton in *The Wild Bunch.* Released in November 1973, on the heels of *The Outfit* and *Executive Action, The Iceman Cometh* became Ryan's final artistic testament, and attention finally was paid: the National Board of Review named him best actor of the year, and the National Society of Film Critics gave him a special award for "a consummate demonstration of acting skill at the end of a long distinguished career."[51]

An even more fitting tribute followed a year later, when John Houseman hosted a performance of Sean O'Casey's *Juno and the Paycock* at the Mark Taper Forum to benefit the Robert and Jessica Ryan Memorial Foundation. A $10,000 grant from Liz Harmon had established the foundation, which was to fund teacher training and instruction of children with learning disabilities, and to institutionalize the social studies program that Jessica and Marie Spottswood had worked so hard to create. Spottswood wrote that the program still was using the books and materials Jessica had written, praising "her able and courageous leadership in piloting the school through a most harassing and difficult period when rival radical factions among parents and teachers came close to destroying it. More than anyone else, she was responsible for Oakwood's survival."[52] Even after the Ryans left Los Angeles, they had maintained their connection to the school.

For such a reserved man, Ryan could be surprisingly open with pen in hand; even on something as simple as an alumni questionnaire, he might hold forth on the state of the world and himself. "Our tendency to become a spectator nation has probably benefited me—nevertheless I deplore it," he wrote on one such form back in November 1956. "I look forward to a world at peace and to my children's lives. I am grateful for my work, my wife, and my children (not in that order)."[53] He always aspired to be an actor, rather than a spectator, in both the political and the theatrical sense, though he would never see a world at peace, and ordering his personal and professional priorities would become more of a challenge than he could have imagined then. The characters Ryan created are all that remain of him now, men for whom shadow is a state of mind.

Acknowledgments

I came to Ryan's work early for someone of my generation. As a freshman at Loyola Academy, a Jesuit school in Wilmette, Illinois, I began my four-year religion curriculum with a class that included a showing and discussion of the 1962 movie *Billy Budd*. My teacher stressed the Christlike sacrifice of young Billy, but this lesson was subverted by the fact that the most charismatic character in the movie was the evil master-of-arms, Mr. Claggart.

The actor, my teacher explained, was Robert Ryan, class of 1927; when I filed down the hallway that housed the school's class photos (passing Bill Murray, class of 1968) and found the portrait of seventeen-year-old Robert Ryan, I could barely reconcile it with the lined, hardened face I had seen on-screen. To begin, then, I thank Rev. James Arimond at Loyola for providing copies of Ryan's earliest published writings, in the school's newspaper and literary magazine, and other background material on his education.

His generosity has been matched by many others who supplied documents, articles, and photographs that inform this account: Dr. James Astman, headmaster of the Oakwood School; Deanna Chew of the La Jolla Playhouse; Sarah Hartwell of Dartmouth College Library; Eddie Muller and Alan K. Rode of the Film Noir Foundation; Vickie Ryan, the actor's daughter-in-law (who provided historical material on the Cheyneys and Cadwaladers); Cheryl S. Spiese and Jean L. Green of the Max Reinhardt Archive at SUNY–Binghamton; Tina Louise Happ of Pritzker Military Library in Chicago; and Vivian Teng of Cinema/Chicago. Above all, I want to thank Peter Jarlett, who provided photographs, audiotaped interviews, and transcriptions amassed by his late brother, Franklin Jarlett, author of *Robert Ryan: A Biography and Critical Filmography* (1990). That book offers a more complete guide to Ryan's work in various media than I have, and I recommend it to those seeking more information.

I am much indebted to the fine research facilities where I conducted my work. In particular I want to thank Martin Gostanian at the Paley Center for Media in Los Angeles, Mark Quigley of the UCLA Film and Television Archive, Julie Graham and Amy Wong of UCLA Performing Arts Special Collections, Maxine Ducey and Mary Huelsbeck of the Wisconsin Center for Film and Theater Research, and Jenny Romero of the Margaret Herrick Library, Fairbanks Center for Motion Picture Study, Beverly Hills. I remember fondly my time researching this project with the Herrick Library's friendly and enthusiastic staff.

This book originated in an October 2009 story in the *Chicago Reader,* "The Actor's Letter," and many *Reader* colleagues contributed their expertise to that project or to this volume: Andrea Bauer, Michael Miner, Jonathan Rosenbaum, Mara Shalhoup, Alison True, Albert Williams, and Kiki Yablon. Dave Kehr, whose early film writing in the *Reader* I much admired, urged me to write this book after reading "The Actor's Letter" and so must be credited with setting it in motion.

My thanks to Chris Linster of Quartet Digital Printing and to my friends and colleagues who read and offered their input on my book proposal and early drafts: Margaret Buchen, Lisa Dombrowski, Joseph C. Heinen, Jonathan Joe, Michael Phillips, Alan Rode, Martin Rubin, Parker Smathers at Wesleyan University Press, and above all my agent, Peter Riva of International Transactions.

I am blessed with family members who aided me in this project. My sister Ruth Ann Jones, a reference librarian, directed me toward countless revealing materials; my sister Julia Macintosh in the UK tracked down reviews of Ryan's 1967 residency at the Nottingham Playhouse; my sister-in-law, Kelsey Beson, translated a key Ryan interview from a French magazine; and my uncle Tom Jones in Louisville nabbed a story from the local *Courier-Journal.* My wife, Margaret, has been a constant source of love and encouragement as this project took over my life (and hers).

Many people were generous with their time in sharing their personal reminiscences of the Ryans and their children: Joe Don Baker, Phil Bauman, Harry Belafonte, Jeff Bridges, Arvin Brown, Rhonda Fleming, Evans Frankenheimer, Charles Haas, Andy Harmon, Toya Harrison, Seymour Hersh,

Marsha Hunt, Stacy Keach, Ramona Lampell, Tina Louise, Mike Metzger, James Naughton, Rev. Lothar Nurnberger, Nehemiah Persoff, Priscilla Ulene, and Jacqueline White.

I'm especially grateful to Lisa Ryan, Cheyney Ryan, and Walker (formerly Timothy) Ryan for their candor and patience as I reconstructed their parents' story. Throughout the process they impressed me as people who shared their parents' desire for privacy but also felt that this story should be told.

Robert Ryan Performances

part one Stage Chronology

TOO MANY HUSBANDS (1940) Belasco Theater, Los Angeles, January 15, 1940.
   Director: Max Reinhardt. Producer: Lloyd D. Mitchell. Playwright: Somerset
   Maugham. Music: Bronislau (aka Bronislaw) Kaper. Cast: Robert Ryan, Maris
   Wrixon, Bruce Bennett, Arno Arno, Ernö Verebes, Adele Neff, Helene Hill, Martin
   Wessner, Millard Vincent, Ralph Freud, Ann Lee.

THE TIME OF YOUR LIFE (1941) Millpond Playhouse, Roslyn, Long Island, June 30
   to July 12, 1941. Director: David Lowe. Producer: David Lowe. Playwright: William
   Saroyan. Cast: Robert Ryan (Joe), Jane Jeffreys, Harald Dyrenforth, James Murray,
   Cameron Mitchell, Jane Morrisey, Joel Steele, Neville Draper. *Note:* Staged during
   the Ryans' summer repertory season at Millpond Playhouse; among the other productions that season were *The Barker* (June 9, 1941), starring Robert Ryan, Jessica
   Cheyney, Edward Thompson, and Kenneth Forbes; *Petticoat Fever* (June 16, 1941),
   starring Ryan and Cheyney; and *Angel Child* (date unknown), starring Ryan, Jane
   Jeffreys, and Cameron Mitchell.

A KISS FOR CINDERELLA (1941) Maplewood Theatre, Maplewood, New Jersey,
   September 18 to 23, 1941. Playwright: J. M. Barrie. Producer: Cheryl Crawford.
   Cast: Luise Rainer, Robert Ryan (Policeman/Prince). *Note:* Ryan and Rainer originated their roles at the Cape Playhouse in Dennis, Massachusetts, before the production moved to the Maplewood Theatre.

CLASH BY NIGHT (1941) Belasco Theatre, New York, December 27, 1941, to Feb-
   ruary 7, 1942. Director: Lee Strasberg. Producer: Billy Rose. Playwright: Clifford
   Odets. Cast: Seth Arnold, Tallulah Bankhead, Ralph Chambers, Lee J. Cobb,
   Stephan Eugene Cole, Harold Grau, John F. Hamilton, Katherine Locke, William
   Nunn, Robert Ryan (Joe W. Doyle), Joseph Schildkraut, Joseph Shattuck, Art
   Smith.

PETTICOAT FEVER (1949) La Jolla Playhouse, La Jolla, California, August 30 to
   September 4, 1949. Director: James Neilson. Playwright: Mark Reed. Cast: Robert

Ryan, Ruth Warrick, Dorothy McGuire, Dan Tobin, Clifford Brooke, Chris-Pin Martin.

BORN YESTERDAY (1950) La Jolla Playhouse, La Jolla, California, July 4 to 9, 1950. Director: James Neilson. Playwright: Garson Kanin. Cast: Marie McDonald, Robert Ryan (Harry Brock), Tom Powers, Whit Bissell, Johnny Call, Paul Maxey, Louise Lorimer.

CORIOLANUS (1954) Phoenix Theatre, New York, New York, opened January 19, 1954. Director: John Houseman. Producers: T. Edward Hambleton, Norris Houghton. Playwright: William Shakespeare. Music: Alex North. Cast: Alan Napier, Robert Ryan (Caius Martius Coriolanus), Lou Polan, Joseph McCaulay, George Fells, Joseph Holland, John Randolph, Will Geer, Mildred Natwick, Lori March, Paula Laurence, John Emery, Jamie Smith, Gene Saks, Jack Klugman, Jerry Stiller, Terry Nardin.

TIGER AT THE GATES (1957) Ivar Theater, Los Angeles, January 29 to February 10, 1957. Director: Harold J. Kennedy. Producer: Harold J. Kennedy. Playwright: Jean Giraudoux. Cast: Robert Ryan, John Ireland, Marilyn Erskine, Ray Danton, Mary Astor, Marianne Stewart, Howard Wendell, Peg La Centra, Milton Parsons, Joel Ashley, Jon Poole, Gene Mekler.

MURDER IN THE CATHEDRAL (1960) Schoenberg Hall, University of California at Los Angeles, January 17 to January 31, 1960. Director: John Houseman. Playwright: T. S. Eliot. Cast: Robert Ryan (Thomas Beckett), John Hoyt, Alan Napier, Pippa Scott, Theodore Marcuse, Ruth Story.

ANTONY AND CLEOPATRA (1960) American Shakespeare Festival Theatre, Stratford, Connecticut, opened July 31, 1960. Director: Jack Landau. Cast: Robert Ryan (Antony), Katharine Hepburn, Douglas Watson, John Harkins, Donald Davis, Patrick Hines, Earle Hyman, Rae Allen, Anne Fielding, John Ragin, Morris Carnovsky, Will Geer, John Myhers, Stephen Strimpell, Clifton James, Claude Woolman, Sada Thompson, Richard Waring, Ted van Griethuysen, Clayton Corzatte.

MR. PRESIDENT (1962) St. James Theatre, New York, New York, October 20, 1962, to June 8, 1963. Director: Joshua Logan. Producer: Leland Hayward. Book: Howard Lindsay, Russel Crouse. Music and lyrics: Irving Berlin. Cast: Nanette Fabray, Robert Ryan (President Stephen Decatur Henderson), David Brooks, Wisa D'Orso, Charlotte Fairchild, Anita Gillette, Stanley Grover, Jack Haskell, John Cecil Holm, Jerry Strickler, Jack Washburn, John Aman.

OTHELLO (1967) Nottingham Playhouse, Nottingham, England, opened September 20, 1967. Director: Noel Willman. Cast: Robert Ryan (Othello), Christopher Hancock, Derek Woodward, John Neville, Terence Knapp, David Neal, Alan Dossor, Ronald Magill, Laurence Harrington, James O'Brien, Ann Bell, Ursula Smith, Christine Welch.

LONG DAY'S JOURNEY INTO NIGHT (1967) Nottingham Playhouse, Nottingham, England, opened September 27, 1967. Director: Michael Rudman. Cast: Robert Ryan (James Tyrone Sr.), Gillian Martell, Anthony Langdon, Alfred Bell, Ursula Smith.

OUR TOWN (1968) Mineola Theater, Mineola, New York, opened September 24,

1968. Director: Edward Hastings. Producers: Martha Scott, Alfred de Liagre Jr., Clifford Stevens. Cast: Henry Fonda, John Beal, Jo Van Fleet, John McGiver, Estelle Parsons, Robert Ryan (Mr. Webb), Katharine Winn.

THE FRONT PAGE (1968) Mineola Theater, Mineola, New York, October 5 to 20, 1968. Director: Leo Brady. Producers: Martha Scott, Alfred de Liagre Jr., Clifford Stevens. Cast: Robert Ryan, John Beal, Mark Bramhall, Henry Fonda, Anthony George, Anne Jackson, John McGiver, Estelle Parsons.

THE FRONT PAGE (1969) Ethel Barrymore Theatre, May 10 to July 5, 1969. Director: Harold J. Kennedy. Producers: Theater 1969 (Edward Albee, Richard Barr, Charles Woodward). Playwrights: Ben Hecht, Charles MacArthur. Cast: Robert Ryan (Walter Burns), Val Avery, Peggy Cass, Bert Convy, James Flavin, Conrad Janis, Harold J. Kennedy, John McGiver, Julia Meade, Doro Merande, Charles White, Tom Atkins, Bruce Blaine, Patrick Desmond, Walter Flanagan, Morison Gampel, Geoff Garland, Will Gregory, Rick Hagan, Scott Hagan, Katharine Houghton, Robert Milli, Don Porter, Ed Riley, Arnold Stang.

THE FRONT PAGE (1969–'70) Ethel Barrymore Theatre, October 18, 1969, to February 28, 1970. Directed by Harold J. Kennedy. Producers: Jay H. Fuchs, Jerry Schlossberg, Albert Zuckerman. Playwrights: Ben Hecht, Charles MacArthur. Cast: Val Avery, Peggy Cass, Bert Convy, Dody Goodman, Helen Hayes, Conrad Janis, John McGiver, Robert Ryan (Walter Burns), James Flavin, Harold J. Kennedy, Charles White, Bruce Blaine, Jack Collard, Patrick Desmond, Walter Flanagan, Joseph George, Will Gregory, Bob Larkin, Kendall March, Robert Milli, Robert Riesel, Ed Riley, Bernie West.

LONG DAY'S JOURNEY INTO NIGHT (1971) Promenade Theatre, New York, New York, April 21 to August 22, 1971. Director: Arvin Brown. Producers: Edgar Lansbury, Jay H. Fuchs, Stuart Duncan, Joseph Beruh. Cast: Robert Ryan (James Tyrone Sr.), Stacy Keach, Geraldine Fitzgerald, James Naughton, Paddy Croft.

part two Film Chronology

THE GHOST BREAKERS (1940) Director: George Marshall. Producer: Arthur Hornblow Jr. Screenwriter: Walter DeLeon, from a play by Paul Dickey and Charles W. Goddard. Photography: Charles Lang. Editor: Ellsworth Hoagland. Music: Ernst Toch. Production and distribution: Paramount Pictures. Release date: June 7, 1940. Running time: 85 minutes. Cast: Bob Hope, Paulette Goddard, Richard Carlson, Paul Lukas, Willie Best, Robert Ryan (Intern, uncredited). Black and white.

QUEEN OF THE MOB (1940) Director: James Hogan. Screenwriters: J. Edgar Hoover, Walter R. Lipman, Horace McCoy, from Hoover's book *Persons in Hiding*. Photography: Theodor Sparkuhl. Editor: Arthur Schmidt. Production and distribution: Paramount Pictures. Release date: June 28, 1940. Running time: 61

minutes. Cast: Ralph Bellamy, J. Carrol Naish, Jeanne Cagney, Richard Denning, Hedda Hopper, Jack Carson, Billy Gilbert, Robert Ryan (Jim, uncredited). Black and white.

GOLDEN GLOVES (1940) Directors: Edward Dmytryk, Felix E. Feist. Producer: Carl Krueger. Screenwriters: Joe Ansen, Lewis R. Foster, Maxwell Shane. Photography: John L. Russell, Henry Sharp. Editors: William F. Claxton, Doane Harrison. Production and distribution: Paramount Pictures. Release date: August 2, 1940. Running time: 66 minutes. Cast: Richard Denning, Jeanne Cagney, J. Carrol Naish, Robert Paige, William Farley, Edward Brophy, Robert Ryan (Pete Wells). Black and white.

NORTH WEST MOUNTED POLICE (1940) Director: Cecil B. DeMille. Producer: Cecil B. DeMille. Screenwriters: Alan Le May, Jesse Laske Jr., C. Gardner Sullivan, from R. C. Fetherstonhaugh's novel *The Royal Canadian Mounted Police*. Photography: W. Howard Green, Victor Milner. Editor: Anne Bauchens. Music: Victor Young. Production and distribution: Paramount Pictures. Release date: October 21, 1940 (Canada); October 22, 1940 (US). Running time: 126 minutes. Cast: Gary Cooper, Madeleine Carroll, Paulette Goddard, Preston Foster, Robert Preston, George Bancroft, Akim Tamiroff, Lon Chaney Jr., George E. Stone, Regis Toomey, Robert Ryan (Constable Dumont). Black and white.

THE TEXAS RANGERS RIDE AGAIN (1940) Director: James Hogan. Screenwriters: William R. Lippman, Horace McCoy. Photography: Archie Stout. Editor: Arthur Schmidt. Production and distribution: Paramount Pictures. Release date: December 13, 1940. Running time: 68 minutes. Cast: Ellen Drew, John Howard, Akim Tamiroff, May Robson, Broderick Crawford, Charley Grapewin, Anthony Quinn, Robert Ryan (Eddie, uncredited). Black and white.

BOMBARDIER (1943) Director: Richard Wallace, Lambert Hillyer (uncredited). Producer: Robert Fellows. Screenwriter: John Twist. Story: John Twist, Martin Rackin. Photography: Nicholas Musuraca, Joseph F. Biroc (uncredited). Editor: Robert Wise. Music: Roy Webb. Production and distribution: RKO Radio Pictures. Release date: May 14, 1943. Running time: 99 minutes. Cast: Pat O'Brien, Randolph Scott, Anne Shirley, Eddie Albert, Walter Reed, Robert Ryan (Joe Connors), Barton MacLane, Leonard Strong, Richard Martin, Russell Wade, James Newill, John Miljan, Charles Russell. Black and white.

THE SKY'S THE LIMIT (1943) Director: Edward H. Griffith. Producer: David Hempstead. Screenwriters: Frank Fenton, Lynn Root, S. K. Lauren (uncredited), William T. Ryder (story, uncredited). Photography: Russell Metty. Editor: Roland Gross. Music: Harold Arlen. Production and distribution: RKO Radio Pictures. Release date: July 13, 1943. Running time: 89 minutes. Cast: Fred Astaire, Joan Leslie, Robert Benchley, Robert Ryan (Reginald Fenton), Elizabeth Patterson, Marjorie Gateson, Freddie Slack and His Orchestra. Black and white.

BEHIND THE RISING SUN (1943) Director: Edward Dmytryk. Producers: Edward Dmytryk (uncredited), Howard Hughes (uncredited). Screenwriter: Emmet Lavery, from the book by James R. Young. Photography: Russell Metty. Editor: Joseph Noriega. Music: Roy Webb. Production and distribution: RKO Radio Pictures. Release date: August 1, 1943. Running time: 88 minutes. Cast: Margo, Tom Neal, J. Carrol Naish, Robert Ryan (Lefty O'Doyle), Gloria Holden, Donald Douglas, George Givot. Black and white.

THE IRON MAJOR (1943) Director: Ray Enright. Producer: Robert Fellows. Screenwriters: Aben Kandel, Warren Duff. Story: Florence E. Cavanaugh. Photography: Robert De Grasse. Editors: Philip Martin Jr., Robert Wise. Music: Roy Webb. Production and distribution: RKO Radio Pictures. Release date: October 25, 1943. Running time: 85 minutes. Cast: Pat O'Brien, Ruth Warrick, Robert Ryan (Father Timothy "Tim" Donovan), Leon Ames, Russell Wade, Bruce Edwards, Richard Martin.

GANGWAY FOR TOMORROW (1943) Director: John H. Auer. Producer: John H. Auer. Screenwriter: Arch Oboler. Story: Aladar Laszlo. Photography: Nicholas Musuraca. Editor: George Crone. Music: Roy Webb. Production and distribution: RKO Radio Pictures. Release date: November 3, 1943. Running time: 69 minutes. Cast: Margo, John Carradine, Robert Ryan (Joe Dunham), Amelita Ward, William Terry, Harry Davenport, James Bell. Black and white.

TENDER COMRADE (1943) Director: Edward Dmytryk. Producer: David Hempstead. Screenwriter: Dalton Trumbo. Photography: Russell Metty. Editor: Roland Gross. Music: Leigh Harline. Production and distribution: RKO Radio Pictures. Release date: December 29, 1943. Running time: 102 minutes. Cast: Ginger Rogers, Robert Ryan (Chris Jones), Ruth Hussey, Patricia Collinge, Mady Christians, Kim Hunter, Jane Darwell, Richard Martin. Black and white.

MARINE RAIDERS (1944) Director: Harold Schuster. Producer: Robert Fellows. Screenwriters: Warren Duff, Jerome Odlum (uncredited). Story: Martin Rackin, Warren Duff. Photography: Nicholas Musuraca. Editor: Philip Martin Jr. Music: Roy Webb. Production and distribution: RKO Radio Pictures. Release date: June 30, 1944. Running time: 90 minutes. Cast: Pat O'Brien, Robert Ryan (Captain Dan Craig), Ruth Hussey, Frank McHugh, Barton MacLane, Richard Martin, Edmund Glover, Russell Wade, Robert Andersen, Michael St. Angel, Martha MacVicar (aka Martha Vickers), Harry Brown. Black and white.

TRAIL STREET (1947) Director: Ray Enright. Producer: Nat Holt. Screenwriters: Norman Houston, Gene Lewis, from the novel by William Corcoran. Photography: J. Roy Hunt. Editor: Lyle Boyer. Music: C. Bakaleinikoff. Production and distribution: RKO Radio Pictures. Release date: February 19, 1947. Running time: 84 minutes. Cast: Randolph Scott, Robert Ryan (Allen), Anne Jeffreys, George "Gabby" Hayes, Madge Meredith, Steve Brodie, Billy House, Virginia Sale, Harry Woods, Phil Warren, Harry Harvey, Jason Robards (Sr.). Black and white.

THE WOMAN ON THE BEACH (1947) Director: Jean Renoir. Producer: Jack J. Gross. Screenwriters: Frank Davis, Jean Renoir. Adaptation: Michael Hogan, from Mitchell Wilson's novel *None So Blind*. Photography: Leo Tover, Harry Wild. Editors: Lyle Boyer, Roland Gross. Music: Hanns Eisler. Production and distribution: RKO Radio Pictures. Release date: June 2, 1947. Running time: 71 minutes. Cast: Joan Bennett, Robert Ryan (Scott), Charles Bickford, Nan Leslie, Walter Sande, Irene Ryan, Glen Vernon, Frank Darien, Jay Norris. Black and white.

CROSSFIRE (1947) Director: Edward Dmytryk. Producer: Adrian Scott. Screenwriter: John Paxton, from Richard Brooks's novel *The Brick Foxhole*. Photography: J. Roy Hunt. Editor: Harry Gerstad. Music: Roy Webb. Production and distribution: RKO Radio Pictures. Release date: July 22, 1947. Running time: 86 minutes. Cast: Robert Young, Robert Mitchum, Robert Ryan (Montgomery), Gloria Grahame, Paul Kelly, Sam Levene, Jacqueline White, Steve Brodie, George Cooper, Richard Benedict, Richard Powers, William Phipps, Lex Barker, Marlo Dwyer.

BERLIN EXPRESS (1948) Director: Jacques Tourneur. Producer: Bert Granet. Screenwriter: Harold Medford. Story: Curt Siodmak. Photography: Lucien Ballard. Editor: Sherman Todd. Music: Frederick Hollander. Production and distribution: RKO Radio Pictures. Release date: May 1, 1948. Running time: 87 minutes. Cast: Merle Oberon, Robert Ryan (Robert Lindley), Charles Korvin, Paul Lukas, Robert Coote, Reinhold Schunzel, Roman Toporow, Peter Von Zerneck, Otto Waldis, Fritz Kortner, Michael Harvey, Richard Powers (aka Tom Keene). Black and white.

RETURN OF THE BAD MEN (1948) Director: Ray Enright. Producer: Nat Holt. Screenwriters: Charles O'Neal, Jack Natteford, Luci Ward. Story: Jack Natteford, Luci Ward. Photography: J. Roy Hunt. Editor: Samuel E. Beetley. Music: Paul Sawtell. Production and distribution: RKO Radio Pictures. Release date: July 17, 1948. Running time: 90 minutes. Cast: Randolph Scott, Robert Ryan (Sundance Kid), Anne Jeffreys, George "Gabby" Hayes, Jacqueline White, Steve Brodie, Richard Powers (aka Tom Keene), Robert Bray, Lex Barker, Walter Reed, Michael Harvey, Dean White, Robert Armstrong, Tom Tyler, Lew Harvey, Gary Gray, Walter Baldwin, Minna Gombell, Warren Jackson, Robert Clarke, Jason Robards (Sr.). Black and white.

THE BOY WITH GREEN HAIR (1948) Director: Joseph Losey. Producer: Stephen Ames, Adrian Scott (uncredited). Screenwriters: Ben Barzman, Alfred Lewis Levitt, from the story by Betsy Beaton. Photography: George Barnes. Editor: Frank Doyle. Music: Leigh Harline. Production and distribution: RKO Radio Pictures. Release date: November 16, 1948. Running time: 82 minutes. Cast: Pat O'Brien, Robert Ryan (Dr. Evans), Barbara Hale, Dean Stockwell, Richard Lyon, Walter Catlett, Samuel S. Hinds, Regis Toomey, Charles Meredith, David Clarke, Billy Sheffield, John Calkins, Teddy Infuhr, Dwayne Hickman, Eilene Janssen. Color.

ACT OF VIOLENCE (1948) Director: Fred Zinnemann. Producer: William H. Wright. Screenwriter: Robert L. Richards. Story: Collier Young. Photography: Robert Surtees. Editor: Conrad A. Nervig. Music: Bronislau (aka Bronislaw) Kaper. Production and distribution: Metro-Goldwyn-Mayer. Release date: December 21, 1948. Running time: 82 minutes. Cast: Van Heflin, Robert Ryan (Joe Parkson), Janet Leigh, Mary Astor, Phyllis Thaxter, Berry Kroeger, Taylor Holmes, Harry Antrim, Connie Gilchrist, Will Wright. Black and white.

CAUGHT (1949) Director: Max Ophuls (aka Max Ophüls). Producer: Wolfgang Reinhardt. Screenwriter: Arthur Laurents, from Libbie Block's novel *Wild Calendar*. Photography: Lee Garmes. Editor: Robert Parrish. Music: Frederick Hollander. Production: Enterprise Productions. Distribution: Metro-Goldwyn-Mayer. Release date: February 17, 1949. Running time: 88 minutes. Cast: James Mason, Barbara Bel Geddes, Robert Ryan (Smith Ohlrig), Frank Ferguson, Curt Bois, Ruth Brady, Natalie Schaefer, Art Smith. Black and white.

THE SET-UP (1949) Director: Robert Wise. Producer: Richard Goldstone. Screenwriter: Art Cohn, from the poem by Joseph Moncure March. Photography: Milton Krasner. Editor: Roland Gross. Music: C. Bakaleinikoff. Production and distribution: RKO Radio Pictures. Release date: March 29, 1949. Running time: 73 minutes. Cast: Robert Ryan (Stoker Thompson), Audrey Totter, George Tobias, Alan Baxter, Wallace Ford, Percy Helton, Hal Fieberling (aka Hal Baylor), Darryl Hickman, Kenny O'Morrison, James Edwards, David Clarke, Phillip Pine, Edwin Max. Black and white.

THE WOMAN ON PIER 13 (1949) Director: Robert Stevenson. Producer: Jack J. Gross. Screenwriters: Charles Grayson, Robert Hardy Andrews. Story: George W. George, George F. Slavin. Photography: Nicholas Musuraca. Editor: Roland Gross. Music: Leigh Harline. Production and distribution: RKO Radio Pictures. Release date: October 8, 1949. Running time: 73 minutes. Cast: Laraine Day, Robert Ryan (Brad Collins aka Frank Johnson), John Agar, Thomas Gomez, Janis Carter, Richard Rober, William Talman, Paul E. Burns, Paul Guilfoyle, G. Pat Collins, Fred Graham, Harry Cheshire, Jack Stoney. Black and white.

THE SECRET FURY (1950) Director: Mel Ferrer. Producer: Jack H. Skirball. Screenwriter: Lionel Houser. Story: Jack R. Leonard, James O'Hanlon. Photography: Leo Tover. Editor: Harry Marker. Music: Roy Webb. Production and distribution: RKO Radio Pictures. Release date: February 21, 1950. Running time: 85 minutes. Cast: Claudette Colbert, Robert Ryan (David McLean), Jane Cowl, Paul Kelly, Philip Ober, Elisabeth Risdon, Doris Dudley, Dave Barbour, Vivian Vance. Black and white.

BORN TO BE BAD (1950) Director: Nicholas Ray. Producer: Robert Sparks. Screenwriter: Edith Sommer, additional dialogue by Robert Soderberg, George Oppenheimer. Adaptation: Charles Schnee, from Anne Parish's novel *All Kneeling*. Photography: Nicholas Musuraca. Editor: Frederic Knudtson. Music: Frederick Hollander. Production and distribution: RKO Radio Pictures. Release date: August 27, 1950. Running time: 94 minutes. Cast: Joan Fontaine, Robert Ryan (Nick Bradley), Zachary Scott, Joan Leslie, Mel Ferrer, Harold Vermilyea, Virginia Farmer, Kathleen Howard, Dick Ryan, Bess Flowers, Joy Hallward, Hazel Boyne, Irvin Bacon, Gordon Oliver. Black and white.

HARD, FAST AND BEAUTIFUL (1951) Director: Ida Lupino. Producer: Collier Young. Screenwriter: Martha Wilkerson, from John R. Tunis's novel *American Girl*. Photography: Archie Stout. Editors: George C. Shrader, William Ziegler. Music: Roy Webb. Production: The Filmmakers. Distribution: RKO Radio Pictures.

Release date: May 23, 1951. Running time: 78 minutes. Cast: Claire Trevor, Sally Forrest, Carleton G. Young, Robert Clarke, Kenneth Patterson, Marcella Cisney, Joseph Kearns, William Hudson, George Fisher, Ida Lupino (uncredited), Robert Ryan (uncredited). Black and white. *Note:* Ryan and Lupino appear as extras in the Seabright tennis match sequence.

BEST OF THE BADMEN (1951) Director: William D. Russell. Producer: Herman Schlom. Screenwriters: Robert Hardy Andrews, John Twist. Story: Robert Hardy Andrews. Photography: Edward Cronjager. Editor: Desmond Marquette. Music: Paul Sawtell. Production and distribution: RKO Radio Pictures. Release date: August 9, 1951. Running time: 84 minutes. Cast: Robert Ryan (Jeff Clanton), Claire Trevor, Robert Buetel, Robert Preston, Walter Brennan, Bruce Cabot, John Archer, Lawrence Tierney, Barton MacLane, Tom Tyler, Robert J. Wilke, John Cliff, Lee MacGregor, Emmett Lynn, Carleton Young. Color.

FLYING LEATHERNECKS (1951) Director: Nicholas Ray. Producer: Edmund Grainger. Screenwriters: James Edward Grant, Beirne Lay Jr. (uncredited). Story: Kenneth Gamet. Photography: William E. Snyder. Editor: Sherman Todd. Music: Roy Webb. Production and distribution: RKO Radio Pictures. Release date: August 28, 1951. Running time: 102 minutes. Cast: John Wayne, Robert Ryan (Captain Carl "Griff" Griffin), Don Taylor, Janis Carter, Jay C. Flippen, William Harrigan, James Bell, Barry Kelley, Maurice Jara, Adam Williams, James Dobson, Carleton Young, Michael St. Angel, Brett King, Gordon Gebert. Color.

THE RACKET (1951) Directors: John Cromwell, Mel Ferrer (uncredited), Tay Garnett (uncredited), Nicholas Ray (uncredited), Sherman Todd (uncredited). Producer: Edmund Grainger. Screenwriters: William Wister Haynes, W. R. Burnett, from the play by Bartlett Cormack. Photography: George E. Diskant. Editor: Sherman Todd. Production and distribution: RKO Radio Pictures. Release date: December 12, 1951. Running time: 89 minutes. Cast: Robert Mitchum, Lizabeth Scott, Robert Ryan (Nick Scanlon), William Talman, Ray Collins, Joyce MacKenzie, Robert Hutton, Virginia Huston, William Conrad, Walter Sande, Les Tremayne, Don Porter, Walter Baldwin, Brett King, Richard Karlan, Tito Vuolo. Black and white.

ON DANGEROUS GROUND (1951) Director: Nicholas Ray. Producer: John Houseman. Screenwriter: A. I. Bezzerides. Adaptation: A. I. Bezzerides, Nicholas Ray, from Gerald Butler's novel *Mad with Much Heart.* Photography: George E. Diskant. Editor: Roland Gross. Music: Bernard Herrmann. Production and distribution: RKO Radio Pictures. Release date: December 17, 1951. Running time: 82 minutes. Cast: Ida Lupino, Robert Ryan (Jim Wilson), Ward Bond, Charles Kemper, Anthony Ross, Ed Begley, Ian Wolfe, Sumner Williams, Gus Schilling, Frank Ferguson, Cleo Moore, Olive Carey, Richard Irving, Pat Prest, A. I. Bezzerides (uncredited). Black and white.

CLASH BY NIGHT (1952) Director: Fritz Lang. Producer: Harriet Parsons. Screenwriter: Alfred Hayes, from the play by Clifford Odets. Photography: Nicholas Musuraca. Editor: George Amy. Music: Roy Webb. Production: Wald-Krasna Productions. Distribution: RKO Radio Pictures. Release date: June 16, 1952. Running time:

105 minutes. Cast: Barbara Stanwyck, Paul Douglas, Robert Ryan (Earl Pfeiffer), Marilyn Monroe, J. Carrol Naish, Silvio Minciotti, Keith Andes. Black and white.

BEWARE, MY LOVELY (1952) Director: Harry Horner. Producer: Collier Young. Screenwriter: Mel Dinelli, from his play *The Man*. Photography: George E. Diskant. Editor: Paul Weatherwax. Music: Leith Stevens. Production: The Film-makers. Distribution: RKO Radio Pictures. Release date: August 7, 1952. Running time: 77 minutes. Cast: Ida Lupino, Robert Ryan (Howard Wilton), Taylor Holmes, Barbara Whiting, James Willmas, O. Z. Whitehead, Dee Pollock, Brad Morrow, Jimmy Mobley, Shelly Lynn Anderson, Ronnie Patterson, Jeanne Eggen-weiler. Black and white.

HORIZONS WEST (1952) Director: Budd Boetticher. Producer: Albert J. Cohen. Screenwriter: Louis Stevens. Photography: Charles P. Boyle. Editor: Ted J. Kent. Music: Joseph Gershenson. Production: Universal-International Pictures. Distribu-tion: Universal Pictures. Release date: October 11, 1952. Running time: 81 minutes. Cast: Robert Ryan (Dan Hammond), Julie Adams, Rock Hudson, Judith Braun, John McIntire, Raymond Burr, James Arness, Dennis Weaver, Frances Bavier, Tom Powers, John Hubbard, Rodolfo Acosta, Douglas Fowley, Walter Reed, Raymond Greenleaf, Dan Poore, Frank Chase, Mae Clarke. Color.

THE NAKED SPUR (1953) Director: Anthony Mann. Producer: William H. Wright. Screenwriter: Sam Rolfe, Harold Jack Bloom. Photography: William Mellor. Edi-tor: George White. Music: Bronislau (aka Bronislaw) Kaper. Production and distri-bution: Metro-Goldwyn-Mayer. Release date: February 6, 1963. Running time: 91 minutes. Cast: James Stewart, Janet Leigh, Robert Ryan (Ben Vandergroat), Ralph Meeker, Millard Mitchell, Denver Pyle. Color.

CITY BENEATH THE SEA (1953) Director: Budd Boetticher. Producer: Albert J. Cohen. Screenwriters: Jack Harvey, Ramon Romero, from Harry E. Rieseberg's book *Port Royal: The Ghost City beneath the Sea*. Photography: Charles P. Boyle. Editor: Edward Curtiss. Music: Joseph Gershenson. Production: Universal-In-ternational Pictures. Distribution: Universal Pictures. Release date: March 11, 1953. Running time: 87 minutes. Cast: Robert Ryan (Brad Carlton), Mala Powers, Anthony Quinn, Suzan Ball, George Mathews, Karel Stepanek, Hilo Hattie, Lalo Rios, Woody Strode, John Warburton, Peter Mamakos, Barbara Morrison, LeRoi Antoine, Leon Lontoc, Marya Marco. Color.

INFERNO (1953) Director: Roy Ward Baker. Producer: William Bloom. Screenwriter: Francis M. Cockrell, from his story "The Waterhole." Photography: Lucien Ballard. Editor: Robert L. Simpson. Music: Paul Sawtell. Production and distribution: 20th Century-Fox. Release date: August 12, 1953. Running time: 83 minutes. Cast: Rob-ert Ryan (Donald Whitley Carson III), Rhonda Fleming, William Lundigan, Larry Keating, Henry Hull, Carl Betz, Robert Burton. Color, 3-D.

ALASKA SEAS (1954) Director: Jerry Hopper. Producer: Mel Epstein. Screenwriters: Walter Doniger, Geoffrey Homes (aka Daniel Mainwaring). Story: Barrett Wil-loughby. Photography: William C. Mellor. Editor: Archie Marshek. Production and distribution: Paramount Pictures. Release date: January 27, 1954. Running time: 78 minutes. Cast: Robert Ryan (Matt Kelly), Jan Sterling, Brian Keith, Gene Barry, Richard Shannon, Ralph Dumke, Ross Bagdasarian, Fay Roope, Timothy Carey, Peter Coe, Jim Hayward, Aaron Spelling. Black and white.

ABOUT MRS. LESLIE (1954) Director: Daniel Mann. Producer: Hal B. Wallis. Screenwriters: Ketti Frings, Hal Kanter, from the novel by Viña Delmar. Photography: Ernest Laszlo. Editor: Warren Low. Music: Victor Young. Production and distribution: Paramount Pictures. Release date: June 27, 1954. Running time: 104 minutes. Cast: Shirley Booth, Robert Ryan (George Leslie), Marjie Millar, Alex Nicol, Sammy White, James Bell, Eilene Janssen, Philip Ober, Harry Morgan, Gale Page, Virginia Brissac, Ian Wolfe, Ellen Corby. Black and white.

HER TWELVE MEN (1954) Director: Robert Z. Leonard. Producer: John Houseman. Screenwriters: William Roberts, Laura Z. Hobson. Story: Louise Baker. Photography: Joseph Ruttenberg. Editor: George Boemler. Music: Bronislau (aka Bronislaw) Kaper. Production and distribution: Metro-Goldwyn-Mayer. Release date: August 11, 1954. Running time: 91 minutes. Cast: Greer Garson, Robert Ryan (Joe Hargrave), Barry Sullivan, Richard Haydn, Barbara Lawrence, James Arness, Rex Thompson, Tim Considine, David Stollery, Frances Bergen, Ian Wolfe. Color.

BAD DAY AT BLACK ROCK (1955) Director: John Sturgess. Producer: Dore Schary. Screenwriter: Millard Kaufman. Adaptation: Don McGuire, from Howard Breslin's story "Bad Time at Honda." Photography: William C. Mellor. Editor: Newell P. Kimlin. Music: André Previn. Production and distribution: Metro-Goldwyn-Mayer. Release date: January 7, 1955. Running time: 81 minutes. Cast: Spencer Tracy, Robert Ryan (Reno Smith), Anne Francis, Dean Jagger, Walter Brennan, John Ericson, Ernest Borgnine, Lee Marvin, Russell Collins, Walter Sande. Color, CinemaScope.

ESCAPE TO BURMA (1955) Director: Alan Dwan. Producer: Benedict Bogeaus. Screenwriters: Talbot Jennings, Hobart Donavan. Story: Kenneth Perkins. Photography: John Alton. Editors: James Leicester, Carlo Lodato. Music: Louis Forbes. Production: Benedict Bogeaus Production. Distribution: RKO Radio Pictures. Release date: April 9, 1955. Running time: 83 minutes. Cast: Barbara Stanwyck, Robert Ryan (Jim Brecan), David Farrar, Murvyn Vye, Lisa Montell, Robert Warwick, Reginald Denny, Robert Cabal, Peter Coe, Alex Montoya, Anthony Numkena. Color, Superscope.

HOUSE OF BAMBOO (1955) Director: Samuel Fuller. Producer: Buddy Adler. Screenwriters: Harry Kleiner, additional dialogue by Samuel Fuller. Photography: Joe MacDonald. Editor: James B. Clarke. Music: Leigh Harline. Production and distribution: 20th Century-Fox. Release date: July 1, 1955. Running time: 103 minutes. Cast: Robert Ryan (Sandy Dawson), Robert Stack, Shirley Yamaguchi, Cameron Mitchell, Brad Dexter, Sessue Hayakawa, Biff Elliott, Sandro Giglio, Elko Hanabusa. Color, CinemaScope.

THE TALL MEN (1955) Director: Raoul Walsh. Producers: William A. Bacher, William B. Hawks. Screenwriters: Sydney Boehm, Frank Nugent, from the novel by Clay Fisher. Photography: Leo Tover. Editor: Louis R. Loeffler. Music: Victor Young. Production and distribution: 20th Century-Fox. Release date: September 22, 1955. Running time: 122 minutes. Cast: Clark Gable, Jane Russell, Robert Ryan (Nathan Stark), Cameron Mitchell, Juan Garcia, Harry Shannon, Emile Meyer, Steve Darrell. Color, CinemaScope.

THE PROUD ONES (1956) Director: Robert D. Webb. Producer: Robert L. Jacks. Screenwriters: Edmund North, Joseph Petracca, from the novel by Verne Athanas. Photography: Lucien Ballard. Editor: Hugh S. Fowler. Music: Lionel Newman. Production and distribution: 20th Century-Fox. Release date: May 1956. Running time: 94 minutes. Cast: Robert Ryan (Marshal Cass Silver), Virginia Mayo, Jeffrey Hunter, Robert Middleton, Walter Brennan, Arthur O'Connell, Ken Clark, Rodolfo Acosta, George Mathews, Fay Roope, Edward Platt, Whit Bissell. Color, CinemaScope.

BACK FROM ETERNITY (1956) Director: John Farrow. Producer: John Farrow. Screenwriter: Jonathan Latimer, from the story by Richard Carroll. Photography: William Mellor. Editor: Eda Warren. Music: Franz Waxman. Production and distribution: RKO Radio Pictures. Release date: September 7, 1956. Running time: 100 minutes. Cast: Robert Ryan (Bill Lonagan), Anita Ekberg, Rod Steiger, Phyllis Kirk, Keith Andes, Gene Barry, Fred Clark, Beulah Bondi, Cameron Prud'Homme, Jesse White, Adele Mara, Jon Provost. Black and white, RKO-Scope.

MEN IN WAR (1956) Director: Anthony Mann. Producer: Sidney Harmon. Screenwriters: Philip Yordan, Ben Maddow (uncredited), from Van Van Praag's novel *Day Without End (Combat)*. Photography: Ernest Haller. Editor: Richard C. Meyer. Music: Elmer Bernstein. Production: Security Pictures. Distribution: United Artists. Release date: September 7, 1956. Running time: 98 minutes. Cast: Robert Ryan (Lieutenant Benson), Aldo Ray, Robert Keith, Phillip Pine, Nehemiah Persoff, Vic Morrow, James Edwards, L. Q. Jones, Scott Marlowe, Adam Kennedy, Race Gentry, Walter Kelley, Anthony Ray, Robert Normand, Michael Miller, Victor Sen Yung. Black and white.

LONELYHEARTS (1958) Director: Vincent J. Donehue. Producer: Dore Schary. Screenwriter: Dore Schary, from Howard Teichmann's play and Nathanael West's original novel *Miss Lonelyhearts*. Photography: John Alton. Editors: Aaron Stell, John Faure. Music: Conrad Salinger. Production: Schary Productions. Distribution: United Artists. Release date: 1958. Running time: 100 minutes. Cast: Montgomery Clift, Robert Ryan (William Shrike), Myrna Loy, Dolores Hart, Jackie Coogan, Mike Kellin, Frank Maxwell, Frank Overton, Onslow Stevens, and introducing Maureen Stapleton. Black and white.

GOD'S LITTLE ACRE (1958) Director: Anthony Mann. Producer: Sidney Harmon. Screenwriter: Philip Yordan, from the novel by Erskine Caldwell. Photography: Ernest Haller. Editor: Richard C. Meyer. Music: Elmer Bernstein. Production: Security Pictures. Distribution: United Artists. Release date: August 13, 1958. Running time: 118 minutes. Cast: Robert Ryan (Ty Ty Walden), Aldo Ray, Buddy Hackett,

Jack Lord, Fay Spain, Vic Morrow, Helen Westcott, Lance Fuller, Rex Ingram, Michael Landon, Russell Collins, Davis Roberts, Janet Brandt, and introducing Tina Louise. Black and white.

DAY OF THE OUTLAW (1959) Director: André de Toth. Producer: Sidney Harmon. Screenwriter: Philip Yordan, from the novel by Lee E. Wells. Photography: Russell Harlan. Editor: Robert Lawrence. Music: Alexander Courage. Production: Security Pictures. Distribution: United Artists. Release date: July 1959. Running time: 92 minutes. Cast: Robert Ryan (Blaise Starrett), Burl Ives, Tina Louise, Alan Marshal, Venetia Stevenson, David Nelson, Nehemiah Persoff, Jack Lambert, Frank DeKova, Lance Fuller, Elisha Cook Jr., Dabbs Greer, Betsey Jones-Moreland, Helen Westcott, Donald Elson, Robert Cornthwaite, Michael McGreevey. Black and white.

ODDS AGAINST TOMORROW (1959) Director: Robert Wise. Producer: Robert Wise. Screenwriters: Abraham Polonsky, Nelson Gidding, from the novel by William P. McGivern. Photography: Joseph Brun. Editor: Dede Allen. Music: John Lewis. Production: HarBel Productions. Distribution: United Artists. Release date: October 15, 1959. Running time: 96 minutes. Cast: Harry Belafonte, Robert Ryan (Earle Slater), Shelley Winters, Ed Begley, Gloria Grahame, Will Kuluva, Kim Hamilton, Mae Barnes, Richard Bright, Carmen De Lavallade, Lew Gallo, Wayne Rogers. Black and white.

ICE PALACE (1960) Director: Vincent Sherman. Producer: Henry Blanke, Harry Kleiner (uncredited). Screenwriter: Harry Kleiner, from the novel by Edna Ferber. Photography: Joseph F. Biroc. Editor: William H. Ziegler. Music: Max Steiner. Production and distribution: Warner Bros. Release date: January 2, 1960. Running time: 143 minutes. Cast: Richard Burton, Robert Ryan (Thor Storm), Martha Hyer, Jim Backus, Carolyn Jones, Ray Danton, Diane McBain. Karl Swenson, Shirley Knight, Barry Kelley, Sheridan Comerate, George Takei, Steve Harris. Color.

THE CANADIANS (1961) Director: Burt Kennedy. Producer: Herman E. Webber. Screenwriter: Burt Kennedy. Photography: Arthur Ibbetson. Editor: Douglas Robertson. Music: Douglas Gamley. Production: Associated Producers, 20th Century-Fox Productions. Distribution: 20th Century-Fox. Release date: March 11, 1961. Running time: 85 minutes. Cast: Robert Ryan (Inspector William Gannon), John Dehner, Torin Thatcher, Burt Metcalfe, John Sutton, Jack Creley, Scott Peters, Richard Alden, Teresa Stratas.

KING OF KINGS (1961) Director: Nicholas Ray. Producer: Samuel Bronston. Screenwriters: Philip Yordan, Ray Bradbury (uncredited narration). Photography: Franz F. Planer, Milton Krasner, Manuel Berenguer. Editors: Harold F. Kress, Renee Lichtig (uncredited). Music: Miklos Rozsa. Production: Samuel Bronston Productions (uncredited). Distribution: Metro-Goldwyn-Mayer. Release date: October 11, 1961. Running time: 168 minutes. Cast: Jeffrey Hunter, Siobhan McKenna, Hurd Hatfield, Ron Randell, Viveca Lindfors, Rita Gam, Carmen Sevilla, Brigid Bazlen, Harry Guardino, Rip Torn, Frank Thring, Guy Rolfe, Royal Dano, Robert Ryan (John the Baptist), Orson Welles (voice-over narration, uncredited). Color, Technirama.

THE LONGEST DAY (1962) Directors: Ken Annakin, Andrew Marton, Bernhard Wicki, Gerd Oswald (uncredited). Producer: Darryl F. Zanuck. Screenwriter: Cornelius Ryan, from his book, with additional scenes by Romain Gary, James Jones, David Pursall, Jack Seddon. Photography: Jean Bourgoin, Walter Wottitz. Editor: Samuel E. Beetley. Music: Maurice Jarre. Production and distribution: 20th Century-Fox. Release date: September 25, 1962. Running time: 178 minutes. Cast: John Wayne, Henry Fonda, Robert Mitchum, Sean Connery, Eddie Albert, Curd Jürgens, Richard Todd, Richard Burton, Peter Lawford, Rod Steiger, Irina Demick, Gert Fröbe, Edmond O'Brien, Kenneth More, Robert Ryan (Brigadier General James M. Gavin). Black and white.

BILLY BUDD (1962) Director: Peter Ustinov. Producer: Peter Ustinov. Screenwriters: Peter Ustinov, DeWitt Bodeen, Robert Rossen (uncredited), from Herman Melville's story "Billy Budd, Sailor" and Louis O. Coxe and Robert H. Chapman's play *Uniform of Flesh*. Photography: Robert Krasker. Editor: Jack Harris. Music: Antony Hopkins. Production: Anglo Allied. Distribution: Allied Artists Pictures. Release date: October 30, 1962. Running time: 123 minutes. Cast: Robert Ryan (John Claggart, Master of Arms), Peter Ustinov, Melvyn Douglas, Paul Rogers, John Neville, David McCallum, Ronald Lewis, Lee Montague, Thomas Heathcote, Ray McAnnally, Robert Brown, John Meillon, Cyril Luckham, Niall McGinnis, Victor Brooks, Barry Keegan, and introducing Terence Stamp. Black-and-white, CinemaScope.

THE INHERITANCE (1964) Director: Harold Mayer. Producer: Harold Mayer. Screenwriter: Millard Lampell. Photography: Edmund B. Gerard, Jesse Paley, Leonard Stark. Editor: Lawrence Silk. Music: George Kleinsinger. Production and distribution: Harold Mayer Productions. Release date: November 8, 1964. Running time: 58 min. Cast: Robert Ryan (narrator). Black and white.

THE CROOKED ROAD (1965) Director: Don Chaffey. Producer: David Henley. Screenwriters: J. Garrison, Don Chaffey. Adaptation: J. Garrison, from Morris L. West's novel *The Big Story*. Photography: Stephen Dade. Editor: Peter Tanner. Music: Bojan Adamic. Production: Argo Film Productions, Triglar Films, Trident Films. Distribution: Seven Arts Pictures. Release date: February 3, 1965. Running time: 92 minutes. Cast: Robert Ryan (Richard Ashley), Stewart Granger, Nadia Gray, Marius Goring, Katherine Woodville, George Coulouris, Robert Rietty, Milan Micic, Demeter Bitenc, Slobodan Dimitrijevic, Murray Kash, Vladimir Bacic, Niksa Stefani. Black and white.

THE SECRET AGENTS (1965) Directors: Christian-Jaque, Werner Klingler, Carlo Lizzani, Terence Young. Producers: Richard Hellman, Eugéne Tucherer. Screenwriters: Philippe Bouvard, Jacques Caborie, Christian-Jaque, Ennio De Concini, Jo Eisinger, Jacques Rémy. Photography: Richard Angst. Editor: Franco Fraticelli. Music: Robert Mellin, Gian Piero Reverberi. Production: American International Pictures, Eichberg-Film, Euro International Film, Fair Film, Franco London Films, Landau/Unger. Distribution: American International Pictures. Release date: June 23,

1965 (France); April 13, 1966 (US). Running time: 118 minutes. Cast: Henry Fonda, Vittorio Gassman, Annie Girardot, Robert Ryan (General Bruce), Bourvil, Peter van Eyck, Maria Grazia Bucella, Jacques Sernas, Robert Hossein. Black and white. *Note:* Released in the United States as *The Dirty Game,* with a running time of 87 minutes and no credit for director Werner Klingler, whose scenes were deleted.

BATTLE OF THE BULGE (1965) Director: Ken Annakin. Producers: Sidney Harmon, Milton Sperling, Philip Yordan. Screenwriters: Philip Yordan, Milton Sperling, John Melson. Photography: Jack Hildyard. Editor: Derek Parsons. Music: Benjamin Frankel. Production: United States Pictures, Cinerama Productions Corp., and Warner Bros. Distribution: Warner Bros. Release date: December 16, 1965. Running time: 167 minutes. Cast: Henry Fonda, Robert Shaw, Robert Ryan (General Grey), Dana Andrews, George Montgomery, Ty Hardin, Pier Angeli, Barbara Werle, Charles Bronson, Hans Christian Blech, Werner Peters, James MacArthur, Telly Savalas. Color, Ultra-Panavision.

THE PROFESSIONALS (1966) Director: Richard Brooks. Producer: Richard Brooks. Screenwriter: Richard Brooks, from Frank O'Rourke's novel *A Mule for the Marquesa.* Photography: Conrad Hall. Editor: Peter Zinner. Music: Maurice Jarre. Production: Pax Enterprises. Distribution: Columbia Pictures. Release date: November 2, 1966. Running time: 117 minutes. Cast: Lee Marvin, Robert Ryan (Hans Ehrengard), Woody Strode, Burt Lancaster, Jack Palance, Ralph Bellamy, Claudia Cardinale, Joe De Santis, Rafael Bertrand, Jorge Martinez de Hoyos, Marie Gomez, José Chavez, Carlos Romero, Vaughn Taylor. Color.

THE BUSY BODY (1966) Director: William Castle. Producer: William Castle. Screenwriter: Ben Starr, from the Donald Westlake novel. Photography: Harold Stine. Editor: Edwin H. Bryant. Music: Vic Mizzy. Production: William Castle Productions. Distribution: Paramount Pictures. Release date: March 12, 1966. Running time: 101 minutes. Cast: Sid Caesar, Robert Ryan (Charley Barker), Anne Baxter, Kay Medford, Jan Murray, Richard Pryor, Arlene Golonka, Charles McGraw, Ben Blue, Dom DeLuise, Bill Dana, Godfrey Cambridge, Marty Ingels, George Jessel. Color.

THE DIRTY DOZEN (1966) Director: Robert Aldrich. Producer: Kenneth Hyman. Screenwriters: Nunnally Johnson, Lukas Heller, from the novel by E. M. Nathanson. Photography: Edward Scaife. Editor: Michael Luciano. Music: Frank De Vol. Production: MKH and Seven Arts Productions. Distribution: Metro-Goldwyn-Mayer. Release date: June 15, 1967. Running time: 150 minutes. Cast: Lee Marvin, Ernest Borgnine, Charles Bronson, Jim Brown, John Cassavetes, Richard Jaeckel, George Kennedy, Trini Lopez, Ralph Meeker, Robert Ryan (Colonel Everett Dasher Breed), Telly Savalas, Donald Sutherland, Clint Walker, Robert Webber. Color.

HOUR OF THE GUN (1967) Director: John Sturges. Producer: John Sturges. Screenwriter: Edward Anhalt. Photography: Lucien Ballard. Editor: Ferris Webster. Music: Jerry Goldsmith. Production: Mirsch-Kappa Production. Distribution: United

Artists. Release date: November 1, 1967. Running time: 100 minutes. Cast: James Garner, Jason Robards, Robert Ryan (Ike Clanton), Albert Salmi, Charles Aidman, Steve Ihnat, Michael Tolan, William Windom, William Schallert, Bill Fletcher, Karl Swenson, Austin Willis, Monte Markham, Richard Bull, Sam Melville, Frank Converse, Jon Voight, Robert Phillips. Color, Panavision.

CUSTER OF THE WEST (1968) Director: Robert Siodmak. Producer: Philip Yordan. Screenwriters: Bernard Gordon, Julian Halevy. Photography: Cecilio Paniagua. Editor: Peter Parasheles, Maurice Rootes. Music: Bernardo Segall. Production: Security Pictures and Cinerama Productions Corp. Distribution: Cinerama Releasing Corporation. Release date: November 9, 1967 (UK); January 24, 1968 (US). Running time: 143 minutes. Cast: Robert Shaw, Mary Ure, Ty Hardin, Jeffrey Hunter, Lawrence Tierney, Marc Lawrence, Kieron Moore, Charles Stalnaker, Robert Hall, Robert Ryan (Sergeant Patrick Mulligan). Color.

A MINUTE TO PRAY, A SECOND TO DIE (1968) Director: Franco Giraldi. Producer: Albert Band. Screenwriters: Louis Garfinkel, Ugo Liberatore, and Albert Band. Photography: Aiace Parolin. Editor: Alberto Gallitti. Music: Carlo Rustichelli. Production: American Broadcasting Company, Documento Film, Selmur Productions. Distribution: Cinerama Releasing Corporation. Release date: May 1, 1968. Running time: 118 minutes. Cast: Alex Cord, Arthur Kennedy, Robert Ryan (New Mexico Governor Lem Carter), Enzo Fiermonte, Renato Romano, Franco Lantieri, Giampiero Albertini, Mario Brega, Nicoletta Machiavelli. Color.

ANZIO (1968) Director: Edward Dmytryk. Producer: Dino De Laurentiis. Screenwriter: H. A. L. Craig. Adaptation: Frank De Felitta, Duilio Coletti, and Giuseppe Mangione, from the book by Wynford Vaughan-Thomas. Photography: Giuseppe Rotunno. Editor: Peter Taylor. Music: Riz Ortolani. Production: Columbia Pictures Corporation and Dino De Laurentiis Cinematografica. Distribution: Columbia Pictures. Release date: July 24, 1968. Running time: 117 minutes. Cast: Robert Mitchum, Peter Falk, Robert Ryan (General Carson), Earl Holliman, Mark Damon, Arthur Kennedy, Reni Santoni, Joseph Walsh, Thomas Hunter, Giancarlo Giannini, Patrick Magee, Arthur Franz. Color.

THE WILD BUNCH (1969) Director: Sam Peckinpah. Producer: Phil Feldman. Screenwriters: Walon Green, Sam Peckinpah. Story: Walon Green, Roy N. Sickner. Photography: Lucien Ballard. Editor: Louis Lombardo. Music: Jerry Fielding. Production and distribution: Warners Bros.–Seven Arts. Release date: June 18, 1969. Running time: 145 minutes. Cast: William Holden, Ernest Borgnine, Robert Ryan (Deke Thornton), Edmond O'Brien, Warren Oates, Jaime Sánchez, Ben Johnson, Emilio Fernández, Strother Martin, L. Q. Jones, Albert Dekker, Bo Hopkins, Dub Taylor, Jorge Russek, Alfonso Arau, Chano Urueta, Sonia Amelio, Aurora Clavel, Elsa Cárdenas. Color.

CAPTAIN NEMO AND THE UNDERWATER CITY (1969) Director: James Hill. Producer: Bertram Ostrer. Screenwriters: Pip Baker, Jane Baker, and R. Wright Campbell, from characters created by Jules Verne. Photography: Alan Hume. Editor: Bill

Lewthwaite. Music: Walter Stott (aka Angela Morley). Production and distribution: Omnia Pictures Ltd., through Metro-Goldwyn-Mayer. Release date: July 1969 (UK); October 7, 1970 (US). Running time: 105 minutes. Cast: Robert Ryan (Captain Nemo), Chuck Connors, Nanette Newman, Luciana Paluzzi, John Turner, Bill Fraser, Kenneth Connor, Alan Cuthbertson, Christopher Hartstone. Color.

THE REASON WHY (1970) Director: Paul Leaf. Screenwriter: From the play by Arthur Miller. Production: Gino Giglio Co. Distribution: Pathé Contemporary Films. Release date: February 13, 1970. Running time: 13 minutes. Cast: Eli Wallach, Robert Ryan (Roger). Color.

LAWMAN (1971) Director: Michael Winner. Producer: Michael Winner. Screenwriter: Gerald Wilson. Photography: Robert Paynter. Editor: Freddie Wilson. Music: Jerry Fielding. Production: Scimitar Films. Distribution: United Artists. Release date: March 11, 1971 (UK); August 4, 1971 (US). Running time: 99 minutes. Cast: Burt Lancaster, Robert Ryan (Cotton Ryan), Lee J. Cobb, Robert Duvall, Sheree North, Albert Salmi, Richard Jordan, John McGiver, Ralph Waite, John Beck, William C. Watson, Walter Brooke, Robert Emhardt, Charles Tyner, J. D. Cannon, Joseph Wiseman, Richard Bull, John Hillerman. Color.

THE LOVE MACHINE (1971) Director: Jack Haley Jr. Producer: M. J. Frankovich. Screenwriter: Samuel Taylor, from the novel by Jacqueline Susann. Photography: Charles B. Lang. Editor: David Blewitt. Music: Artie Butler. Production: Frankovich Productions, Columbia Pictures Corporation. Distribution: Columbia Pictures. Release date: August 14, 1971. Running time: 109 minutes. Cast: Dyan Cannon, Robert Ryan (Gregory Austin), Jackie Cooper, David Hemmings, Shecky Greene, William Roerick, Maureen Arthur, Clinton Greyn, Sharon Farrell, Alexandra Hay, Eve Bruce, Greg Mullavey, Edith Atwater, Gene Baylos, Ben Lessy, Elizabeth St. Clair, Claudia Jennings, John Phillip Law, and introducing Jodi Wexler. In color.

AND HOPE TO DIE (1972) Director: René Clément. Producer: Serge Silberman. Screenwriter: Sébastien Japrisot, from David Goodis's novel *Black Friday*. Photography: Edmond Richard. Editor: Roger Dwyre. Music: Francis Lai. Production: Greenwich Film Productions. Distribution: 20th Century-Fox. Release date: September 15, 1972 (France); November 29, 1972 (US). Running time: 99 minutes. Cast: Jean-Louis Trintignant, Robert Ryan (Charley), Lea Massari, Aldo Ray, Jean Gaven, Tisa Farrow. Color.

LOLLY-MADONNA XXX (1973) Director: Richard Sarafian. Producer: Rodney Carr-Smith. Screenwriter: Rodney Carr-Smith and Sue Grafton, from Grafton's novel *The Lolly-Madonna War*. Photography: Philip H. Lathrop. Editor: Tom Rolf. Music: Fred Myrow. Production and distribution: Metro-Goldwyn-Mayer. Release date: February 21, 1973. Running time: 103 minutes. Cast: Rod Steiger, Robert Ryan (Pap Gutshall), Jeff Bridges, Scott Wilson, Katherine Squire, Joan Goodfellow, Tresa Hughes, Gary Busey, Randy Quaid, Season Hubley. Color.

THE OUTFIT (1973) Director: John Flynn. Producer: Carter DeHaven. Screenwriter: John Flynn, from the novel by Richard Stark (aka Donald E. Westlake).

Photography: Bruce Surtees. Editor: Ralph E. Winters. Music: Jerry Fielding. Production and distribution: Metro-Goldwyn-Mayer. Release date: October 1973. Running time: 86 minutes. Cast: Robert Duvall, Karen Black, Joe Don Baker, Timothy Carey, Richard Jaeckel, Sheree North, Felice Orlandi, Marie Windsor, Jane Greer, Henry Jones, Joanna Cassidy, Tom Reese, Elisha Cook, Bill McKinney, Anita O'Day, Archie Moore, Tony Young, Roland La Starza, Edward Ness, Roy Roberts, Toby Andersen, Robert Ryan (Mailer). Color.

EXECUTIVE ACTION (1973) Director: David Miller. Producer: Edward Lewis. Screenwriter: Dalton Trumbo. Story: Donald Freed, Mark Lane. Photography: Robert Steadman. Editor: George Grenville. Music: Randy Edelman. Production: Wakeford/Orloff. Distribution: National General Pictures. Release date: November 7, 1973. Running time: 91 minutes. Cast: Burt Lancaster, Robert Ryan (Robert Foster), Will Geer, Gilbert Green, John Anderson, Paul Carr, Colby Chester, Walter Brooke, Ed Lauter. Color.

THE ICEMAN COMETH (1973) Director: John Frankenheimer. Producer: Ely Landau. Screenwriter: Thomas Quinn Curtiss, from the play by Eugene O'Neill. Photography: Ralph Woolsey. Editor: Harold F. Kress. Production and distribution: The American Film Theatre. Release date: November 10, 1973. Running time: 239 minutes. Cast: Lee Marvin, Fredric March, Ryan (Larry Slade), Jeff Bridges, Bradford Dillman, Sorrell Booke, Hildy Brooks, Nancy Juno Dawson, Evans Evans, Martyn Green, Moses Gunn, Clifton James, John McLiam, Stephen Pearlman, Tom Pedi, George Voskovec, Don McGovern, Bart Burns. Color.

part three Notable Radio and Television Broadcasts

Ryan acted on radio in the late 1940s and early 1950s (on the CBS thriller anthology *Suspense* and the Mutual Broadcasting System's Christian dramatic series *Family Theater*) and on television in the late 1950s and early 1960s (on such anthology series as *Goodyear Theatre, Alcoa Theatre, Zane Grey Theater,* and *Kraft Suspense Theatre*). A more complete list of Ryan's TV appearances (including talk shows with Dick Cavett, David Frost, David Susskind, Johnny Carson, Jack Paar, and Steve Allen) can be found online at the Internet Movie Database. Franklin Jarlett's *Robert Ryan: A Biography and Critical Filmography* has a detailed inventory of Ryan's episodic TV work, as well as his voluminous narrations and audio recordings. But following are Ryan's more significant radio and TV performances.

HOLLYWOOD FIGHTS BACK (1947) A live program protesting the House Un-American Activities Committee's investigation into communist subversion of the movie industry. Broadcast: October 26, 1947, ABC Radio. Cast: Charles Boyer, Judy Garland, Gene Kelly, Lauren Bacall, Joseph Cotten, Peter Lorre, June Havoc, John Huston, Danny Kaye, Marsha Hunt, Walter Wanger, Cornel Wilde, Melvyn Douglas, Richard Conte, Evelyn Keyes, Burt Lancaster, Paul Henreid, William

Holden, Robert Ryan, Florence Eldridge, Myrna Loy, Robert Young, Lucille Ball, Van Heflin, Henry Morgan, Keenan Wynn, Humphrey Bogart, John Beal, Edward G. Robinson, Paulette Goddard, Norman Corwin, Audie Murphy, William Wyler, Fredric March, John Garfield, Deems Taylor, Harlow Shapley, Artie Shaw, Arthur Garfield Hayes, Elbert Thomas, Harley Kilgore, Archibald MacLeish, Claude Pepper, Glen Taylor, Vincent Price, John Rankin, J. Parnell Thomas. *Note:* Archived at the Paley Center for Media, New York and Los Angeles.

CROSSFIRE (1948) A live radio adaptation of the RKO film, for the CBS anthology series *Suspense.* Broadcast: April 10, 1948, CBS Radio. Running time: 60 minutes. Cast: Robert Young, Robert Mitchum, Robert Ryan (Montgomery), George Cooper, William Phipps.

ADLAI STEVENSON CAMPAIGN RALLY (1952) A live program from Madison Square Garden, complete with Ryan's delayed entrance as master of ceremonies. Broadcast: October 29, 1952, WABD-TV, New York City. Running time: 30 minutes. Cast: Lauren Bacall, Robert Ryan, Kenny Delmar, George Hall, Richard Rodgers, Oscar Hammerstein, Al Capp, Channing Tobias, Mercedes McCambridge, Lew Parker, Al Kelly, Montgomery Clift, Tallulah Bankhead, Louis Calhern, Benay Venuta, Humphrey Bogart, Carl Sandburg, George Jessel, James A. Farley. *Note:* Archived at the Paley Center for Media, New York and Los Angeles. Black and white.

THE ROBERT RYAN STORY (1953) A fanciful reenactment of Ryan's career for the NBC series *The Hollywood Story,* with actors playing his mother, his wife, and his mentor, Max Reinhardt, among others. Broadcast: November 28, 1953, NBC Radio. Running time: 30 minutes. *Note:* Archived at the Wisconsin Center for Film and Theater Research, Madison, Wisconsin.

LINCOLN'S DOCTOR'S DOG (1955) A filmed episode of the NBC anthology series *Screen Directors Playhouse.* Director: H. C. Potter. Teleplay: Christopher Morley. Photography: James Wong Howe. Editor: G. E. Luckenbacher. Broadcast: December 14, 1955, NBC-TV. Running time: 30 minutes. Cast: Robert Ryan (Abraham Lincoln), Charles Bickford, Richard Long, Willis Bouchey, Howard Wendell, Johnny Lee, Paul Keast, Mack Williams, John Craven, Dennis King Jr. Black and white.

THE GREAT GATSBY (1958) A taped performance for the CBS anthology series *Playhouse 90.* Director: Franklin Schaffner. Producer: Martin Manulis. Adaptation: David Shaw, from the novel by F. Scott Fitzgerald. Music: Milton Anderson. Broadcast: June 26, 1958, CBS-TV. Running time: 88 minutes. Cast: Robert Ryan (Jay Gatsby), Rod Taylor, Jeanne Crain, Patricia Barry, Phillip Reed, Virginia Grey, Barry Atwater. Black and white. *Note:* Archived at the Paley Center for Media, New York and Los Angeles.

30TH ANNUAL ACADEMY AWARDS A live program from the RKO Pantages Theatre in Hollywood; Ryan and actor Wendell Corey present the award for Best Costume Design. Director: Alan Handley. Producer: Jerry Wald. Broadcast: March 26, 1958, NBC-TV. Running time: 120 minutes. Black and white. *Note:* Archived at the Paley Center for Media, New York and Los Angeles.

"A CALL FROM . . ." (1960) A documentary on the United Nations' World Refugee Year. Directors: Jack Orbison, William F. Wallace. Producer: Marsha Hunt. Writer: Robert Presnell Jr. Broadcast: February 10, 1960, KCOP-TV, Los Angeles. Running time: 60 minutes. Cast: Steve Allen, Harry Belafonte, Richard Boone, Spring Byington, Jeff Chandler, Bing Crosby, Burl Ives, Louis Jourdan, Phyllis Kirk, Paul Newman, David Niven, Robert Ryan, Jean Simmons, Joanne Woodward. Black and white. *Note:* Archived at the UCLA Film and Television Archive, Los Angeles. Restored in 2009 as *A Call from the Stars.*

THE SNOWS OF KILIMANJARO (1960) A live performance from CBS Television City in Los Angeles, for the anthology series *Buick-Elektra Playhouse.* Director: John Frankenheimer. Producer: Gordon Duff. Teleplay: A. E. Hotchner, from the story by Ernest Hemingway. Broadcast: March 25, 1960, CBS-TV. Running time: 87 minutes. Cast: Robert Ryan (Harry Walters), Ann Todd, James Gregory, Liliane Montevecchi, Brock Peters, Janice Rule, Mary Astor, Clancy Cooper, Norma Crane, Clegg Hoyt, Albert Paulson, Frank Puglia. Black and white. *Note:* Archived at the Paley Center for Media, New York and Los Angeles.

THE BELL TELEPHONE HOUR (1964) Ryan hosts this musical variety program, performing the narration to Aaron Copland's *A Lincoln Portrait.* Director: Sid Smith. Producer: Charles Andrews. Broadcast: February 11, 1964, NBC-TV. Running time: 60 minutes. Cast: Robert Ryan, Al Hirt, The Brothers Four, Joan Sutherland, Donald Voorhees, Suzanne Farrell, Patricia Neary, Conrad Ludlow. Color. *Note:* Archived at the Paley Center for Media, New York and Los Angeles.

THE COMPLETE STORY: WORLD WAR I (1964–65) A twenty-six-episode documentary series, produced by CBS News and narrated by Ryan. Music: Morton Gould. Broadcast debut: September 22, 1964, CBS-TV. Total running time: 660 minutes. Black and white. *Note:* Released on DVD by CBS DVD home video.

THE PRESIDENCY: A SPLENDID MISERY (1964) Ryan provides the voice of Abraham Lincoln for this historical documentary. Broadcast: September 23, 1964, CBS-TV. Total running time: 60 minutes. Cast: Dana Andrews, Ed Begley, Sidney Blackmer, Macdonald Carey, James Daly, Fredric March, E. G. Marshall, Herbert Marshall, Gary Merrill, Dan O'Herlihy, Jason Robards, Robert Ryan. Black and white.

GUILTY OR NOT GUILTY (1966) A filmed TV pilot that was ultimately broadcast on the NBC anthology series *Bob Hope Presents the Chrysler Theatre.* Broadcast: March 9, 1966, NBC-TV. Running time: 60 minutes. Directors: Roland Kibbee, David Lowell Rich. Producer: Richard Lewis. Teleplay: Evan Hunter, Roland Kibbee, Guthrie Lamb. Cast: Richard Beymer, Robert Duvall, Leif Erickson, Diana Hyland, Leslie Nielsen, Robert Ryan (Andrew Dixon), Pippa Scott. Color.

INAUGURAL EVENING AT FORD'S THEATRE (1968) A live program from Ford's Theatre in Washington, DC. Broadcast: January 30, 1968, CBS-TV. Running time: 59 minutes. Producer: Don Hewitt. Cast: Roger Mudd, Hubert Humphrey, Helen Hayes, Fredric March, Robert Ryan, Henry Fonda, Harry Belafonte, Nina Foch,

Andy Williams, Richard Crenna, Patricia Brooks, Odetta, Carmen De Lavallade. Color. *Note:* Archived at the Paley Center for Media, New York, and the UCLA Film and Television Archive, Los Angeles.

SIMON AND GARFUNKEL: SONGS OF AMERICA (1969) Ryan delivers a brief introduction to the program. Broadcast: November 30, 1969, CBS-TV. Running time: 53 minutes. Director: Charles Grodin. Producers: Paul Simon, Arthur Garfunkel, Mike Jackson. Photography: Abbot Mills, Peter Powell. Editors: Luke Bennett, Ellen Giffard. Cast: Paul Simon, Art Garfunkel, Charles Grodin. Color. *Note:* Released as part of the Columbia/Legacy CD/DVD reissue of *Bridge Over Troubled Water.*

THE FRONT PAGE (1970) A taped performance of the play by Ben Hecht and Charles MacArthur, with some cast members from the 1969 Broadway production. Director: Alan Handley. Producer: Lewis Freedman. Production: Metromedia Producers Corporation, Plumstead Playhouse. Broadcast: January 31, 1970, Hughes Sports Network. Running time: 90 minutes. Cast: Robert Ryan (Walter Burns), George Grizzard, Helen Hayes, Vivian Vance, Estelle Parsons, Harold J. Kennedy, Susan Watson, John McGiver, Charles White. Color.

THE MAN WITHOUT A COUNTRY (1973) A TV movie, for the series *ABC Movie of the Week.* Director: Delbert Mann. Producer: Norman Rosemont. Screenwriter: Sidney Carroll, from the story by Edward Everett Hale. Photography: Andrew Laszlo. Editor: Gene Milford. Production: Norman Rosemont Enterprises, American Broadcasting Company. Broadcast: April 24, 1973, ABC-TV. Running time: 78 minutes. Cast: Cliff Robertson, Beau Bridges, Peter Strauss, Robert Ryan (Lieutenant Commander Vaughan), Walter Abel, Geoffrey Holder, John Cullum. Color.

Notes

Introduction

1. Harold Kennedy, *No Pickle, No Performance: An Irreverent Theatrical Excursion from Tallulah to Travolta* (Garden City, NY: Doubleday, 1978), 125.

2. Martin Scorsese, "Scorsese Screens," *TCM Now Playing,* November 2013, 11.

3. Margaret McManus, "Robert Ryan Speaks Out on Reagan," *Bridgeport (Connecticut) Telegram,* November 6, 1966.

4. Millard Lampell, interview with Franklin Jarlett, March 10, 1987, private collection.

5. Robert Ryan, as told to Jane Kesner Ardmore, "What Makes an Actor Tick?" (ca. 1957), Jane Ardmore Papers, Margaret Herrick Library Special Collections, Academy of Motion Picture Arts and Sciences, Beverly Hills, California.

one Inferno

1. "Chicago Makes Kaiser's Wake Wild Bedlam." *Chicago Tribune*, November 12, 1918, 1, 3.

2. Robert Ryan, "The Full Text of Ryan's Letter," *Chicago Reader,* October 29, 2009, http://www.chicagoreader.com/chicago/actor-robert-ryans-letter-to-his-children /Content?oid=1223014.

3. *Illinois Political Directory 1899* (Chicago: W. L. Bodine, 1899), 144.

4. Ryan, "The Full Text of Ryan's Letter."

5. Ibid.

6. Ibid.

7. Ibid.

8. Ibid.

9. Ibid.

10. Jeanne Stein, "Robert Ryan: Unlike Most Handsome Actors He Was Willing to Be a Heavy," *Films in Review* 9, no. 1 (January 1968): 9.

11. William M. Tuttle Jr., *Race Riot: Chicago in the Red Summer of 1919* (New York: Atheneum, 1970), 10.

12. Ryan, "The Full Text of Ryan's Letter."

13. Ibid.

14. Ibid.

15. *Loyola Prep,* June 1926, 67.

16. Ryan, "The Full Text of Ryan's Letter."

17. Ibid.

18. Ibid.

19. Lupton A. Wilkinson, "These Fathers!" *Motion Picture,* n.d., Robert Ryan clipping file, Wisconsin Center for Film and Theater Research, Madison, Wisconsin.

20. Roger Biles, *Big City Boss in Depression and War: Mayor Edward J. Kelly of Chicago* (DeKalb: Northern Illinois University Press, 1984), 9.

21. Elmer Lynn Williams, *The Fix-It Boys: The Inside Story of the New Deal and the Kelly-Nash Machine* (Chicago: Elmer Lynn Williams, 1940), 22.

22. Jessica Ryan, "Campaign–'52, or A Camera's-Eye View from Two Odd Birds" (ca. 1970), private collection.

23. "12 Dead, 16 Saved, in Tunnel," *Chicago Daily News,* April 14, 1931, 1, 3.

24. Ibid.

25. "12 Rescued in Disaster," *Chicago Evening Post,* April 14, 1931, 1, 3.

26. Williams, *The Fix-It Boys,* 62.

27. "Coroner's Jury Goes Through Death Tunnel," *Chicago Daily News,* April 15, 1931, 3.

28. "Little Chance to Fix Tunnel Disaster Blame," *Chicago American,* April 15, 1931, 1, 2.

29. Tina Louise, telephone interview with author, July 15, 2012; Lisa Ryan, interview with author, San Francisco, April 17, 2011.

30. Irv Kupcinet, "Kup's Column," *Chicago Sun-Times,* April 7, 1949.

31. J. M. Waldreck, "Ryan the Rip-Roaring Adventurer" n.p., n.d., Robert Ryan clipping file, Wisconsin Center for Film and Theater Research, Madison, Wisconsin.

32. Stein, "Robert Ryan," 10.

33. Wilkinson, "These Fathers!"

34. Captain James McNamara (chairman, Maritime Industry Museum, Fort Schuyler, New York), telephone interview with author, July 1, 2012.

35. Ryan, "The Full Text of Ryan's Letter."

36. Jessica Ryan, "Campaign–'52."

37. June Skinner Sawyers, *Chicago Portraits* (Chicago: Loyola University Press, 1991), 140.

38. Williams, *The Fix-It Boys,* 31.

39. Dartmouth College Class of 1932 newsletter (ca. March 1945), Dartmouth Alumni File, Dartmouth College, Hanover, New Hampshire.

40. "Robert Ryan Dies of Cancer," *Newark Star-Ledger,* July 12, 1973, 43.

41. Wilkinson, "These Fathers!"

42. Autographed program for *Dear Brutus,* May 6, 1938, private collection.

43. *Loyola Prep,* 78.

44. Stein, "Robert Ryan," 13.

45. William Shakespeare, *King Lear,* ed. G. Blakemore Evans. *The Riverside Shakespeare* (Boston: Houghton Mifflin, 1974), 1.4.288–89. References are to act, scene, and line.

two The Mysterious Spirit

1. William Shakespeare, *Hamlet,* ed. G. Blakemore Evans. *The Riverside Shakespeare* (Boston: Houghton Mifflin, 1974), 1.5.106–109.

2. Fredda Duddley, "Romancing with Ryan," *Photoplay,* April 1944, 104.

3. "Living the Life of Ryan," *Screen Guide,* January 1950.

4. "The Robert Ryan Story," NBC Radio's *The Hollywood Story* (November 28, 1953), Wisconsin Center for Film and Theater Research, Madison, Wisconsin. Audio recording.

5. George Wellworth and Alfred G. Brooks, ed., *Max Reinhardt: A Centennial Festschrift, 1873–1973* (Binghamton, NY: Max Reinhardt Archives, 1973), 129.

6. Wellworth and Brooks, *Max Reinhardt,* 129.

7. Ibid., 1.

8. Ibid., 5.

9. Ibid., 75.

10. "Robert Ryan's Advice to Would-Be Actors," *Salt Lake City Deseret News,* November 30, 1951.

11. Wellworth and Brooks, *Max Reinhardt,* 110.

12. Jeanne Stein, "Robert Ryan: Unlike Most Handsome Actors He Was Willing to Be a Heavy," Films in Review 9, no. 1 (January 1968): 13.

13. Jessica Ryan, "Recollections of a Pioneer Grandmother" (ca. 1970), private collection.

14. Jessica Ryan, "If School Keeps" (ca. 1970), private collection.

15. William Shakespeare, *The Merchant of Venice,* ed. G. Blakemore Evans. *The Riverside Shakespeare* (Boston: Houghton Mifflin, 1974), 4.1.186–87. References are to act, scene, and line.

16. Jessica Ryan, "Recollections of a Pioneer Grandmother."

17. Robert Ryan, "I'm Gambling with My Career," *Movieland,* August 1947, 42.

18. Ibid.

19. Helen Louise Walker, "Portrait of a Happy Man," *Movielan*d, December 1949, 76.

20. Marsha Hunt, telephone interview with author, February 9, 2011.

21. Edward Dmytryk, *It's a Hell of a Life But Not a Bad Living: A Hollywood Memoir* (New York: Times Books, 1978), 48.

22. Sidney Skolsky, "Tintypes," *Hollywood Citizen-News,* June 24, 1954.

23. Cheyney Ryan, *The Chickenhawk Syndrome: War, Sacrifice, and Personal Responsibility* (Lanham, MD: Rowman and Littlefield, 2009), x–xi.

24. "Acts of Birth: Robert Ryan," *Films and Filming,* March 1971, 29.

25. Robert Wallsten, interview with Franklin Jarlett, March 1986, private collection.

26. Denis Brian, *Tallulah, Darling: A Biography of Tallulah Bankhead* (New York: Macmillan, 1972), 93.

27. Ibid., 114.

28. Ibid., 120.

29. Tallulah Bankhead, *Tallulah: My Autobiography* (New York: Harper and Brothers, 1952), 245.

30. Lee Israel, *Miss Tallulah Bankhead* (New York: G. P. Putnam's Sons, 1972), 213.

31. Joel Lobenthal, *Tallulah! The Life and Times of a Leading Lady* (New York: Regan Books, 2004), 336.

32. Brian, *Tallulah, Darling,* 118.

33. "Pare Lorentz Picks American Odysseus," *Brooklyn Eagle,* July 14, 1942, 4.

34. Patricia Bosworth, "Robert Ryan: In Search of Action," *New York Times,* June 1, 1969, 1, 7.

three Bombs Away

1. John Houseman, *Run-Through* (New York: Simon and Schuster, 1972), 484.

2. Edward Dmytryk, *It's a Hell of a Life, but Not a Bad Living: A Hollywood Memoir* (New York Times Books, 1978), 54.

3. "How Much? RKO Wants to Know from Lorentz," *Variety,* July 22, 1942, 3.

4. Robert Ryan to A. J. Dickerson (mid-1945), Dartmouth Alumni File, Dartmouth College, Hanover, New Hampshire.

5. "Movies Are Put in Essential Class by Draft Ruling," *New York Times,* February 9, 1942, 1.

6. "Special Draft Deferment Creates Furor in Hollywood," *Los Angeles Times,* February 11, 1942, A2.

7. Joe McCarthy, "Antic Arts: Robert Ryan" (ca. 1963), private collection.

8. Pat O'Brien, *The Wind at My Back: The Life and Times of Pat O'Brien* (Garden City, NY: Doubleday, 1964), 271.

9. Joe McCarthy, "Antic Arts."

10. Dmytryk, *It's a Hell of a Life,* 56.

11. Fredda Dudley, "Romancing with Ryan," *Photoplay,* April 1944, 103.

12. Jessica Ryan, "Marine Ryan," *Movieland,* October 1944, 31.

four You Know the Kind

1. Jessica Ryan, "Marine Ryan," *Movieland,* October 1944, 32.

2. Robert Witty and Neil Morgan, *Marines of the Margharita* (San Diego: Frye and Smith, 1970), 10.

3. "Living the Life of Ryan," *Screen Guide,* January 1950.

4. Robert Ryan to commandant of the Marine Corps, August 25, 1944, National Personnel Records Center, St. Louis, Missouri.

5. Robert Ryan to A. J. Dickerson (mid-1945), Dartmouth Alumni File, Dartmouth College, Hanover, New Hampshire.

6. Dartmouth College Class of 1932 newsletter (ca. March 1945), Dartmouth Alumni File, Dartmouth College, Hanover, New Hampshire.

7. Richard Brooks, *The Brick Foxhole* (New York: Harper and Brothers, 1945), viii.

8. Ibid., 29.

9. Ibid.

10. Douglass K. Daniels, *Tough as Nails: The Life and Films of Richard Brooks* (Madison: University of Wisconsin Press, 2011), 34.

11. Robert Ryan to A. J. Dickerson (mid-1945), Dartmouth Alumni File, Dartmouth College, Hanover, New Hampshire.

12. Jessica Ryan, *The Man Who Asked Why* (Garden City, NY: Doubleday, Doran, 1945), 7.

13. U.S. Marine Corps report of medical survey for Pvt. Robert Ryan (September 8, 1945), National Archives and Records Administration, Washington, DC.

14. Cheyney Ryan, interview with author, Eugene, Oregon, April 15, 2011.

15. Jeanne Stein, "Robert Ryan: Unlike Most Handsome Actors He Was Willing to Be a Heavy," *Films in Review* 9, no. 1 (January 1968): 19.

16. Bert Cardullo, ed., *Jean Renoir: Interviews* (Jackson, MS: University of Jackson Press, 2005), 173. From Rui Nogueira and Francois Truchaud, *Sight and Sound* 37, no. 2 (Spring 1968): 25.

17. Jean Renoir, *My Life and My Films* (New York: Atheneum Publishers, 1974), 244.

18. Rui Nogueira and Nicoletta Zalaffi, "A Bastard's Long Career: Meeting with Robert Ryan," *Cinema 70* (April 1970): 50.

19. Cardullo, *Jean Renoir,* 173.

20. John Paxton to Clay Steinman, Keith Kelly, and Mario Falsetto (ca. July 1977), John Paxton Papers, Margaret Herrick Library Special Collections, Academy of Motion Picture Arts and Sciences, Beverly Hills, California.

21. Robert Ryan, "I'm Gambling with My Career," *Movieland,* August 1947.

22. Robert Ryan, "My Role in Crossfire," *Daily Worker,* July 20, 1947, Southern edition.

23. Ryan, "I'm Gambling with My Career."

24. N. Peter Rathvon memo to Dore Schary (February 12, 1947), Dore Schary Papers, Wisconsin Center for Film and Theater Research, Madison, Wisconsin.

25. Dore Schary, *Heyday* (Boston, Toronto: Little, Brown, 1979), 157.

26. Edward Dmytryk, *On Screen Directing* (Boston: Focal Point Press, 1984), 86.

27. Lee Server, *Robert Mitchum: "Baby I Don't Care"* (New York: St. Martin's Press, 2001), 135.

28. Clay Steinman, Keith Kelly, and Mario Falsetto to John Paxton, June 29, 1977, John Paxton Papers, Margaret Herrick Library Special Collections, Academy of Motion Picture Arts and Sciences, Beverly Hills, California.

29. Ryan, "I'm Gambling with My Career."

1. Cheyney Ryan, interview with author, Eugene, Oregon, April 15, 2011.

2. "Jeep Hunt," *Photoplay,* June 1947, 102.

3. "A-Hunting We Will Go," *Screen Guide,* November 1947, 65.

4. Lynn Bowers, "Gentle Heel" n.p., n.d., Robert Ryan clipping file, Wisconsin Center for Film and Theater Research, Madison, Wisconsin.

5. Bert Granet, "Berlin Express Diary," *Screen Writer,* May 1948, 12.

6. Herb Lightman, "The Story of Filming 'Berlin Express,'" *American Cinematographer,* July 1948, 232.

7. Bert Granet, letter draft n.p., n.d., Bert Granet Papers, Margaret Herrick Library Special Collections, Academy of Motion Picture Arts and Sciences, Beverly Hills, California.

8. Ibid.

9. Charles Higham and Roy Moseley, *Princess Merle: The Romantic Life of Merle Oberon* (New York: Coward-McCann, 1983), 183–84.

10. Robert Ryan, "We're Not Quitting," *Screen Guide,* May 1948, 84.

11. Ibid., 55.

12. Granet, "Berlin Express Diary," 12.

13. Ryan, "We're Not Quitting," 85.

14. Ibid., 85.

15. Ibid., 84.

16. Harold J. Kennedy, *No Pickle, No Performance: An Irreverent Theatrical Excursion from Tallulah to Travolta* (Garden City, NY: Doubleday, 1978), 127.

17. Advertisement, *Variety,* July 30, 1947.

18. Ryan, "We're Not Quitting," 87.

19. Ibid.

20. "RKO's Sensitive Pick, 'Crossfire,' Looks Well Over the Sales Hump," *Variety,* October 15, 1947, 7.

21. Elliot E. Cohen, "Letter to the Movie-Makers: The Film Drama as a Social Force," *Commentary,* August 1947, 112.

22. Robert Ryan, "My Role in Crossfire," *Daily Worker,* July 20, 1947, Southern edition.

23. Robert Ryan, "Don't Play It Safe" n.p., n.d., Robert Ryan clipping file, Wisconsin Center for Film and Theater Research, Madison, Wisconsin.

24. Dore Schary, *Heyday: An Autobiography* (Boston and Toronto: Little, Brown, 1979), 157–58.

25. Jennifer Langdon, "Americanism on Trial," chap. 9 in *Caught in the Crossfire: Adrian Scott and the Politics of Americanism in 1940s Hollywood* (Gutenberg-e.org), para. 33.

26. Jessica Ryan, notes for "Campaign–'52" (ca. 1970), private collection.

27. A. M. Sperber and Eric Lax, *Bogart* (New York: William Morrow, 1994), 36.

28. Larry Ceplar and Steven Englund, *The Inquisition in Hollywood: Politics in the Film Community, 1930–1960* (Garden City, NY: Anchor Press/Doubleday, 1980), 273.

29. Langdon, *Caught in the Crossfire,* chap. 9, para. 26.

30. ABC Radio's *Hollywood Fights Back,* original radio broadcast, October 26, 1948. Old Time Radio Catalogue, otrcat.com.

31. Edward Dmytryk, *Odd Man Out: A Memoir of the Hollywood Ten* (Carbondale and Edwardsville: Southern Illinois University Press, 1996), 73.

32. House Committee on Un-American Activities, *Hearings Regarding the Communist Infiltration of the Motion Picture Industry,* 80th Cong., 1st sess., 1947, public law 601, sect. 121, subsect. Q(2). https://archive.org/stream/hearingsregardin1947aunit /hearingsregardin1947aunit_djvu.txt.

33. Herman A. Lowe, "Big D.C. Whodunit: Who Killed That Red Probe? See Resumption in Dec.," *Variety,* November 5, 1947, 3, 18.

34. "Chatter—Hollywood," *Variety,* October 29, 1947, 63.

35. Schary, *Heyday,* 369.

36. "Bogart Terms Wash. Trip a 'Foolish' Move," *Variety,* December 3, 1947, 5, 18.

37. Higham and Moseley, *Princess Merle,* 184.

38. Louella O. Parsons, "In Hollywood with Louella O. Parsons" n.p., February 29, 1948, Robert Ryan clipping file, Wisconsin Center for Film and Theater Research, Madison, Wisconsin.

39. Jessica Ryan, notes for "Campaign–'52."

40. Jessica Ryan, "Campaign–'52, or A Camera's-Eye View from Two Odd Birds" (ca. 1970), private collection.

41. Ibid.

42. Jessica Ryan, notes for "Campaign–'52."

43. "Portrait of a Happy Man," *Movieland,* December 1949, 76.

44. Philip Dunne, interview with Franklin Jarlett, June 12, 1987, private collection.

45. Jessica Ryan, notes for "Campaign–'52."

46. "Ryan for 'Glory,'" *Variety,* November 5, 1947, 4.

47. Norman Cousins, "Modern Man Is Obsolete," *Saturday Review,* August 18, 1945, 8.

48. Lisa Ryan, telephone interview with author, May 9, 2010.

49. Dmytryk, *Odd Man Out,* 99.

six Caught

1. Thomas Schatz, *The Genius of the System: Hollywood Filmmaking in the Studio Era* (New York: Pantheon Books, 1988), 411–12.

2. "Despite Rathvon's Balm to Aides, They're Still Uneasy on Hughes Buy," *Variety,* May 19, 1948, 5.

3. "No RKO Changes Due, Schary Assures Help," *Variety,* June 9, 1948, 3.

4. Arthur Noletti Jr., "Conversation with Fred Zinnemann," in *Fred Zinnemann: Interviews,* ed. Gabriel Miller (Jackson: University Press of Mississippi, 2005), 116.

5. Fred Zinnemann, *A Life in the Movies: An Autobiography* (New York: Charles Scribner's Sons, 1992), 74.

6. Robert Surtees, "The Story of Filming 'Act of Violence,'" *American Cinematographer* (August 1948): 268.

7. Dore Schary, *Heyday: An Autobiography* (Boston and Toronto: Little, Brown, 1979), 171.

8. "Hollywood's Economy Jitters," *Variety,* July 14, 1948, 1.

9. Betty Lasky, *RKO, the Biggest Little Major of Them All* (Englewood Cliffs, NJ: Prentice Hall, 1984), 216–17.

10. "RKO Closure Shrinks Backlog," *Variety,* February 9, 1949, 5.

11. Lisa Ryan, telephone interview with author, May 26, 2010.

12. Franklin Jarlett, *Robert Ryan: A Biography and Critical Filmography* (Jefferson, NC: McFarland, 1994), 35.

13. Arthur Laurents, *Original Story by: A Memoir of Broadway and Hollywood* (New York: Knopf, 2000), 140.

14. Ibid., 143.

15. "Inside Stuff—Pictures," *Variety,* August 4, 1948, 16.

16. Robert Wallsten, interview with Franklin Jarlett, May 1986, private collection; also Jarlett, *Robert Ryan,* 89.

17. Lutz Bacher, *Max Ophuls in the Hollywood Studios* (Brunswick, NJ: Rutgers University Press, 1996), 237.

18. Joseph Moncure March, *The Wild Party / The Set-Up / A Certain Wildness* (Freeport, ME: Bond Wheelwright, 1968), 53.

19. Ibid., 153.

20. Robert Ryan, interview with Tony Thomas (1960), Margaret Herrick Library Special Collections, Academy of Motion Picture Arts and Sciences, Beverly Hills, California.

21. George Stevens Jr., *Conversations with the Great Moviemakers of Hollywood's Golden Age at the American Film Institute* (New York: Knopf, 2006), 465.

22. Richard C. Keenan, *The Films of Robert Wise* (Lanham, MD: Scarecrow Press, 2007), 43–44.

23. Robert Ryan, "The Role I Liked Best . . . ," *Saturday Evening Post,* July 15, 1950, 68.

24. Ibid.

25. Ibid.

26. Arthur (Weegee) Fellig column, *Los Angeles Mirror,* November 26, 1948.

27. Jessica Ryan, notes for "Campaign–'52" (ca. 1970), private collection.

28. Jarlett, *Robert Ryan,* 40.

29. Jessica Ryan, notes for "Campaign–'52."

30. Philip Dunne, oral history, Margaret Herrick Library Special Collections, Academy of Motion Picture Arts and Sciences, Beverly Hills, California, 69.

31. Jessica Ryan, notes for "Campaign–'52."

32. Ibid.

33. Michael Ciment, *Conversations with Losey* (New York: Methuen, 1985), 81.

34. Ben Barzman, "Pour Joe," *Positif,* no. 293/4 (July–August 1985): 11, in David Caute, *Joseph Losey: A Revenge on Life* (New York: Oxford University Press, 1994), 87.

35. "After 150G Preparation, 'Boy' Goes sans Haircut," *Variety,* September 1, 1948, 2.

36. Ciment, *Conversations with Losey,* 81.

37. Bosley Crowther, review of *The Boy with Green Hair, New York Times Book Review,* January 13, 1949, 26.

38. Cheyney Ryan, interview with author, Eugene, Oregon, April 15, 2011.

39. Ciment, *Conversations with Losey,* 82.

40. Patrick McGilligan, *Backstory 2: Interviews with Screenwriters of the 1940s and 1950s* (Berkeley: University of California Press, 1991), 197.

41. Bernard Eisenschitz, *Nicholas Ray: An American Journey* (Berkeley: University of California Press, 1993), 121.

42. Gregory G. Hewett, *The Heavy: The Somewhat Noir Life of Thomas Gomez, Hollywood's Quintessential Character Actor* (forthcoming).

43. RKO production file for *The Woman on Pier 13,* UCLA Special Collections, University of California at Los Angeles, Los Angeles, California.

44. Cheyney Ryan, interview with author, Eugene, Oregon, April 15, 2011.

seven. Learning by Doing

1. Jessica Ryan, notes for "Campaign–'52" (ca. 1970), private collection.

2. Jessica Ryan to Dido and Jean Renoir, n.d., Jean Renoir Papers, UCLA Special Collections, University of California at Los Angeles, Los Angeles, California.

3. Jessica Ryan, "If School Keeps" (ca. 1970), private collection.

4. Erskine Johnson, "Lazy Newcomers Irk Ryan," *Los Angeles Mirror News,* December 2, 1959.

5. Bob Thomas, "Male Cheesecake! Robert Ryan Comments on New Trend," *Hollywood Citizen-News,* July 11, 1949.

6. Laraine Day, oral history, Margaret Herrick Library Special Collections, Academy of Motion Picture Arts and Sciences, Beverly Hills, California, 201.

7. Cheyney Ryan, interview with author, Eugene, Oregon, April 15, 2011.

8. Reba and Bonnie Churchill, "Ryan Goes Romantic" n.p., n.d., Robert Ryan clipping file, Wisconsin Center for Film and Theater Research, Madison, Wisconsin.

9. Bernard Eisenschitz, *Nicholas Ray: An American Journey* (Berkeley: University of California Press, 1993), 127.

10. Ibid., 129.

11. Patrick McGilligan, *Nicholas Ray: The Glorious Failure of an American Director* (New York: HarperCollins, 2011), 176.

12. Eisenschitz, *Nicholas Ray,* 513.

13. Franklin Jarlett, *Robert Ryan: A Biography and Critical Filmography* (Jefferson, NC: McFarland, 1994), 43.

14. "Inside Stuff—Pictures," *Variety,* December 7, 1949, 18.

15. Eisenschitz, *Nicholas Ray,* 130.

16. Richard B. Jewell, *The* RKO *Story* (New York: Arlington House, 1982), 143.

17. Michel Ciment, *Conversations with Losey* (New York: Methuen, 1985), 79.

18. Gerald Butler, *Mad with Much Heart* (New York: Rinehart, 1946), 6.

19. Butler, *Mad with Much Heart,* 121.

20. Lee Server, *Screenwriter: Words Become Pictures* (Pittstown, NJ: Main Street Press, 1987), 40.

21. Eisenschitz, *Nicholas Ray,* 155.

22. Joseph I. Breen to Harold Melniker, March 23, 1950, RKO production file for *On Dangerous Ground,* UCLA Special Collections, University of California at Los Angeles, Los Angeles, California.

23. Joseph I. Breen to Harold Melniker, March 20, 1950, RKO production file for *On Dangerous Ground,* UCLA Special Collections, University of California at Los Angeles, Los Angeles, California.

24. Eisenschitz, *Nicholas Ray,* 156.

25. Lamont Johnson, interview with Franklin Jarlett, August 17, 1986, private collection; also Franklin Jarlett, *Robert Ryan: A Biography and Critical Filmography* (Jefferson, NC: McFarland, 1990), 62.

26. Norma H. Goodhue, "Crowded Schools Do Good Job Despite Difficulties," *Los Angeles Times,* February 26, 1950, 1, 3.

27. Jessica Ryan, "If School Keeps."

28. Ibid.

29. Ibid.

30. Peer J. Oppenheimer, "A Film Hero Fights for Better Schools," *New Haven Sunday Register,* August 7, 1960, 12.

31. Jessica Ryan, "If School Keeps."

32. Ibid.

33. Larry Ceplair and Steven Englund, *The Inquisition in Hollywood: Politics in the Film Community, 1930–1960* (Garden City, NY: Anchor Press/Doubleday, 1980), 362–63.

34. Greg Mitchell, *Tricky Dick and the Pink Lady: Richard Nixon vs. Helen Gahagan Douglas—Sexual Politics and the Red Scare* (New York: Random House, 1998), 215.

35. Jessica Ryan, notes for "Campaign–'52."

36. Eisenschitz, *Nicholas Ray,* 162.

37. Nicholas Ray, *I Was Interrupted: Nicholas Ray on Making Movies* (Berkeley: University of California Press, 1993), 106.

38. Franklin Jarlett, *Robert Ryan: A Biography and Critical Filmography* (Jefferson, NC: McFarland, 1990), 39.

39. Ray, *I Was Interrupted.*

40. Robert Ryan, open letter to parents in North Hollywood, January 1951, Oakwood School Archives, North Hollywood, California.

41. Jessica Ryan, "If School Keeps."

42. John Dewey, "My Pedagogic Creed," in *The Essential Dewey,* vol. 1: *Pragmatism, Education, Democracy,* ed. Larry A. Hickman and Thomas M. Alexander (Bloomington and Indianapolis: Indiana University Press, 1998), 230.

43. Elsie M. Walker and David T. Johnson, *Conversations with Directors* (Lanham, MD: Scarecrow Press, 2008), 209.

44. Franklin Jarlett, *Robert Ryan: A Biography and Critical Filmography* (Jefferson, NC: McFarland, 1990), 39.

45. Robert Ryan, "How Do You Remember All Those Words?" (ca. 1957), Jane Ardmore Papers, Margaret Herrick Library Special Collections, Academy of Motion Picture Arts and Sciences, Beverly Hills, California.

46. *Flying Leathernecks* publicity, Lincoln Quarberg Papers, Margaret Herrick Library Special Collections, Academy of Motion Picture Arts and Sciences, Beverly Hills, California.

47. Extension of Remarks of Hon. Richard M. Nixon of California in the Senate of the United States (Monday, August 27, 1951), Lincoln Quarberg Papers, Margaret Herrick Library Special Collections, Academy of Motion Picture Arts and Sciences, Beverly Hills, California.

48. Jessica Ryan, "If School Keeps."

49. Ibid.

50. Howard McClay, "He Didn't Look Like an Actor—But," *Los Angeles Daily News,* May 20, 1952.

eight The Whiz Kids

1. Louis Berg, "Gentle Irishman," *Los Angeles Times,* February 4, 1951.

2. Peter Bogdanovich, *Fritz Lang in America* (New York: Praeger, 1969), 81.

3. Rui Nogueira and Nicoletta Zalaffi, "A Bastard's Long Career: Meeting with Robert Ryan," *Cinema 70* (April 1970): 50–51.

4. Axel Madsen, *Stanwyck* (New York: HarperCollins, 1994), 291.

5. Jane Ellen Wayne, *Marilyn's Men: The Private Life of Marilyn Monroe* (New York: St. Martin's Press, 1992), 49.

6. Bogdanovich, *Fritz Lang in America,* 82.

7. Richard Buskin, *Blonde Heat: The Sizzling Screen Career of Marilyn Monroe* (New York: Billboard Books, 2001), 96.

8. Ibid., 95.

9. Ella Smith, *Starring Miss Barbara Stanwyck* (New York: Crown Publishers, 1984), 233.

10. Lisa Ryan, e-mail to author, April 14, 2014.

11. Louella O. Parsons, "Robert Ryan: Nice Man to Have Around the Movies," *Los Angeles Examiner,* February 10, 1952.

12. Cheyney Ryan, interview with author, Eugene, Oregon, April 15, 2011.

13. Harriet Parsons, "Battle-Scarred Ryan Is Home," *Los Angeles Herald-Examiner,* December 12, 1965, 1, 5.

14. Jessica Ryan, "If School Keeps" (ca. 1970), private collection.

15. Ibid., 68.

16. Cheyney Ryan, interview with author, Eugene, Oregon, April 15, 2011.

17. "Films' Biggest Mystery—RKO," *Variety,* February 20, 1952, 3, 12.

18. "Hughes' Commie Blast Viewed as Cue to Exit RKO; Mayer Report Up Again," *Variety,* April 9, 1952, 3, 29.

19. Janet Leigh, *There Really Was a Hollywood* (Garden City, NY: Doubleday, 1984), 159.

20. Jane Morris, "He Makes Living His Business" n.p., December 1952, Robert Ryan alumni file, Dartmouth College Library, Hanover, New Hampshire.

21. Michael Munn, *Jimmy Stewart: The Truth Behind the Legend* (Fort Lee, NJ: Barricade Books, 2006), 215.

22. Leigh, *There Really Was a Hollywood,* 159.

23. Nogueira and Zalaffi, "A Bastard's Long Career," 57–58.

24. Jessica Ryan, "If School Keeps."

25. Jessica Ryan, "Campaign–'52."

26. Porter McKeever, *Adlai Stevenson: His Life and Legacy* (New York: William Morrow, 1989), 215–16.

27. Jessica Ryan, "Campaign–'52."

28. Robert Ryan, as told to Dick Pine, "The Trouble with Me Is," *Movieland,* June 1951, 21, 79.

29. Jessica Ryan, "Campaign–'52."

30. Jessica Ryan, notes for "Campaign–'52."

31. Jessica Ryan, "Campaign–'52."

32. Jessica Ryan, notes for "Campaign–'52."

33. Ibid.

34. Robert Wallsten, interview with Franklin Jarlett, May 1986, private collection.

35. Jessica Ryan, notes for "Campaign–'52."

36. Cheyney Ryan, interview with author, Eugene, Oregon, April 15, 2011.

37. Jessica Ryan, notes for "Campaign–'52."

38. Roy Ward Baker, *The Director's Cut: A Memoir of 60 Years in Film and Television* (London: Reynolds and Hearn, 2000), 82.

39. Ibid., 83.

40. Rhonda Fleming, e-mail to author, August 21, 2012.

41. "Acts of Birth: Robert Ryan," *Films and Filming,* March 1971, 28.

42. M. Nichols, "Robert Ryan—Hero and Heel," *Coronet,* January 1960, 16.

43. John Houseman, *Front and Center* (New York: Simon and Schuster, 1979), 423.

44. Jessica Ryan, "If School Keeps."

45. Charles Haas, interview with author, Studio City, California, April 20, 2011.

46. Ibid.

47. Jessica Ryan, "If School Keeps."

48. Charles Haas, interview with author.

49. Jeanne Stein, "Robert Ryan: Unlike Most Handsome Actors He Was Willing to Be a Heavy," *Films in Review* (January 1968): 21.

50. Albert Hackett, interview with Franklin Jarlett, August 1986, private collection; also Glenn Loney, "In the Words of Robert Ryan," *Cue,* July 11, 1970, 11.

51. Houseman, *Front and Center,* 438.

nine Rum, Rebellion, and Ryan

1. John Houseman, *Front and Center* (New York: Simon and Schuster, 1979), 436.

2. William Shakespeare, *Coriolanus,* in *The Riverside Shakespeare,* ed. G. Blakemore Evans (Boston: Houghton Mifflin, 1974), 1.1.170–72, 82–84. References are to act, scene, and line.

3. Shakespeare, *Coriolanus,* 3.1.138–39.

4. Denis Brian, *Tallulah, Darling: A Biography of Tallulah Bankhead* (New York: Macmillan, 1972), 84–85.

5. Howard McClay, "Shakespeare Summons Bob Ryan," *Los Angeles Daily News,* March 24, 1954.

6. Houseman, *Front and Center,* 437.

7. Robert Ryan, as told to Naomi Engelsman, "Backstage with Us Ryans," *Parents* (September 1954): 130.

8. George Shea, "Shakespeare on Treason," review of *Coriolanus, Wall Street Journal,* January 21, 1954, 10.

9. Brooks Atkinson, "Again, the Phoenix," review of *Coriolanus, New York Times Book Review,* January 24, 1954, X1.

10. Jessica Ryan, "If School Keeps" (ca. 1970), private collection.

11. Ibid., 130.

12. Howard Breslin, "Bad Time at Honda," *American* (January 1947): 41, 136.

13. Ibid., 138.

14. Kenneth MacKenna, interoffice memo to Dore Schary, June 10, 1954, Dore Schary Papers, Wisconsin Center for Film and Theater Research, Madison, Wisconsin.

15. Tom Weaver, *They Fought in the Creature Features* (Jefferson, NC: McFarland, 1995), 163.

16. "Acts of Birth: Robert Ryan," *Films and Filming,* March 1971, 27.

17. Glenn Lovell, *Escape Artist: The Life and Films of John Sturges* (Madison: University of Wisconsin Press, 2008), 103.

18. James Curtis, *Spencer Tracy* (London: Hutchinson, 2011), 673.

19. Cheyney Ryan, interview with author, Eugene, Oregon, April 15, 2011.

20. Lisa Ryan, telephone interview with author, October 3, 2009.

21. Erskine Johnson column, *Los Angeles Daily News,* July 7, 1951.

22. Ryan, "Backstage with Us Ryans," 128.

23. Jessica Ryan, "If School Keeps."

24. James Naughton, telephone interview with author, July 18, 2012.

25. Millard Lampell, interview with Franklin Jarlett, March 10, 1987, private collection.

26. Cheyney Ryan, interview with author, Eugene, Oregon, September 22, 2012.

27. Roy Norr, "Cancer by the Carton," *Reader's Digest,* September 1952, 739.

28. John O'Hara, review of *Bad Day at Black Rock, Collier's,* March 18, 1955.

29. Robert Hatch, review of *Bad Day at Black Rock, Nation,* February 19, 1955, 165.

30. Samuel Fuller, *A Third Face: My Tale of Writing, Fighting, and Filmmaking* (New York: Knopf, 2002), 317.

31. Fuller, *A Third Face,* 315.

32. Rui Nogueira and Nicoletta Zalaffi, "A Bastard's Long Career: Meeting with Robert Ryan," *Cinema 70* (April 1970): 56.

33. Lee Server, *Sam Fuller: Film Is a Battleground* (Jefferson, NC: McFarland, 1994), 115.

34. Fuller, *A Third Face,* 316.

35. Jessica Ryan to Dido and Jean Renoir, April 8, 1955, Jean Renoir Papers, UCLA Special Collections, University of California at Los Angeles, Los Angeles, California.

36. William Otterburn-Hall, "A Good Bad Man Is Hard to Find," *Louisville Courier-Journal and Times,* June 7, 1970, E4.

37. Cheyney Ryan, interview with author, Eugene, Oregon, September 22, 2012.

38. Otterburn-Hall, "A Good Bad Man Is Hard to Find."

ten The Gates of War

1. Robert Ryan, as told to Jane Kesner Ardmore, "What Makes an Actor Tick?" (ca. 1957), Jane Ardmore Papers, Margaret Herrick Library Special Collections, Academy of Motion Picture Arts and Sciences, Beverly Hills, California.

2. Jane Morris, "He Makes Living His Business" n.p., December 1952. Robert Ryan alumni file, Dartmouth College Library, Hanover, New Hampshire.

3. Philip Yordan, interview with Franklin Jarlett, October 27, 1986, private collection; also Franklin Jarlett, *Robert Ryan: A Biography and Critical Filmography* (Jefferson, NC: McFarland, 1990), 48.

4. Patrick McGilligan, *Backstory 2: Interviews with Screenwriters of the 1940s and 1950s* (Berkeley: University of California Press, 1991), 361.

5. Ibid., 181.

6. Ibid., 182.

7. Ibid., 357.

8. Robert Ryan, as told to Jane Kesner Ardmore, "What Makes an Actor Tick?" (ca. 1957), Jane Ardmore Papers, Margaret Herrick Library Special Collections, Academy of Motion Picture Arts and Sciences, Beverly Hills, California.

9. Toya Harrison, interview with author, Studio City, California, April 20, 2011.

10. Chalmers M. Roberts, "Adlai Calls for All-Out Final Drive," *Washington Post and Times Herald,* October 21, 1956, A1.

11. Cheyney Ryan, interview with author, Eugene, Oregon, April 15, 2011.

12. *Dartmouth Alumnus,* December 1956, Dartmouth Alumni File, Dartmouth College, Hanover, New Hampshire.

13. Jean Giraudoux, *Tiger at the Gates,* trans. Christopher Fry (London: Samuel French, 1955), 25.

14. Ibid., 11.

15. Ibid., 48.

16. Harold J. Kennedy, *No Pickle, No Performance: An Irreverent Theatrical Excursion from Tallulah to Travolta* (Garden City, NY: Doubleday, 1978), 128.

17. Ibid., 129.

18. "Actor Robert Ryan's Mother Injured by Auto," *Los Angeles Times,* February 2, 1957.

19. Kennedy, *No Pickle, No Performance,* 128.

20. Richard L. Coe, "Here's One Not to Miss," review of *Men in War, Washington Post,* March 9, 1957, D9.

21. Philip Scheuer, "Suspense Pulses in 'Men in War,'" *Los Angeles Times,* January 13, 1957, F1.

22. "Expansion Program on at Oakwood," *San Fernando Valley Mirror-News,* May 30, 1957.

23. Lamont Johnson, interview with Franklin Jarlett, August 17, 1986, private collection; also Franklin Jarlett, *Robert Ryan: A Biography and Critical Filmography* (Jefferson, NC: McFarland: 1990), 66.

24. Marie Spottswood, "Such a Resource in One Individual," in *A Memorial Tribute for the Robert and Jessica Ryan Memorial,* November 3, 1974, Oakwood School archives, North Hollywood, California.

25. Robert Wallsten, interview with Franklin Jarlett, May 1986, private collection.

26. Erskine Caldwell, *God's Little Acre* (Athens: University of Georgia Press, 1995), 88.

27. "Harmon-Mann Solicit No Seal for 'God's Little Acre,' Tell Why," *Variety,* April 3, 1957, 10.

28. Philip Yordan, interview with Franklin Jarlett, October 27, 1986, private collection.

29. Lisa Ryan, interview with author, San Francisco, California, April 17, 2011.

30. Robert Ryan to Corey Ford, October 28, 1957, Dartmouth Boxing Club File, Dartmouth College, Hanover, New Hampshire.

31. Albert Schweitzer, "Declaration of Conscience," *Saturday Review,* May 18, 1957, 20.

32. Norman Cousins, interview with Franklin Jarlett, June 1, 1987, private collection; also Jarlett, *Robert Ryan*, 108.

33. Joseph Wershba, "Outspoken Actor," *New York Post*, March 7, 1963.

34. Nathanael West, *Miss Lonelyhearts and Day of the Locust* (New York: New Directions, 1962), 1.

35. Jeanne Stein, "Robert Ryan: Unlike Most Handsome Actors He Was Willing to Be a Heavy," *Films in Review* 9, no. 1 (January 1968): 22.

36. Lisa Ryan, interview with author, San Francisco, California, April 17, 2011.

37. Patricia Bosworth, *Montgomery Clift: A Biography* (New York: Harcourt Brace Jovanovich, 1978), 300.

38. Cheyney Ryan, interview with author, Eugene, Oregon, April 15, 2011.

39. James Kotsilibas-Davis and Myrna Loy, *Myrna Loy: Being and Becoming* (New York: Knopf, 1987), 287.

40. Stanley Kaufmann, "Far East and Far Off," review of *Lonelyhearts, New Republic*, February 2, 1959, 21.

41. Dwight Macdonald, "No Art and No Box Office," *Esquire* (March 1959): 66.

42. Pat O'Brien, *The Wind at My Back* (Garden City, NY: Doubleday, 1964), 309.

43. "Public, Not Producers, Guilty of Typing Actors: Bob Ryan," *Variety*, May 23, 1958.

44. "Sees Participation Deal as 'Income Roulette,'" *Motion Picture Herald*, October 24, 1959.

45. Anthony Slide, ed., *De Toth on De Toth: Putting the Drama in Front of the Camera* (London: Faber and Faber, 1996), 142.

46. Philip Yordan, interview with Franklin Jarlett, October 27, 1986, private collection.

47. Franklin Jarlett, *Robert Ryan: A Biography and Critical Filmography* (Jefferson, NC: McFarland, 1990), 103.

eleven Beautiful Creatures

1. Andy Harmon, telephone interview with author, May 17, 2012.

2. Cheyney Ryan, interview with author, Eugene, Oregon, September 22, 2012.

3. Jessica Ryan, "Woman: The Mythless American" (ca. 1970), private collection.

4. Cheyney Ryan, interview with author, Eugene, Oregon, September 22, 2012.

5. Cheyney Ryan, telephone interview with author, September 26, 2009.

6. Robert Ryan, "I Didn't Want to Play a Bigot," *Ebony*, (November 1959): 68–69.

7. Don Alpert, "Ryan: 1 in 50 Critics Knows," *Los Angeles Times*, December 3, 1961.

8. Harry Belafonte, telephone interview with author, October 10, 2012.

9. Ibid.

10. Ryan, "I Didn't Want to Play a Bigot," 69.

11. Robert Wise, interview with Franklin Jarlett, February 18, 1986, private collection.

12. Shelley Winters, *Shelley II: The Middle of My Century* (New York: Simon and Schuster, 1989), 263–64.

13. Cheyney Ryan, interview with author, Eugene, Oregon, September 22, 2012.

14. Robert Ryan, "The Full Text of Ryan's Letter," *Chicago Reader,* October 29, 2009, http://www.chicagoreader.com/chicago/actor-robert-ryans-letter-to-his-children/Content?oid=1223014.

15. Lisa Ryan, interview with author, San Francisco, California, April 17, 2011.

16. Cheyney Ryan, interview with author, Eugene, Oregon, April 15, 2011.

17. Lamont Johnson, interview with Franklin Jarlett, August 17, 1986, private collection; also Franklin Jarlett, *Robert Ryan: A Biography and Critical Filmography* (Jefferson, NC: McFarland, 1990), 48.

18. Sidney Skolsky, "An Interview with Robert Ryan," n.d., n.p., Sidney Skolsky Papers, Margaret Herrick Library Special Collections, Academy of Motion Picture Arts and Sciences, Beverly Hills, California.

19. Bill Becker, "Focus on the Forty-Ninth State," *New York Times,* September 27, 1959, sec. 2, p. 7.

20. Skolsky, "An Interview with Robert Ryan."

21. John L. Scott, "Ryan Lifts Self by His 'Heels,'" *Los Angeles Times,* October 25, 1959, E1.

22. "Film Stars Join in Nuclear Plea," *New York Times,* October 20, 1959, 45.

23. Ibid.

24. Ibid.

25. John Houseman, *Final Dress* (New York: Simon and Schuster, 1982), 196.

26. T. S. Eliot, *Murder in the Cathedral* (New York: Harcourt Brace, 1935), 83.

27. Philip K. Scheuer, "Eliot Verse Play Well Staged, Acted," review of *Murder in the Cathedral, Los Angeles Times,* January 21, 1960, C9.

28. Eliot, *Murder in the Cathedral,* 49.

29. Cecil Smith, "At the UCLA Theater Group, the Ordinary Was a Rarity," *Los Angeles Times,* May 14, 1981, Q7.

30. Harold Hildebrand, "Robert Ryan Speaks Out," *Los Angeles Examiner,* October 11, 1961.

31. Marsha Hunt, telephone interview with author, February 9, 2011.

32. "Directed by John Frankenheimer: The Seminar," *Museum of Television and Radio Seminar Series*, Paley Center for Media, Los Angeles, January 18, 1996. Video recording.

33. "A Conversation with John Frankenheimer," Museum of Television and Radio Seminar Series, Paley Center for Media, Los Angeles, September 24, 1977. Video recording.

34. "Directed by John Frankenheimer: The Seminar."

35. Ibid.

36. Ibid.

37. Alpert, "Ryan: 1 in 50 Critics Knows."

38. Harold Hildebrand, "Ryan's 'Between' Films," *Los Angeles Examiner,* October 8, 1961.

39. Bernard Eisenschitz, *Nicholas Ray: An American Journey* (Minneapolis: University of Minnesota Press, 1990), 369.

40. C. Gregory Jensen, "The Actor Who Will Play Christ," *Family Weekly*, December 25, 1960, 11–13.

41. Lisa Ryan, interview with author, San Francisco, California, April 17, 2011.

42. Jesse Zunser, "Stratford: Ryan, Hepburn, et al.," *Cue*, July 30, 1960, 8.

43. Raymond J. Buck, "A Rare Kind of Movie Star," *Dartmouth Varsity*, October 1960, 30.

44. Judith Crist, "Katharine Hepburn Stars in 'Antony and Cleopatra,'" *New York Herald Tribune*, August 1, 1960, 8.

45. Cheyney Ryan, interview with author, Eugene, Oregon, April 15, 2011.

46. Rich, review of *The Canadians, Variety*, March 8, 1961, 6.

47. Cheyney Ryan, interview with author, Eugene, Oregon, April 15, 2011.

48. Norman Cousins, interview with Franklin Jarlett, June 1, 1987, private collection.

49. Milton S. Katz, *Ban the Bomb: A History of SANE, the Committee for a Sane Nuclear Policy, 1957–1985* (New York: Greenwood Press, 1986), 61.

50. Mike Metzger, telephone interview with author, March 9, 2011.

51. Peter Ustinov, *Dear Me* (Boston: Atlantic Monthly Press, 1977), 311.

52. Herman Melville, *Billy Budd and The Piazza Tales* (New York: Barnes and Noble Classics, 2006), 40.

53. Melville, *Billy Budd*, 41–42.

54. Louis O. Coxe and Robert Chapman, *Billy Budd* (New York: Hill and Wang, 1962), 30, 33.

55. Terence Stamp, audio commentary, *Billy Budd*, Warner Bros., 2007, DVD.

56. Hank Werba, "'Billy Budd' Budget Item: Dramamine," *Variety*, June 28, 1961, 17.

twelve The Longest Day

1. *Milwaukee Journal*, January 13, 1963.

2. Lisa Ryan, telephone interview with author, May 4, 2010.

3. Cheyney Ryan, telephone interview with author, October 17, 2013.

4. Joseph Wershba, "Outspoken Actor," *New York Post*, March 7, 1963.

5. Marsha Hunt, telephone interview with author, February 9, 2011.

6. "Actor Threatened with Bomb Attack," *Hollywood Citizen-News*, February 5, 1962.

7. Ibid.

8. Philip Dunne, *Take Two: A Life in Movies and Politics* (New York: Limelight Editions, 1992), 268.

9. Cheyney Ryan, interview with author, Eugene, Oregon, April 15, 2011.

10. Sue Chambers, "Robert Ryan—Heavy and Hero," *Milwaukee Journal*, January 13, 1963.

11. Dorothy Manners, "His Knees Knock in Broadway Tempo," *Los Angeles Herald-Examiner*, July 8, 1962.

12. Joshua Logan, *Movie Stars, Real People, and Me* (New York: Delacorte Press, 1978), 173–74.

13. Bob Lardine, "This Dove Is a Tough Bird," *New York Sunday News,* August 27, 1967, 4.

14. Logan, *Movie Stars, Real People, and Me,* 177.

15. Les Carpenter, "'Mr. Prez' Leaves D.C. Better Than When JFK Saw It," *Variety,* October 17, 1962.

16. Cornelia Otis Skinner, *Life with Lindsay and Crouse* (Boston: Houghton Mifflin, 1985), 226.

17. Jessica Ryan, *America—Dream or Nightmare?* (ca. 1970), private collection.

18. Harry Belafonte, telephone interview with author, October 10, 2012.

19. Joe McCarthy, "Antic Arts: Robert Ryan" (ca. 1963), private collection.

20. Lisa Ryan, interview with author, San Francisco, California, April 17, 2011.

21. McCarthy, "Antic Arts: Robert Ryan."

22. Robert Wallsten, interview with Franklin Jarlett, June 14, 1986, private collection; also Franklin Jarlett, *Robert Ryan: A Biography and Critical Filmography* (Jefferson, NC: McFarland, 1990), 126.

23. Cheyney Ryan, interview with author, Eugene, Oregon, September 22, 2012.

24. Ibid..

25. Harry Belafonte, telephone interview with author, October 10, 2012.

26. "Establish Free Southern Theatre for Summer Sked in Jackson, Miss., Then Local Groups, Touring Units," *Variety,* April 8, 1964, 79, 82.

27. "November 22, 1963: In Search of an Answer," *Executive Action,* Warner Bros., 2007, DVD.

28. Lisa Ryan, interview with author, San Francisco, April 17, 2011.

29. Cheyney Ryan, interview with author, Eugene, Oregon, April 15, 2011.

30. Philip K. Scheuer, "Robert Ryan Lifts Veil on Yugoslavia," *Los Angeles Times,* August 11, 1964.

31. Ibid.

32. Robert Ryan to chairman, Stars for SANE (ca. July 1964), Dore Schary Papers, Wisconsin Center for Film and Theater Research, Madison, Wisconsin.

33. Millard Lampell, interview with Franklin Jarlett, March 10, 1987, private collection.

34. Cheyney Ryan, interview with author, Eugene, Oregon, April 15, 2011.

35. Scheuer, "Robert Ryan Lifts Veil on Yugoslavia."

36. Harriet Parsons, "Battle-Scarred Ryan Is Home," *Los Angeles Herald-Examiner,* December 12, 1965, 5. Parsons, daughter of gossip columnist Louella Parsons, earlier had produced Ryan's RKO feature *Clash by Night* (1952).

37. Lampell, interview with Franklin Jarlett.

38. Philip Yordan, interview with Franklin Jarlett, October 27, 1986, private collection; also Jarlett, *Robert Ryan,* 135.

39. Lampell, interview with Franklin Jarlett; also Jarlett, *Robert Ryan,* 90.

1. Woody Strode and Sam Young, *Goal Dust: The Warm and Candid Memoirs of a Pioneer Black Athlete and Actor* (Lanham, MD: Madison Books, 1990), 227.

2. Douglass K. Daniel, *Tough as Nails: The Life and Films of Richard Brooks* (Madison: University of Wisconsin Press, 2011), 166.

3. Strode, *Goal Dust,* 230.

4. Phil Yordan, interview with Franklin Jarlett, October 27, 1986, private collection.

5. Philip Dunne, interview with Franklin Jarlett, August 24, 1987, private collection; also Michael Winner, *Winner Take All: A Life of Sorts* (London: Robson Books, 2004), 63.

6. Gary Fishgall, *Against Type: The Biography of Burt Lancaster* (New York: Scribner's, 1995), 244.

7. Virginia E. Rodgers, "Robert Ryan: 'A Most Un-Actor-Like Actor,'" *New Bedford (Massachusetts) Standard-Times,* July 22, 1965.

8. Lisa Ryan, interview with author, San Francisco, April 17, 2011.

9. Richard T. Stout, *People* (New York: Harper and Row, 1970), 43.

10. Jessica Ryan, notes for "Campaign–'52" (ca. 1970), private collection.

11. Margaret McManus, "Robert Ryan Speaks Out on Reagan," *Bridgeport (Connecticut) Telegram,* November 6, 1966.

12. Jessica Ryan, notes for "Campaign–'52."

13. Dwayne Epstein, *Lee Marvin: Point Blank* (Tucson: Schaffer Press, 2013), 171.

14. Lisa Ryan, interview with author, San Francisco, California, April 17, 2011.

15. Bert Reisfeld, *Wieder Wildwestfilme in Hollywood,* radio broadcast (ca. November 1967), Margaret Herrick Library, Academy of Motion Picture Arts and Sciences, Beverly Hills, California. Audio recording.

16. McManus, "Robert Ryan Speaks Out on Reagan."

17. Ken Furie, "Robert Ryan on Everything but Birth Control," *Dartmouth,* April 21, 1967.

18. Jessica Ryan to Jean Renoir (ca. May 1967), Jean Renoir Papers, UCLA Special Collections, University of California at Los Angeles, Los Angeles, California.

19. Philip Yordan, interview with Franklin Jarlett, October 27, 1986, private collection; also Franklin Jarlett, *Robert Ryan: A Biography and Critical Filmography* (Jefferson, NC: McFarland, 1990), 142.

20. Lisa Ryan, interview with author, San Francisco, California, April 17, 2011.

21. Philip Yordan, interview with Franklin Jarlett; also Jarlett, *Robert Ryan,* 77.

22. Robert Ryan to Dore Schary, August 5, 1967, Dore Schary Papers, Wisconsin Center for Film and Theater Research, Madison, Wisconsin.

23. Furie, "Robert Ryan on Everything but Birth Control."

24. Daniel Rosenthal, "Fifty Years at the Cutting Edge," *London Times,* February 19, 1999, 35.

25. Alvin Shuster, "Robert Ryan Plays *Othello* Abroad for $150 a Week," *New York Times,* October 18, 1967, 37.

26. John Peter, "John Neville as Iago," review of *Othello, London Times,* September 22, 1967, 7.

27. John Peter, "Embattled Family," review of *Long Day's Journey into Night, London Times,* September 28, 1967, 6.

28. "Legitimate: Asides and Ad-Libs," *Variety,* April 12, 1967, 70.

29. Robert Ryan to Lisa Ryan (ca. November 1967), private collection.

30. Bob Lardine, "This Dove Is a Tough Bird," *New York Sunday News,* August 27, 1967, 4.

31. Cheyney Ryan, interview with author, Eugene, Oregon, April 15, 2011.

32. Millard Lampell, interview with Franklin Jarlett, March 10, 1987, private collection.

33. Ibid.

34. Lisa Ryan, interview with author, San Francisco, April 17, 2011.

35. Lampell, interview with Franklin Jarlett; also Jarlett, *Robert Ryan,* 144.

36. Patricia Bosworth, "Robert Ryan: In Search of Action," *New York Times,* June 1, 1969, sec. 2, pp. 1, 7.

37. Hersh, telephone interview with author.

38. Arthur Herzog, *McCarthy for President* (New York: Viking Press, 1969), 10.

39. "Unforeseen Eugene," *Time,* March 22, 1968, 15.

40. Hersh, telephone interview with author.

41. Stout, *People,* 177.

42. Marshall Fine, *Bloody Sam: The Life and Films of Sam Peckinpah* (New York: Donald I. Fine, 1991), 130.

43. Movie Body Counts Boards, accessed September 10, 2012, http://movie bodycounts.proboards.com/index.cgi?board=finished&action=display&thread=629.

44. Bob Thomas, *Golden Boy: The Untold Story of William Holden* (New York: St. Martin's Press, 1983), 166.

45. Robert Ryan to Jean Renoir (ca. August 1968), Jean Renoir Papers, UCLA Special Collections, University of California at Los Angeles, Los Angeles, California.

46. Cheyney Ryan, telephone interview with author, September 26, 2009.

fourteen My Good Bad Luck

1. Jessica Ryan, "My Name Is Robert Ryan" (ca. 1969), private collection.

2. Betty Friedan, *The Feminine Mystique: Twentieth Anniversary Edition* (New York: Dell, 1983), 21.

3. "Understanding and Coping with Anxiety—Rollo May," www.existentialanalysis .org.uk/assets/articles/Understanding_and_Coping_with_Anxiety_Rollo_May _transcription_Martin_Adams.pdf.

4. Jessica Ryan, *Woman—The Mythless American* (ca. 1970), private collection.

5. Ibid.

6. Ramona Lampell, telephone interview with author, May 18, 2012.

7. Ibid.

8. Millard Lampell, interview with Franklin Jarlett, March 10, 1987, private collection.

9. Cheyney Ryan, interview with author, Eugene, Oregon, April 15, 2011.

10. Lampell, interview with Franklin Jarlett.

11. Harold J. Kennedy, *No Pickle, No Performance: An Irreverent Theatrical Excursion from Tallulah to Travolta* (Garden City, NY: Doubleday, 1978), 136.

12. Ibid.

13. Ibid.

14. Bob Lardine, "This Dove Is a Tough Bird," *New York Sunday News,* August 27, 1967, 4.

15. Lisa Ryan, interview with Franklin Jarlett, February 23, 1986, private collection.

16. William MacAdams, *Ben Hecht: The Man Behind the Legend* (New York: Charles Scribner's Sons, 1990), 107.

17. Ben Hecht and Charles MacArthur, *The Front Page* (New York: Samuel French, 1928), 30.

18. Walter Kerr, "After 41 Years, It's Still Page One," *New York Times,* May 25, 1969, D1.

19. Patricia Bosworth, "Robert Ryan: In Search of Action," *New York Times,* June 1, 1969.

20. Lenore Rottenberg, "No Wonder," *New York Times,* August 17, 1969, D23.

21. Aljean Harmetz, "'Man Was a Killer Long Before He Served a God,'" *New York Times,* August 31, 1969, D9.

22. Darwin Willard, "Just a Movie," *New York Times,* September 14, 1969, D36.

23. Arnold M. Auerbach, "The Wildest Bunch of All," *New York Times,* August 17, 1969, D11.

24. Vincent Canby, "Violence and Beauty Mesh in 'Wild Bunch,'" *New York Times,* June 26, 1969, 45.

25. Cheyney Ryan, interview with author, Eugene, Oregon, April 11, 2011.

26. Joe McGinniss, *The Selling of the President* (New York: Penguin Books, 1988), 240–41.

27. Jessica Ryan, *America—Dream or Nightmare?: American Myths of Power, Aggression and Violence* (ca. 1970), private collection.

28. "Acts of Birth: Robert Ryan," *Films and Filming,* March 1971, 26.

29. William Otterburn-Hall, "A Good Bad Man Is Hard to Find," *Louisville Courier-Journal,* June 7, 1970, E4.

30. Arthur Miller, *Collected Plays 1964–1972,* ed. Tony Kushner (New York: Library of America, 2012), 283.

31. Ibid., 281.

32. Ibid., 285.

33. "The Harmony Game" (video documentary) on *Bridge over Troubled Water,* Columbia/Legacy Video, 2011, CD/DVD.

34. Otterburn-Hall, "A Good Bad Man Is Hard to Find."

35. Michael Winner, *Winner Take All: A Life of Sorts* (London: Robson Books, 2004), 143.

36. Harry Belafonte, telephone interview with author, October 10, 2012.

37. Jessica Ryan, "Campaign–'52, or A Camera's-Eye View from Two Odd Birds" (ca. 1970), private collection.

38. Robert Wallsten, interview with Franklin Jarlett, May 1986, private collection.

39. "Acts of Birth: Robert Ryan," *Films and Filming,* March 1971, 26.

40. Robert Ryan to Mr. Kemeny, March 23, 1971, Dartmouth Alumni File, Dartmouth College, Hanover, New Hampshire.

41. Lisa Ryan, interview, "Lucy Talks Movies," www.podtech.net/home/3848 /robert-ryan-and-dana-andrews-had-daughters.

42. Cheyney Ryan, interview with author, Eugene, Oregon, April 15, 2011.

43. Bob Thomas, "Robert Ryan Fights Back After Tragic Two Years," *Milwaukee Journal,* August 25, 1972.

44. James Naughton, telephone interview with author, July 18, 2012.

45. Arvin Brown, interview with Franklin Jarlett, September 3, 1986, private collection; also Franklin Jarlett, *Robert Ryan: A Biography and Critical Filmography* (Jefferson, NC: McFarland: 1990), 59.

46. Eugene O'Neill, *Long Day's Journey into Night* (New Haven: Yale University Press, 1956), 150.

47. Brown, interview with Franklin Jarlett; also Jarlett, *Robert Ryan,* 162.

48. Naughton, telephone interview with author.

49. Brown, interview with Franklin Jarlett.

50. Walter Kerr, "Do the Tyrones Live Here?," *New York Times,* May 2, 1971, D3.

51. Arvin Brown, interview with Franklin Jarlett; also Franklin Jarlett, *Robert Ryan,* 160.

52. Naughton, telephone interview with author.

53. Stacy Keach, telephone interview with author, July 18, 2012; Naughton, telephone interview with author.

54. Arvin Brown, telephone interview with author, November 1, 2012.

55. Lisa Ryan, interview with author, San Francisco, California, April 17, 2011.

56. Brown, interview with Franklin Jarlett.

57. Robert Ryan, "The Next Time You Want to Do a Play" (ca. July 1971), private collection.

58. Brown, interview with Franklin Jarlett; also Jarlett, *Robert Ryan,* 162, 164, 87.

59. Lisa Ryan, interview with author, San Francisco, California, April 17, 2011.

60. "Ryan-Buddy Hackett for Mexican 'Quixote,'" *Variety,* March 29, 1972, 38.

61. Pete Hamill, "For Robert Ryan," *New York Post,* July 13, 1973.

62. Bob Thomas, "Robert Ryan Fights Back After Tragic Two Years," *Milwaukee Journal,* August 25, 1972.

63. Ramona Lampell, telephone interview with author, May 18, 2012.

1. Jean Renoir to Robert Ryan, May 25, 1972, Jean Renoir Papers, UCLA Special Collections, University of California at Los Angeles, Los Angeles, California.

2. Mary Murphy, "Robert Ryan—A New Life on Borrowed Time," *Los Angeles Times,* September 5, 1972, 1, 12.

3. Robert Ryan to Jean Renoir, July 20, 1972, Jean Renoir Papers, UCLA Special Collections, University of California at Los Angeles, Los Angeles, California.

4. Murphy, "Robert Ryan—A New Life on Borrowed Time."

5. Franklin Jarlett, *Robert Ryan: A Biography and Critical Filmography* (Jefferson, NC: McFarland, 1990), 164.

6. Ramona Lampell, telephone interview with author, May 18, 2012.

7. Jarlett, *Robert Ryan,* 165.

8. Millard Lampell, interview with Franklin Jarlett, March 10, 1987, private collection.

9. Cheyney Ryan, interview with author, Eugene, Oregon, September 22, 2012.

10. Lisa Ryan, interview with author, San Francisco, California, April 17, 2011.

11. Arvin Brown, interview with Franklin Jarlett, September 3, 1986, private collection.

12. Arvin Brown, telephone interview with author, November 1, 2012.

13. Cheyney Ryan, interview with author, Eugene, Oregon, September 22, 2012.

14. Edward Everett Hale, "The Man without a Country," *Atlantic,* December 1863, http://www.theatlantic.com/magazine/archive/1863/12/the-man-without-a-country/308751/?single_page=true.

15. Louis Sheaffer, *O'Neill: Son and Artist,* vol. 2 (New York: Cooper Square Press, 1973), 492.

16. Eugene O'Neill, *The Iceman Cometh* (New York: Vintage International, 1999), 9.

17. John Frankenheimer, interview with Franklin Jarlett, May 25, 1987, private collection; also Jarlett, *Robert Ryan,* 165.

18. "Jeff Bridges: The Dude Abides," Public Broadcasting System's *American Masters,* January 12, 2011.

19. Jeff Bridges, telephone interview with author, November 2, 2012.

20. Arvin Brown, interview with Franklin Jarlett.

21. Evans Frankenheimer, interview with Franklin Jarlett, May 30, 1987, private collection.

22. John Frankenheimer to Lisa Ryan, December 14, 1973, private collection.

23. Robert Ryan, "How Do You Remember All Those Words?" (ca. 1957), Jane Ardmore Papers, Margaret Herrick Library, Academy of Motion Picture Arts and Sciences, Beverly Hills, California.

24. Bridges, telephone interview with author.

25. O'Neill, *The Iceman Cometh,* 23.

26. Dwayne Epstein, *Lee Marvin: Point Blank* (Tucson: Schaffner Press, 2013), 196.

27. John Frankenheimer, interview with Franklin Jarlett; also Jarlett, *Robert Ryan*, 168.

28. O'Neill, *The Iceman Cometh,* 9.

29. Charles Champlin, "Robert Ryan: In Memoriam," *Los Angeles Times,* July 12, 1973, sec. 4, p. 1.

30. Philip Yordan, interview with Franklin Jarlett, October 27, 1986, private collection.

31. "Phil Yordan into Tele Corp of America; Red Silverstein Sales Chief Beyond U.S.," *Variety,* July 4, 1973, 14.

32. Yordan, interview with Franklin Jarlett.

33. Joe Don Baker, telephone interview with author, January 25, 2014.

34. Champlin, "Robert Ryan."

35. Albert Hackett, interview with Franklin Jarlett, August 1986, private collection.

36. Sue Cameron, "Robert Ryan Signed for Broadway Star Role in 'Shenandoah,'" *Hollywood Reporter,* June 29, 1973.

37. Cheyney Ryan, interview with author, Eugene, Oregon, April 15, 2011.

38. "November 22, 1963: In Search of an Answer," *Executive Action,* Warner Bros., 2007, DVD.

39. Evans Frankenheimer, interview with Franklin Jarlett, May 30, 1987, private collection.

40. John Frankenheimer, interview with Franklin Jarlett.

41. Larry Goebel, "Robert Ryan," *Los Angeles Times,* July 18, 1973, sec. 2, p. 6.

42. Cheyney Ryan, interview with author, Eugene, Oregon, April 15, 2011.

43. Mary Murphy, "Robert Ryan—A New Life on Borrowed Time," *Los Angeles Times,* September 5, 1972, 1, 12.

44. "Chatter: Broadway," *Variety,* July 18, 1973, 109.

45. Millard Lampell, interview with Franklin Jarlett, March 10, 1987, private collection.

46. "Private Services for Robert Ryan, Burial in Chicago," *Hollywood Reporter,* July 13, 1973.

47. "Robert Ryan Estate Left to Children," *Los Angeles Times,* July 22, 1973, sec. 1, p. 15.

48. Pete Hamill, "For Robert Ryan," *New York Post,* July 13, 1973.

49. Champlin, "Robert Ryan."

50. Paul D. Zimmerman, *Newsweek,* November 12, 1973.

51. "Film Critics Soc. Award for Ryan," *Hollywood Reporter,* January 30, 1974.

52. Marie Spottswood, "Such a Resource in One Individual," in *A Memorial Tribute for the Robert and Jessica Ryan Memorial,* November 3, 1974, Oakwood School archives, North Hollywood, California.

53. Dartmouth College, Twenty-five-Year Report Biographical Data Sheet (ca. 1956), Dartmouth Alumni File, Dartmouth College, Hanover, New Hampshire.

Selected Bibliography

Books

Bacher, Lutz. *Max Ophuls in the Hollywood Studios.* Brunswick, NJ: Rutgers University Press, 1996.

Bacon, Margaret Hope. *Mothers of Feminism: The Story of Quaker Women in America.* San Francisco: Harper and Row, 1986.

Baker, Roy Ward. *The Director's Cut: A Memoir of 60 Years in Film and Television.* London: Reynolds and Hearn, 2000.

Bankhead, Tallulah. *Tallulah: My Autobiography.* New York: Harper and Brothers, 1952.

Bernstein, Walter. *Inside Out: A Memoir of the Blacklist.* New York: Knopf, 1996.

Biles, Roger. *Big City Boss in Depression and War: Mayor Edward J. Kelly of Chicago.* DeKalb: Northern Illinois University Press, 1984.

———. "Edward J. Kelly: New Deal Machine Builder," in *The Mayors: The Chicago Political Tradition,* ed. Paul M. Green and Melvin G. Holli. Carbondale and Edwardsville: Southern Illinois University Press, 1995.

Block, Libbie. *Wild Calendar.* New York: Knopf, 1946.

Bogdanovich, Peter. *Fritz Lang in America.* New York: Praeger, 1969.

Borgnine, Ernest. *Ernie: The Autobiography.* New York: Citadel Press, 2005.

Bosworth, Patricia. *Montgomery Clift: A Biography.* New York: Harcourt Brace Jovanovich, 1978.

Brian, Denis. *Tallulah, Darling: A Biography of Tallulah Bankhead.* New York: Macmillan, 1972.

Brooks, Richard. *The Brick Foxhole.* New York: Harper and Brothers, 1945.

Bushkin, Richard. *Blonde Heat: The Sizzling Screen Career of Marilyn Monroe.* New York: Billboard Books, 2001.

Butler, Gerald. *Mad with Much Heart.* New York: Rinehart, 1946.

Callahan, Dan. *Barbara Stanwyck: The Miracle Woman.* Jackson: University of Mississippi Press, 2012.

Cardullo, Bert, ed. *Jean Renoir: Interviews.* Jackson: University of Mississippi Press, 2005.

Caute, David. *Joseph Losey: A Revenge on Life.* New York: Oxford University Press, 1994.

Ceplair, Larry, and Steven Englund. *The Inquisition in Hollywood: Politics in the Film Community, 1930–1960.* Garden City, NY: Anchor Press/Doubleday, 1980.

Chatfield, Charles, ed. *Peace Movements in America.* New York: Schocken Books, 1973.

Ciment, Michael. *Conversations with Losey.* New York: Methuen, 1985.

Compo, Susan. *Warren Oates: A Wild Life.* Lexington: University Press of Kentucky, 2009.

Curcio, Vincent. *Suicide Blonde: The Life of Gloria Grahame.* New York: William Morrow, 1989.

Curtis, James. *Spencer Tracy.* London: Hutchinson, 2011.

Daniel, Douglass K. *Tough as Nails: The Life and Films of Richard Brooks.* Madison: University of Wisconsin Press, 2011.

De Toth, André. *De Toth on De Toth: Putting the Drama in Front of the Camera.* Edited by Anthony Slide. London: Faber and Faber, 1996.

Dmytryk, Edward. *It's a Hell of a Life but Not a Bad Living: A Hollywood Memoir.* New York: Times Books, 1978.

———. *Odd Man Out: A Memoir of the Hollywood Ten.* Carbondale and Edwardsville: Southern Illinois University Press, 1996.

———. *On Screen Directing.* Boston: Focal Press, 1984.

Dombrowki, Lisa. *The Films of Samuel Fuller: If You Die, I'll Kill You!* Middletown, CT: Wesleyan University Press, 2008.

Dontai, William. *Ida Lupino: A Biography.* Lexington: University Press of Kentucky, 1996.

Dunne, Philip. *Take Two: A Life in Movies and Politics.* New York: Limelight Editions, 1992.

Eisenschitz, Bernard. *Nicholas Ray: An American Journey.* Berkeley: University of California Press, 1993.

Eliot, T. S. *Murder in the Cathedral.* New York: Harcourt Brace, 1935.

Epstein, Dwayne. *Lee Marvin: Point Blank.* Tucson, AZ: Schaffner Press, 2013.

Fine, Marshall. *Bloody Sam: The Life and Films of Sam Peckinpah.* New York: Donald I. Fine, 1991.

Fishgall, Gary. *Against Type: The Biography of Burt Lancaster.* New York: Charles Scribner's Sons, 1995.

Flynn, George O. *The Draft, 1940–1973.* Lawrence: University Press of Kansas, 1993.

Fonda, Henry, as told to Howard Teichmann. *Fonda: My Life.* New York: New American Library: 1981.

Fontaine, Joan. *No Bed of Roses.* New York: William Morrow, 1978.

Frankenheimer, John, and Charles Champlin. *John Frankenheimer: A Conversation.* Burbank, CA: Riverwood Press, 1995.

Freedland, Michael, with Barbara Paskin. *Hollywood on Trial: McCarthyism's War against the Movies.* London: Robson Books, 2007.

Friedan, Betty. *The Feminine Mystique: Twentieth Anniversary Edition.* New York: Dell, 1983.

Fuller, Samuel, with Christa Fuller and Jerome Henry Rudes. *A Third Face: My Tale of Writing, Fighting, and Filmmaking.* New York: Knopf, 2002.

Fury, David. *Maureen O' Sullivan: "No Average Jane."* Minneapolis: Artist's Press, 2006.

Gill, Brendan. *Tallulah.* New York: Holt, Rinehart and Winston, 1972.

Giraudoux, Jean. *Tiger at the Gates.* Translated by Christopher Fry. London: Samuel French, 1955.

Hagen, Ray, and Laura Wagner. *Killer Tomatoes: Fifteen Tough Film Dames.* Jefferson, NC: McFarland, 2004.

Hannsberry, Karen Burroughs. *Femme Noir: Bad Girls of Film.* Jefferson, NC: McFarland, 1998.

Haut, Woody. *Heartbreak and Vine: The Fate of Hardboiled Writers in Hollywood.* London: Serpent's Tail, 2002.

Hecht, Ben, and Charles MacArthur. *The Front Page.* New York: Samuel French, 1928.

Herr, Christopher J. *Clifford Odets and American Political Theater.* Westport, CT: Praeger, 2003.

Herzog, Arthur. *McCarthy for President.* New York: Viking Press, 1969.

Hickman, Larry A., and Thomas M. Alexander, eds. *The Essential Dewey.* Vol. 1, *Pragmatism, Education, Democracy.* Bloomington and Indianapolis: Indiana University Press, 1998.

Higham, Charles, and Roy Moseley. *Princess Merle: The Romantic Life of Merle Oberon.* New York: Coward-McCann, 1983.

Hirsch, Foster. *Joseph Losey.* Boston: Twayne, 1980.

Hoberman, J. *The Dream Life: Movies, Media, and the Mythology of the Sixties.* New York: New Press, 2003.

Houseman, John. *Final Dress.* New York: Simon and Schuster, 1983.

———. *Front and Center.* New York: Simon and Schuster, 1979.

———. *Run-Through.* New York: Simon and Schuster, 1972.

Illinois Political Directory 1899. Chicago: W. L. Bodine, 1899.

Israel, Lee. *Miss Tallulah Bankhead.* New York: G. P. Putnam's Sons, 1972.

Jarlett, Franklin. *Robert Ryan: A Biography and Critical Filmography.* Jefferson, NC: McFarland, 1994.

Jewell, Richard B. *The RKO Story.* New York: Arlington House, 1982.

Katz, Milton S. *Ban the Bomb: A History of SANE, the Committee for a Sane Nuclear Policy, 1957–1985.* New York: Greenwood Press, 1986.

Keenan, Richard C. *The Films of Robert Wise.* Lanham, MD: Scarecrow Press, 2007.

Kennedy, Harold J. *No Pickle, No Performance: An Irreverent Theatrical Excursion from Tallulah to Travolta.* Garden City, NY: Doubleday, 1978.

Kotsilibas-Davis, James, and Myrna Loy. *Myrna Loy: Being and Becoming.* New York: Knopf, 1987.

LaFeber, Walter. *The Deadly Bet: LBJ, Vietnam, and the 1968 Election.* New York: Rowan and Littlefield, 2005.

Langdon, Jennifer E. *Caught in the Crossfire: Adrian Scott and the Politics of Americanism in 1940s Hollywood.* New York: American Historical Association and Columbia University Press, 2008. Accessed on www.Gutenberg-e.org.

Lasky, Betty. *RKO: The Biggest Little Major of Them All.* Englewood Cliffs, NJ: Prentice Hall, 1984.

Laurents, Arthur. *Original Story by: A Memoir of Broadway and Hollywood.* New York: Knopf, 2000.

Leahy, James. *The Cinema of Joseph Losey.* Holland: Tantivy Press, 1967.

Leemann, Sergio. *Robert Wise on His Films: From Editing Room to Director's Chair.* Los Angeles: Silman-James Press, 1995.

Leider, Emily W. *Myrna Loy: The Only Good Girl in Hollywood.* Berkeley: University of California Press, 2011.

Leigh, Janet. *There Really Was a Hollywood.* Garden City, NY: Doubleday, 1984.

Lewis, David Levering. *King: A Biography.* Urbana: University of Illinois Press, 1970.

Lobenthal, Joel. *Tallulah! The Life and Times of a Leading Lady.* New York: Regan Books, 2004.

Logan, Joshua. *Movie Stars, Real People, and Me.* New York: Delacorte Press, 1978.

Lovell, Glenn. *Escape Artist: The Life and Films of John Sturges.* Madison: University of Wisconsin Press, 2008.

MacAdams, William. *Ben Hecht: The Man Behind the Legend.* New York: Charles Scriber's Sons, 1990.

McGilligan, Patrick. *Backstory 2: Interviews with Screenwriters of the 1940s and 1950s.* Berkeley: University of California Press, 1991.

———. *Nicholas Ray: The Glorious Failure of an American Director.* New York: HarperCollins, 2011.

McGinniss, Joe. *The Selling of the President.* New York: Penguin Books, 1988.

McKeever, Porter. *Adlai Stevenson: His Life and Legacy.* New York: William Morrow, 1989.

Melville, Herman. *Billy Budd and the Piazza Tales.* New York: Barnes and Noble Classics, 2006.

Merriner, James L. *Grafters and Goo Goos: Corruption and Reform in Chicago, 1833–2003.* Carbondale: Southern Illinois University Press, 2004.

Miller, Arthur. *Collected Plays 1964–1982.* New York: Library of America, 2012.

Miller, Dan B. *Erskine Caldwell: The Journey from Tobacco Road.* New York: Knopf, 1995.

Mitchell, Greg. *Tricky Dick and the Pink Lady: Richard Nixon vs. Helen Gahagan Douglas—Sexual Politics and the Red Scare.* New York: Random House, 1998.

Morley, Sheridan. *Shall We Dance: The Life of Ginger Rogers.* New York: St. Martin's Press, 1995.

Moss, Marilyn Ann. *Raoul Walsh: The True Adventures of Hollywood's Legendary Director.* Lexington: University Press of Kentucky, 2011.

Muller, Eddie. *Dark City: The Lost World of Film Noir.* New York: St. Martin's Press, 1998.

O'Brien, Pat. *The Wind at My Back: The Life and Times of Pat O'Brien.* Garden City, NY: Doubleday, 1964.

O'Neill, Eugene. *Long Day's Journey into Night.* New Haven: Yale University Press, 1956.

Petersen, Virgil W. *Barbarians in Our Midst.* Boston: Little, Brown, 1952.

Pratley, Gerald. *The Films of John Frankenheimer: Forty Years in Film.* Cranbury, NJ: Lehigh University Press, 1998.

Ray, Nicholas. *I Was Interrupted: Nicholas Ray on Making Movies.* Berkeley: University of California Press, 1993.

Reilly, John H. *Jean Giraudoux.* Boston: Twayne Publishers, 1978.

Reinhardt, Gottfried. *The Genius: A Memoir of Max Reinhardt.* New York: Knopf, 1979.

Renoir, Jean. *Jean Renoir: Letters.* Edited by David Thompson and Lorraine LoBianco. London: Faber and Faber, 1994.

———. *My Life and My Films.* New York: Atheneum, 1974.

Ross, Stephen J. *Hollywood Left and Right: How Movie Stars Shaped American Politics.* New York: Oxford University Press, 2011.

Ryan, Cheyney. *The Chickenhawk Syndrome: War, Sacrifice, and Personal Responsibility.* Lanham, MD: Rowman and Littlefield, 2009.

Ryan, Jessica. *Exit Harlequin.* Garden City, NY: Doubleday, 1947.

———. *The Man Who Asked Why.* Garden City, NY: Doubleday, Doran, 1945.

Sandbrook, Dominic. *Eugene McCarthy and the Rise and Fall of American Liberalism.* New York: Anchor Books, 2005.

Schary, Dore. *Heyday: An Autobiography.* Boston and Toronto: Little, Brown, 1979.

Schatz, Thomas. *The Genius of the System: Hollywood Filmmaking in the Studio Era.* New York: Pantheon Books, 1988.

Server, Lee. *Robert Mitchum: "Baby I Don't Care."* New York: St. Martin's Press, 2001.

———. *Sam Fuller: Film Is a Battleground.* Jefferson, NC: McFarland, 1994.

Shakespeare, William. *The Tragedy of Coriolanus.* In *The Riverside Shakespeare,* edited by G. Blakemore Evans. Boston: Houghton Mifflin, 1974.

Skinner, Cornelia Otis. *Life with Lindsay and Crouse.* Boston: Houghton Mifflin, 1976.

Sperber, A. M., and Eric Lax. *Bogart.* New York: William Morrow, 1994.

Stack, Robert, with Mark Evans. *Straight Shooting.* New York: Macmillan, 1980.

Stamp, Terence. *Double Feature.* London: Bloomsbury, 1989.

Stevens, George, Jr. *Conversations with the Great Moviemakers of Hollywood's Golden Age at the American Film Institute.* New York: Knopf, 2006.

Stout, Richard T. *People.* New York: Harper and Row, 1970.

Strode, Woody, and Sam Young. *Goal Dust: The Warm and Candid Memoirs of a Pioneer Black Athlete and Actor.* Lanham, MD: Madison Books, 1990.

Tucker, David C. *Shirley Booth: A Biography and Career Record.* Jefferson, NC: McFarland, 2008.

Tuttle, William M., Jr. *Race Riot: Chicago in the Red Summer of 1919.* New York: Atheneum, 1970.

Ustinov, Peter. *Dear Me.* Boston: Atlantic Monthly Press, 1977.

Walsh, Raoul. *Each Man in His Own Time.* New York: Farrar, Straus and Giroux, 1974.

Wayne, Jane Ellen. *Marilyn's Men: The Private Life of Marilyn Monroe.* New York: St. Martin's Press, 1992.

Weaver, Tom. *They Fought in the Creature Features.* Jefferson, NC: McFarland, 1995.

Wellworth, George E., and Alfred G. Brooks, eds. *Max Reinhardt: A Centennial Festschrift, 1873–1973.* Binghamton, NY: Max Reinhardt Archive, 1973.

West, Nathanael. *Miss Lonelyhearts and Day of the Locust.* New York: New Directions, 1962.

Williams, Elmer Lynn. *The Fix-It Boys: The Inside Story of the New Deal and the Kelly-Nash Machine.* Chicago: Elmer Lynn Williams, 1940.

Williams, Tony. *Body and Soul: The Cinematic Vision of Robert Aldrich.* Lanham, MD: Scarecrow Press, 2004.

Winner, Michael. *Winner Take All: A Life of Sorts.* London: Robson Books, 2004.

Winters, Shelley. *Shelley II: The Middle of My Century.* New York: Simon and Schuster, 1989.

Witty, Robert, and Neil Morgan. *Marines of the Margarita.* San Diego. Calif.: Frye and Smith, 1970.

Zinnemann, Fred. *A Life in the Movies: An Autobiography.* New York: Charles Scribner's Sons, 1992.

Periodicals

"Actor Robert Ryan's Mother Injured by Auto." *Los Angeles Times,* February 2, 1957.

"Actor Threatened with Bomb Attack." *Hollywood Citizen-News,* February 5, 1962.

"Actor to Build Vacation Home in Holderness." *Lakes Region Trader,* November 6, 1968.

"Actor's Son Gets Jail Term, Fine." *Los Angeles Herald-Examiner,* November 11, 1970.

"Acts of Birth: Robert Ryan." *Films and Filming,* March 1971.

"A-Hunting We Will Go." *Screen Guide* 5, no.3 (November 1947).

"Amateur Critics Lift Ryan to Stardom with 'Rave Cards.'" *New York Herald Tribune,* May 28, 1944.

"At Home with Robert Ryan." *New York Sunday News,* September 25, 1960.

"'B'Way for Peace' Show Realizes over $100,000." *Variety,* January 24, 1968.

"Bob Ryan in Boxing Roles." *Boston Sunday Advertiser,* December 8, 1957.

"Bob Ryan, KPFK Get Threats." *Los Angeles Herald-Examiner,* February 5, 1962.

"Bob Ryan May Sell." *Variety,* December 24, 1958.

"Brady, Hastings to Stage 'Town,' 'Page' for Plumstead, Mineola." *Variety,* August 14, 1968.

"Broadway Hit Comes to TV." *Los Angeles Times,* January 30, 1970.

"Caldwell Novel for UA Roster." *Variety,* January 30, 1957.

"Camera Debut." *Los Angeles Times,* August 28, 1952.

"'The Canadians' under Eady Plan." *Variety,* November 30, 1960.

"Chatter: Broadway." *Variety,* July 18, 1973.

"Chin-Up Guy." *Movie Stars Parade* 4 no.5 (April 1944): 40.

"Coroner's Jury Goes through Death Tunnel." *Chicago Daily News,* April 15, 1931.

"'Crossfire': Thriller with a Dynamite Punch." *Cue,* July 26, 1947.

"Death Takes Mother of Robert Ryan." *Los Angeles Times,* March 15, 1963.

"Establish Free Southern Theatre for Summer Sked in Jackson, Miss., Then Local Groups, Touring Units." *Variety,* April 8, 1964.

"Expansion Program on at Oakwood." *San Fernando Valley Mirror-News,* May 30, 1957.

"Extraordinary Properties on the Market." *Architectural Digest,* March 1998.

"Film Critics Soc. Award for Ryan." *Hollywood Reporter,* January 30, 1974.

"Film Stars Join in Nuclear Plea." *New York Times,* October 20, 1959.

"Films' Biggest Mystery—RKO." *Variety,* February 20, 1952.

"Guthrie Memorial Salute Nets 7-1/2 G from 2 SRO Perfs. at Carnegie Hall." *Variety,* January 24, 1968.

"Harmon-Mann Solicit No Seal for 'God's Little Acre,' Tell Why." *Variety,* April 3, 1957.

"Hollywoodites Join in Study of Actor Lore; Yen Stage Presentation." *Variety,* February 26, 1958.

"Hughes' Commie Blast Viewed as Cue to Exit RKO; Mayer Report Up Again." *Variety,* April 9, 1952.

"Hush-Filming on Kennedy Killing." *Variety,* June 6, 1973.

"Inside Stuff—Pictures." *Variety,* December 7, 1949.

"International: International Sound Track." *Variety,* December 22, 1971.

"John Beal, Carol Teitel to Expand 'Journey' Sked." *Variety,* July 14, 1971.

"John Ryan, Pioneer Joliet Merchant, Dies." *Chicago Tribune,* May 27, 1919.

"Jug Bob Ryan's Son." *Variety,* November 11, 1970.

"'Juno' Will Aid Ryan Memorial." *Hollywood Reporter,* October 8, 1974.

"Just for Variety." *Variety,* April 19, 1973.

"Just for Variety." *Variety,* April 26, 1973.

"Just for Variety." *Variety,* May 1, 1973.

"The Kelly-Nash Political Machine." *Fortune* 14, no. 1 (August 1936): 47–126.

"Legitimate: Asides and Ad-Libs." *Variety,* April 12, 1967.

"Legitimate: N.Y. Critics' Poll Results." *Variety,* July 21, 1971.

"Leone Prepping $5,000,000 Saga." *Variety,* January 10, 1968.

"Living the Life of Ryan." *Screen Guide,* January 1950.

"Little Chance to Fix Tunnel Disaster Blame." *Chicago American,* April 15, 1931.

"Long Lunches, Cocktails, Censorship but Spain Grows as Show Biz Center." *Variety,* June 6, 1960.

"Many Top Names Asked to Explain." *Variety,* May 21, 1952.

"Marie Spottswood: Guided Oakwood School Growth." *Los Angeles Times,* June 26, 1987.

"Movieland Events." *Los Angeles Times,* April 2, 1955.

"Movies Are Put in Essential Class by Draft Ruling." *New York Times,* February 9, 1942.

"MPC, Plumstead Tie on Teleplay Specs with Xerox Backing." *Variety,* July 16, 1969.

"'Mr. President' Spurns More Boston Orders." *Variety,* August 1, 1962.

"N.Y. Critics Rave: 'Billy Budd' Break for Allied Artists." *Variety,* November 7, 1962.

"New 'Front Page' to Cost $20,000." *Variety,* April 9, 1969.

"One Minute Interviews." *Hollywood Citizen-News,* November 5, 1953.

"Opinions of an Actor." *Hollywood Citizen-News,* January 23, 1948.

"Parade in Loop Launches Movie about Marines." *Chicago Tribune,* August 14, 1951.

"Pare Lorentz Picks American Odysseus." *Brooklyn Eagle,* July 14, 1942.

"Phil Yordan into Tele Corp of America: Red Silverstein Sales Chief beyond U.S." *Variety,* July 4, 1973.

"Plumstead Group Aims 3 Revivals for Next Season." *Variety,* May 21, 1969.

"Posthumous Award Given to Actor Robert Ryan." *Boxoffice,* February 4, 1974.

"Private Services for Robert Ryan, Burial in Chicago." *Hollywood Reporter,* July 13, 1973.

"Public, Not Producers, Guilty of Typing Actors: Bob Ryan." *Variety,* May 23, 1958.

"Radio Station, Actor's Home Guarded after Bomb Threat." *Los Angeles Times,* February 6, 1962.

"Robert Ryan Estate Left to Children." *Los Angeles Times,* July 22, 1973.

"Robert Ryan Pilot for NBC-TV Rolling at U." *Variety,* October 21, 1964.

"Robert Ryan Speaks." *Los Angeles Daily News,* October 22, 1947.

"Robert Ryan to Appear with British Repertory." *Hollywood Reporter,* February 13, 1967.

"Robert Ryan's Advice to Would-Be Actors." *Salt Lake City Deseret News,* November 30, 1951.

"Robert Ryan's Spiel." *Variety,* January 22, 1964.

"Rugged Ryan." *Movie Play,* January 1947.

"Ryan—Buddy Hackett for Mexican 'Quixote.'" *Variety,* March 29, 1972.

"Ryan for 'Glory.'" *Variety,* November 4, 1947.

"Ryan Project Will Benefit." *Los Angeles Times,* October 23, 1974.

"Salute of the Week: Robert Ryan." *Cue,* May 10, 1969.

"Saskatchewan Socialist Backing for Mounties' Film with Bob Ryan." *Variety,* September 28, 1960.

"Savalas Inks 3-Film Deal with Scotia Int'l." *Variety,* July 7, 1971.

"Search for 'Typical American' for Screen a Six Months' Job." *New York Herald Tribune,* April 19, 1942.

"See 'Set-Up' Scoring Close Verdict over 'Champion' in Suit." *Variety,* May 11, 1949.

"Sees Participation Deal as 'Income Roulette.'" *Motion Picture Herald,* October 24, 1959.

"Set Guthrie Memorial at Carnegie Hall, N.Y." *Variety,* January 10, 1968.

"Show Biz Names from Paris, B'Way and H'wood Perform at D.C. March." *Variety,* September 4, 1963.

"Special Draft Deferment Creates Furor in Hollywood." *Los Angeles Times,* February 11, 1942.

"Teachers Learn from Students at Hollywood Private School." *Pasadena Star-News,* September 4, 1957.

"Threaten to Bomb Bob Ryan's Home." *Variety,* February 5, 1962.

"Timothy Ryan, Contractor, Dies at 61; Rites Tomorrow." *Chicago Tribune,* April 28, 1936.

"12 Dead, 16 Saved, in Tunnel." *Chicago Daily News,* April 14, 1931.

"21 Rescued in Disaster." *Chicago Evening Post,* April 14, 1931.

"UCLA Theatre Division Plans 3 Play Evenings." *Variety,* July 20, 1960.

"Understanding and Coping with Anxiety—Rollo May." Audio recording, *Psychology Today,* 1978. www.existentialanalysis.org.uk/assets/articles/Understanding_and _Coping_with_Anxiety_Rollo_May_transcription_Martin_Adams.pdf.

"Unforeseen Eugene." *Time,* March 22, 1968.

"Unknown British Actor Playing Billy Budd." *Variety,* June 7, 1961.

"Wald-Krasna Unit Still Stalled at RKO; Former Ill." *Variety,* March 19, 1952.

"Youngstein's Shuttle; 7 Properties Shape." *Variety,* September 30, 1964.

"Yugoslavia Sets Coproductions." *Variety,* July 8, 1964.

Alpert, Don. "Ryan: 1 in 50 Critics Knows." *Los Angeles Times,* December 3, 1961.

Auerbach, Arnold. "The Wildest Bunch of All." *New York Times,* August 17, 1969.

Becker, Bill. "Focus on the Forty-Ninth State." *New York Times,* September 27, 1959.

Benjamin, George. "What a Man!" *Modern Screen,* October 1944.

Berg, Louis. "Gentle Irishman." *Los Angeles Times,* February 4, 1951.

Bergstrom, Janet. "Oneiric Cinema: *The Woman on the Beach.*" *Film History* 11 (1999): 114–25.

Bosworth, Patricia. "Robert Ryan: In Search of Action." *New York Times,* June 1, 1969.

Breslin, Howard. "Bad Time at Honda." *American Magazine,* January 1947.

Brogan, Phil F. "Valley of No Return Doesn't Stop Brogan." *Bend Bulletin,* November 12, 1958.

Buck, Raymond J. "A Rare Kind of Movie Star." *Dartmouth Varsity,* October 1960.

Cameron, Sue. "Robert Ryan Signed for Broadway Star Role in 'Shenandoah.'" *Hollywood Reporter,* June 29, 1973.

Carpenter, Les. "Lincoln Program Dramatic Opener for Famous Ford's Theatre, Wash." *Variety,* February 7, 1968.

———. "'Mr. Prez' Leaves D.C. Better Than When JFK Saw It." *Variety,* October 17, 1962.

Chambers, Sue. "Robert Ryan—Heavy and Hero." *Milwaukee Journal,* January 13, 1963.

Champlin, Charles. "Robert Ryan: In Memoriam." *Los Angeles Times,* July 12, 1973.

Churchill, Reba, and Bonnie Churchill. "Mister Velvet." *Movie Stars Parade,* April 1948.

Coe, Richard. "Visitor Ryan." *Washington Post and Times Herald,* October 20, 1956.

Cohen, Elliot E. "Letter to the Movie-Makers: The Film Drama as a Social Force." *Commentary* 4, no. 2 (August 1947).

Cousins, Norman. "Modern Man Is Obsolete." *Saturday Review,* August 18, 1945.

Crist, Judith. "Katharine Hepburn Stars in 'Anthony and Cleopatra.'" *New York Herald Tribune,* August 1, 1960

Cuffs, John. "Robert Ryan: Villain Extraordinary." *Films and Filming,* July 1961.

Dudley, Fredda. "Romancing with Ryan." *Photoplay,* April 1944.

Fellig, Arthur (Weegee). Column for *Los Angeles Mirror,* November 26, 1948.

Friedman, Lester D. "A Very Narrow Path: The Politics of Edward Dmytryk." *Literature/Film Quarterly* 12, no. 4 (October 1984): 214–24. In Elsie M. Walker and David T. Johnson, *Conversations with Directors.* Lanham, MD: Scarecrow Press, 2008.

Funke, Lewis. "Robert Ryan's 'Journey.'" *New York Times,* March 7, 1971.

Furie, Ken. "Robert Ryan on 'Everything but Birth Control.'" *Dartmouth,* April 21, 1967.

Gent, George. "Ryan Sees Something of Himself in O'Neill's People." *New York Times,* April 5, 1971.

Goebel, Larry. "Robert Ryan." *Los Angeles Times,* July 18, 1973.

Granet, Bert. "Berlin Express Diary." *Screen Writer,* May 1948.

Grant, Ila S. "Ila Finds That Movie Making Is Hard Work." *Bend Bulletin,* November 22, 1958.

Greenberg, Abe. "Rugged Robert Ryan Speaks Up." *Hollywood Citizen-News,* July 19, 1966.

Grenquist, Peter C. "'Stranger Than Fiction' Ryan Stops Changing." *Dartmouth,* March 17, 1950.

Hamill, Pete. "For Robert Ryan." *New York Post,* July 13, 1973.

Harmetz, Aljean. "'Man Was a Killer Long before He Served a God.'" *New York Times,* August 31, 1969.

Harris, Radie. "Broadway Ballyhoo." *Hollywood Reporter,* June 17, 1969.

Heyn, Howard C. "Friend of the Underdog: Bob Ryan Favors Stories about Hard-Knock People." Associated Press [ca. 1949]. Robert Ryan file, Margaret Herrick Library, Beverly Hills, California.

Hildebrand, Harold. "Robert Ryan Speaks Out." *Los Angeles Examiner,* October 11, 1961.

———. "Ryan's 'Between' Films." *Los Angeles Examiner,* October 8, 1961.

Hopper, Hedda. "Robert Ryan Awaits Stork's Third Visit." *Los Angeles Times,* August 25, 1951.

Hunt, Gerry. "Maureen O'Sullivan Tells of Her Secret Romance with the Late Robert Ryan." *National Enquirer,* December 23, 1973.

Jensen, C. Gregory. "The Actor Who Will Play Christ." *Family Weekly*, December 25, 1960.

Johnson, Arnold [photog]. "Rugged!" *Movie Life,* August 1948.

Johnson, Erskine. "Lazy Newcomers Irk Ryan." *Los Angeles Mirror News,* December 2, 1959.

———. Untitled column. *Los Angeles Daily News,* July 7, 1951.

Jones, J. R. "The Actor's Letter." *Chicago Reader,* October 29, 2009.

Kerr, Walter. "After 41 Years, It's Still Page One." *New York Times,* May 25, 1969.

———. "Do the Tyrones Live Here?" *New York Times,* May 2, 1971.

Kupcinet, Irv. "Kup's Column." *Chicago Sun-Times,* April 7, 1949, 45.

Lardine, Bob. "This Dove Is a Tough Bird." *New York Sunday News,* August 27, 1967.

Lightman, Herb A. "The Story of Filming 'Berlin Express.'" *American Cinematographer* 29, no. 7 (July 1948).

Lowe, Herman A. "Big D.C. Whodunit: Who Killed That Red Probe? See Resumption in Dec." *Variety,* November 5, 1947.

Nichols, M. "Robert Ryan—Hero and Heel." *Coronet* 47, no.16 (January 1960).

Macdonald, Dwight. "No Art and No Box Office." *Esquire,* March 1959.

MacPherson, Virginia. "Why Shouldn't the Kids Be Actors?—Ryan." *Los Angeles Daily News,* January 1, 1951.

Manners, Dorothy. "His Knees Knock in Broadway Tempo." *Los Angeles Herald-Examiner,* July 8, 1962.

———. "Ryan's Courage Faces Sorrow." *Los Angeles Herald-Examiner,* July 24, 1972.

McClay, Howard. "He Didn't Look Like an Actor—But." *Los Angeles Daily News,* May 20, 1952.

———. "It's Always Nice to Have Something Going for You." *Los Angeles Daily News,* June 30, 1953.

———. "Shakespeare Summons Bob Ryan." *Los Angeles Daily News,* March 24, 1954.

McManus, Margaret. "Robert Ryan Speaks Out on Reagan." *Bridgeport (Connecticut) Telegram,* November 6, 1966.

McMurtry, Charles. "Ex-Dartmouth Athlete Stars in First Movie Role." *Worcester Telegram,* May 12, 1942.

Meyers, Joe. "Whatever Happened to Robert Ryan?" *Connecticut Post,* August 28, 1994.

Moskowitz, Gene. "Serge Silberman: France to Quebec." *Variety,* October 20, 1971.

Moss, Morton. "Buoyancy and Bounce." *Los Angeles Herald-Examiner,* January 29, 1970.

Murphy, Mary. "Robert Ryan—A New Life on Borrowed Time." *Los Angeles Times,* September 5, 1972.

Nogueira, Rui, and Nicoletta Zalaffi. "A Bastard's Long Career: Meeting with Robert Ryan." *Cinema 70* (April 1970). Translation by Kelsey Beson.

Oppenheimer, Peer J. "A Film Hero Fights for Better Schools." *New Haven Sunday Register,* August 7, 1960.

Parsons, Harriet. "Battle-Scarred Ryan Is Home." *Los Angeles Herald-Examiner,* December 12, 1965.

Parsons, Louella O. "In Hollywood with Louella O. Parsons." *Los Angeles Examiner,* February 29, 1948.

———. "Robert Ryan: Nice Man to Have around the Movies." *Los Angeles Examiner,* February 10, 1952.

Roberts, Chalmers M. "Adlai Calls for All-Out Final Drive." *Washington Post and Times Herald,* October 21, 1956.

Rode, Alan K. "'First Is First and Second Is Nobody': The Philip Yordan Story." *Noir City Sentinel,* November-December 2009.

Rodgers, Virginia E. "Robert Ryan: 'A Most Un-Actor-Like Actor.'" *New Bedford (Massachusetts) Standard-Times,* July 22, 1965.

Ryan, Jessica. "Marine Ryan." *Movieland* 4, no. 9 (October 1944).

Ryan, Robert. "Acts of Birth." *Films and Filming,* March 1971.

Ryan, Robert, as told to Naomi Engelsman. "Backstage with Us Ryans." *Parents' Magazine,* September 1951.

Ryan, Robert. "'Front Page' Puts Him on Broadway." *Hollywood Citizen-News,* May 22, 1969.

———. "I Didn't Want to Play a Bigot." *Ebony,* November 1959.

———. "I'm Gambling with My Career." *Movieland,* August 1947.

———. "'Just an Actor,' Says Robert Ryan." *Hollywood Citizen-News,* February 18, 1970.

———. "My Role in Crossfire." *Worker,* July 20, 1947. Southern edition.

———. "The Role I Liked Best . . ." *Saturday Evening Post,* July 15, 1950.

———. "We're Not Quitting!" *Screen Guide,* May 1948.

———. "What Is Proper Speech?" *New York Times,* October 24, 1965.

Ryan, Robert, as told to Loney, Glenn. "In the Words of Robert Ryan." *Cue,* January 11, 1970.

Ryan, Robert, as told to Pine, Dick. "The Trouble with Me Is . . ." *Movieland,* June 1951.

Schary, Dore. "Letter from a Movie-Maker: 'Crossfire' as a Weapon against Anti-Semitism." *Commentary,* October 1947.

Scheuer, Philip K. "Robert Ryan Lifts Veil on Yugoslavia." *Los Angeles Times,* August 11, 1964.

Schumach, Murray. "Art's Call Heard by Robert Ryan." *New York Times,* February 5, 1960.

Schweitzer, Albert. "Declaration of Conscience." *Saturday Review,* May 18, 1957.

Scott, John L. "Good or Bad; Robert Ryan Plays Either." *Los Angeles Times,* August 10, 1947.

———. "Play Features All-Star Cast." *Los Angeles Times,* January 27, 1957.

———. "Ryan Lifts Self by His 'Heels.'" *Los Angeles Times,* October 25, 1959.

Scott, Vernon. "Ryan Works Again Despite Cancer." *Los Angeles Herald-Examiner,* August 27, 1972.

Shuster, Alvin. "Robert Ryan Plays *Othello* Abroad for $150 a Week." *New York Times,* October 18, 1967.

Skolsky, Sidney. "Tintypes." *Hollywood Citizen-News,* October 16, 1947.

———. "Tintypes." *Hollywood Citizen-News,* June 24, 1954; *New York Post,* June 27, 1954.

———. "Tintypes." *Hollywood Citizen-News,* October 8, 1959.

Smallwood, Frank. "Ryan '32 Tops Career as *Crossfire's* Killer." *Dartmouth,* January 28, 1948.

Smith, Cecil. "At the UCLA Theater Group, the Ordinary Was a Rarity." *Los Angeles Times,* May 14, 1981.

———. "Medicine for 'Tired and Shabby' Theater." *Los Angeles Times,* January 22, 1961.

Smith, Darr. Untitled column. *Los Angeles Daily News,* February 17, 1949.

Stein, Jeanne. "Robert Ryan: Unlike Most Handsome Actors He Was Willing to Be a Heavy." *Films in Review* 9, no. 1 (January 1968).

Stinson, Charles. "UCLA to Present Eliot Masterpiece." *Los Angeles Times,* January 17, 1960.

Surtees, Robert. "The Story of Filming 'Act of Violence.'" *American Cinematographer,* August 1948.

Thomas, Bob. "Male Cheesecake! Robert Ryan Comments on New Trend." *Hollywood Citizen-News,* July 11, 1949.

———. "Tots' School Begun by Film Star Thrives." *Los Angeles Mirror News,* July 24, 1958.

Vallee, William Lynch. "Movie Life of Robert Ryan." *Dartmouth Varsity,* ca. 1949.

Walker, Helen Louise. "Portrait of a Happy Man." *Movieland,* December 1949.

Werba, Hank. "'Billy Budd' Budget Item: Dramamine." *Variety,* June 28, 1961.

———. "Dmytryk Repeats History as 'Anzio' Restaged Yanks' Liberation of Rome." *Variety,* August 23, 1967.

Wershba, Joseph. "Outspoken Actor." *New York Post,* March 7, 1963.

Wheatley, James H. "Boxing Team to 'Set-up' Is Circuit for Ryan '32." *Dartmouth,* April 30, 1949.

Whitman, Alden. "Robert Ryan, Actor, Dies at 63." *New York Times,* July 12, 1973.

Williams, Dick. "Over Hill, Dale, A-Golfing We Go with Slicer Robert Ryan." *Los Angeles Mirror,* February 8, 1950.

Williams, Whitney. "Be Smart: Send Screen Stars to Japan for Personals, Protect U.S. Films—Bob Ryan's Advice." *Variety*, March 30, 1955.

Zolotow, Sam. "'Front Page' Here as Benefit in May." *New York Times,* January 8, 1969.

———. "New Group Forms at Theater on L.I." *New York Times,* August 1, 1968.

———. "The Plumstead to Offer in Fall 3 Pulitzer Plays." *New York Times,* May 21, 1969.

Zunser, Jesse. "Stratford: Ryan, Hepburn, et al." *Cue,* July 30, 1960.

Zylstra, Freida. "From Chicago Sandhog to Hollywood Star: Robert Ryan." *Chicago Tribune,* July 19, 1950.

Unpublished Manuscripts

Harmon, Sidney. "Robert Ryan."

Jarlett, Franklin. Interview transcriptions for *Robert Ryan: A Biography and Critical Filmography:* Arvin Brown (September 3, 1986), Norman Cousins (June 1, 1987), Philip Dunne (June 12 and August 24, 1987), Evans Frankenheimer (May 30, 1987), John Frankenheimer (May 25, 1987), Albert Hackett (August 1986), John Houseman (spring 1986), Lamont Johnson (August 17, 1986), Harold J. Kennedy (March 20, 1986), Millard Lampell (March 10, 1987), Harold Mayer (August 1986), Cheyney Ryan (February 20 and March 15, 1986), Lisa Ryan (February 23, 1986, and September 1, 1987), Timothy Ryan (February 2 and March 20, 1986; June 6 and August 26, 1987), Virginie van Bark (March 5, 1986), Robert Wallsten (May 1986), Robert Wise (February 18, 1986), and Philip Yordan (October 27, 1986). In the case of discrepancies between the transcribed interviews and Jarlett's published text, priority was given to the transcriptions.

McCarthy, Joe. "Antic Arts: Robert Ryan." 1963.

Ryan, Jessica. "America—Dream or Nightmare?: American Myths of Power, Aggression and Violence," ca. 1970.

———. "Campaign–'52, or A Camera's-Eye View from Two Odd Birds," notes and text, ca. 1970.

———. "If School Keeps," ca. 1970.

———. "Recollections of a Pioneer Grandmother," ca. 1970.

———. "Woman: The Mythless American," outline and text, ca. 1970.

Ryan, Robert. "How Do You Remember All Those Words?," n.d. Jane Ardman Papers, Margaret Herrick Library, Academy of Motion Picture Arts and Sciences, Beverly Hills, California.

———. "The Next Time You Want to Do a Play." 1971.

———. Untitled essay on American culture. 1968.

———. "What Makes an Actor Tick?," n.d. Jane Ardman Papers, Margaret Herrick Library, Academy of Motion Picture Arts and Sciences, Beverly Hills, California.

Selected Archival Resources

DARTMOUTH COLLEGE LIBRARY, DARTMOUTH COLLEGE,
HANOVER, NEW HAMPSHIRE.

Dartmouth Boxing Club file: (1) Robert Ryan to Corey Ford, July 24, 1957. (2) Robert Ryan to Corey Ford, October 28, 1957.

Robert Ryan alumnus file: (1) Robert Ryan to A. J. Dickerson, mid-1945. (2) Five excerpts from Dartmouth College Class of 1932 newsletter, 1940–1947. (3) Excerpt from Dartmouth College Class of 1932 newsletter, March 19, 1962. (4) Dartmouth alumni office biographical data sheet, ca. 1956. (5) Dartmouth alumni records office questionnaire, ca. September 1967. (6) Robert Ryan to Mr. Kemeny of Dartmouth College alumni office, March 23, 1971. (7) Dartmouth College alumni records office questionnaire, ca. 1972.

MARGARET HERRICK LIBRARY, ACADEMY OF MOTION PICTURES ARTS AND SCIENCES, BEVERLY HILLS, CALIFORNIA.

Audiovisual archive: (1) Robert Ryan, interview with Tony Thomas, audio recording, ca. 1960. (2) Robert Ryan, interview with Bert Reisfeld for German radio program *Wieder Wildwestfilme in Hollywood,* ca. 1967.

Bert Granet Papers: Granet, unaddressed letter draft regarding production of *Berlin Express,* n.d.

Hedda Hopper Papers: Robert Ryan, interview with Hedda Hopper for column promoting *King of Kings,* June 14, 1960.

History of Cinema: Hollywood and the Production Code collection: Stephen S. Jackson to David Hopkins of Enterprise Productions regarding *Caught,* February 12, 1948.

John Huston Papers: (1) SANE letter from Robert Ryan and Steve Allen to Huston, February 9, 1960. (2) SANE document, "Suggestions for Platform Hearings of the Democratic National Committee," July 7, 1960.

John Paxton Papers: (1) Clay Steinman to Paxton, June 29, 1977. (2) Clay Steinman and Keith Kelly, interview questions for Paxton, July 1, 1977. (3) Paxton to Clay Steinman and Keith Kelly, July 14, 1977. (4) Paxton to Clay Steinman, Keith Kelly, and Mario Falsetto, n.d.

John Sturges Papers: Sturges to cast and crew of *The Law and Tombstone* (aka *Hour of the Gun*), October 15, 1966.

Lincoln Quarberg Papers: Congressional statement of Congressman Richard M. Nixon on the release of *Flying Leathernecks,* August 27, 1951.

Motion Picture Association of America Production Code Administration Files: (1) Joseph I. Breen to William Gordon of RKO Radio Pictures regarding *The Woman on the Beach,* March 28, 1945. (2) Joseph I. Breen to Harold Melniker of RKO Radio Pictures regarding *On Dangerous Ground,* March 20, 1950; March 23, 1950; and May 2, 1950. (3) Geoffrey M. Shurlock to Hal Wallis of Paramount Pictures regarding *About Mrs. Leslie,* June 17, 1954. (4) Joseph I. Breen to Hal Wallis regarding *About Mrs. Leslie,* August 20, 1953. (5) Geoffrey M. Shurlock to Hal Wallis regarding *About Mrs. Leslie,* August 24, 1953.

Sidney Skolsky Papers: Interview with Robert Ryan for "Tintypes" column to promote *The Ice Palace,* ca. January 1960.

OAKWOOD SCHOOL, NORTH HOLLYWOOD, CALIFORNIA.

1. Robert Ryan to parents in North Hollywood and Studio City, California, January 1951.
2. Material pertaining to background of the Ryan Center, The Robert and Jessica Ryan Memorial, 1972–1975.

PALEY CENTER FOR MEDIA, LOS ANGELES, CALIFORNIA.

1. "Directed by John Frankenheimer: The Seminar." *Museum of Television and Radio Seminar Series.* Video recording, January 18, 1996.
2. "A Conversation with John Frankenheimer." *Museum of Television and Radio Seminar Series.* Video recording, September 24, 1997.

MAX REINHARDT ARCHIVES AND LIBRARY, SUNY–BINGHAMTON, BINGHAMTON, NEW YORK.

Four addresses to students and faculty at the Max Reinhardt School of the Theater: June 1938; June 27, 1938; July 12, 1938; and September 12, 1938.

UCLA FILM AND TELEVISION ARCHIVE, UNIVERSITY OF CALIFORNIA AT LOS ANGELES, LOS ANGELES, CALIFORNIA.

(1) *A Call from . . .* (aka *A Call from the Stars*). Video recording, February 10, 1960. Television Collection, inventory number DVD 4142 T. (2) *It Could Be You.* Video recording, November 7, 1959. Television Collection, inventory no. DVD 10465.

UCLA LIBRARY SPECIAL COLLECTIONS, UNIVERSITY OF CALIFORNIA AT LOS ANGELES, LOS ANGELES, CALIFORNIA.

Jean Renoir Papers: (1) Jessica Ryan to Dido and Jean Renoir, ca. March 1948. (2) Jessica Ryan to Dido and Jean Renoir, April 8, 1955. (3) Jessica Ryan to Jean Renoir, ca. May 1967. (4) Robert Ryan to Jean Renoir, ca. August 1968. (5) Jean Renoir to Robert Ryan, May 25, 1972. (6) Robert Ryan to Jean Renoir, July 20, 1972.

WISCONSIN CENTER FOR FILM AND THEATER RESEARCH, MADISON, WISCONSIN.

Patrick McGilligan Papers: Interview with Dore Schary.
Robert Ryan clipping file: Autographed fan questionnaire in Ryan's hand, February 7, 1942.
Dore Schary Papers: (1) Peter Rathvon to Dore Schary regarding *Crossfire,* February 12, 1947. (2) Research on anti-Japanese violence for *Bad Day at Black Rock,* October 26, 1953. (3) Audience comments from preview of *Bad Day at Black Rock,* Encino Theatre, Encino, California, October 14, 1954. (4) MGM summary of British reviews for *Bad Day at Black Rock,* March 21, 1955. (5) Robert Ryan to Dore Schary, November 16, 1959. (6) Robert Ryan remarks to New York SANE event, Town Hall, New York City, March 10, 1963. (7) Robert Ryan to the chairman of "Stars for SANE," ca. 1965. (8) Robert Ryan to Dore Schary, August 5, 1967. (9) SANE brochure, "Some Things You Should Know." (10) Form letter from Robert Ryan and Steve Allen to Dore Schary, January 29, 1960. (11) SANE program for Steve Allen testimonial dinner, November 15, 1962.

Index

Wesleyan Film

A SERIES FROM WESLEYAN UNIVERSITY PRESS
Edited by Lisa Dombrowski and Scott Higgins
ORIGINATING EDITOR: Jeanine Basinger

J.R. JONES is the film editor for the *Chicago Reader*, where his work has appeared since 1996 and won multiple awards from the Association of Alternative Newsmedia. His writing has also appeared in the *Chicago Sun-Times, New York Press, Kenyon Review*, Noir City, and *Da Capo Best Music Writing 2000*, edited by Peter Guralnick. J.R. Jones lives in Chicago.